Managerial Economics: Theories and Applied Principles

Managerial Economics: Theories and Applied Principles

Edited by
Swena Lesley

Willford Press
www.willfordpress.com

Published by Willford Press,
118-35 Queens Blvd., Suite 400,
Forest Hills, NY 11375, USA

ISBN: 978-1-68285-467-9

Cataloging-in-Publication Data

Managerial economics : theories and applied principles / edited by Swena Lesley.
p. cm.
Includes bibliographical references and index.
ISBN 978-1-68285-467-9
1. Managerial economics. 2. Economics. I. Lesley, Swena.

HD30.22 .M36 2018
330--dc23

For information on all Willford Press publications
visit our website at www.willfordpress.com

WILLFORD PRESS

Printed in China.

Contents

Preface

The application of the concepts and analysis of economies for problem solving in management related issues is known as managerial economics. Risk analysis, capital budgeting and pricing analysis are some of the significant areas where managerial economics is applied. This book studies, analyses and upholds the pillars of managerial economics and its utmost significance in modern times. Some of the diverse topics covered herein address the varied branches that fall under this discipline. It attempts to assist those with a goal of delving into the field of managerial economics.

The information contained in this book is the result of intensive hard work done by researchers in this field. All due efforts have been made to make this book serve as a complete guiding source for students and researchers. The topics in this book have been comprehensively explained to help readers understand the growing trends in the field.

I would like to thank the entire group of writers who made sincere efforts in this book and my family who supported me in my efforts of working on this book. I take this opportunity to thank all those who have been a guiding force throughout my life.

Editor

1

Corruption, Political Instability and Economic Development in the Economic Community of West African States (ECOWAS): Is There a Causal Relationship?

Nurudeen Abu[1], Mohd Zaini Abd Karim[1], Mukhriz Izraf Azman Aziz[2]

ABSTRACT Despite the abundant research on economic development, corruption and political instability, little research has attempted to examine whether there is a causal relationship among them. This paper examines the causal relationship among corruption, political instability and economic development in the ECOWAS using the Granger causality test within a multivariate cointegration and error-correction framework for the 1996-2012 period. The findings indicate that political instability Granger-causes economic development in the short term, while political instability and economic development Granger-cause corruption in the long term. In addition, we employed the forecast error variance decomposition and impulse response function analyses to investigate the dynamic interaction between the variables. The results demonstrate positive unidirectional Granger causality from political instability to economic development in the short term and positive unidirectional Granger causality from political instability and economic development to corruption in the long term in ECOWAS countries. Thus, ECOWAS governments should employ policies to promote political stability in the region.

KEY WORDS: Corruption, Political instability, Economic development, ECOWAS

[1] Othman Yeop Abdullah Graduate School of Business, Univeristi Utara Malaysia, 06010 Sintok, Kedah, Malaysia; [2]School of Economics, Finance and Banking, Univeristi Utara Malaysia, 06010 Sintok, Kedah, Malaysia

Introduction

There is broad consensus that the Economic Community of West African States (ECOWAS) is one of the least developed regions in the world. Furthermore, the region has continued to face rising corruption and political instability, which in turn contribute to the region's underdevelopment through adverse effects on government revenue, production, savings, investment, growth, income distribution and poverty (see Aisen & Veiga, 2013; Asiedu & Freeman, 2009; Alesina & Perotti, 1996; Edwards, 1996; Fosu, 1992; Ghura, 2002; Gyimah-Brempong, 2002; Gyimah-Brempong & Dapaah, 1996; Gyimah-Brempong & Traynor, 1999; Oto-Peralías, Romero-Ávila, & Usabiaga, 2013). Although researchers have established that corruption is harmful to an economy (see Gyimah-Brempong, 2002;

Correspondence concerning this article should be addressed to: **Mohd Zaini Abd Karim**, Othman Yeop Abdullah Graduate School of Business, Universiti Utara Malaysia, 06010 Sintok, Kedah, Malaysia. E-mail: agrivetent@gmail.com

Mauro, 1995), we have observed the coexistence of high levels of corruption and economic development in some Asian countries, such as China. This observation is not surprising, as Leff (1964) and Huntington (1968) suggested that corruption can have positive impact on the economy via increased efficiency in countries where the bureaucracy is inefficient and constitutes a barrier to investment. This statement reflects the "grease the wheels" hypothesis. For instance, entrepreneurs pay bribes to government officials (grease the wheels) to reduce the time that they spend in queues to obtain business permits, licenses or contract approval. This system in turn increases efficiency and investment and, as a result, economic growth (Méon & Sekkat, 2005). In addition, Goldsmith (1999) cited cases in which entrepreneurs greased the wheels and won contracts even at inflated prices, thus facilitating construction of the intercontinental railway system in the United States.

However, the level of economic development (or income level) plays an important role in promoting or reducing corruption and political instability. Mauro (1995) noted that low-income (less developed) countries tend to be corrupt and politically unstable. Hence, higher-income countries (with improvements in economic conditions) tend to have lesser corruption (Montinola & Jackman, 2002; Van Rijckeghem & Weder, 2001; Schumacher, 2013) and higher political stability (Adelman & Morris, 1968; Helliwell, 1994). Corruption and political instability, including economic development, seem to reinforce one another, at least in the ECOWAS region. Whereas the military allude to corruption and poor economic conditions, among other things, for seizing power or staging a coup, it has also been accused of engaging in massive corruption and failing to bring the majority of citizens out of poverty (Edi, 2006). Moreover, some scholars hold the view that corruption is an important determinant of political instability (Mauro, 2004; Mbaku & Paul, 1989). Other authors claim that political instability accounts for the high level corruption found in many countries (Billger & Goel, 2009; Campbell & Saha, 2013; Park, 2003; Serra, 2006; Shabbir & Anwar, 2007; Zhang, Cao, & Vaughn, 2009) and that political stability tends to moderate the adverse effects of corruption in an economy (Habib & Zurawicki, 2001).

The various reports of Transparency International (TI), which publishes the corruption perception index (CPI), suggest that most ECOWAS countries are highly corrupt. Of the 15 countries in the ECOWAS region, only Cape Verde is among the top 50 in the TI ranking in the past few years. Similarly, the Political Risk Service International Country Risk Guide (ICRG) political risk rating, which reflects the extent of political uncertainty, demonstrates that ECOWAS countries are politically unstable. Many ECOWAS countries have had an average rating of less than 60% for several years, indicating that they have been experiencing serious political problems.

Despite the abundant research on economic development, corruption and political instability, few attempts have been made to examine whether there is a causal relationship among them. Most studies have focused on the relationship between two of the variables, while studies examining the association among the three variables are almost non-existent. For instance, researchers have investigated the causal effects of the relationships between corruption and development/growth (Bentzen, 2012; Blackburn & Forgues-Puccio, 2007; Gyimah-Brempong, 2002; Mauro, 1995; Ugur & Dasgupta, 2011), political instability and development/growth (Aisen & Veiga, 2013; Alesina et al., 1996; Comeau, 2003; Fosu, 2002a, 2002b; Mbaku, 1988), and corruption and political conditions (Mbaku & Paul, 1989; Montinola & Jackman, 2002). To our knowledge, this work is the first attempt to investigate the causal relationship among corruption, political instability, and economic development within a multivariate cointegration and error-correction framework in ECOWAS countries. An investigation of the causal relationship between corruption/political instability and economic development, for instance, is highly important because it provides useful information on which variables governments should emphasize. If the results of the causality test reveal that corruption causes political instability, then authorities can employ measures to reduce corruption to attain higher political stability. However, if the results indicate that it is political instability that precedes corruption, then governments can design policies to promote political stability with the goal of making society corruption-free. Similarly, if the causality test suggests that economic development causes corruption and/or political instability, then governments can implement policies that enhance development to lower corruption and/or promote political stability. It is important to mention that regardless of which hypothesis is true, employing a single policy of economic development or political stability may not be sufficient to solve other problems in ECOWAS countries. Therefore, causality test results can help in prioritizing the policies to be employed. Hence, the main objective of this paper is to examine the causal relationship among corruption, political instability and economic development in ECOWAS countries. The remainder of the paper is organized as follows. Section two reviews the relevant literatures. Section three describes the theoretical framework and model, and section four presents and discusses the results. Finally, section five concludes the paper.

Review of relevant literature

Most studies on corruption, political instability and economic development have focused on their causes and consequences. In fact, some authors have found political factors and/or the level of development (income level) to be important determinants of corruption. For instance, Park (2003) employed multiple regression analysis to examine the determinants of corruption across countries. The author discovered that economic freedom, socio-political stability, a tradition of law abidance and national cultures are the major factors explaining corruption in the countries considered in his study. Del Monte and Papagni (2007) evaluated the factors responsible for high levels of corruption in Italy during the 1963–2001 period using statistics on crimes against regional public administration. The empirical evidence illustrated that the main causes of corruption include government consumption, the level of development, party concentration, the presence of voluntary organizations, and absenteeism in national elections. Zhang et al. (2009) investigated the structural determinants of corruption using data from several sources, and their findings suggested that corruption is influenced to a greater extent by social support, the types of government and inequality. Furthermore, many studies have demonstrated that higher levels of democracy lead to lower levels of corruption (see Billger & Goel, 2009; Campbell & Saha, 2013; Emerson, 2006; Goldsmith, 1999; Iwasaki & Suzuki, 2012; Lederman, Loayza, & Soares, 2005; Serra, 2006; Shabbir & Anwar, 2007).

Meanwhile, some studies have established that corruption has a damaging impact on political conditions in a country, whereas others have concluded that higher economic development tends to reduce the level of political crisis in a society. For example, Mbaku and Paul (1989) found a positive relationship between rent seeking (corruption) and destabilization of political activities. Habib and Zurawicki (2001) concluded that corruption has an adverse effect on both domestic and foreign investments and found that the degree of openness and political stability of the host country moderates the influence of corruption. Montinola and Jackman (2002) discovered that corruption is lesser in dictatorships than in partially democratized countries. In addition, they found that higher levels of democracy reduce corruption. Other important determinants of corruption include membership in the Oil Producing and Exporting Countries (OPEC) and low wages for public sector employees in low-income countries. Claderon and Chong (2006) confirmed that democratic regimes have a negative association with rent seeking behavior in Uruguay. Moreover, a number of studies have shown that an improvement in economic development (or a higher growth rate) tends to reduce the political instability in a country (see Bollen & Jackman, 1985; Gasiorowski, 1998; Gupta, Madhavan & Blee, 1998; Gyimah-Brempong & Traynor, 1999).

The impact of corruption and political instability on economic development or growth has also been empirically investigated. Some studies have confirmed a negative impact of corruption on growth (see Gyimah-Brempong, 2002; Mauro, 1995; Ugur & Dasgupta, 2011). For instance, Mauro (1995) examined the impact of corruption on economic growth across countries using OLS and TSLS estimators. The author found that corruption has a negative impact on economic growth. Gyimah-Brempong (2002) employed a dynamic panel estimator to evaluate the effect of corruption on economic growth and income distribution in African countries. The author discovered that corruption decreases economic growth directly and indirectly via reduced investment in physical capital. Ugur and Dasgupta (2011) employed fixed effects and random effects weighted means to examine the effect of corruption across countries. Their results revealed that corruption has a negative effect on per capita GDP growth. Studies that have also found a negative impact

Table 1. A Summary of the Literature on Corruption, Political Instability and Economic Development

Author(s)	Objective(s)	Empirical evidence
Park (2003)	Examined the determinants of corruption across countries	Socio-political stability leads to lower corruption
Serra (2006)	Investigated the determinants of corruption in 62 countries	Higher levels of political instability are associated with higher corruption, while the length of preservation of democratic institutions has a negative relationship with corruption
Shabbir and Anwar (2007)	Evaluated economic and non-economic determinants of corruption in 41 developing countries	The level of economic development has a negative effect on corruption
Billger and Goel (2009)	Determined whether greater democracy and economic freedom lead to less corruption in nearly 100 countries	Greater democracy reduces corruption
Lederman et al. (2005)	Examined the determinants of corruption with a primary focus on political institutions that increase accountability across countries from 1975 to 1999	Democracies along with parliamentary systems, political stability, and freedom of press are negatively related to corruption
Mbaku and Paul (1989)	Tested the hypothesis that corruption destabilizes political activities in African countries	Corruption leads to the destabilization of political activities
Bollen and Jackman (1985)	Examined economic and non-economic determinants of political democracy in a sample of almost 100 countries	Economic development was significant in all regression analyses
Gupta et al. (1998)	Analyzed the relationship among democracy, political instability and economic growth in a sample of 120 countries	Growth in income per capita has a positive impact on democracy, but the effect on political violence is negative
Gyimah-Brempong and Traynor (1999)	Explored the relationship between political instability and economic growth in SSA	Higher economic growth leads to lesser political instability
Gyimah-Brempong (2002)	Evaluated the impact of corruption on economic growth and income distribution in African countries	Corruption decreases economic growth directly and indirectly via reduced investment in physical capital
Ugur and Dasgupta (2011)	Examined the effect of corruption across countries	Corruption has a negative effect on per capita GDP growth.
Anoruo and Braha (2005)	Investigated the impact of corruption on economic growth in 18 African countries	Corruption reduces economic growth directly by slowing productivity and indirectly by lowering investment
Aisen and Veiga (2013)	Assessed the effect of political instability on economic growth in a sample of 169 countries from 1960 to 2004	Higher political instability leads to lower GDP per capita growth rates via its effect on productivity growth as well as physical and human capital accumulation
Okafor et al. (2014)	Investigated the impact of corruption in a sample of 48 SSA countries from 1996 to 2008	Corruption has a significant negative relationship with economic development
Del Monte and Papagni (2007)	Evaluated the factors responsible for high corruption in Italy during the 1963-2001 period	Level of economic development has a significant impact on corruption
Butkiewicz and Yanikkaya (2006)	Estimated the relationship between economic growth and five measures of democracy in 100 countries from 1970 to 1999	Democratic countries have higher growth rates

Table 1. A Summary of the Literature on Corruption, Political Instability and Economic Development (Continued)

Author(s)	Objective(s)	Empirical evidence
Fosu (2002)	Studied the different effects of various elite political instability situations (which include coups d'état, abortive coups or coup plots) on economic growth in 31 SSA countries from 1960 to 1986	Abortive coups and coup plots rather than successful coups have a negative effect on economic growth
Mbaku (1988)	Examined the impact of political instability on economic development in SSA countries	Lack of political stability has negatively impacted economic performance
Ades and Chua (1997)	Evaluated the effect of regional instability on economic growth in 98 countries from 1960 to 1985	Existence of negative spillovers in politically unstable neighboring countries
Alesina et al. (1996)	Investigated the relationship between political instability and GDP per capita growth in a sample of 113 countries from 1950 to 1982	Growth tends to be lower in countries and periods with a strong tendency for government collapse

of corruption on economic growth include the works of Mo (2001), Anoruo and Braha (2005), and Farooq et al. (2013). Similarly, others have confirmed a negative association between corruption and economic development (Bentzen, 2012; Blackburn & Forgues-Puccio, 2007; Okafor, Smith, & Ujah, 2014).

Some researchers have also found a negative effect of political instability on growth (see Asteriou & Price, 2001; Comeau, 2003; Devereux & Wen, 1998; Butkiewicz & Yanikkaya, 2006). For example, Devereux and Wen (1998) developed a simple model that relates political instability to the share of government spending in GDP and economic growth for a group of 52 countries during the 1960-1985 period. The authors discovered that political instability dampens economic growth but increases the share of government spending in GDP. Asteriou and Price (2001) employed GARCH-M models to examine the effect of political instability on economic growth in the United Kingdom from 1961 to 1997. The authors found a strong negative effect of political instability on growth. Comeau (2003) tested the hypothesis that socio-political instability has a negative effect on growth in a group of countries selected from the Latin American and East Asian regions. The author discovered that socio-political instability has a negative impact on growth. Butkiewicz and Yanikkaya (2006) estimated the relationship between economic growth and five measures of democracy using panel data for 100 countries during the 1970-1999 period. The results suggested that democratic countries have higher growth rates.

Many studies have found that political instability has a negative effect on economic growth (see Ades & Chua, 1997; Aisen & Veiga, 2013; Alesina et al., 1996; Asteriou & Siriopoulos, 2000; Campos & Karanasos, 2008; Fosu, 2002; Mbaku, 1988). However, Butkiewicz and Yanikkaya (2005) found a weak relationship between socio-political instability and economic growth. The authors also discovered that the impact of socio-political instability is higher in more developed and highly democratic states. A summary of the literature review is presented in table 1.

The literature review clearly indicates that researchers have not paid adequate attention to the issue of causality among corruption, political instability and economic development. Thus, this paper attempts to contribute to the literature by investigating the causal relationship among the variables in ECOWAS countries.

Theoretical framework and model

Scholars have made attempts to theoretically establish a link among corruption, political instability, and economic development. In explaining the connection between corruption, political instability and economic growth, for instance, Mauro (2000) described a scenario in which an individual politician sets a high bribe rate. The attendant widespread corruption will have adverse effects on economic performance (that is, sluggish economic growth), leading to the collapse of the government. For example, corruption among government officials or bureaucrats reduces the amount of social services such as healthcare and education that alleviate poverty and inequality (Gupta, Davoodi, & Alonso-Terme, 2002) and therefore leads to social discontent, protests, strikes, and political violence. Sustained dissatisfaction among citizens will lead to a collapse of (or a change in) government. In developed countries, a change in government occurs through the electioneering process (Gyimah-Brempong & Dapaah, 1996) and in line with constitutional provisions. By contrast, in developing countries such as those in the ECOWAS, an unconstitutional change in government through military intervention has always been the case. Military takeover in the ECOWAS region appears to be the norm rather than exception (Edi, 2006), and it tends to have a destabilizing impact on political stability in these countries because of their fragile political structures (Adelman & Morris, 1968).

Moreover, frequent changes in government induce public or elected officials to practice rent-seeking behavior because of the high uncertainty surrounding their tenure of office. In a previous study, Shleifer and Vishny (1993) cited in Park (2003) argued that if public officials realize that their term in office will be short-lived because of political instability, they will become irresponsible and become involved in rent-seeking behavior. Using the same line of argument, Park (2003) opined that high uncertainty and anxiety among public officials (arising from political instability) would lead them to seek gain through corrupt means to protect their social status even after they no longer have their positions. Moreover, in explaining Lipset and Raab's (1970) concept of "status strain", Park (2003) emphasized that the fear of a decline in status will compel people to do anything (including engage in corrupt behaviors) to maintain their status and property.

Economic development (or income level) largely promotes or reduces corruption and political instability in a country. Mauro (1995) proposed that low-income countries are likely to be corrupt and politically unstable. In fact, low income levels or civil servant wages encourage rent-seeking behavior because people see corruption as an opportunity to improve their socio-economic well-being. By contrast, an improvement in economic conditions (such as higher wages or income) tends to lower corruption (Montinola & Jackman, 2002; Van Rijckeghem & Weder, 2001; Schumacher, 2013). Similarly, declining economic fortunes encourages discontent and socio-political instability. However, higher economic development, such as higher incomes, improves people's well-being and promotes political stability (Adelman & Morris, 1968; Helliwell, 1994).

Meanwhile, economic development can be influenced by the level of corruption and political instability through their negative impact on savings, investment and production, among other effects. For instance, political instability disrupts production activity, reduces investment and negatively influences economic performance (Alesina & Perotti, 1996; Aisen & Veiga, 2013; Alesina et al., 1996). According to Butkiewicz and Yanikkaya (2005), one of the best measures to improve the economic well-being of people in the poorest nations is to prevent political instability. In the same vein, corruption discourages investment and production, leading to sluggish growth (Asiedu & Freeman, 2009; Gyimah-Brempong, 2002; Mauro, 1995). Thus, corruption, political instability and economic development appear to cause each other. Given the issues discussed above, we hypothesize the following:

1: Political instability and economic development do not Granger-cause corruption.
2: Corruption and economic development do not Granger-cause political instability.
3: Corruption and political instability do not Granger-cause economic development.

To estimate the relationship between the variables, we formulate three models in which corruption (COR), political instability (POL) and economic development (PCY) are specified as a function of the other variables. That is,

$$COR_{it} = \alpha_0 + \alpha_1 POL_{it} + \alpha_2 PCY_{it} + U_{1it} \quad 1$$

$$POL_{it} = \beta_0 + \beta_1 COR_{it} + \beta_2 PCY_{it} + U_{2it} \quad 2$$

$$PCY_{it} = \delta_0 + \delta_1 COR_{it} + \delta_2 POL_{it} + U_{3it} \quad 3$$

Where i refers to a given country and t a given year; α_i, β_i and δ_i are coefficients; and U is the error term.

The data used in this paper were obtained from three main sources: TI, ICRG and the World Bank's World Development Indicators (WDI). Specifically, data on political instability were collected from the ICRG. Political instability has been measured by the number of successful coups, the number of people killed in domestic mass violence incidents as a fraction of the total population, the number of attempted but unsuccessful coups, or the number of politically motivated assassinations (Alesina & Perotti, 1996). Unfortunately, such (rich) data are not available for most ECOWAS countries for a considerable number of years. Moreover, the objective indices are not without shortcomings. For instance, frequent changes in government, which is an indication of political instability (Edwards, 1996), may give the wrong information about the political conditions in a country. Mauro (1995) noted that although Italy had more than fifty changes in government between 1945 and 1995, the country remained relatively stable during the period. Thus, we captured political instability by using the ICRG political risk rating (index). Although the ICRG index is subjective, it has been increasingly used in empirical research and has been found be highly associated with economic variables (see Erb, Harvey, & Viskanta, 1996; Hayakawa, Kimura, & Lee, 2013). The index measures the extent of political instability or uncertainty in a country, and its components include political leadership, military role in politics, external conflicts, the role of organized religion in politics, racial and national tension, law and order, political terrorism, civil war, and political party development. The index ranges from 0% (indicating higher political instability) to 100% (indicating higher political stability), and it has been employed in previous studies (see Abu et al., 2013; Erb et al., 1996; Hayakawa et al., 2013; Heaney & Hooper, 1999; Linder & Santiso, 2002).

Corruption is difficult to measure/quantify, and what is perceived as a norm in one country at one point in time may be considered corruption in other countries. Also, given that most corrupt practices are regarded as unlawful activities, they occur in secrecy. Thus, it is difficult to measure/quantify them. Moreover, the only objective measure of corruption that is available is the number of individuals who have been convicted of engaging in corrupt practices. However, higher conviction rates (as in the case of Singapore and Hong Kong) do not necessarily imply that corruption is higher but may indicate the effectiveness of the judiciary and anti-corruption agencies in detecting and prosecuting offenders (Lambsdorff, 1999; 2006). Given the weakness of such objective data, corruption perception indices (subjective data) have been widely used. Furthermore, because of the lack of adequate measurements of corruption, one may resort to using corruption perception indices (Gyimah-Brempong, 2002). In this study, therefore, we employed the TI corruption perception index (CPI) that has been employed in many empirical studies as a measure of corruption. The CPI reveals the extent to which a country is perceived to be corrupt. This index is also a reflection of the depth and frequency of corruption (Swaleheen, 2007), and it ranges from 0 (very corrupt) to 10 (very clean).

Corruption perception indices are not completely devoid of criticism. For instance, as reported by Williams and Siddique (2008) cited in Swaleheen (2007), some researchers have questioned the importance of the CPI for year-to-year comparisons. They have argued that the increase in the number of countries covered by the index over time has resulted in additional new data sources and improvements in the precision of estimates of the incidence of corruption, which could disturb the continuity of an index. However, Lambsdorff (1999) allayed this fear and likened the problem to that typically encountered when designing the price index for a basket of goods while the composition of the basket is constantly changing. Often referred to as a composite index, the CPI has two main advantages (Méon & Sekkat, 2005). For instance, because basic indicators are constructed based on subjectivity, they may be biased. The composite index can help to cancel out the biases, thereby resulting in the determination of the average opinion on corruption. Second, given that the composite index is an aggregate of several other indices, it facilitates data availability for larger samples of countries. The corruption perception indices have been found to be reliable because of their high correlations with important economic variables, suggesting that spuriousness is not a problem (Blackburn et al., 2010). The index has been employed in recent studies (Blackburn et al., 2010; Gyimah-Brempong, 2002; Swaleheen, 2007).

Table 2. Panel Unit Root Test Results for the Variables

Variables	Fisher-ADF		Fisher Phillips-Perron	
	Level	First difference	Level	First difference
POL	-1.0684 (0.1427)	-7.1952*** (0.0000)	-2.0456 (0.2004)	-10.3496*** (0.0000)
COR	3.6992 (0.9999)	-5.6420*** (0.0697)	4.8088 (1.0000)	-6.2817*** (0.0000)
PCY	5.9814 (1.0000)	-5.7279*** (0.0000)	7.9195 (1.0000)	-2.9273*** (0.0017)

Note: POL refers to political instability, COR refers to corruption, and PCY refers to economic development. The numbers in parentheses are probability values. *** indicate a rejection of the null hypothesis of the unit root at the 1% significance level.

Economic development is captured by income (GDP) per capita. Studies have used income per capita as a proxy for economic development (see Bentzen, 2012; Bollen & Jackman, 1985). Data on GDP per capita were obtained from the WDI. This paper considers ECOWAS countries (excluding Cape Verde and Benin because of unavailable data on political instability) and covers the 1996-2012 period. Although Benin and Cape Verde are not included in our analysis, their exclusion may not have had any serious effects on the results. For instance, countries with similar characteristics (such as the level of development) are considered in our analysis. Cape Verde has the highest GDP per capita ($4,000) in the ECOWAS region, followed by Ghana ($3,300) and Nigeria (2,700), which are included in the analysis. Similarly, Cote D'Ivoire ($1,700) has almost the same GDP per capita as Benin ($1,600).

Results

Having specified the respective models, we conducted a unit root test to ascertain whether the series used in this study are stationary. Standard economic theory requires series to be stationary prior to estimating their relationship to avoid generating spurious results. Fisher augmented Dickey-Fuller (Fisher-ADF) and Fisher Phillips-Perron (Fisher-PP) statistics were employed to test the unit root properties of the series. The results of the unit root test are presented in table 2.

The table clearly indicates that the series have a unit root at level but are stationary at the first difference. This outcome supports the claim that many macroeconomic variables are non-stationary at level but stationary after the first difference (Nelson & Plosser, 1982). Our next task is to investigate if there is a long-term equilibrium relationship (cointegration) between the series using the Pedroni residual cointegration test (Pedroni, 1999). The Pedroni statistics tests (seven of them) were used to investigate whether the error process of the estimated equation is stationary and to test the null hypothesis of no cointegration against the alternative of cointegration. The first four statistics test the null hypothesis of no cointegration for all cross-sectional units (within a dimension), while the other three statistics test the null hypothesis of no cointegration based on pooling between dimensions. The existence of cointegration suggests that the estimated relationship is not spurious. In addition, if the tests reveal the presence of cointegration, then causality will exist in at least one direction (Granger, 1986). The results of the cointegration test are presented in table 3.

Given that the variables are cointegrated, we took another step to determine the direction of causality between them. Granger (1969) proposed that variable X is said to "Granger cause" variable Y if and only if Y is better predicted by past values of X than by using past values of Y in either case. In other words, if X helps in forecasting Y, we can conclude that X Granger-causes Y. Thus, our main objective here is to examine whether current values of the individual dependent varble can be predicted by past values of the explanatory variables. To employ the Granger causality test for the variables, we estimated the following multivariate vector error-correction models (VECM):

$$\Delta COR_{it} = \alpha_0 + \sum_{j=1}^{J}\alpha_1 \Delta POL_{it-j} + \sum_{j=1}^{J}\alpha_2 \Delta PCY_{it-j} + \\ + \sum_{j=1}^{J}\alpha_3 \Delta COR_{it-j} + \phi_1 ECT_{t-1} + U_{4it} \qquad 4$$

Table 3. Results of the Pedroni Residual Cointegration Test

Statistics (Within dimension)	**Value**
Panel v-statistic	-1.2027
Panel rho-statistic	2.5870
Panel PP-statistic	-2.2122**
Panel ADF-statistic	-1.7342**

Statistics (Between dimensions)	**Value**
Group rho-statistic	3.5304
Group PP-statistic	-4.2650***
Group ADF-statistic	-2.2412**

Note: POL refers to political instability, COR refers to corruption, and PCY refers to economic development. ** and *** indicate a rejection of the null hypothesis of no cointegration at the 5% and 1% significance levels, respectively.

Table 4. Results of Granger Causality Test

Dependent variable	**ΔCOR_t**	**ΔPOL_t**	**ΔPCY_t**	**ECT_{t-1}**
ΔCOR_{it}	-	1.6508	2.5074	-0.1882**
ΔPOL_{it}	0.3609	-	0.0411	-0.0580
ΔPCY_{it}	0.0197	11.2356***	-	-0.0243

Note: ** and *** indicate a rejection of the null hypothesis of no Granger causality at the 5% and 1% significance levels, respectively.

$$\Delta POL_{it} = \beta_0 + \sum_{j=1}^{J} \beta_1 \Delta COR_{it-j} + \sum_{j=1}^{J} \beta_2 \Delta PCY_{it-j} + + \sum_{j=1}^{J} \beta_3 \Delta POL_{it-j} + \phi_2 ECT_{t-1} + U_{5it} \quad 5$$

$$\Delta PCY_{it} = \delta_0 + \sum_{j=1}^{J} \delta_1 \Delta COR_{it-j} + \sum_{j=1}^{J} \delta_2 \Delta POL_{it-j} + + \sum_{j=1}^{J} \delta_3 \Delta PCY_{it-j} + \phi_3 ECT_{t-1} + U_{6it} \quad 6$$

Where COR_{it} and COR_{it-j} represent the current and lagged values of corruption, POL_{it} and POL_{it-j} are the current and lagged values of political instability, and PCY_{it} and PCY_{it-j} are the current and lagged values of the level of economic development, respectively. Additionally, Δ is the first-difference operator, and U_{it} are the residuals. Moreover, ECT_{t-1} is the one period lag of the error-correction term, and the statistical significance of the ECT_{t-1} is used to determine the long-term causality.

The results of the Granger causality tests reported in table 4 indicate that there is short-term unidirectional causality from political instability to economic development, while there is long-term unidirectional causality from political instability and economic development to corruption. This result implies that political instability Granger-causes economic development in the short term and that both economic development and political instability Granger-cause corruption in the long term in ECOWAS countries.

Forecast Error Variance Decomposition Analysis

The Granger causality analysis conducted above is limited to the 1996-2012 period, but it does not consider the dynamic interaction of the variables beyond that period. In an attempt to understand the dynamic relationship among corruption, political instability and economic development outside of the sample period of 1996-2012, we performed a forecast error variance decomposition analysis (FEVD) (Sims, 1980). The FEVD is useful in assessing the amount of variation in a variable caused by its own shock and by shocks to other variables. In the short term, a larger percentage of the variation in a variable results from its own shock, while in the long term, the impact of shocks on other variables increases. Each of the variables in the system is disturbed by one standard deviation.

The results of the variance analysis presented in table 5 indicate that corruption is the most exogenous variable, followed by political instability and economic development. In the second year, for instance, 98.53%, 98.47% and 98.04% of the variations in the forecast error variance for corruption, political instability and economic development, respectively, is explained by its own shock. In explaining the shocks to corruption, political instability is more important than economic development in both the short and long term. Specifically, political instability explains 1.00% of the variations in corruption, while economic development accounts for 0.46% of the variations in corruption in the second year. Moreover, political instability explains 7.97% and 17.73% of the variations in corruption in the fifth and tenth years compared with the contributions of economic development at 4.53% and 14.65% during the same period.

Furthermore, corruption is more important than economic development in explaining shocks to political instability in both the short and long term. In the second year, for instance, 1.43% of the variation in political instability is explained by corruption, but economic development accounts for 0.10% of the variation in political instability. Similarly, corruption explains 8.35% and 20.81% of the variations in political instability, but the contribution of economic development to variations in political instability is 0.61% and 1.02% in the fifth and fifteenth year, respectively. Moreover, corruption is more important than political instability in explaining shocks to economic development in the short and long term. In the second year, for instance, corruption accounts for 1.95% whereas political instability explains 0.32% of the variation in economic development. In the same vein, corruption accounts for 0.76% and 0.55% of the variation in economic development, while political instability explains 0.27% and 0.35% of this variation in the tenth and fifteenth year, respectively.

Impulse Response Function Analysis

The causality tests conducted earlier provide information only on the direction of causality among the variables; these tests do not indicate whether the sign of the relationship is positive or negative. In addition, causality tests are unable to explain how much time is needed for the impacts to occur in the system. To this end, we conducted impulse response function analysis (IRF) to trace how each variable responded to a shock to the other variables in the system. The IRF results for corruption, political instability and economic development in response to a one-standard-deviation shock in corruption, political instability and economic development over the 15-year period are reported in table 6.

The results of the IRF reveal that over a period of fifteen years, a one-standard-deviation shock to political instability exerts a positive impact on corruption. A shock to political instability has a positive impact on corruption for the first five years, but between the tenth and fifteenth year, the impact declines but remains near the positive region. Similarly, a shock to economic development has a positive impact on corruption between the first and fifteenth years. Regarding the response of political instability to a shock in corruption and economic development, the results illustrate that a shock to corruption exerts a positive effect on political instability, but the impact declines continuously over the fifteen-year period and remains near the positive region. A shock to economic development has a negative impact on political instability, but the effect decreases over the fifteen-year period. Furthermore, the results demonstrate that a shock to corruption exerts a negative impact on economic development, while a shock to political instability exerts a positive impact on economic development over the fifteen-year period. Although the impact of

Table 5. Results of the Variance Decomposition Analysis

Relative Variance of COR				Relative Variance of POL				Relative Variance of PCY			
Years	COR	POL	PCY	Years	COR	POL	PCY	Years	COR	POL	PCY
1	100.00	0.00	0.00	1	0.03	99.97	0.00	1	1.95	0.32	97.72
2	98.53	1.00	0.46	2	1.43	98.47	0.10	2	1.67	0.29	98.04
3	95.61	2.95	1.44	3	3.60	96.17	0.27	3	1.46	0.26	98.28
4	91.77	5.39	2.84	4	6.00	93.55	0.45	4	1.29	0.25	98.46
5	87.50	7.97	4.53	5	8.35	91.04	0.61	5	1.16	0.24	98.60
10	67.62	17.73	14.65	10	16.75	82.23	1.02	10	0.76	0.27	98.97
15	53.42	21.33	25.24	15	20.81	78.17	1.02	15	0.55	0.35	99.10

Note: Cholesky ordering: COR, POL and PCY

Table 6. Results of the Impulse Response Function Analysis

Response of COR				Response of POL				Response of PCY			
Years	COR	POL	PCY	Years	COR	POL	PCY	Years	COR	POL	PCY
1	0.31	0.00	0.00	1	0.05	2.80	0.00	1	-12.90	5.23	91.33
2	0.24	0.04	0.03	2	0.44	2.44	-0.12	2	-11.08	4.69	92.88
3	0.19	0.06	0.05	3	0.70	2.17	-0.19	3	-9.78	4.48	94.65
4	0.15	0.08	0.06	4	0.86	1.96	-0.24	4	-8.84	4.49	96.60
5	0.13	0.09	0.07	5	0.96	1.81	-0.25	5	-8.14	4.67	98.70
10	0.08	0.10	011	10	1.00	1.36	-0.21	10	-6.46	6.60	110.70
15	0.06	0.09	0.14	15	0.86	1.12	-1.11	15	-5.77	9.07	124.75

Note: Cholesky ordering: COR, POL and PCY

political instability fell between the first and second years, it shows a rising trend from the third to fifteenth years.

In sum, the empirical results indicate that there is positive causality running from political instability to economic development in the short term and from political instability and economic development to corruption in the long term in ECOWAS countries. In separate studies, Fosu (1992, 2001, 2002a, 2002b) confirmed that political instability is deleterious to economic growth in Sub-Saharan African (SSA) countries. For instance, Fosu (1992) found the adverse impact of political instability in SSA to be almost 33 percent of GDP growth over the 1960-1986 period. Similarly, Fosu (2002b) discovered that political instability adversely affected the transfer of economic growth to human development (measured as a change in an index of life expectancy and literacy) between 1970 and 1985. Many years of political instability (military intervention in politics) have contributed to the poor economic performance of ECOWAS countries such as Nigeria. Between 1960 and 1995, Nigeria failed to make any meaningful economic progress (given its potential) because of numerous military takeovers. In addition to military coups, conflicts caused primarily by armed rebels have been on the rise since the 1990s in Liberia, Sierra Leone, Guinea-Bissau, Mali, Cote D'Ivoire and, more recently, in Nigeria. Such rising conflict has led to the displacement and destruction of human and physical capital, thus further contributing to the underdevelopment of the region.

Moreover, military rulers in the ECOWAS region have been blamed to a greater extent for the institutionalization of corruption as evident in some countries. The various military regimes alluded to corruption as one of the reasons that they seized power (Edi, 2006). Furthermore, Nigeria's former military rulers have been accused of stealing and mismanaging several billions of dollars belonging to the country. Recently, the Swiss government returned some of the funds alleged to have been looted by the late General Sani Abacha to the Nigerian government. Similarly, General Ibrahim Babangida was accused of mismanaging US$12 billion of oil windfalls while he headed the military Junta for 8 years in Nigeria. Moreover, after 15 years of democracy, the political class has also had its fair share of corruption-related activities. Many former governors and cabinet members have been investigated for helping themselves to state resources. For instance, a former governor of the oil-rich Delta state in Nigeria (James Ibori) was convicted and consequently sentenced to 13 years in prison by the British government for stealing public funds. In the same vein, high-ranking military officers in Guinea Bissau have been accused of not only legitimizing corruption but they aiding drug trafficking along the shores of their country.

Conclusion and recommendations

Given that less developed ECOWAS countries are corrupt and politically unstable, it is important to examine the interaction among economic development, corruption and political instability in these countries. This paper examines the causal relationship among corruption, political instability, and economic development in ECOWAS countries within a multivariate cointegration and error-correction framework. The Pedroni cointegration test reveals that the variables are cointegrated, indicating the existence of a long-term equilibrium relationship among corruption, political instability, and economic development. Having confirmed the existence of cointegration, we investigated the direction of causality between the variables using the VECM. The results illustrate that there is short-term unidirectional causality from political instability to economic development, while in the long term, causality runs from economic development and political instability to corruption in ECOWAS countries.

Moreover, we employed the FEVD and IRF to examine the dynamic interaction among corruption, political instability and economic development in ECOWAS outside the sample period of 1996-2012. The FEVD confirmed that corruption, political instability and economic development are endogenous. Political instability is the most important variable accounting for shocks in corruption, while corruption is the most important variable accounting for shocks in political instability and economic development. Furthermore, the IRF illustrated that a shock to political instability and economic development has a positive effect on corruption. Additionally, a shock to corruption has a positive impact on political instability, while a shock to economic development has a negative effect on political instability. In addition, a shock to political instability has a positive effect on economic development, whereas a shock to corruption has a negative impact on economic development. Thus, there is positive unidirectional causality from political instability and economic development to corruption in the long term and positive unidirectional causality from political instability to economic development in the short term in ECOWAS countries.

The findings of this study suggest that years of political instability have contributed to the high rate of corruption and underdevelopment in ECOWAS countries. Researchers have confirmed that corruption increases with political instability (see Lederman et al., 2005; Leite & Weidmann, 1999; Park, 2003). Likewise, other proxies of political instability have also been found to be correlated with corruption. For instance, it has been observed that democracy (as measured by press freedom) is negatively related to corruption (Brunetti & Weder, 2003; Lederman et al., 2005). Similarly, improvements in civil liberty reduce corruption (Lederman et al., 2005). In addition, higher levels of decentralization reduce corruption by bringing government closer to the people and ensuring that government officials can be held accountable when the need arises (Fisman & Gatti, 2002). Furthermore, political instability destroys physical capital and displaces human capital (Le, 2004), disrupts production activity (Aisen & Veiga, 2013), and encourages the violation of property rights, including lack of guarantee for contracts (Svensson, 1998). All of these consequences adversely affect the economy (Aisen & Veiga, 2013; Alesina et al., 1996).

High levels of corruption and underdevelopment in ECOWAS have been blamed on political instability primarily resulting from many years of military rule (including ethno-religious crises). For instance, Edi (2006) posited that the failure to improve socio-economic conditions and high corruption, among other factors, led to reoccurring military takeovers in ECOWAS countries. Based on our findings, ECOWAS governments should employ policies to promote political stability to improve economic development and reduce corruption in the region. However, as we stated in the introduction, the use of a single policy option of political stability may not be sufficient to achieve higher levels of economic development and to eliminate corruption from ECOWAS countries.

References

Abu, N., Karim, M.Z.A., & Aziz, M.I.A. (2013). Low savings rates in the Economic Community of West African States (ECOWAS): The role of the political instability-income interaction. *South East European Journal of Economics and Business*, 8 (2), 53-63.

Adelman, I., & Morris, C. T. (1968). An econometric model of socio-economic and political change in underdeveloped countries. *American Economic Review*, 58 (5), 1184-1218.

Ades, A., & Chua, H. B. (1997). Thy neighbor's curse: Regional instability and economic growth. *Journal of Economic Growth*, 2 (3), 279-304.

Aisen, A., & Veiga, F. J. (2013). How does political instability affect economic growth?. *European Journal of Political Economy*, 29, 151-167.

Alesina, A., & Perotti, R. (1996). Income distribution, political instability and investment. *European Economic Review*, 40 (6), 1203-1228.

Alesina, A., Ozler, S., Roubini, N., & Swagel, P. (1996). Political instability and economic growth. *Journal of Economic Growth*, 1 (2), 189-212.

Anoruo, E., & Braha, H. (2005). Corruption and economic growth: The African experience. *Journal of Sustainable Development in Africa*, 7 (1), 43-55.

Asiedu, E. (2006). Foreign direct investment in Africa: The role of natural resources, market size, government policy, institutions and political instability. *World Economy*, 29 (1), 63-77.

Asiedu, E., & Freeman, J. (2009). The effect of corruption on investment growth: Evidence from firms in Latin America, Sub-Saharan Africa, and transition countries, *Review of Development Economics*, 13 (2), 200-214.

Asteriou, D., & Price, S. (2001). Political instability and economic growth: UK time series evidence. *Scottish Journal of Political Economy*, 48 (4), 383-399.

Asteriou, D., & Siriopoulos, C. (2000). The role of political instability in stock market development and economic growth: The case of Greece. *Economic Notes*, 29 (3), 355-374.

Bentzen, J. S. (2012). How bad is corruption? Cross-country evidence of the impact of corruption on economic prosperity. *Review of Development Economics*, 16 (1), 167-184.

Billger, S. M., & Goel, R. K. (2009). Do existing corruption levels matter in controlling corruption?: Cross-country quantile regression estimates. *Journal of Development Economics*, 90 (2), 299-305.

Blackburn, K., & Forgues-Puccio, G. F. (2007). Distribution and development in a model of misgovernance. *European Economic Review*, 51 (6), 1534-1563.

Bollen, K. A., & Jackman, R. W. (1985). Economic and noneconomic determinants of political democracy in the 1960s. *Research in Political Sociology*, 1, 27-48.

Brunetti, A. & Weder, B. (2003). A free press is bad news for corruption. *Journal of Public Economics*, 87 (7-8), 1801-1824.

Butkiewicz, J. L., & Yanikkaya, H. (2005). The impact of sociopolitical instability on economic growth: Analysis and implications. *Journal of Policy Modeling* 27 (5), 629-645.

Butkiewicz, J. L., & Yanikkaya, H. (2006). Institutional quality and economic growth: Maintenance of the rule of law or democratic institutions, or both? *Economic Modelling*, 23 (4), 648-661.

Campbell, N., & Saha, S. (2013). Corruption, democracy, and Asia-Pacific countries. *Journal of the Asia Pacific Economy*, 18 (2), 290-303.

Campos, N. F., & Karanasos, M. G. (2008). Growth, volatility and political instability: Non-linear time-series evidence for Argentina, 1896–2000. *Economics Letters*, 100 (1), 135-137.

Claderon, C., & Chong, A. (2006). Do democracies breed rent-seeking behaviour? *Journal of Policy Reform*, 9 (4), 247-260.

Comeau, L. (2003). The political economy of growth in Latin America and East Asia: Some empirical evidence. *Contemporary Economy Policy*, 21 (4), 476-489.

Del Monte, A., & Papagni, E. (2007). The determinants of corruption in Italy: Regional panel data analysis. *European Journal of Political Economy*, 23 (2), 379-396.

Devereux, M. B., & Wen, J. F. (1998). Political instability, capital taxation, and growth. *European Economic Review*, 42 (9), 1635-1651.

Edi, E. (2006). Pan West Africanism and political instability in West Africa: Perspectives and reflections. *The Journal of Pan African Studies*, 1 (3), 7-31.

Edwards, S. (1996). Why are Latin America's savings rates so low? An international comparative analysis, *Journal of Development Economics*, 51 (1), 5-44.

Emerson, P. M. (2006). Corruption, competition and democracy. *Journal of Development Economics*, 81 (1), 193-212.

Erb, C. B., Harvey, C. R., & Viskanta, T. E. (1996). Political risk, financial risk and economic risk. *Financial Analysts Journal*, 52 (6), 29-46.

Farooq, A., Shahbaz, M., Arouri, M., & Teulon, F. (2013). Does corruption impede economic growth in Pakistan?. *Economic Modelling*, 35, 622-633.

Fisman, R. & Gatti, R. (2002). Decentralization and corruption: Evidence across countries. *Journal of Public Economics*, 83 (3), 325-345.

Fosu, A. K. (1992). Political instability and economic growth: Evidence from Sub-Saharan Africa. *Economic Development and Cultural Change*, 40 (4), 829-841.

Fosu, A. K. (2001). Political instability and economic growth in developing economies: Some specification empirics. *Economics Letters*, 70 (2), 289-294.

Fosu, A. K. (2002a). Political instability and economic growth: Implications of coup events in Sub-Saharan Africa. *American Journal of Economics and Sociology*, 61 (1), 329-348.

Fosu, A. K. (2002b). Transforming economic growth to human development in Sub-Saharan Africa: The role of elite political instability. *Oxford Development Studies*, 30 (1), 9-19.

Gasiorowski, M. J. (1998). Macroeconomic conditions and political instability: An empirical analysis. *Studies in Comparative International Development*, 33 (3), 3-17.

Ghura, D. (2002). Tax revenue in Sub-Saharan Africa: Effects of economic policies and corruption. In G. T. Abed, S. Gupta (Eds.), *Governance, Corruption, and Economic Performance* (pp. 369-395). Washington, DC: International Monetary Fund.

Goldsmith, A. A. (1999). Slapping the grasping hand. *American Journal of Economics and Sociology*, 58 (4), 865-883.

Granger, C. W. J. (1969). Investigating causal relations by econometric models and cross spectral methods. *Econometrica*, 37 (3), 424-438.

Granger, C. W. J. (1986). Development in the study of cointegrated economic variables. *Oxford Bulletin of Economics and Statistics*, 48 (3), 213-228.

Gupta, S., Davoodi, H., & Alonso-Terme, R. (2002). Does corruption affect income inequality and poverty? Economics of Governance, 3 (1), 23-45.

Gupta, D. K., Madhavan, M. C., & Blee, A. (1998). Democracy, economic growth and political instability: an integrated perspective. *The Journal of Socio-Economics*, 27 (5), 587-611.

Gyimah-Brempong, K. (2002). Corruption, economic growth, and income inequality in Africa. *Economics of Governance*, 3 (3), 183-209.

Gyimah-Brempong, K., & Dapaah, A. S. (1996). Non elite political instability and economic growth: Evidence from Sub-Saharan Africa. *Journal of Economic Development*, 21 (1), 181-210.

Gyimah-Brempong, K. & Traynor, T. L. (1999). Political instability, investment and economic growth in Sub-Saharan Africa. *Journal of African Economies*, 8 (1), 52-86.

Habib, M., & Zurawicki, L. (2001).Country-level investments and the effect of corruption- Some empirical evidence. *International Business Review*, 10 (6), 687-700.

Hayakawa, K., Kimura, F., & Lee, H. H. (2013). How does country risk matter for foreign direct investment? *The Developing Economies,* 5 (1), 60-78.

Heaney, R., & Hooper, V. (1999). World, regional and political risk influences upon Asia Pacific equity market returns. *Australian Journal of Management,* 24 (2), 131-142.

Helliwell, J. F. (1994). Empirical linkages between democracy and economic growth. *British Journal of Political Science,* 24 (2), 225-248.

Huntington, S. P. (1968). *Political order in changing societies.* New Haven, CT: Yale University Press.

Iwasaki, I., & Suzuki, T. (2012). The determinants of corruption in transition economies. *Economics Letters,* 114 (1), 54-60.

Lambsdorff, J. G. (1999, October). The Transparency International corruption perceptions index 1999: Framework document. *Transparency International, Berlin.* Retrieved from http://www.icgg.org/downloads/1999_CPI_FD.pdf

Lambsdorff, J. G. (2006). The validity and precision of subjective indicators (CPI). In C. Sampford, A. Shacklock, C. Connors, & F. Galtung (Eds.), *Measuring Corruption* (pp. 81-99). Aldershot, UK: Ashgate Publishing Company.

Le, Q. V. (2004). Political and economic determinants of private investment. *Journal of International Development,* 16 (4), 589-604.

Lederman, D., Loayza, N. V., & Soares, R. R (2005). Accountability and corruption: Political institutions matter. *Economics & Politics,* 17 (1), 1-35.

Leff, N. H. (1964). Economic development through bureaucratic corruption. *American Behavioral Scientist,* 8 (3), 8-14.

Leite, C. A. & Weidmann, J. (1999). Does mother nature corrupt?: Natural resources, corruption, and economic growth (Working Paper No. 99/85). International Monetary Fund.

Linder, A., & Santiso, C. (2002). Assessing the predictive power of country risk ratings and governance indicators (Working Paper No. 0202). School of Advanced International Studies. The Johns Hopkins University.

Lipset, S. M., & Raab, E. (1970). *The politics of unreason: Right-wing extremism in America, 1790-1970.* New York, NY: Harper & Row.

Mauro, P. (1995). Corruption and growth. *Quarterly Journal of Economics,* 110 (3), 681-712.

Mauro, P. (2004). The persistence of corruption and slow economic growth. *International Monetary Fund Staff Papers,* 51 (1), 1-18.

Mbaku, J. M. (1988). Political instability and economic development in Sub-Saharan Africa:
Some recent evidence. *Review of Black Political Economy,* 17 (1), 89-111.

Mbaku, J. M., & Paul, C. (1989). Political instability in Africa: A rent-seeking approach. *Public Choice Public Choice,* 63 (1), 63-72.

Méon, P. G., & Sekkat, K. (2005). Does corruption grease or sand the wheels of growth? *Public Choice,* 122 (1-2), 69-97.

Mo, P. H. (2001). Corruption and economic growth. *Journal of Comparative Economics,* 29 (1), 66-79.

Montinola, G. A., & Jackman, R.W. (2002). Sources of corruption: A cross-country study. *British Journal of Political Science,* 32 (1), 147-170.

Nelson, C. R., & Plosser, C. I. (1982). Trends and random walks in macroeconomic time series: Some evidence and implications. *Journal of Monetary Economics,* 10 (2), 139-162.

Okafor, C. E., Smith, M., & Ujah, N. (2014). Kleptocracy, nepotism, kakistrocracy: Impact of corruption in Sub-Saharan African countries. *International Journal of Economics and Accounting,* 5 (2), 97-115.

Oto-Peralías, D., Romero-Ávila, D., & Usabiaga, C. (2013). Does fiscal decentralization mitigate the adverse effects of corruption on public deficits? *European Journal of Political Economy,* 32, 205-231.

Park, H. (2003). Determinants of corruption: A cross-national analysis. *Multinational Business Review,* 11 (2), 29-48.

Pedroni, P. (1999). Critical values for cointegration tests in heterogeneous panels with multiple regressors. *Oxford Bulletin of Economics and Statistics,* 61, 653-670.

Serra, D. (2006). Empirical determinants of corruption: A sensitivity analysis. *Public Choice,* 126 (1), 225-256.

Schumacher, I. (2013). Political stability, corruption and trust in politicians. *Economic Modelling,* 31, 359-369.

Shabbir, G., & Anwar, M. (2007). Determinants of corruption in developing countries. *The Pakistan Development Review,* 46 (4), 751-764.

Shleifer, A., & Vishny, R. (1993). Corruption. *Quarterly Journal of Economics,* 108 (3), 599-617.

Sims, C. A. (1980). Macroeconomics and Reality. *Econometrica,* 48 (1), 1-48.

Svensson, J. (1998). Investment, property rights and political instability: Theory and evidence. *European Economic Review,* 42 (7), 1317-1341.

Swaleheen, M. (2007). Corruption and investment choices: A panel data study. *Kyklos,* 60 (4), 601-616.

Ugur, M., & Dasgupta, N. (2011). Corruption and economic growth: A meta-analysis of the evidence on low-income countries and beyond (MPRA 31226). University Library of Munich, Germany.

Van Rijckeghem, C., & Weder, B. (2001). Bureaucratic corruption and the rate of temptation: Do wages in the civil service affect corruption, and by how much? *Journal of Development Economics,* 65 (2), 307-331.

Williams, A., & Siddique, A. (2008). The use (and abuse) of governance indicators in economics: A review. *Economics of Governance,* 9 (2), 131-175.

Zhang, Y., Cao, L., & Vaughn, M. S. (2009). Social support and corruption: Structural determinants of corruption in the world. *Australian & New Zealand Journal of Criminology,* 42 (2), 204-217.

2

Innovations and Fighting Global Economic Problems

Natalia G. Vovchenko[1], Olga B. Ivanova[1], Elena D. Kostoglodova[1], Marina O. Otrishko[1], Olga S. Dzhu[1]

ABSTRACT The authors proffer the hypothesis that the most important issue in all of the previously studied global economic problems is the imperfection of the production process. Innovations stimulate the improvement of the production process and provide solutions to global economic problems. Thus, the purpose of this article is to verify this hypothesis and determine the role of innovations in overcoming global economic problems. To verify the hypothesis, the authors use analysis of causal connections, problem and systemic analysis, economic and mathematical modeling, and a developed proprietary economic and mathematical model of the production process. The authors conduct an analysis of global economic problems at present and in perspective and determine the role of innovations in overcoming these global economic problems. The offered hypothesis is proven, and it is substantiated, based on the problem of resource limitations, disproportions of economic growth, and crises in the global economy, that innovations play an important role in solving global economic problems. For example, innovations lead to improvements in the production process because the consumption of resources is reduced and the volume of manufactured goods is increased, which solves the problem of resource limitations. Furthermore, the implementation of production innovations in enterprises in the least developed countries stimulates their economic development and reduces the level of countries' differentiation in the global economy. Accordingly, the authors determine the directions of development with respect to the innovation activities of modern enterprises for overcoming global economic problems, and they develop an algorithm for the development of the modern global economy.

KEY WORDS: innovations, global economic problems, global economy, crisis, limitations of resources

[1]Rostov State Economic University, Russia

Introduction

The globalization of the world economy stimulates the expansion and unification of the goals and interests of various countries with respect to the creation of a world economy. In the new millennium, humankind faces a global problem that influences each member of the global economy, and thus, it can be solved only by the joint efforts of the global community. There are several important global economic problems.

- The problem of limited resources for the manufacturing of necessary goods. This extends from the interactions between humankind and the environment and includes issues such as the lack of natural resources, the impossibility to satisfy the demand for human resources (famine, disease, etc.), the depletion of nat-

Correspondence concerning this article should be addressed to: Natalia G. Vovchenko, Department of Finance, Rostov State Economic University (RINH), 69 Bolshaya Sadovaya St. Rostov-on-Don 344007 Russian Federation. E-mail: natalia-vovchenk@rambler.ru

ural resources, and the worsening of the global ecological situation. The problem of the differentiation of countries in the global economy with respect to their level of economic development is deeply rooted in the formation of the modern global economy and is exemplified by the superiority of some countries over others; this problem stems from issues of post-war development in the global economy and is manifested in the presence of the most economically developed countries, which are leaders in the global economy, and underdeveloped countries, which are actually referred to as developing countries as they strive to overcome the developed countries;
- The problem of the cyclic development of the global economy, which contributes to the aptness of an economy for crises. The market model of the economy in most countries of the world stimulates the emergence of periodic failures, which, having emerged in one country, are distributed to all countries of the world under the influence of globalization processes and under conditions of close cooperation and strong interdependence of economies.

These problems determine the outline of the modern global economy and the limitations of its further development. There is a high level of interest in this study because of these problems and the causal connections to their development, the search for the methods and means to solve them, and role of various factors in overcoming them.

The authors offer the hypothesis that the most important cause of all of the studied global economic problems is the imperfection of the production process. Innovations stimulate the perfection of the production process and ensure the solving of the global economic problems. The purpose of the article is to verify the offered hypothesis and determine possibilities and perspectives to overcome these global economic problems through the development of innovations. The achievement of this goal supposes the following successive solutions to the main problems:

- analyze the causes of the global economic problems;
- determine the possibilities to solve these problems by implementing innovations in production;
- examine the key barriers to the implementation of innovations in production in developing countries using modern Russia as an example;
- determine the perspective directions for the development of innovative activity of modern enterprises to overcome the global economic problems and develop the mechanism for the innovational development of the modern global economy.

Literature review

Global economic problems are examined in a number of studies by modern researchers. At present, there are many hypotheses as to the reasons for the emergence of these problems and the factors that allow them to be overcome. These issues are examined in the works of such authors as (Grigoreva, 2015; Gubaidullina, 2015; Melnik, Orlov, Bondarenko, Melnik, & Grekova, 2015; Yegireddy, Panda, Rout, & Bonthu, 2015). The most important reasons for the emergence of global economic problems include the irrational spending of resources (Omelchenko, 2015), the active development of industry (Gerards, 2015), and the irresponsible attitude towards issues of environmental protection.

The problem of limited resources is one of the most ancient of economic problems and is the reason for the emergence of economics as a science aimed at the search for a solution to this problem. It is studied in works of such authors as (Pogodaeva, Zhaparova, Rudenko, & Skripnuk, 2015; Waisová, 2013). Despite the fact that resources are either renewable or non-renewable, they should be spent effectively due to their strict limitations (Visser, Ohan, & Enns, 2015).

The problems of disproportionate economic growth and the differentiation in the levels of economic development of various countries in the global economy have only recently been actualized, but they have already attracted attention and become the basis for multiple lines of research, among which are the works of (Bhanumurthy & Singh, 2013; Bozkurt, Erdem, Ero⊠lu, & 2015; Caporale & Spagnolo, 2012; Gehringer, 2014; Jahfer & Inoue, 2014). Due to the uniqueness of these economic systems, their economic development assumes various directions at different rates (Al Mamun & Sohag, 2015), which causes the problem of disproportionate economic growth in the global economy (Popkova, Zubakova, Bogdanov, Yakovleva, & Nebesnay, 2013). This problem can be solved by reducing the rates of development of the leading countries or by quickening the rates of economic development in underdeveloped countries (Popkova, Yurev, Stepicheva, & Denisov, 2015).

The problem of the cyclic character of development of the global economy, which is built on the basis of the market principle and is subject to the periodic emergence of global crises, became the foundation of the well-known studies of N. Kondratyev, which, having not lost their sense of reality, are reconsidered in the works of Grinin, Devezas, and Korotayev (2012) and such researchers as (Aytaç, Rankin, & İbikoğlu, 2015; Guttmann, 2015; Heinrich, Kobayashi, & Bryant, 2016; McMaster, 2015; Rodriguez, Turmo, & Vara, 2014; Zhao, Jiang, & Li, 2015).

Due to the spontaneity and unpredictability of market processes in the modern global economy, crisis phenomena emerge from time to time (Galbraith, 2015) and are then succeeded by economic growth (Capello, Caragliu, & Fratesi, 2015). It should be noted that after a crisis, the economy usually realizes higher rates and levels of development (Hieronymi, 2016).

The role and significance of innovations in the development and production of specific enterprises, countries, and the modern global economy on the whole, the possibilities and perspectives of further innovational development of the global economy, and the transition of various countries to an innovational path of economic development are analyzed in the works of such scientists as (Coccia, 2015; Donate, Peña, & Sánchez de Pablo, 2016; Kolychev & Prokhorov, 2015; Rumyantsev, 2014; Vasin & Gamidullaeva, 2015). The implementation of innovations requires a high level of development in science and education (Ng, Kanagasundram, Wong, & Chandran, 2015); financing science and education may allow the underdeveloped countries to close the gap between themselves and the developed economies (Filinova, Filinov, Pogodina, Lunev, & Luneva, 2015).

The most important problems associated with transitioning to innovational paths of development in various countries include traditional thinking, unfavorable business climates, and lack of investment resources (Turriago-Hoyos, Thoene, Bernal-Torres, & Alfonso-Lizarazo, 2015). Despite the popularity, research, multiple hypotheses, and extensive elaboration on the topic of global economic development, scientists have not yet come to a unified opinion as to the reasons for the emergence of global economic problems and have not yet found the means to resolve them, either separately or as a whole, even with the help of universal instrumentarium.

Thus, it is necessary to conduct further research and to offer new hypotheses. This article is devoted to the development of the topic of global economic problems and the verification of the hypothesis that the problems can be solved by increasing the innovational activities of modern enterprises.

Method

To verify the offered hypothesis, the authors adopt the method of analysis of causal connections, the method of problem and systemic analysis, and the method of economic and mathematical modeling. According to the authors of this research, economic and mathematical modeling of the production process takes the following form:

$$PP=(HR+MR+CR)*TP \qquad (1)$$

where PP – production process;
HR – human resources;
MR – material resources;
CR – capital resources;
TP – technology of production.

Though this is not a model of production factors, there is a certain similarity in that the production process model includes all of the main factors except entrepreneurial capability because the entrepreneur does not participate directly in the production process, but rather only organizes it.

Formula (1) indicates that the spending of resources is predetermined by the technology of production, where human resources are the investing of human labor in the production of goods and material resources are raw materials used in production.

Capital resources reflect the financial facets and include investments in production. The technology of production, which includes the production of equipment, determines the manner in which the various resources can be combined to enhance the speed of the production of goods (time spent). The authors also use systemic and problem analysis, analysis of causal connections, synthesis, induction, deduction, and formalization.

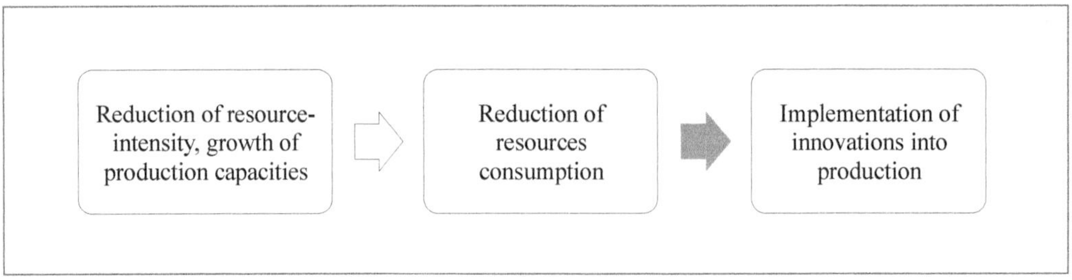

Figure 1. Process of solving the problem of limited resources in the global economy with the help of implementation of innovations into production

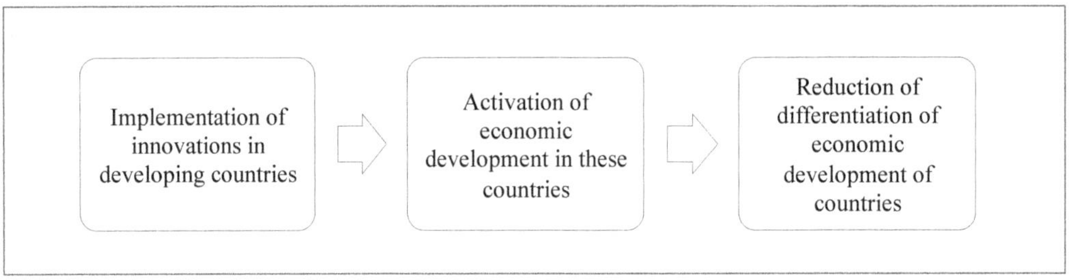

Figure 2. Process of solving the problem of disproportions of economic development of countries in the global economy with the help of implementation of innovations into production

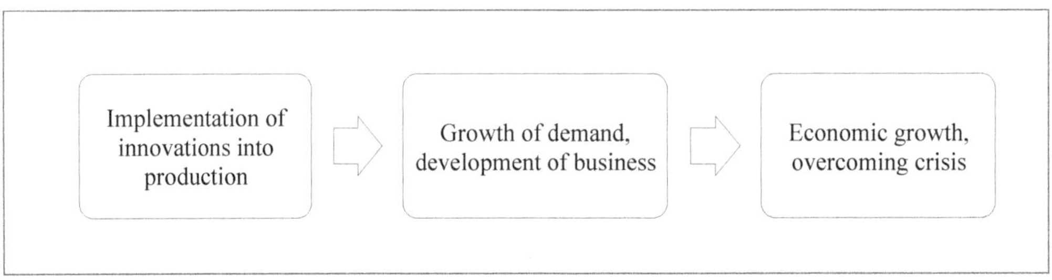

Figure 3. The process of solving the problem of crisis phenomena in the global economy by implementing innovations in production

Results

A deep and thorough study conducted to analyze the causes of global economic problems reveals that the most important cause of all studied global economic problems is imperfection in the production process. Thus, the problem of limited resources is caused, on the one hand, by the limitations in natural inheritance, which are within the control of humankind, and the peculiarities of the environment, and on the other hand, by the high resource intensity associated with modern production.

The cause of differentiation among countries regarding the level of economic development is based on the of different levels of GDP due to varied levels of production development among them. Furthermore, the cyclic development of the global economy and its aptitude to manage crises is manifested in the reduction of the rates of economic growth, which in turn are determined by the development of production.

The possibility to solve these problems is found in the implementation of innovations in production.

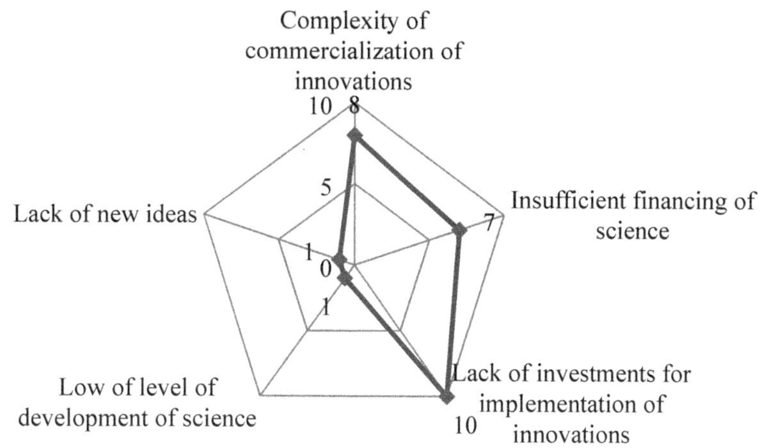

Figure 4. Key barriers on the way for implementation of innovations into production in Russia, 2014
Adapted from "Scientific research and innovations. Russia in numbers. 2015", by Rosstat (2015). Retrieved from http://www.gks.ru/free_doc/doc_2016/rusfig/rus16.pdf

Therefore, it is necessary to examine the production processes before and after the implementation of innovations. During the initial use of technology in the production process, production factors are used and combined, which leads to a certain set of goods.

It is impossible to reduce the resource intensity of production and increase production capacities without changing production technologies. Consider, for example, the invention and implementation of the conveyor, a significant innovation that changed the production process at the beginning of the 20th century.

As a result of the creation and implementation of innovations in production in the short-term, there is an improvement in production technology as well as a growth in the expenditures of capital resources, as the modernization of equipment requires significant resources.

However, the expenses with respect to human resources are reduced significantly due to the automatization of production. Moreover, expenditures for material resources (raw materials) are also reduced due to the implementation of technology in production.

For example, as a result of the use of the conveyor technology, there was a significant reduction in human resources and a moderate reduction in expenses related to material resources. It is noted, however, that the reduction in spending for material resources may not have been a direct consequence of the invention of the conveyor, but it may be the result of the implementation of other innovations. This example reflects the implementation of innovation in production.

The spending of capital resources increased significantly due to the need to attract huge investments to modernize equipment, and production technology developed considerably. As a result, the volume of manufactured goods increased significantly, thus resolving the problem of a lack of goods and helping to meet the needs of society by, for example, reducing famine and providing drinking water and medicine.

In the long term, after the successful implementation of innovations, investments are returned and the spending of capital resources is reduced due to the decreased need for labor and material resources. Furthermore, as a result of the implementation of innovations, there is a reduction in the resource intensity of production and an increase in production capacities, thus substantiating the premise that the primary role of innovation is to solve the global economic problem of limited resources (Fig. 1). The implementation of in-

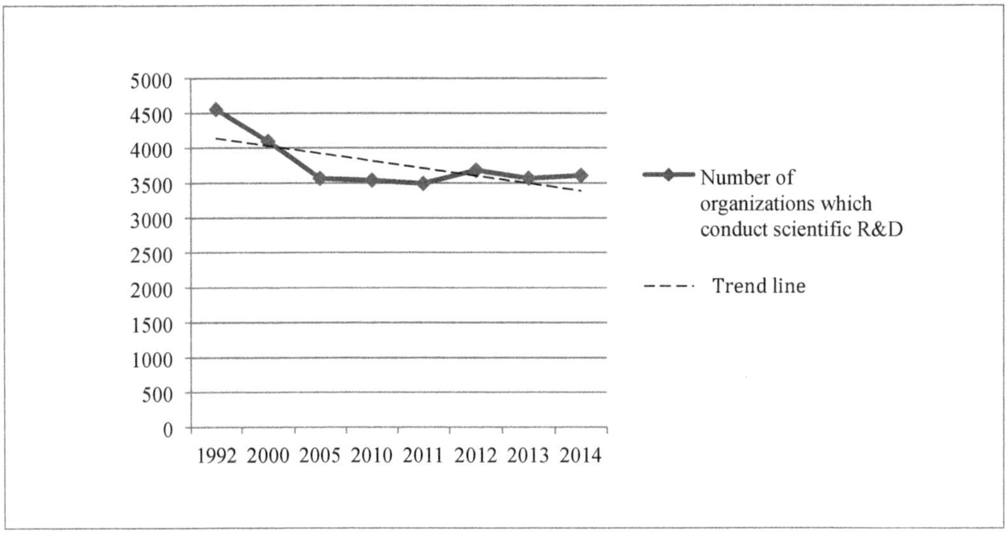

Figure 5. Dynamics of the number of innovational enterprises in Russia in 1992-2014
Adapted from "Scientific research and innovations. Russia in numbers. 2015", by Rosstat (2015). Retrieved from http://www.gks.ru/free_doc/doc_2016/rusfig/rus16.pdf

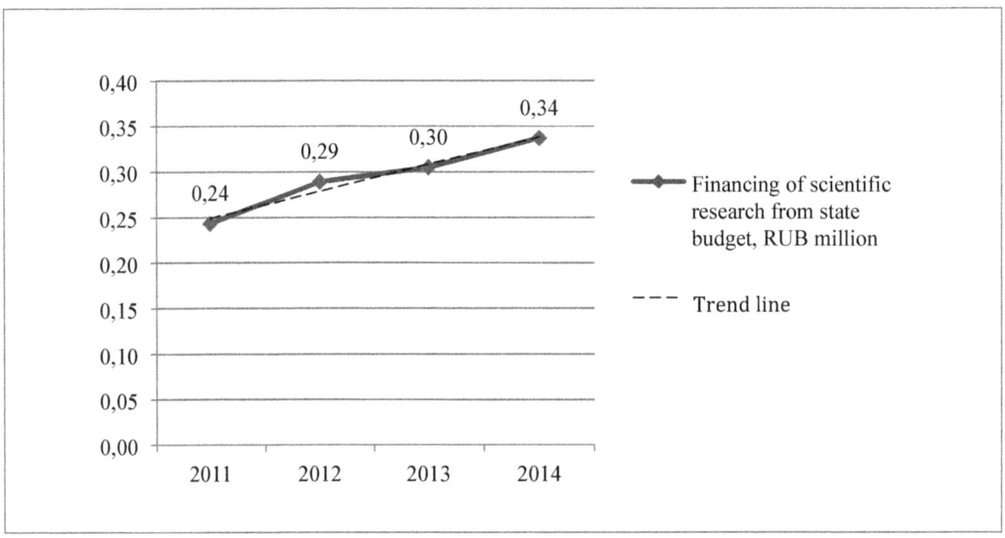

Figure 6. Dynamics of the share of spending for financing of science in the structure of Russian GDP in 2011-2014
Adapted from "Scientific research and innovations. Russia in numbers. 2015", by Rosstat (2015). Retrieved from http://www.gks.ru/free_doc/doc_2016/rusfig/rus16.pdf

novations in the least developed countries stimulates the development of production in these countries and increases their GDP. As a result, active economic development of these countries occurs, which leads to a reduction in the level of differentiation among the countries and thus contributes to solving the problem of disproportionate economic growth in the global economy (Fig. 2). Enterprises that manufacture in-

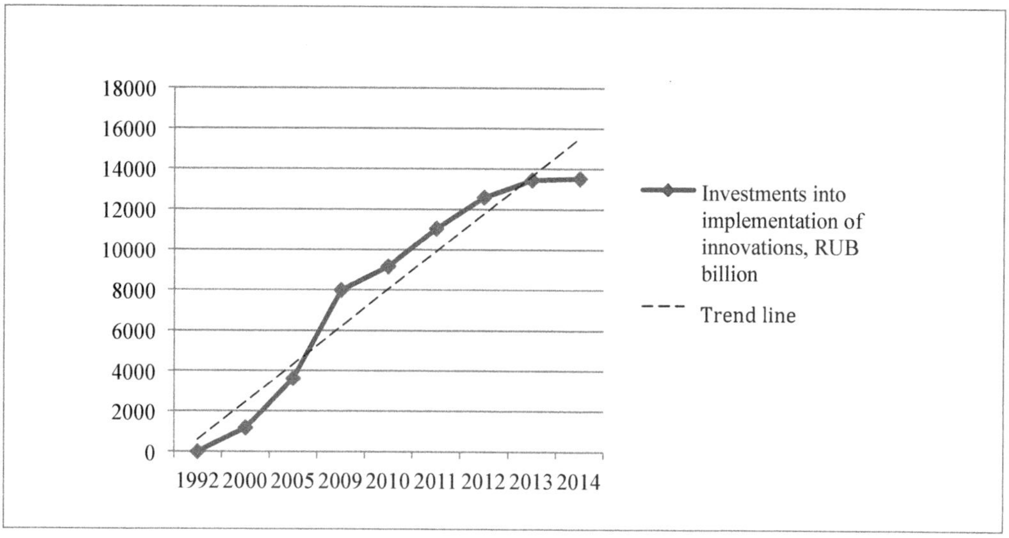

Figure 7. Dynamics of investments into implementation of innovations in Russia in 1992-2014
Adapted from "Scientific research and innovations. Russia in numbers. 2015", by Rosstat (2015). Retrieved from http://www.gks.ru/free_doc/doc_2016/rusfig/rus16.pdf

novational products have advantages when compared to other companies, as they put less expensive, better, or completely new products on the market that are in greater demand – due to the above reasons – than the products of other enterprises.

Furthermore, these innovations are adopted by other enterprises, which results in increased demand and business, even under conditions of a decline in the population's income and, correspondingly, a reduction in purchasing power.

As a result, profits grow, which leads to revenues for the state budget. These revenues then create possibilities for the further stimulation of economic development. Thus, the consequences of the crisis are overcome, and the global economy is able to overcome the recession (Fig. 3).

We consider the key barriers to the implementation of innovations in production in developing countries from the perspective modern Russia. The obstacles on the path to the development of innovations in developing countries are, as a rule, the lack of financing for science; the complexity of the commercialization of innovations; the lack of investments, which are needed to implement innovations; the low level of science development; and the lack of new ideas. Based on the statistical information obtained from the Federal State Statistics Service, the key barriers to the implementation of innovations in production in Russia in 2014 have been determined (Fig. 4). As presented in Fig. 4, the most serious impediments when building an innovation economy in modern Russia were the lack of financing for science, the complexity of the commercialization of innovations, and the lack of necessary investments to implement innovations. This is, again, clearly reflected in Figs. 5 to 7.

As evidenced in Fig. 5, the number of innovational enterprises in Russia has declined by 20% over the past two decades, and, as presented in Fig. 6, the share of investment in financing scientific research constituted less than 1% over the period of 2011 to 2014. Fig. 7 indicates that investments in the implementation of innovations in Russia increased between 1992 and 2013 but then decreased in 2014, revealing a negative tendency.

Based on the determined problems, the most prescriptive strategies for the development of innovational activities in modern enterprises to overcome global economic problems are as follows:

- provide favorable conditions for the creation of innovations in developing countries;
- provide favorable conditions for the commercialization of innovations in developing countries;

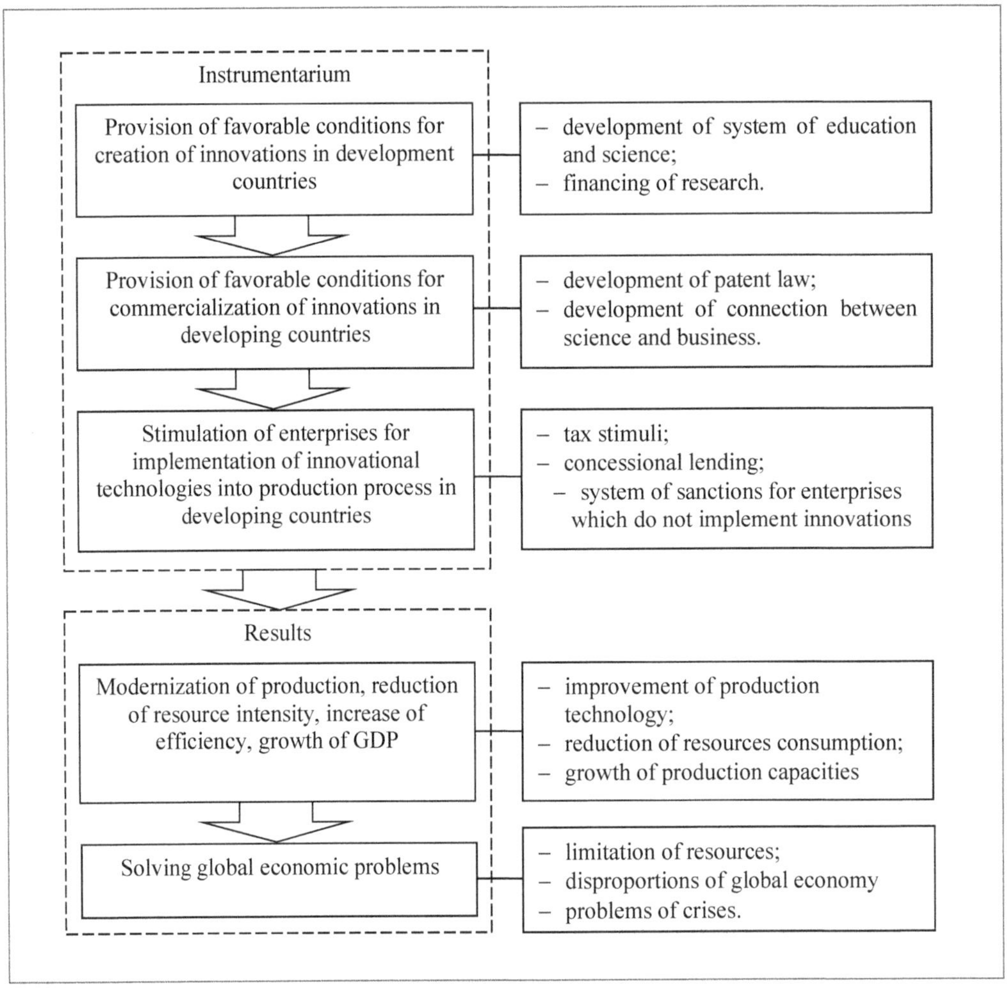

Figure 8. Algorithm of the innovational development of the modern global economy

- stimulate enterprises to implement innovational technologies in the production processes in developing countries.

To actualize these strategies, this research offers a proprietary mechanism for innovational development in the modern global economy, as presented in Fig. 8.

Conclusion

Thus, as a result of the conducted research, the offered hypothesis was proven and, by referencing the problems of limited resources, disproportionate economic growth, and crises in the global economy, it was substantiated that the development of innovations is a perspective tool for solving global economic problems.

Innovations lead to improvements in the production process such that the consumption of resources decreases and the volume of manufactured goods increases, which leads to solving the problem of limited resources. The implementation of innovations in production at the enterprise level in the least developed countries stimulates their economic development and reduces the level of differentiation among countries in the global economy.

Under the conditions of recession, the economy does not develop, and economic growth stagnates. Accordingly, innovations create the stimulus for the development of the global economy, which ensures that the global economic crisis is overcome and solves the problem of the cyclic development of the global economy.

The most serious problems affecting the building of an innovational economy in Russia are the lack of financing for science, the complexity of the commercialization of innovations, and the lack of investments necessary to implement innovations.

To remove these barriers and build an innovation economy, this research offers an algorithm for the innovational development of a modern global economy that stimulates the increase of innovational activity in developing countries and the solving of global economic problems.

This research is built on the study of the role of innovation in solving three large economic problems that include the totality of global issues. Accordingly, this predetermines the limitations of the results of the research based on the problems chosen for analysis.

Therefore, it is expedient to conduct further research in this sphere to determine the role of innovations in solving global economic problems using the examples of other negative phenomena in the global economy, particularly the examples of the problems of ecological security and military threats to the global economy.

References

Al Mamun, M., & Sohag, K. (2015). Revisiting the dynamic effect of foreign direct investment on economic growth in LDCs. *International Journal of Economic Policy in Emerging Economies, 8*(2), 97-118.

Aytaç, I. A., Rankin, B. H., & İbikoğlu, A. (2015). The social impact of the 2008 global economic crisis on neighborhoods, households, and individuals in Turkey. *Social Indicators Research, 124*(1), 1-19.

Bhanumurthy, N. R., & Singh, P. (2013). Financial sector development and economic growth in Indian states. *International Journal of Economic Policy in Emerging Economies, 6*(1), 47-63.

Bozkurt, Ö. G., Erdem, C., & Ero⊠lu, I. (2015). Identifying the factors affecting the economic growth of oil-producing countries. *International Journal of Trade and Global Markets, 8* (2), 97-111.

Capello, R., Caragliu, A., & Fratesi, U. (2015). Global trends and the economic crisis: Future alternative European growth strategies. *Technological Forecasting and Social Change, 98*, 120-136.

Caporale, G.M., & Spagnolo, N. (2012). Stock market, economic growth and EU accession: Evidence from three CEECs. *International Journal of Monetary Economics and Finance, 5*(2), 183-191.

Coccia, M. (2015). General sources of general purpose technologies in complex societies: Theory of global leadership-driven innovation, warfare and human development. *Technology in Society, 42*, 199-226.

Donate, M. J., Peña, I., & Sánchez de Pablo, J. D. (2016). HRM practices for human and social capital development: Effects on innovation capabilities. *The International Journal of Human Resource Management, 27*(9), 928-953.

Filinova, N. V., Filinov, V. P., Pogodina, O. N., Lunev, V. A., & Luneva, E. V. (2015). The socio-economic foundations of the development of contemporary economic innovations. *Asian Social Science, 11*(6), 250-260.

Galbraith, J. K. (2015). *Inequality and instability: A study of the world economy just before the great crisis. Inequality and Instability: A Study of the World Economy Just Before the Great Crisis*, Oxford, UK: Oxford University Press.

Gehringer, A. (2014). Financial liberalisation, financial development and productivity growth: An overview. *International Journal of Monetary Economics and Finance, 7*(1), 40-65.

Gerards, J. (2015). The ecthr's response to fundamental rights issues related to financial and economic difficulties: The problem of compartmentalisation. *Netherlands Quarterly of Human Rights, 33*(3), 274-292.

Grigoreva, E. A. (2015). Problems of institutional provision of the state's economic security. *Mediterranean Journal of Social Sciences, 6*(3), 499-503.

Grinin L., Devezas T., & Korotayev A. (2012). Kondratieff's Mystery. Kondratieff Waves. In L. E. Grinin, T. C. Devezas, & A. V. Kortayev (Eds.), *Kondratieff waves: Dimensions and perspectives at the dawn of the 21st century* (pp. 5-22). Volgograd: Uchitel.

Gubaidullina, T. N. (2015). Systemic approach in the study of problems of territories's sustainable ecological and economic development. *Mediterranean Journal of Social Sciences, 6* (1S3), 232-236.

Guttmann, R. (2015). Chronic macro-economic and financial imbalances in the world economy: A meta-economic view. Revista de Economia Politica, 35(2), 203-226.

Heinrich, K., Kobayashi, Y., & Bryant, K. A. (2016). Public opinion and foreign aid cuts in economic crises. *World Development, 77*, 66-79.

Hieronymi, O. (2016). The crisis of international finance, the Eurozone and economic growth. In S. P. S. Rossi, & R. Malavi (Eds.), Financial crisis, bank behaviour and credit crunch (pp. 3-18). Berlin: Springer.

Jahfer, A., & Inoue, T. (2014). Financial development, foreign direct investment and economic growth in Sri Lanka. *International Journal of Economic Policy in Emerging Economies, 7*(1), 77-93.

Kolychev, V. D., Prokhorov, I. V. (2015). Conception, technology and methods of development of university system of innovation projects commercialization based on effectuation. *Asian Social Science, 11*(8), 44-51.

McMaster, R. (2015). The "illusion" or "paradigm blindness" of economics: Ethical challenges to economic thought from the financial crisis. In T. H. Jo & F. S. Lee (Eds.), *Marx, Veblen, and the Foundations of Heterodox Economics: Essays in Honor of John F. Henry* (pp. 155-175). London, UK: Routledge.

Melnik, M. S., Orlov, L. F., Bondarenko, A. V., Melnik, E. D.,Grekova, K. P. (2015). The Problems of Modern Economic Development: The Fundamental Mechanics. *Mediterranean Journal of Social Sciences, 6*(3), 646-653.

Ng, B. K., Kanagasundram, T., Wong, C. Y., Chandran, V. G. R. (2015). Innovation for inclusive development in Southeast Asia: The roles of regional coordination mechanisms. *The Pacific Review, 2*(1), 1- 30.

Omelchenko, K. Y. (2015). Model for economic indicators forecasting with a dual problem. Actual Problems of Economics, *164*(2), 437-441.

Pogodaeva, T. V., Zhaparova, D. V., Rudenko, D. Y., Skripnuk, D. F. (2015). Innovations and socio-economic development: Problems of the natural resources intensive use regions. *Mediterranean Journal of Social Sciences, 6*(1), 129-135.

Popkova, E. G, Zubakova, N. N., Bogdanov, D. V., Yakovleva, E. A, Nebesnay, A. Y. (2013). Measurement of economic growth as a factor of development of strategies of economic transformation. *World Applied Sciences Journal, 25*(2), 264-269.

Popkova, E. G., Yurev, V., Stepicheva, O., Denisov, N. (2015). Transformation and concentration of intellectual capital as a factor of economic growth in the modern economy. *Regional and Sectoral Economic Studies, 15*(1), 53-60.

Rodriguez, A., Turmo, J., & Vara, O. (2014). Financial crisis and the failure of economic theory. Abington, UK: Routlege.

Rosstat (2015). Scientific research and innovations. Russia in numbers. 2015: Bulletin of Rosstat. Retrieved from Rosstat. (2015). *Russia in numbers. Scientific research and innovations 2015: Bulletin of Rosstat.* Retrieved from http://www.gks.ru/free_doc/doc_2015/rusfig/rus-15.pdf

Rumyantsev, A. A. (2015). Science and innovation space of a macroregion: Prospects of innovative territorial development. *Studies on Russian Economic Development, 26*(4), 379-387.

Turriago-Hoyos, A., Thoene, U., Bernal-Torres, C., Alfonso-Lizarazo, E. (2015). Product innovation, research and development and technology acquisition: A case study of the industrial sector in Colombia. *Institutions and Economies, 7*(2), 85-119.

Vasin, S. M., Gamidullaeva, L. A. (2015). Development a basic model of the innovation system. *Review of European Studies, 7*(11), 175-183.

Visser, T. A. W., Ohan, J. L., Enns, J. T. (2015). Temporal cues derived from statistical patterns can overcome resource limitations in the attentional blink. *Attention, Perception, and Psychophysics, 77*(5), 1585-1595.

Waisová, Š. (2013). Od hrozby k příležitosti: Vede nedostatek environmentálních zdrojů ke spolupráci? [From Threat to opportunity: Does a lack of environmental resources lead to cooperation?]. *Mezinarodni Vztahy, 48*(3), 32-61.

Yegireddy, N. K., Panda, S., Rout, U. K., Bonthu, R. K. (2015). Selection of control parameters of differential evolution algorithm for economic load dispatch problem. In L. C. Jain, H. S. Behera, J. K. Mandal, & D. P. Mohapatra (Eds.), Computational Intelligence in Data Mining (Vol. 3, pp. 251-260). New Delhi: Springer India.

Zhao, X., Jiang, X., Li, Z. (2015). The impact of the economic crisis on the financial performance of multinational corporations. *International Review of Economics and Finance, 37*, 55-68.

3

An Allocation Analysis of Polish Household Savings Invested in Financial Assets, 2003 – 2014

Wiesław Dębski[1], Bartosz Świderski[2]

ABSTRACT

This article addresses the allocation of Polish household savings that are invested in financial assets. As an economic category, these savings are very important in every country because they determine investments in the national economy, thereby influencing a country's further economic growth and development. From this point of view, investigating both the allocation of personal savings and their structure is essential because they change due to changing economic circumstances, changing situations in the world's financial markets, especially in the stock exchange markets, and the development of financial markets. The main purpose of this article is to analyze the changes in the allocation of savings in Polish households and the structure of their investment in financial assets. These changes, which are empirically observed, result from the circumstances of the national economy, which affect the behavior of investors in the stock market and determine the interest rate levels. The analysis is conducted on the basis of trend models with variations of parameters. The analysis has been carried out for the period Q4 2003 – Q3 2014.

KEY WORDS: savings of the Polish households, financial assets, analysis of allocation and its structure, trend models with variations of parameters

[1] University of Finance and Management in Warsaw - Management and Finance, Poland; [2] Warsaw University of Life Sciences - Faculty of Applied Informatics and Mathematics, Department of Applied Informatics, Poland

Introduction

The savings of households are a very important economic category in any economy and influence its development. The allocation of these savings is particularly essential, thus making it the subject matter of this paper. Personal savings have a direct impact on economic investment. The allocation of these savings attests to the inflow of capital to those sectors (branches) of the economy that, based on the savings investor's evaluation, are capable of showing the highest rates of return on the investment, i.e., they are the most profitable. Such sectors are frequently also the most innovative of the economy and, in turn, exert the most profound influence on economic growth, thus also determining its development. The allocation and *de facto* investment of household savings in the economy may occur through the banking sector (indirect investment) or the financial market (direct investment). In Poland, the overwhelming majority

Correspondence concerning this article should be addressed to: **Wiesław Dębski**, University of Finance and Management in Warsaw - Management and Finance, 55 Pawia Str., 01-030 Warsaw, Poland. E-mail: wdebski@vizja.pl

of personal savings is allocated through the banking sector, which is done primarily through bank deposits, which the bank later uses for lending. Although the financial market develops as a result (in the midst of the second decade of the 21st century, the Polish financial market is considered quite well-developed), more and more of the savings are allocated directly, i.e., investments made in shares or debt securities of companies. A certain amount of personal savings is also allocated indirectly through the financial market, which is done through various types of mutual fund agencies, such as investment, pension, and capital funds that are managed by life insurance undertakings. Numerous factors determine the allocation of household savings and its structure; however, first and foremost, they are contingent upon economic and demographic factors and on the psychological attributes of an investor, though we do not examine the latter two factors. Among the economic factors, those that directly shape the economy are the most important because they also influence the stock market and interest rate levels (although the basic interest rate is set by the central bank of Poland, its level is largely dependent on economic circumstances).

The chief purpose of this paper is to analyze the allocation of personal savings to financial assets in Poland and the changes to the structure of this allocation. The analysis was based on quarterly financial accounts that were drafted by the National Bank of Poland in the period 2003Q4-2014Q3. The analysis assumed a macroeconomic perspective, which is econometric in character, and was conducted based on a trend model with a variety of parameters, which were estimated using the ordinary least squares (OLS) method. The analyzed period encompassed times of prosperity and economic slowdown, the latter of which was caused by the financial crisis starting in 2007, as well as the period of recovery from this crisis. During this period, changes in the country's economic circumstances led primarily to changes in the stock market and interest rates, which exerted a direct influence on the structure of the allocation of household savings invested in financial assets. Using sample cases, the main objective of this study is to determine the extent of those changes. The intention is to determine the extent of the decreasing proportion of household savings being allocated to bank deposits and debt securities, the extent of the simultaneous growth of the proportion of these savings being allocated to shares and mutual funds, and vice versa. The present study is a continuation of research initiated by Dębski (2009) and Dębski and Świderski (2011). Research on the allocation of personal savings to various assets has also been carried out by several authors, including (Bergstresser & Poterba, 2004; Brennan & Xia, 2002; Campbell, Chan, & Viceira, 2003; Gomes & Michaelides, 2005; Horneff et al., 2009; Milevsky & Young, 2007; Shoren & Sialm, 2004) and in Poland (Anioła & Gołaś, 2012a; Rytelewska & Kłopocka, 2010).

1. Household savings – methodological aspects

In macroeconomics, household savings are defined as the difference between a household's available personal income and its expenditure on ongoing consumption. These are the ongoing savings of the population, which represent an increase in the total personal savings in a given year and are a resource because they are the sum of both the ongoing savings and the aggregated savings from the past. The total household savings may be composed of tangible assets in which the household has invested, such as real estate, art, gold, and jewelry, and the household's financial assets, such as cash, bank deposits, securities, and shares in mutual funds. This paper analyzes the structure of the allocation of household savings in financial assets and the changes to this structure by examining the financial market's approach to allocating these savings and the corresponding changes to the approach. Over time, the structure of allocation undergoes changes that are due to not only the changing circumstances of the market but also the use of personal savings as a resource. In a given period (a quarter or a year), a change may occur in the consequences of withdrawing part of one's savings from the financial market and allocating them to purchase tangible assets, or vice versa. In a given period, a household's total savings may also become smaller if they are withdrawn from investment and devoted to ongoing consumption.

The theory of economics that is supported by numerous empirical studies argues that the fundamental factor determining the amount of a household's ongoing savings is the household's propensity to save, which is most frequently seen as the ratio of these savings in a given year to the disposable income, a measure that is also referred to as the savings rate. An individual's (household) propensity to save results predominantly from the willingness to defer current consumption until a later date. The relevant economic literature pays particular attention to the motives behind saving that inspire an individual, their psychological traits that encourage saving, or demographic factors. Although this paper does not address the microeconomic perspective, we cite examples of the following relevant papers: (Anioła & Gołaś, 2012b; Börsch-Supan, 2003; Brandstaetter & Gueth, 2000; Canova, Rattazzi, & Webley, 2005; Duesenbury, 1952; Fisher & Montalto, 2010; Kirsanova & Sefton, 2007).

Many researchers have examined the propensity to save from a macroeconomic perspective by looking at the entire population (all households). These studies were dependent on manifold factors, entertained by various theories on saving. An overall review may of the research has been provided by Rytelewska (2008) and Beverly and Sherraden (1999), among others. The theories clearly indicate that the basic factor determining an increase in ongoing savings, which is a direct consequence of a household's propensity to save, is the population's personal disposable income (as already noted by J. Keynes (1985, p. 122)), which is directly expressed in the yearly national income. The personal disposable incomes of the population is equal to the personal incomes minus taxes paid (see Carroll, 2001). Regarding theories about savings that measure the dependence of personal savings on personal incomes, the most prominent ones are the income theory by Keynes (1985), the life-cycle hypothesis by Modigliani (Modigliani & Brumberg, 1955), and the permanent income hypothesis by Friedman (1957). Countless economists have conducted research in this regard, including (Bunting, 2009; Han & Sherraden, 2009; Liberda, 2000; Sherraden, Schreiner, & Beverly, 2003).

Interest rates are another important factor that influences the increase in household savings. In models accounting for personal savings, the interest rate is typically expressed as the real interest rate of bank deposits, which can be seen in models of the national economy (Welfe, 2013) or in models of the national economy's financial sector (Dębski, 1990; Łapińska-Sobczak, 1997). When this rate increases, more funds are placed in various types of bank accounts, and fewer funds are allocated to the financial market's equity instruments, such as shares of companies or mutual funds. In turn, a decrease in this rate causes a reverse effect, i.e., a decrease in the proportion of savings placed in banks and an increase in the proportion of savings allocated to shares and investment funds.

Moreover, the precautionary motive should be mentioned as one of the factors that stimulates an increase in household savings, as already noticed by Keynes (1985). The consequence of this motive is intentional saving, whether for the purpose of buying a house or apartment, securing retirement funds, educating children, or otherwise, as well as cashless transactions that directly influence the amount of funds that the population holds in its bank accounts. An additional factor stimulating household savings is the monetary policy of the central bank. An expansionary program that leads to the intensification of commercial bank lending will result in greater investments, which will result in an increase in personal incomes and household savings. In turn, if the central bank pursues a restrictive policy, the results will be inverse.

In Poland, the savings rate in the period under examination ranged between 7.7% (2003) and 10.0% (2007) and started to fall gradually, reaching 6.4% in 2008, 6.3% in 2010, and 3.7% in 2013. As research shows (Anioła, Gołaś, 2012a, p. 27; Rytelewska, 2008, p. 417), the rate in the period 2003-2007 was higher than those of the United States, Great Britain, Canada, and many other countries; however, countries such as Germany, France, and Italy had an interest rate higher than Poland's. Beginning in 2008, the savings rate in Poland began to decline. In the countries belonging to the Euro Area, the rate was higher in the whole period under analysis, at approximately 14%.

There is no doubt that in any country whose chief function is to mobilize capital, the development of the financial market contributes to an increase in personal savings and to changes in the structure of their allocation. Greater savings leads to economic growth, which leads to an increase in savings by contributing to an increase in people's personal incomes (feedback in the economy). Over the past 25 years, following the country's political transformation, the development of Poland's financial market has been accompanied by significant changes to the structure of household savings. As demonstrated by Dębski (2009), the proportion of personal savings that is allocated to the banking sector has gradually declined during this period, and the proportion of these savings that is allocated through the financial market has risen. This shift occurred as a result of a structural transformation of the Polish economy, which led to the establishment of a stock exchange, as well as mutual funds, such as investment, pension and capital funds that are managed by life insurance undertakings. Considerable development of these practices has undoubtedly contributed to a substantial increase in long-term savings of households in Poland.

2. Discussion of empirical results

2.1. Household savings in Poland and their allocation to financial assets between 2003 and 2014

Household savings, apart from the money intended for the purchase of various tangible assets, may be allocated to a diverse range of financial assets. This article analyzes the structure of those assets, which might be bank deposits, various types of securities or equity interests, and/or investments made through a mutual funds agency. Table 1 presents the overall level of household savings accumulated in the types of financial assets enumerated above, along with the respective allocation of these assets in the period 2003-2014.

Table 1 demonstrates that at the end of 2003, the household savings allocated to all types of financial assets in Poland amounted to PLN 401.5 billion, which was 47.5% of the Gross Domestic Product (GDP). In the first quarter of 2008, this amount rose to PLN 843 billion and was almost 70% of the GDP. Thus, the increase is twofold and very significant. Considering the increase in prices (the CPI index) in this period, which amounted to 12.5%, an actual increase of 86.6% was achieved. In turn, as a proportion of the GDP, the financial assets held by the population grew by over 20 percentage points (pp.). Such a substantial increase in the value of household savings that were allocated to financial assets was a consequence of that period's prosperous economic circumstances, including the flourishing stock market, because the stock index WIG (the main Warsaw stock exchange index) rose from 20820.1 (at the end of 2003) to 66077.7 (at the end of the second quarter of 2007), which was a multiplication of 2.9 times. Beginning in the second quarter of 2008, the amount of financial assets held by the population began to fall, reaching PLN 639 billion at the end of the first quarter of 2009. Beginning in the second quarter of 2009, the assets began to grow again (although there was a slight reduction during the second, third, and fourth quarters of 2011), until the end of 2013, when they reached PLN 1203.3 billion, which was 72.4% of the GDP. This indicates that at the end of 2013, the proportion of financial assets held by households in Poland exceeded the proportion from the end of the first quarter of 2008 by slightly more than 2 pp.

In comparison to the end of 2003, the level of personal savings allocated to financial assets at the end of 2013 tripled in nominal value; if inflation is considered, the increase amounts to 127.4% (the WIG index rose by 146% at that time). Thus, the increase in financial assets held by the population that occurred during that period was very significant. Even if unquoted shares and other equity interests (i.e., assets that are subject not to market but to accounting valuation) are excluded from the total sum of the population's financial assets, at the end of 2003, the level of the population's remaining financial assets amounted to PLN 238.3 billion, which constituted 28.2% of the GDP. At the end of 2013, these financial assets reached PLN 913.3 billion, which was nearly 55% of the GDP and represented an increase of 26.8 pp. As a result, the nominal growth rate reached 283%; the real one was 191%. Thus, these increases were greater than the total of the financial assets, which certainly denotes a rise in the population's interest in allocating its savings to various types of market financial instruments.

During the first quarter of 2014, the level of household financial assets fell to PLN 1084 billion due to a reform of the pension system (approximately 50% of the funds invested in treasury bonds by open-ended pension funds were shifted to the Social Insurance Company (ZUS), which meant that those funds were withdrawn from the financial market). At the end of the study period (2014Q3), the size of the assets was PLN 1111.4 billion, which constituted a nominal increase of 176.8% and, compared to the end of 2003, a real increase of nearly 110%.

Table 1. Allocation of financial assets of households (in PLN billion)

Period	Cash	Deposits	Debt securities	Quoted shares	Unquoted shares and other equity interests	Shares and other equity interests	Shares in invest-ment funds	Life insurance and annuity entitle-ments	Pension entitle-ments	Total financial assets
1	2	3	4	5	6	5 +6	7	8	9	10
2003Q4	46.2	62.8	11.6	11.6	163.2	174.8	30.7	30.1	45.4	401.5
2004Q1	46.7	63.5	11.6	13.1	182.7	195.8	32.5	31.2	50.5	431.7
Q2	46.8	63.5	11.8	12.5	184.7	197.2	29.6	32.3	52.5	433.7
Q3	46.2	63.8	12.6	14.6	188.3	202.9	29.1	33.5	57.3	445.4
Q4	46.5	65.4	11.6	19.1	205.9	225.0	30.2	35.2	63.0	476.9
2005Q1	46.6	70.7	11.3	18.5	214.8	233.3	33.6	35.6	69.0	500.2
Q2	48.8	75.0	10.7	18.0	214.3	232.2	37.2	37.9	74.6	516.4
Q3	49.8	76.7	10.7	21.7	232.2	253.9	44.5	39.7	84.0	559.2
Q4	51.3	83.5	9.9	24.9	228.2	253.2	51.6	41.2	88.5	579.1
2006Q1	52.9	88.3	10.1	29.8	227.5	257.3	60.9	43.4	97.6	610.5
Q2	58.3	94.9	9.1	31.1	194.1	225.2	62.3	45.9	101.0	596.6
Q3	60.9	98.6	8.7	37.0	209.1	246.1	69.1	48.2	109.1	640.8
Q4	63.4	109.4	8.8	50.5	213.5	264.0	79.6	51.8	120.7	697.5
2007Q1	65.1	116.8	8.6	56.8	259.7	316.5	94.9	56.1	132.2	790.3
Q2	68.1	119.4	8.0	69.6	280.7	350.3	113.0	60.0	143.4	862.1
Q3	70.1	125.7	8.3	65.5	277.0	342.4	112.8	60.3	144.8	864.4
Q4	71.3	137.6	7.6	59.8	248.6	308.5	109.9	61.2	145.7	841.8
2008Q1	72.4	147.3	7.8	53.7	271.6	325.3	85.4	61.1	143.7	843.0
Q2	76.2	154.0	7.3	43.2	203.0	246.1	76.2	65.2	141.9	766.9
Q3	76.9	152.8	8.2	40.0	213.8	253.8	65.6	68.5	145.1	770.8
Q4	84.1	144.5	9.0	28.4	157.0	185.4	53.5	66.2	143.5	686.3
2009Q1	84.5	156.2	8.0	26.5	111.3	137.9	45.9	64.1	142.5	639.0
Q2	86.7	168.3	7.2	34.1	144.7	178.7	55.0	62.5	158.6	717.0
Q3	84.0	173.3	6.6	39.3	172.7	212.0	59.6	64.7	174.2	774.4
Q4	83.9	185.1	6.2	41.1	179.3	220.4	66.2	65.6	185.6	813.0
2010Q1	83.3	192.7	9.9	46.0	216.1	262.1	67.4	65.9	199.1	880.4
Q2	88.1	206.0	7.7	44.5	171.3	215.8	62.4	65.4	200.8	846.2

Table 1. Allocation of financial assets of households (in PLN billion) (Continued)

Period	Cash	Deposits	Debt securities	Quoted shares	Unquoted shares and other equity interests	Shares and other equity interests	Shares in invest-ment funds	Life insurance and annuity entitle-ments	Pension entitle-ments	Total financial assets
Q3	86.7	208.7	7.3	50.2	210.8	261.0	67.2	69.4	217.5	917.8
Q4	87.8	225.7	6.9	52.1	179.7	231.8	70.3	71.6	229.7	923.8
2011Q1	87.5	231.5	7.0	55.3	198.6	253.9	70.8	71.9	237.5	960.2
Q2	90.3	230.9	6.1	50.5	179.5	230.0	70.3	73.0	245.8	946.4
Q3	95.3	226.7	7.2	40.8	183.2	224.0	60.9	68.4	230.9	913.5
Q4	97.7	233.4	7.9	39.6	180.2	219.7	58.8	67.4	233.6	918.5
2012Q1	95.6	233.9	8.1	40.7	214.9	255.7	62.9	70.8	247.2	974.4
Q2	99.6	234.9	8.2	36.6	208.8	245.4	62.8	72.8	250.9	974.6
Q3	98.9	230.3	10.2	35.7	238.1	273.7	63.4	72.9	262.8	1012.1
Q4	98.5	236.6	9.1	37.9	251.1	289.0	67.8	74.4	280.9	1056.3
2013Q1	102.2	254.1	5.0	37.3	262.7	300.0	70.6	74.4	281.2	1087.6
Q2	108.7	269.4	5.0	38.1	246.6	284.7	74.6	73.2	284.5	1100.0
Q3	109.2	274.3	4.7	43.2	296.5	339.7	79.1	75.3	304.8	1187.0
Q4	110.3	278.6	4.4	45.5	290.0	335.4	85.6	76.3	312.6	1203.3
2014Q1	113.0	282.3	4.2	45.2	310.5	355.7	87.3	76.0	165.6	1084.0
Q2	117.0	285.3	4.4	44.6	293.6	338.2	90.9	77.1	166.3	1079.2
Q3	120.4	284.6	4.2	44.2	311.8	356.0	94.7	78.8	172.8	1111.4

Source: (NBP, 2015)

Taking into account the structure of household savings allocated to financial assets, which is presented in table 2, one may note that the biggest component is composed of shares and other equity interests, i.e., equity financial instruments. The smallest portion of these instruments are decidedly shares that are quoted in the organized market (the regulated market and the alternative trading system in Poland). At the end of 2003, the percentage of those instruments was 2.89; it started to slowly climb up to 8.07% (2007Q2) and then fell to reach less than 4% at the end of the third quarter of 2014. Although such a significant improvement in the market circumstances accounts for the increase in this proportion during the first period and the decrease during the first years of the financial crisis is also justified, the decrease in this proportion that occurred between 2012 and 2013 is difficult to rationalize because the WIG index rose by 15% at that time and the rediscount rate of the central bank was declining.

The proportion of shares unquoted in an organized market and other equity interests is unquestionably higher than the proportion of shares quoted in that market. Altogether, the percentage of both these items in the period under examination was approximately 45%. It was the highest at the end of 2004 (47.18%) but started to fall and reached 21.58% (2009Q1); it rose again to a level slightly above 32% in 2014. During this period, the rise in the proportion of household savings invested in unquoted equity instruments should be associated with a relatively good and constantly improving situation in the Polish market.

The second largest component in the structure of household savings allocated to financial assets is deposits, which includes funds that are placed in accounts of monetary financial institutions and cash accounts in brokerage offices. At the end of 2003, the level of deposits was 15.63%. Small reductions, including some fluctuations, began to occur, and by the end of the second quarter of 2007, this proportion amounted to 13.85%. This decline was indubitably connected with the ongoing improvement in the stock market and a decrease in interest rates (the WIG index rose 2.9 times, whereas the rediscount rate of the central bank (NBP) fell from 7% (2004Q4) to 4.25% (2007Q1)). The rise in the stock market index and the decrease in the interest rate on bank deposits made it more attractive to allocate funds to securities, in comparison to bank deposits, which resulted in a portion of the deposits being moved directly to the stock exchange (as demonstrated above) or to mutual funds. Following the outbreak of the financial crisis and as the circumstances on the stock exchange were deteriorating (the WIG index fell by 8.6% at the end of 2007Q3 compared to the level at the end of 2007Q2 and by 63.6% at the end of 2009Q1) and the rediscount rate was increasing (starting from 2007Q2 and in the second and third quarters of 2008, it reached 6.25%), the proportion of bank deposits held by households began to rise and reached 24.44% at the end of the first quarter of 2009. This proportion began to decline again, reaching 21.89% at the end of the first quarter of 2010, while the rediscount rate fell to 3.75%, which then remained around the level of 24% or slightly higher during the period 2010Q2-2012Q2. At that time, the rediscount rate increased to 5%, and the stock market suffered some turbulence, especially in the second half of 2011. The percentage of deposits then fell to 22.40% (2012Q4). In 2014, it climbed back to the level of approximately 26%, which resulted from decreased interest rates (the rediscount rate slumped to 2.25%), although it is difficult to explain this fact because the WIG index rose by 15.6% in that period. If cash is added to the deposits, it may be noted that the percentage of both of those components of the total financial assets held by households in 2014 was approximately 35%, which was the largest proportion in the study period. In contrast, the proportion of cash and deposits among the total financial assets that were reduced by unquoted shares and other equity interests in 2014 was approximately 51%.

The investment of personal savings in debt securities (both short- and long-term) constituted the smallest proportion among the other possibilities of allocation to financial assets. This portion was the highest between 2003 and 2004, when it amounted to approximately 2.7%. At that time, the rediscount rate of the NBP was relatively high, ranging from 5.75% (2003Q4) to 7.0% (2004Q4), and it then began to gradually fall until it reached 0.37% (2014Q3). As mentioned above, a clearly positive correlation with the decreasing rediscount rate is unmistakable.

The means of allocation of personal savings to financial assets discussed so far may be jointly referred to as a direct investment, i.e., it is made single-handedly by a household. The funds invested in such a way represented a proportion of the total savings allocated to financial assets during the study period, ranging from slightly more than 62% at the end of 2003, to approximately 47% in the first quarter of 2009, and then to 58% at the end of the third quarter of 2014, which indicates that the investment amount followed first a downward and then an upward trend. If the proportion of personal savings held in cash, which was quite stable during the study period because it oscillated approximately 10% (one exception is the period 2007Q1-2008Q1, when it was approximately 8%) is added to that, it may be stated that the remaining portion of the savings was allocated in an indirect manner, i.e., through capital, pension, and investment funds – mutual funds.

The household savings that were allocated to investment funds as a proportion of the total financial assets during the study period were subject to the most violent fluctuations as the circumstances of the stock market were changing, which is normal because these investment funds invest large portions of their funds in the stock exchange. Thus, this proportion first increased from slightly over 7.5% (2003Q4) to slightly over 13% (in the three last quarters of 2007); it then began to fall gradually until it reached 6.26% (2012Q3)

Table 2. Structure of the allocation of financial assets held by households (in percentages)

Period	Cash	Deposits	Debt securities	Quoted shares	Unquoted shares and other equity interests	Shares and other equity interests	Shares in invest-ment funds	Life insurance and annuity entitle-ments	Pension entitle-ments	Total financial assets
1	2	3	4	5	6	5 + 6	7	8	9	10
2003Q4	11.51	15.63	2.87	2.89	40.66	43.55	7.64	7.51	11.30	100.0
2004Q1	10.81	14.70	2.68	3.03	42.32	45.35	7.54	7.22	11.69	100.0
Q2	10.78	14.65	2.72	2.88	42.59	45.47	6.82	7.45	12.10	100.0
Q3	10.37	14.32	2.83	3.28	42.27	45.55	6.54	7.53	12.87	100.0
Q4	9.74	13.72	2.42	4.00	43.19	47.18	6.34	7.38	13.21	100.0
2005Q1	9.32	14.14	2.26	3.69	42.95	46.64	6.72	7.12	13.79	100.0
Q2	9.44	14.53	2.08	3.48	41.49	44.97	7.20	7.33	14.44	100.0
Q3	8.91	13.71	1.91	3.88	41.52	45.40	7.95	7.11	15.02	100.0
Q4	8.86	14.42	1.70	4.31	39.41	43.72	8.90	7.12	15.28	100.0
2006Q1	8.66	14.47	1.65	4.88	37.27	42.14	9.98	7.11	15.99	100.0
Q2	9.78	15.91	1.53	5.21	32.54	37.74	10.43	7.69	16.93	100.0
Q3	9.51	15.39	1.36	5.78	32.63	38.40	10.78	7.52	17.03	100.0
Q4	9.08	15.68	1.27	7.24	30.60	37.84	11.41	7.42	17.30	100.0
2007Q1	8.24	14.78	1.09	7.18	32.86	40.05	12.01	7.10	16.73	100.0
Q2	7.90	13.85	0.93	8.07	32.56	40.63	13.10	6.96	16.64	100.0
Q3	8.11	14.54	0.96	7.57	32.04	39.62	13.05	6.98	16.75	100.0
Q4	8.46	16.34	0.91	7.11	29.54	36.65	13.06	7.27	17.31	100.0
2008Q1	8.59	17.47	0.93	6.37	32.22	38.59	10.13	7.25	17.05	100.0
Q2	9.94	20.08	0.95	5.63	26.47	32.10	9.94	8.50	18.50	100.0
Q3	9.98	19.82	1.06	5.19	27.73	32.92	8.51	8.88	18.83	100.0
Q4	12.26	21.06	1.32	4.14	22.88	27.02	7.80	9.64	20.90	100.0
2009Q1	13.22	24.44	1.25	4.15	17.42	21.58	7.19	10.03	22.30	100.0
Q2	12.09	23.47	1.01	4.75	20.18	24.93	7.67	8.71	22.13	100.0
Q3	10.84	22.38	0.85	5.08	22.30	27.38	7.70	8.35	22.50	100.0
Q4	10.32	22.77	0.76	5.06	22.05	27.11	8.15	8.07	22.82	100.0
2010Q1	9.46	21.89	1.12	5.23	24.55	29.77	7.65	7.49	22.61	100.0
Q2	10.41	24.35	0.91	5.26	20.24	25.50	7.38	7.73	23.73	100.0

Table 2. Structure of the allocation of financial assets held by households (in percentages) (Continued)

Period	Cash	Deposits	Debt securities	Quoted shares	Unquoted shares and other equity interests	Shares and other equity interests	Shares in invest-ment funds	Life insurance and annuity entitle-ments	Pension entitle-ments	Total financial assets
Q3	9.45	22.73	0.79	5.47	22.97	28.44	7.32	7.57	23.69	100.0
Q4	9.50	24.43	0.75	5.64	19.45	25.09	7.61	7.75	24.86	100.0
2011Q1	9.11	24.11	0.73	5.76	20.68	26.44	7.38	7.49	24.74	100.0
Q2	9.54	24.40	0.65	5.34	18.97	24.31	7.43	7.71	25.97	100.0
Q3	10.43	24.82	0.79	4.46	20.06	24.53	6.66	7.49	25.28	100.0
Q4	10.63	25.41	0.86	4.31	19.61	23.92	6.40	7.34	25.43	100.0
2012Q1	9.82	24.01	0.84	4.18	22.06	26.24	6.45	7.27	25.37	100.0
Q2	10.22	24.10	0.84	3.76	21.42	25.18	6.45	7.47	25.74	100.0
Q3	9.77	22.76	1.00	3.52	23.52	27.05	6.26	7.20	25.96	100.0
Q4	9.32	22.40	0.86	3.59	23.77	27.36	6.42	7.04	26.59	100.0
2013Q1	9.40	23.37	0.46	3.43	24.15	27.58	6.49	6.84	25.86	100.0
Q2	9.88	24.49	0.46	3.46	22.42	25.88	6.78	6.66	25.86	100.0
Q3	9.20	23.11	0.39	3.64	24.98	28.62	6.66	6.34	25.67	100.0
Q4	9.17	23.15	0.37	3.78	24.10	27.87	7.12	6.34	25.98	100.0
2014Q1	10.42	26.05	0.38	4.17	28.64	32.81	8.05	7.01	15.27	100.0
Q2	10.84	26.44	0.40	4.13	27.20	31.34	8.43	7.14	15.41	100.0
Q3	10.83	25.60	0.37	3.97	28.05	32.03	8.52	7.09	15.55	100.0

Source: authors' estimations based on NBP, 2015

and then increased again to 8.52% (2014Q3). This fluctuation demonstrates that investment funds lose relatively more than stock exchange indices do in a bear market as the phenomenon of mass withdrawal and relocation of money from these funds to banks takes place. In contrast, placing household savings in pension funds (open-ended pension funds, employee pension funds, individual pension accounts, and pension schemes) was rising in importance, predominantly because saving in pension funds was compulsory. Therefore, the proportion of these savings allocated to pension funds grew steadily from 11.30% (2003Q4) to 25.98% at the end of 2013, with a small slump during the bear market in 2007. At the beginning of 2014, this proportion was slightly over 15% because a reform of Poland's pension system was implemented, which involved withdrawing approximately 50% of the funds that the open-ended pension funds had invested in treasury bonds, transferring them to the Social Insurance Company (ZUS), and gradually relocating to this institution the funds that were held by people who were 10 years under the retirement age. Moreover, compulsory participation in open-ended funds was abolished. The household savings allocated to life insurance undertakings (mainly through capital funds and life annuity contracts) made up approximately 7% of the total financial assets of the population during the study period (this proportion was a bit higher between 2008 and 2009 and even reached 10% at the end of the first quarter of 2009).

2.2. Analysis of changes to the structure of savings allocated to financial assets

The changes made to the structure of savings allocated to financial assets in Poland occurring throughout the study period (2003Q4-2014Q3) were analyzed using an econometric trend model with variations of parameters. The model was as follows:

$$Y_t = a + bT + cU + dUT + \varepsilon_t$$

or $$\ln(Y_t) = a + b\ln(T) + cU + dU\ln(T) + \varepsilon_t$$

where

Y_t – a given component of financial assets expressed in percentages in period t,

T – time variable (trend),

U – dummy variable taking the value 1 from the period of parameter change up to 2014Q3 and the value 0 in the remaining periods,

ε_t – random term in period t,

a, b, c, d – structural parameters.

Both a linear model and a power model were tested and estimated using the classic method of least squares. The period of variation in parameter was determined iteratively (with the trial and error method) based on the criterion of minimum residual sum of squares in the estimated model. In most of the estimated models, this period was the first or second quarter of 2008, which was when the latest financial crisis began. A change in the structure of household savings allocated to financial assets could have been expected with a high degree of certainty in this period. Determination of this period (which divided the sample into two sub-samples) served to appropriately define the dummy variable, U, that belonged to the set of explanatory variables of the model presented above. Variation in the parameters of the model, especially the one standing by the time variable, was tested in this way.

The trend model presented above was employed to analyze changes to the structure of allocation of personal savings to financial assets, as enumerated in the quarterly financial accounts that were drafted by the National Bank of Poland as follows: cash, deposits, debt securities, quoted shares, unquoted shares and other equity interests, shares and other equity interests (a sum of the two preceding items), shares in investment funds, life insurance and annuity entitlements, and pension entitlements. The estimation results for the model of these components with the OLS method are presented in table 3.

The results suggest that when the financial crisis began in the global economy in 2007-2008, quite substantial changes occurred in the structure of household savings that were allocated to financial assets in Poland. In general, the thesis confirms that both in a period of prosperity, with a decrease in interest rates, and during a bull market, the proportion of savings allocated to shares quoted on the organized market and to investment funds increases and the proportion of savings allocated to deposits and debt securities and the proportion of cash in the total financial assets both decrease. In contrast, in the period of adverse circumstances and during a bear market, i.e., when the investment risk rises as well and the interest rates go up, the proportion of personal savings allocated to deposits and debt securities and the proportion of cash both grow, but the proportion of savings allocated to shares quoted on the organized market and investment funds decreases.

For instance, based on the results shown in table 3, it may be concluded that the proportion of household savings allocated to shares quoted on the organized market in the period 2003Q4-2007Q4 rose on average by 0.3428 percentage points (pp.) each quarter and that at the beginning of 2008Q1, it started to go down by an average of 0.0742 pp. on a quarterly basis (0.3428-0.4170). For the proportion of savings allocated to investment funds, the result was similar. In the period 2003Q4-2007Q4, it grew on a quarterly basis by an average of 0.4607 pp. Beginning in 2008Q1, it began to decline by 0.0598 pp. (0.4607-0.5205). The proportion of unquoted shares and other equity interests in the population's total financial assets behaved differently: it fell on quarterly basis by an average of 0.9463 pp. between 2003Q4 and 2008Q4 and then started to grow by an average of 0.3116 pp. (1.2579-0.9463). As indicated in table 2, this proportion began

Table 3. Estimation results for the trend model (variables expressed in percentages)

Name of variable	Period of variation in parameters	Function	a (pval)	b (pval)	c (pval)	d (pval)	R2	DW (pval)
Cash	2008Q2	power	2.470 (0.000)	-0.120 (0.000)	0.353 (0.096)	-0.027 (0.666)	0.561	0.911 (0.000)
Deposits	2008Q2	power	2.663 (0.000)	0.018 (0.316)	-0.159 (0.337)	0.173 (0.001)	0.943	1.295 (0.002)
Debt securities	2008Q1	linear	3.066 (0.000)	-0.137 (0.000)	-1.426 (0.000)	0.109 (0.000)	0.960	1.145 (0.000)
Quoted shares	2008Q1	linear	1.885 (0.000)	0.343 (0.000)	4.989 (0.000)	-0.417 (0.000)	0.800	0.687 (0.000)
Unquoted shares and other equity interests	2009Q1	linear	45.921 (0.000)	-0.946 (0.000)	-33.647 (0.000)	1.258 (0.000)	0.933	1.103 (0.000)
Shares and other equity interests	2008Q4	linear	48.142 (0.000)	-0.659 (0.000)	-27.871 (0.000)	0.866 (0.000)	0.927	1.280 (0.001)
Shares in mutual funds	2008Q1	linear	5.234 (0.000)	0.461 (0.000)	4.119 (0.000)	-0.520 (0.000)	0.795	0.407 (0.000)
Life insurance and annuity entitlements	2008Q2	power	2.012 (0.000)	-0.013 (0.347)	1.375 (0.000)	-0.384 (0.000)	0.767	1.007 (0.000)
Pension entitlements	2014Q1	linear	11.538 (0.000)	0.406 (0.000)	-1.963 (0.951)	-0.270 (0.715)	0.959	0.432 (0.000)

Source: authors' estimations.
a, b, c, d – estimates of structural parameters of the model,
p-val – minimum significance level that allows the hypothesis on the lack of significance (α=0 for the linear function) of the parameter under analysis to be rejected,
R2 – coefficient of determination,
DW – estimate of Durbin-Watson statistic.

to grow quite significantly at the beginning of 2012Q3. In contrast the proportion of personal savings allocated to debt securities in the total financial assets decreased by an average of 0.1370 pp. in the period 2003Q4-2007Q4. Beginning in 2008Q1, the reduction was limited to 0.0277 pp. (0.1370-0.1093). In turn, the estimated model for deposits revealed that their proportion in the total financial assets of households between 2003Q4-2008Q1 rose on a quarterly basis at a rate of 0.0181% (this result may be a slightly misleading value due to the statistical insignificance of this interpretation). Next, the proportion started to increase to a higher rate of 0.1725 pp., which is in agreement with the thesis formulated above that the proportion of personal deposits should have grown in the period in which the financial crisis occurred and that investment risk increased substantially. It is worth noting that this proportion clearly rose between 2013 and 2014 (see table 2), i.e., in the period when the rediscount rate of the NBP was very low. The reason for these circumstances may only be the high investment risk that was caused by political factors, i.e., the war in Ukraine.

In contrast, the proportion of funds allocated to pension entitlements in the period under examination behaved differently from the proportions of household savings allocated to financial assets discussed above. This occurred because such allocations are long-term investments with no possibility of withdrawing funds, to which contributions are increasingly larger on systemic and compulsory bases. However, a change in the structure of the allocation of savings has been noted in this case as well. The change was brought about at the beginning of 2014, when the reform of open-ended pension funds was implemented, as mentioned above. The presented results demonstrate that the proportion of household savings allocated to all pension funds in the period 2003Q4-2013Q4 grew on a quarterly basis by an average of 0.4061 pp. Beginning in 2014Q1, the increase was reduced by 0.2704 pp. (as mentioned above, this decline was a consequence of both the withdrawal of approximately 50% of the contributions from open-ended pension funds and the abolishment of mandatory contributions to those funds). The proportion of savings allocated to life insurance (life insurance policies) and annuity entitlements decreased in the period 2003Q-2008Q1 at a quarterly rate of 0.0132%, which is a statistically insignificant interpretation. Starting in 2008Q2, the decrease deepened by 0.3836 pp. When evaluating the data in column 8 of table 2, one may note that this proportion was decreasing throughout virtually the entire period of analysis, with the exception of 2008Q2-2009Q2, when it increased significantly.

Regarding a general substantive-statistical interpretation of the estimated models, it may be stated that it is positive in most cases because the signs of the estimated structural parameters are correct from an economic point of view. Further, with the exception of a small number of cases, their interpretations are statistically significant, which may be inferred from the p-val values placed under the structural parameter estimations provided in table 3. The coefficients of determination (R2) are also relatively high as an estimation of variables expressed as a percentage proportion; apart from three cases, the Durbin-Watson (DW) statistics indicate the non-existence of autocorrelation of the random term.

Conclusion

This examination has demonstrated that as the financial market and economic circumstances developed in Poland, the structure of allocation of household savings to financial assets underwent quite significant changes between 2003 and 2014. The analysis revealed that changes to this structure had a relatively strong dependency on the current market circumstances. The study showed that along with the improvement of the economic condition in Poland, which led, among other things, to an increase in the stock market share prices and a decrease in interest rates, the proportion of personal savings allocated to shares quoted on an organized market and mutual funds increased, and the proportion of savings allocated to deposits and debt securities decreased. However, in adverse economic circumstances that led to a bear market and an increase in interest rates, the proportions discussed above displayed contrasting behavior. Thus, the structure of the allocation of household savings to financial assets in the period under examination underwent changes. In Poland, such a change occurred with the commencement of the global financial crisis in 2007-2008. Empirical research has shown the depth of those changes in regards to the particular components of household savings that are allocated to financial assets.

References

Anioła, P., Gołaś, Z. (2012a), Zastosowanie wielowymiarowych metod ststystycznych w typologii strategii oszczędnościowych gospodarstw domowych w Polsce [Application of Multidimensional Statistical Methods in the Typology of Saving Strategies of Polish Households]. Materialy i Studia NBP, Zeszyt 282. Retrieved from https://www.nbp.pl/publikacje/materialy_i_studia/ms282.pdf

Anioła, P., & Gołaś, Z. (2012b). Differences in the level and structure of household indebtedness in the EU countries. *Contemporary Economics, 6*(1), 46-59.

Bergstresser, D., & Poterba, J. (2004). Asset allocation and asset location: household evidence from the survey of consumer finances, *Journal of Public Economics, 88*(9-10), 1893-1915.

Beverly, S. G., & Sherraden, M. (1999). Institutional determinants of savings: Implication for low – income households and public policy. *Journal of Socio – Economics, 28*(4), 457-473.

Börsch-Supan, A. (Ed.). (2003). Life - cycle savings and public policy: A cross - national study in six countries. New York, NY: Academic Press.

Brandstaetter, H., & Gueth, W. (2000). A psychological approach to individual differences in Intertemporal Consumption Patterns. *Journal of Economic Psychology, 21*(5), 465-479.

Brennan, M. J., & Xia, Y. (2002). Dynamic asset allocation under inflation. *Journal of Finance, 57*(3), 1201-1238.

Bunting, D. (2009). The saving decline: Macro - facts, micro - behavior. *Journal of Economic Behaviour and Organisation, 70*(1-2), 282-295.

Campbell, J. Y, Chan, Y. L., & Viceira, L. M. (2003). A multivariate model of strategic asset allocation. *Journal of Financial Economics, 67*(1), 41-80.

Canova, L., Rattazzi, A. M. M., & Webley, P. (2005). The hierarchical structure of saving motives. *Journal of Economic Psychology, 26*(1), 21-34.

Carroll, C. D. (2001). Precautionary Saving and the Marginal Propensity to Consume Out of Permanent Income (Working Papers No. 8233). National Bureau of Economic Research. Retrieved from http://www.nber.org/papers/w8233.pdf

Dębski, W. (1990). *Model pieniężnych dochodów i wydatków ludności Polski: ekonometryczna analiza, symulacje* [Model of cash income and expenditure of the Polish population - the econometric analysis, simulation]. Łódź: Wydawnictwo Uniwersytetu Łódzkiego.

Dębski, W. (2009). Alokacja oszczędności ludności w Polsce w latach 2003 - 2008 [The allocation of personal savings in Poland in the years 2003 - 2008]. *Zeszyty Naukowe Uniwersytetu Szczecińskiego. Ekonomiczne Problemy Usług, 38,* 421-428.

Dębski, W., & Świderski, B. (2011). Change in the Allocation Structure of Personal Savings Invested in Financial Assets in Poland, 2003 - 2009. *Transformations in Business & Economics, 10*(1), 81-97.

Duesenbury, J. S. (1952). Income, savings and the theory of consumer behavior.. Cambridge, MA: Harvard University Press.

Fisher, P. J., & Montalto, C. P. (2010). Effect of saving motives and horizon on saving behaviours. *Journal of Economic Psychology, 31*(1), 92-105.

Friedman, M. (1957). Theory of the Consumption Function. Princeton, NJ: Princeton University Press

Gomes, F., & Michaelides, A. (2005). Optimal life - cycle asset allocation: Understanding the empirical evidence. *Journal of Finance, 60(2),* 869-904.

Han, C. K., & Sherraden, M. (2009). Do institutions really matter for saving among low - income households? A comparative approach. *Journal of Socio - Economics, 38*(3), 475-483.

Horneff, W. J., Maurer, R., Mitchel, O. S., & Stamos, M. Z. (2009). Asset allocation and location over the life cycle with investment - linked survival - contingent payouts. *Journal of Banking & Finance, 33(9),* 1688-1699.

Keynes, J. M. (1985). Ogólna teoria zatrudnienia, procentu i pieniądza [The General Theory of Employment, Interest and Money]. Warszawa: PWN.

Kirsanova, T., & Sefton, J. (2007). A comparison of national saving rates in the UK, US and Italy. *European Economic Review, 51*(8), 1998-2028.

Liberda, B. (2000). Oszczędzanie w gospodarce polskiej [Savings in the Polish economy]. Warszawa: Dom Wydawniczy Bellona.

Łapińska-Sobczak, N. (1997). Makromodel sektora finansowego: studium ekonometryczne dla gospodarki polskiej [Financial sector macromodel: econometric study of the Polish economy]. Łódź: Wydawnictwo Uniwersytetu Łódzkiego.

Milevsky, M., & Young, V. (2007). Annuitization and asset allocation. *Journal of Economic Dynamics and Control, 31*(9), 3138-3177.

Modigliani F., & Brumberg R. (1955). Utility analysis and the consumption function: An interpretation of cross-section data. In K. K. Kurihara (Ed.), Post-Keynesian Economics (pp. 388-436). London, UK: George Allen and Unwin.

National Bank of Poland (2015). Kwartalne rachunki finansowe Narodowego Banku Polskiego [National Bank of Poland quarterly financial accounts] Available from www.nbp.pl/home.aspx?f=statystyka/pieniezna_i_bankowa/krt.html

Rytelewska, G. (2008). Gospodarstwa domowe [Households]. In B. Pietrzak, Z. Polański, B. Woźniak (Eds.), System finansowy w Polsce [Financial system in Poland] (Vol. 2, pp. 399-433). Warsaw: Wydawnictwo Naukowe PWN.

Rytelewska, G., Kłopocka, A. (2010). Wpływ czynników demograficznych na poziom i strukturę oszczędności gospodarstw domowych w Polsce

[Influence of demographic factors on the level and structure of household savings in Poland]. *Bank i Kredyt, 41*(1), 57-80.

Sherraden, M., Schreiner, M., & Beverly, S. (2003). Income, institutions, and saving performance in individual development accounts. *Economic Development Quarterly, 17*(1), 95-112.

Shoren, J. B., & Sialm, C. (2004). Asset location in tax – deferred and conventional savings accounts. *Journal of Public Economics, 88*(1-2), 23-38.

Welfe, W. (2013). Macroeconometric Models. Berlin: Springer Verlag.

4

Financial Systems and Economic Growth: Empirical Evidence from Australia

Sheilla Nyasha[1], Nicholas M Odhiambo[1]

ABSTRACT This paper examines the dynamic impact of both bank- and market-based financial development on economic growth in Australia during the period from 1980 to 2012. The study uses the autoregressive distributed lag (ARDL) bounds testing approach to examine this linkage. Unlike certain previous studies, this study uses both bank- and market-based financial development indices to measure the level of financial sector development in Australia. These indices were computed using the means-removed average method. The empirical results of this study show that while bank-based financial development has a short-run positive impact on economic growth in Australia, market-based financial development has no significant impact on economic growth, both in the short run and in the long run. These results imply that, in Australia, it is of paramount importance to concentrate on pro-banking sector policies, at least in the short run, to stimulate growth.

KEY WORDS: Australia, bank-based financial development, market-based financial development, economic growth

[1]University of South Africa, Department of Economics, South Africa

Introduction

Although there is rich literature on the finance-growth nexus, the bulk of such literature is on the relationship between bank-based financial development and economic growth. Only a handful of studies provide coverage on the relationship between market-based financial development and economic growth. However, even in studies that have explored the economic growth impact of market-based financial development, the conclusions are far from conclusive.

In the finance-growth literature, there is evidence in support of a positive relationship between financial development and economic growth (Akinlo & Akinlo, 2009; Adu, Marbuah, & Mensah, 2013; Bernard & Austin, 2011; Goldsmith, 1969; Hassan, Sanchez, & Yu, 2011; Kargbo & Adamu, 2009; King & Levine, 1993; Levine & Zervos, 1996; Odedokun, 1996). Despite such overwhelming evidence, some studies conclude that bank-based and market-based financial development have a negative impact on economic growth (Adu *et al.*, 2013; Bernard and Austin, 2011; Buffie, 1984; De Gregorio and Guidotti, 1995; Ujunwa and Salami, 2010; Van Wijnbergen, 1983). In addition to these two contrasting groups of empirical evidence,

Correspondence concerning this article should be addressed to: **Sheilla Nyasha,** University of South Africa, Department of Economics, P.O Box 392 UNISA 0003 Pretoria Pretoria Gauteng 0003 South Africa. E-mail: sheillanyasha@gmail.com

there is a third group that concludes that financial development has no significant impact on economic growth (Andersen & Tarp, 2003; Lucas, 1988; Ram, 1999; Stern, 1989).

In this context, the current study aims to examine the impact of bank-based and market-based financial development on economic growth using data for Australia over the period from 1980 to 2012. The study period was dictated by the availability of the stock market data. This study differs fundamentally from most of the previous studies on the finance-growth nexus in a number of ways. Firstly, it splits financial development into bank- and market-based components, and it focuses on the impact of each component on economic growth. Secondly, the study uses the indices of bank- and market-based financial development, which are created from a wide range of bank- and market-based financial development indicators. The use of these indices ensures that the financial landscape of the studied country is captured as accurately as possible, unlike in most other studies in which one or two bank-based financial development indicators are used to capture a whole financial system. Thirdly, this study uses the recently developed autoregressive distributed lag (ARDL) bounds approach to cointegration, which is appropriate even when a sample size is too small (see also Odhiambo, 2008). Finally, contrary to the bulk of the previous studies that have over-relied on cross-sectional data, which may not have adequately addressed country-specific issues, this study uses time-series data analysis methods to address country-specific issues (see also Ghirmay, 2004; Odhiambo, 2009).

The study focuses on Australia because the country has not received much individual coverage in terms of the finance-growth nexus research in recent years. Australia also makes an interesting case study because of its recent visibility as one of the leading economies and its distinguished resilience in the context of the recent global financial crises. Australia has one of the best-developed financial systems in the world. Both the bank- and the market-based financial segments of the financial sector are equally well developed.

At the top of the Australian financial system is the Reserve Bank of Australia, which is the country's central bank. The Reserve Bank of Australia is responsible for monetary policy and related matters, and it ensures that the Australian financial fundamentals are in order (Reserve Bank of Australia, 2013). The Australian banking sector is stable, and its banks are well capitalized in the context of a sound and effective supervisory environment (Bologna (2010). From the market-based financial side, the Australian stock market is made up of three stock exchanges, namely, the Australian Securities Exchange Group, the National Stock Exchange of Australia, and the Asian Pacific Stock Exchange. These stock exchanges were born out of a string of stock exchanges that merged over time. Of the three, the Australian Securities Exchange Group is the largest.

As with any other financial sector, over the years, the Australian financial sector has undergone a wide range of reforms. According to Perkins (1989), the financial reform period can be divided into three phases: (i) A fully regulated era, which lasted into the late 1960s; (ii) a phase of attempted reform during the 1970s; and (iii) a reformed era, which began during the 1980s and continues into the present. In the banking sector, these reforms concentrated on improving legal, judiciary, regulatory and supervisory environments, promoting financial liberalization, rehabilitating financial infrastructure, restoring bank soundness and improving financial services for consumer protection. From the stock market perspective, the reforms focused on addressing the legal, regulatory, judiciary and supervisory aspects of the market, as well as the transformation of the trading environment. These wide-ranging reforms resulted in a well-developed financial sector, which is competitive and globally recognized.

The remainder of the article is set forth as follows. The next section provides a review of the related literature. The data, variable descriptions and model specifications are covered in section three. The results are set forth and discussed in section four, and some concluding remarks are drawn in section five.

Review of the Related Literature

Although the relationship between financial development and economic growth has received widespread attention in the modern history of economics, the conclusions have been far from conclusive. The finance-growth nexus debate can be traced to the work of Schumpeter (1911) during the early 20th Century. The thrust of the debate has been whether financial development has any impact on economic growth, and, if it has, whether the impact is positive or negative.

Table 1. Studies Showing the Nature of Impact of Bank and Market-based Financial Development on Economic Growth

Author(s)	Region/Country	Results
	Panel 1: Bank-Based Financial Development and Economic Growth	
De Gregorio & Guidotti, 1995	A large number of countries	Positive impact (in a large cross-country sample)
Odedokun, 1996	LDCs - 71 developing countries	Positive impact (in 85% of the 71 countries)
Ahmed & Ansari, 1998	India, Pakistan and Sri Lanka	Positive impact
Allen & Ndikumana, 2000	8 countries in Southern Africa – Botswana, Lesotho, Mauritius, Malawi, Swaziland, South Africa, Zambia and Zimbabwe	Positive impact
Güryay et al., 2007	Northern Cyprus	Positive impact (though negligible)
Kargbo & Adamu, 2009	Sierra Leone	Positive impact
Hassan et al., 2011	Low- and middle-income countries	Positive impact
Adu et al., 2013	Ghana	Positive impact (when credit to the private sector as ratio to GDP and total domestic credit are used as proxies of financial development)
De Gregorio & Guidotti, 1995	A large number of countries	Negative impact (in Latin America)
Odedokun, 1996	LDCs - 71 developing countries	Negative impact (in 15% of the 71 countries)
Adu et al., 2013	Ghana	Negative impact (when broad money stock to GDP ratio is used as proxies of financial development)
Ram, 1999	95 countries	No impact
Andersen & Tarp, 2003	74 countries	No impact
	Panel 2: Market-Based Financial Development and Economic Growth	
Levine & Zervos, 1996	41 countries	Positive impact
Caporale et al., 2003	Four developing countries (Chile, Korea, Malaysia and the Philippines)	Positive impact
Bekaert et al., 2005	A large number of countries	Positive impact
Adjasi & Biekpe, 2006	14 African countries	Positive impact
Nurudeen, 2009	Nigeria	Positive impact
Akinlo & Akinlo, 2009	Seven countries in sub-Saharan Africa	Positive impact
Ujunwa & Salami, 2010	Nigeria	Positive impact (when stock market development is proxied by stock market size and turnover ratios)
Bernard & Austin, 2011	Nigeria	Positive impact (when stock market development is proxied by turnover ratio)
Ujunwa & Salami, 2010	Nigeria	Negative impact (when stock market development is proxied by total value of shares traded)
Bernard & Austin, 2011	Nigeria	Negative impact (when stock market development is proxied by market capitalization and value traded ratios)

Table 2. Variable Description

Variable	Description
y	Growth rate of real gross domestic product. It is a proxy for economic growth.
BD	An index of bank-based financial development, calculated as a means-removed average of M2, M3 and credit provided to the private sector by financial intermediaries. It is a proxy for bank-based financial development (see also Demirguc-Kunt and Levine, 1996)
MD	An index of market-based financial development, which is a means-removed average of stock market capitalization, stock market traded value and stock market turnover. It is a proxy for market-based financial development (see also Demirguc-Kunt and Levine, 1996)
IN	Investment, calculated as gross fixed capital formation as a percentage of GDP.
SA	Gross savings as a percentage of GDP
TO	Trade openness, which is the sum of the share of total imports in GDP and the share of total exports in GDP

To date, the overwhelming empirical evidence has been in favor of Schumpeter's (1911) notion that financial development has a positive impact on economic growth. From the bank-based financial development perspective, Odedokun (1996), Ahmed and Ansari (1998), Christopoulos and Tsionas (2004), Güryay, Şafakli, & Tüzel, (2007), Kargbo and Adamu (2009), Yonezawa and Azeez (2010), Hassan *et al.* (2011), and Adu *et al.* (2013), among other studies, have found evidence in support of the positive impact of bank-based financial development on economic growth in various countries. From the market-based financial development perspective, Levine and Zervos (1996), Caporale, Howells, & Soliman (2003), Bekaert, Harvey, & Lundblad, (2005), Adjasi and Biekpe (2006), Nurudeen (2009), Akinlo and Akinlo (2009), Ujunwa and Salami (2010) and Bernard and Austin (2011), among others studies, have reinforced the argument that market-based financial development has a positive impact on economic growth.

Despite overwhelming evidence that bank-based and market-based financial development have a positive impact on economic growth, alternative views still exist. There are a number of studies that provide evidence in support of the negative impact of financial development on economic growth. De Gregorio and Guidotti (1995), Bolbol, Fatheldina, & Omranb (2005) and Adu *et al.* (2013) found evidence of a negative relationship between bank-based financial development and economic growth in certain isolated instances, while Ujunwa and Salami (2010) and Bernard and Austin (2011) provide evidence that market-based financial development has a negative impact on economic growth in certain countries.

In addition to the strong view that there is a relationship between financial development (both bank- and market-based) and economic growth, irrespective of whether this relationship is positive or negative, there have been a few studies that suggest that financial development, whether bank- or market-based, has no impact on economic growth. These studies provide evidence in support of the notion that financial development and economic growth are not related, and they are two different phenomena that are independent of one another. Such studies include Ram (1999) and Andersen and Tarp (2003).

Table 1 summarizes the empirical studies on the impact of bank-based and market-based financial development on economic growth. Panel 1 shows studies on bank-based financial development and economic growth, while Panel 2 presents a summary of studies on market-based financial development and economic growth.

Data, Variable Description and Model Specification

Data

The annual time series data that are utilized in this study cover the period from 1980 to 2012; and were obtained from the World Bank Economic Indicators and the International Financial Statistics Year Books (IFS, various issues).

Variable Description

The description of the variables that are used in this study is given in Table 2.

The annual growth rate of real GDP is used as a proxy for economic growth (y). This proxy has been used extensively in the literature (Majid, 2008; Odedokun, 1996; Shan & Jianhong, 2006; Wood, 1993). Financial development, on the other hand, is proxied by bank-based and market-based financial indicators. In the modern literature, bank-based financial development is proxied by various indicators, as is market-based financial development. Thus, to produce an assessment of the overall level of "bank development" and "stock market development" within a country, an index was developed that averages the information that is contained in the individual indicators.

To this end, financial development is proxied by bank-based and market-based financial indicators. Bank-based financial development is proxied by a bank-based financial development index (BD), which is constructed from three bank-based financial development variables – namely M2 to nominal GDP (M2), M3 to nominal GDP (M3), and domestic credit to private sector divided by nominal GDP (C).

Market-based financial development, on the other hand, is proxied by a market-based financial development index (MD). This index was constructed from three market-based financial development variables, namely, stock market capitalization (CAP), the total value of stocks traded (TV) and turnover ratio (TOR). To compute a conglomerate index of bank-based financial development, the means-removed values of the three indicators of bank development were averaged in a two-step procedure (see also Demirguc-Kunt and Levine, 1996). Firstly, the means-removed values of M2 to nominal GDP (M2), M3 to nominal GDP (M3) and domestic credit to private sectors to nominal GDP (C) were computed. The means-removed value of variable X is defined as Xm = [X – mean (X)] / [ABS (mean (X))], where ABS (z) refers to the absolute value of z. For the mean (X), the average value of X over the 1980-2012 period was used.

Secondly, a simple average of the means-removed M2 to nominal GDP, M3 to nominal GDP and domestic credit to private sectors to nominal GDP, was taken to obtain an overall index of bank-based financial development (BD). The conglomerate index of market-based financial development (MD) was constructed in the same way.

In addition to the real GDP growth rate (y) and the financial development indicators (BD and MD), three other variables were introduced in the model. These additional variables comprise: the share of investment in GDP (IN), the share of savings in GDP (SA), and trade openness (TO). These three variables were included in the above model to fully specify the model. According to growth theory, the three additional variables exert a positive impact on economic growth; hence, their coefficients are also expected to be positive.

The Model

The empirical model that is used in this study to test the impact of bank-based and market-based financial development on economic growth is specified as follows:

$$y_t = \alpha_0 + \alpha_1 BD_t + \alpha_2 MD_t + \alpha_3 IN_t + \alpha_4 SA_t + \alpha_5 TO_t + + \varepsilon_t \ldots\ldots\ldots\ldots\ldots\ldots\ldots\ldots\ldots\ldots\ldots\ldots (i)$$

Where α_0 is a constant, α_1 - α_5 are respective regression coefficients and ε_t is the error term.

The ARDL model based on the specified empirical model in equation (i) is expressed as follows:

$$\Delta y_t = \alpha_0 + \sum_{i=1}^{n} \alpha_{1i} \Delta y_{t-i} + \sum_{i=0}^{n} \alpha_{2i} \Delta BD_{t-i} + \sum_{i=0}^{n} \alpha_{3i} \Delta MD_{t-i} + $$
$$+ \sum_{i=0}^{n} \alpha_{4i} \Delta IN_{t-i} + \sum_{i=0}^{n} \alpha_{5i} \Delta SA_{t-i} + \sum_{i=0}^{n} \alpha_{6i} \Delta TO_{t-i} + \Phi_1 y_{t-1} +$$
$$\Phi_2 BD_{t-1} + \Phi_3 MD_{t-1} + \Phi_4 IN_{t-1} + \Phi_5 SA_{t-1} + \Phi_6 TO_{t-1} +$$
$$+ \mu_{1t} \ldots\ldots\ldots\ldots\ldots\ldots\ldots (ii)$$

Where: α_0 is a constant, α_1 - α_6 and Φ_1 - Φ_6 are respective regression coefficients; Δ is the difference operator; n is the lag length; and μ_t is the white noise error term.

The associated ARDL-based error correction model is specified as follows:

$$\Delta y_t = \alpha_0 + \sum_{i=1}^{n} \alpha_{1i} \Delta y_{t-i} + \sum_{i=0}^{n} \alpha_{2i} \Delta BD_{t-i} + \sum_{i=0}^{n} \alpha_{3i} \Delta MD_{t-i} +$$
$$+ \sum_{i=0}^{n} \alpha_{4i} \Delta IN_{t-i} + \sum_{i=0}^{n} \alpha_{5i} \Delta SA_{t-i} + \sum_{i=0}^{n} \alpha_{6i} \Delta TO_{t-i} +$$
$$+ \delta ECM_{t-1} + \mu_t \ldots\ldots\ldots (iii)$$

Table 3. Unit Root Tests for all Variables

Phillips-Perron (PP)				
Variable	Stationarity of all Variables in Levels		Stationarity of all variables in First Difference	
	Without Trend	With Trend	Without Trend	With Trend
y	-5.173***	-5.034***	–	–
BD	0.571	-2.672	-6.952***	-7.958***
MD	-1.285	-2.685	-6.479***	-6.460***
IN	-1.934	-1.874	-5.067***	-8.661***
SA	-1.786	-0.946	-4.448***	-6.297***
TO	-0.624	-3.257*	-7.439***	-7.167***
Perron, 1997 (PPURoot)				
Variable	Stationarity of all Variables in Levels		Stationarity of all variables in First Difference	
	Without Trend	With Trend	Without Trend	With Trend
y	-4.186	-4.247	-8.019***	-8.223***
BD	-5.983	-5.035	-6.998***	-7.307***
MD	-3.994	-4.171	-6.700***	-7.024***
IN	-4.839	-5.012	-5.542**	-5.771**
SA	-4.102	-4.032	-6.036***	-5.958**
TO	-4.284	-4.131	-6.652***	-6.548***

Note:*, ** and *** denote stationarity at 10%, 5% and 1% significance levels, respectively

Unit Roots, Cointegration and Impact Analysis

Unit Root Tests

The variables were first subjected to unit root tests using the Phillips-Perron (PP) unit root test. To allow for possible structural breaks in data, the Perron (1997) unit root test (PPURoot) was also utilized. The detailed results of the unit root tests for all of the variables are presented in Table 3.

After being differenced once, the results that are reported in Table 3 show that all of the variables became conclusively stationary. Although the ARDL technique does not require that variables be pre-tested for unit roots, the stationarity test provides guidance as to whether the ARDL analysis is suitable because it is only applicable for the analysis of variables that are integrated of order zero or one. In this case, all of the variables are integrated of either order zero or one. As a result, the ARDL bounds testing method can be used in the estimation of the model.

ARDL Bounds-Testing Approach

The cointegration analysis in this study is based on the fairly newly developed ARDL bounds testing approach because of the numerous advantages that it offers over other alternative empirical analysis methods. First, the ARDL test has superior small sample properties when compared to the other conventional methods of testing cointegration (Pesaran and Shin, 1999). Thus, the ARDL test is suitable even when the sample size is small. Second, the ARDL method employs only a sin-

Table 4. Bounds F-Test for Cointegration

Dependent Variable	Function		F-statistic		Cointegration Status	
y	F(y|BD, MD, IN, SA, TO)		5.760***		Cointegrated	
			Asymptotic Critical Values			
Pesaran et al. (2001), p.300, Table CI(iii)	1%		5%		10%	
	I(0)	I(1)	I(0)	I(1)	I(0)	I(1)
Case III	3.41	4.68	2.62	3.79	2.26	3.35

Note: *** denotes statistical significance at 1% level

gle reduced-form equation, unlike the conventional cointegration methods that estimate the long-run relationships within a context of a system of equations (see also Duasa, 2007). Third, the technique provides unbiased estimates of the long-run model and valid t statistics even when some of the regressors are endogenous (see also Odhiambo, 2008). Finally, this technique can be employed regardless of whether the regressors are integrated of the same order or not, as long as they are integrated of an order of not more than one. Therefore, the ARDL approach is considered to be well-suited for the analysis of the impact of bank- and market-based financial development on economic growth in this paper. The method has also been increasingly used in recent empirical research.

Bounds F-Test for Cointegration

This section examines the long-run relationship between the variables in the specified model using the ARDL bounds testing approach. First, the order of lags on the first differenced variables in equation (ii) was determined. Finally, a bounds F-test was applied to equation (ii) to establish the existence of a long-run relationship between the variables under study. The results of the bounds F-test are displayed in Table 4.

The results of the ARDL bounds test for cointegration, which are displayed in Table 4, show that the calculated F-statistic of 5.760 is higher than the critical values that were reported by Pesaran, Shin, & Smith (2001) in Table CI(iii) Case III at a 1% significance level. Hence, it can be concluded that the variables in the specified empirical model are cointegrated.

Impact Analysis

Because y, BD, MD, IN, SA and TO are cointegrated, the ARDL procedure is used in the estimation of the model. The optimal lag-length for the specified model was determined using the Akaike information criterion (AIC) or the Bayesian information criterion (BIC). The optimal lag-length that was selected based on BIC was ARDL(1,1,0,1,0,0). The BIC-based model was chosen because it was more parsimonious than the AIC-based model. The long-run and short-run results of the selected model are reported in Table 5 Panel 1 and Panel 2, respectively.

The empirical results that are reported in Table 5 reveal that, in Australia, the impact of bank-based financial development on economic growth is time variant; while it is positive in the short run, it is negative in the long run. The positive impact is confirmed by the bank-based financial development coefficient in Panel 2, which is positive and statistically significant, as expected, while the negative impact is supported by the bank-based financial development coefficient in Panel 1, which is statistically significant but negative. Although the long-run bank-based financial development coefficient for Australia has an unexpected sign, it is not unique to this study. Several other studies have shown evidence of a negative association between the two (Adu *et al.*, 2013; De Gregorio & Guidotti, 1995).

Further, the results that are displayed in Table 5 show that market-based financial development has no significant impact on economic growth in Australia, irrespective of whether the model is estimated in the long run or in the short run. This finding is confirmed by the coef-

Table 5. Empirical Results of the Estimated ARDL Model

Panel 1: Long-Run Results	**Dependent variable is y**			
Regressor	Co-efficient	Standard Error	T-Ratio	Probability
C	9.14	10.18	0.90	0.380
BD	-0.11**	0.04	-2.66	0.014
MD	0.02	0.02	1.03	0.316
IN	-0.60	0.43	-1.40	0.178
SA	0.49*	0.28	1.75	0.096
TO	-0.02	1.17	-0.13	0.897
Panel 2: Short-Run Results	**Dependent variable is Δy**			
Regressor	Co-efficient	Standard Error	T-Ratio	Probability
ΔBD	0.14**	0.06	2.44	0.023
ΔMD	0.02	0.02	1.12	0.277
ΔIN	0.24	0.37	0.65	0.523
ΔSA	0.48**	0.22	2.13	0.045
ΔTO	-0.02	0.16	-0.13	0.895
ecm(-1)	-0.97***	0.18	-5.33	0.000
R-Squared	0.815 R-Bar-Squared	0.731		
SE of Regression	1.160 F-Stat F(6,24)	12.550[0.000]		
Residual Sum of Squares	26.923 DW statistic	1.816		
Akaike Info. Criterion	-50.945 Schwarz Bayesian Criterion	-57.951		

Notes: *, ** and *** denote stationarity at 10%, 5% and 1% significance levels, respectively; Δ=first difference operator.

Table 6. Diagnostic Tests

LM Test Statistic	**Results [Probability]**
Serial Correlation: CHSQ(1)	0.560[0.454]
Heteroscedasticity: CHSQ (1)	2.488[0.115]
Normality: CHSQ (2)	4.240[0.086]
Functional Form: CHSQ(1)	0.967[0.326]

ficient of market-based financial development in Panels 1 and 2, which is insignificant. Thus, from these results, it can be concluded that, in Australia, it is bank-based financial development rather than market-based financial development that propels the real sector.

Other results reveal that, in Australia, savings have a positive impact on economic growth, both in the long run and in the short run. However, the long-run and short-run coefficients of investment and trade openness have been found to be insignificant. The results also reveal that the coefficient of ECM (-1) is negative and statistically significant, as expected.

The regression of the underlying ARDL model fits well, as is indicated by an R-squared of 81.5%. The

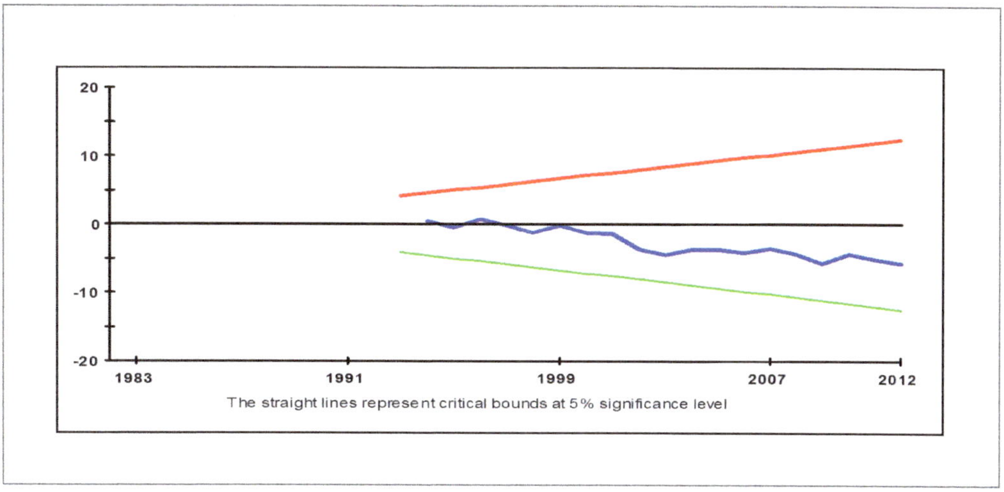

Figure 1. Plot of Cumulative Sum of Recursive Residuals

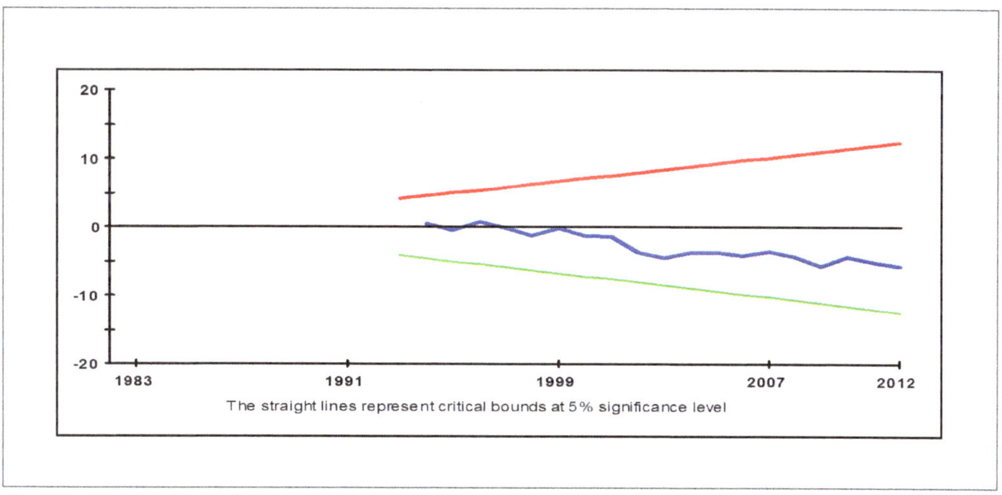

Figure 2. Plot of Cumulative Sum of Squares of Recursive Residuals

results of the diagnostic tests that were performed for serial correlation, functional form, normality and heteroscedasticity are displayed in Table 6, and they show that the model passed all of the tests except normality. However, an inspection of the Cumulative Sum of Recursive Residuals (CUSUM) and the Cumulative Sum of Squares of Recursive Residuals (CUSUMSQ) graphs in Figures 1 and 2, respectively, shows that there is stability, and there is no systematic change identified in the coefficients at a 5% significance level over the study period. The CUSUM and CUSUMSQ graphs, therefore, confirm that the parameters in this model are stable over the sample period.

Concluding Remarks

This paper examined the impact of bank- and market-based financial development on economic growth in Australia during the period from 1980 to 2012 using the

ARDL bounds testing approach. Unlike some previous studies, the paper used bank-based and market-based financial development indices to measure the level of bank-based and market-based financial development. These indices were constructed using the means-removed average method. The empirical results show that, in Australia, bank-based financial development only has a positive impact on economic growth in the short run. In the long run, its impact on economic growth is largely negative. These results imply that, in order to stimulate growth in Australia, it is of paramount importance to concentrate more on the pro-banking sector policies, at least in the short run. These results also show that the relationship between financial development (whether bank-based or market-based) and economic growth is not clear-cut; as it is proxy-dependent and time-variant. Hence, the notion that both bank- and market-based financial development have a positive impact on economic growth calls for further scrutiny.

References

Adjasi, C. K. D., & Biekpe, N. B. (2006). Stock market development and economic growth: The case of selected African countries. *African Development Review, 18*(1), 144-161.

Adu, G., Marbuah, G., & Mensah, J. T. (2013). Financial development and economic growth in Ghana: Does the measure of financial development matter? *Review of Development Finance, 3*(4), 192-203.

Ahmed, S. M., & Ansari, M. I. (1998). Financial sector development and economic growth: The South-Asian experience. *Journal of Asian Economics, 9*(3), 503-517.

Akinlo, A. E., & Akinlo, O. O. (2009). Stock market development and economic growth: Evidence from seven sub-Sahara African countries. *Journal of Economics and Business, 61*(2), 162-171.

Allen, D. S., & Ndikumana, L. (2000). Financial intermediation and economic growth in Southern Africa. *Journal of African Economies, 9*(2), 132-160.

Andersen, T. B., & Tarp, F. (2003). Financial liberalization, financial development and economic growth in LDCs. *Journal of International Development,* 15(2), 189-209.

Bekaert, G., Harvey, C., & Lundblad, C. (2005). Does financial liberalization spur growth? *Journal of Financial Economics, 77*(1), 3-55.

Bernard, A. U., & Austin, A. (2011). The role of stock market development on economic growth in Nigeria: A time-series analysis. *African Research Review, 5*(6), 213-230.

Bolbol, A. A., Fatheldina, A., & Omranb, M. M. (2005). Financial development, structure, and economic growth: The case of Egypt, 1974 - 2002. *Research in International Business and Finance*, 19, 171-194.

Bologna, P. (2010). Australian banking system resilience: What should be expected looking forward? An international perspective (*Working Paper* No. 10/228). International Monetary Fund.

Buffie, E. F. (1984). Financial repression, the new structuralists, and stabilisation policy in semi-industrialized economics. *Journal of Development Economics, 14*(3), 305-322.

Caporale, G. M., Howells, P. G. A., & Soliman, A. M. (2003). Stock market development and economic growth: The causal linkage. *Journal of Economic Development, 29*(1), 33-50.

Christopoulos, D. K., & Tsionas, E. G. (2004). Financial development and economic growth: evidence from panel unit root and cointegration tests. *Journal of Development Economics, 73*(1), 55-74.

De Gregorio, J., & Guidotti, P. E. (1995). Financial development and economic growth. *World Development, 23*(3), 433-448.

Demirguc-Kunt, A., & Levine, R. (1996). Stock market development and financial intermediaries: Stylized facts. *World Bank Economic Review, 10*(2), 291-321.

Duasa, J. (2007). Determinants of Malaysian trade balance: An ARDL bounds testing approach. *Journal of Economic Cooperation, 28*(3), 21-40.

Ghirmay, T. (2004). Financial development and economic growth in sub-Saharan African countries: Evidence from time series analysis. *African Development Review, 16*(3), 15–432.

Goldsmith, R. W. (1969). *Financial Structure and Development*, New Haven, CT: Yale University Press.

Güryay, E., Şafakli, O. V., & Tüzel, B. (2007). Financial development and economic growth: Evidence from Northern Cyprus. *International Research Journal of Finance and Economics, 8*(2), 57-62.

Hassan, K. M., Sanchez, B., & Yu, J. (2011). Financial development and economic growth: New evidence from panel data. *The Quarterly Review of Economics and Finance, 51*(1), 88-104.

Kargbo, S. M., & Adamu, P. A. (2009). Financial development and economic growth in Sierra Leone. *West African Journal of Monetary and Economic Integration*, 9(2), 30-61.

King, R. G., & Levine, R. (1993). Finance and growth: Schumpeter might be right. *Quarterly Journal of Economics, 108*(3), 717-737.

Levine, R., & Zervos, S. (1996). Stock market development and long run growth. *World Bank Economic Review, 10*(2), 323-340.

Lucas, R. (1988). On the mechanism of economic development. *Journal of Monetary Economics,* 22(1), 3-42.

Majid, M. S. A. (2008). Does financial development matter for economic growth in Malaysia? An ARDL bound testing approach. *Journal of Economic Cooperation, 29*(1), 61-82.

Nurudeen, A. (2009). Does stock market development raise economic growth? Evidence from Nigeria. *The Review of Finance and Banking, 1*(1), 15-26.

Odedokun, M. O. (1996). Alternative econometric approaches for analyzing the role of the financial sector in economic growth: Time-series evidence from LDCs. *Journal of Development Economics, 50*(1), 119-146.

Odhiambo, N. M. (2008). Financial depth, savings and economic growth in Kenya: A dynamic causal linkage. *Economic Modelling, 25*(4), 704-713.

Odhiambo, N. M. (2009). Finance-growth nexus and inflation dynamics in Kenya: An empirical investigation. *Savings and Development, 33*(1), 7-25.

Perkins, J. N. O. (1989). *The Deregulation of the Australian Financial System: The Experience of the 1980s.* Melbourne: Melbourne University Press.

Perron, P. (1997). Further evidence on breaking trend functions in macroeconomic variables. *Journal of Econometrics, 80*(2), 355-385.

Pesaran, M. H., & Shin, Y. (1999). An autoregressive distributed lag modeling approach to cointegration analysis. In S. Strøm (Ed.), *Econometrics and economic theory in the 20th century: The Ragnar Frisch Centennial Symposium . Econometric society monographs* (Vol. 31, pp. 1-31). Cambridge, UK: Cambridge University Press.

Pesaran, M. H., Shin, Y., & Smith, R. (2001). Bound Testing Approaches to the Analysis of Level Relationship. *Journal of Applied Econometrics, 16*(3), 289-326.

Ram, R. (1999). Financial development and economic growth: Additional evidence. *Journal of Development Studies, 35*(4), 164-174.

Reserve Bank of Australia. (2013). Various issues. Available from http://www.rba.gov.au

Schumpeter, J. A. (1911). *The Theory of Economic Development*, Harvard University Press, Cambridge, MA.

Shan, J., & Jianhong, Q. (2006). Does financial development 'lead' economic growth? The case of China. *Annals of Economics and Finance*, 1, 231-250.

Stern, N. (1989). The economics of development: a survey. *Economic Journal, 99*(397), 597-685.

Ujunwa, A., & Salami, O.P. (2010). Stock market development and economic growth: Evidence from Nigeria. *European Journal of Economics, Finance and Administrative Sciences, 25*, 44-53.

Van Wijnbergen, S. (1983). Credit policy, inflation and growth in a financially repressed economy. *Journal of Development Economics, 13*(1), 45-65.

Wood, A. (1993). Financial development and economic growth in Barbados: Causal evidence. *Savings and Development, 17*(4), 379-390.

Yonezawa, Y., & Azeez, A. A. (2010). Financial systems and economic performance: a cross country analysis. *Global Economy and Finance Journal, 3*(2), 107-121.

Competitiveness and Resilience of the productive districts in Sicily. The behavior of the Sicilian production areas during the economic crisis

Michele Sabatino[1]

ABSTRACT

"Resilience" refers to the ability of companies to adapt their strategies in response to economic circumstances that change from time to time. This definition seems appropriate to explain the behavior of the Sicilian productive districts in light of the recent economic crisis. These meta-producing districts of Sicily merit further study, particularly in terms of the concept of resilience and its accompanying economic dynamics. The Sicilian Region has recognized these productive districts, which represent an attempt to use industrial policy to promote various types of mergers among companies. This regional strategy could have been a useful tool to induce the production system to direct its decisions toward forms of integration and inter-company collaboration that would also strengthen the previously begun processes of local development. The crisis reduced any regional policy aspirations and above all decimated the numerous small enterprises that might have represented the backbone of the proto-districts. After an initial methodological and historical reconstruction, the present study focuses on the Sicilian production areas – with particular reference to the industrial area – from the first years of their establishment and regional recognition to those latter years marked by the economic crisis. Thus, we evaluate the degree of resilience of the different districts and their competitive capacities. Arguing about competitiveness and resilience means, on one hand, to understand what the factors are that combine to reduce the vulnerability of a territory and a production system and on the other hand, to identify strategies to increase financing for the same factors that are crucial to a region's economic growth.

KEY WORDS: resilience, productive district, regional strategy, economic crisis

[1]KORE University of Enna, Italy

Introduction

The current international financial crisis has severely affected Italy and its economy. The austerity policies that are required – which involve reducing the public debt – have also made it more difficult to develop local economies, particularly lagging economies such as Sicily's.

The manufacturing districts promoted by the Sicilian Region are the main subject of this paper and appear to be a reality in motion for almost ten years; as such, they can help promote local development in this particularly difficult economic context. At the end of the past decade, recognizing the productive districts

Correspondence concerning this article should be addressed to: Michele Sabatino, KORE University of Enna, Via Donna nuova 109 – 94100 Enna
Email: michele.sabatino@unikore.it

promoted by the Sicilian Region represented the industrial policy's attempt at promoting types of mergers between companies inside a regional context; in this context, applying the latest methods to mapping the Italian districts (Sforzi, 2009) left the entire island unguarded, although these embryonic forms of proto-districts or districts were already present.

The economic crisis and de-industrialization processes underway in Italy and Sicily seem not only to have set aside any aspirations of regional industrial policy but also to have decimated the universe of micro and small enterprises that might represent the backbone of the recognized proto-districts.

In the most recent economic literature, the term resilience refers to the ability of companies to adapt their strategies in response to changes in economic situations that arise from time to time (Christopherson, Michie, & Tyler, 2010). This definition seems particularly suited to explaining the behavior of the Sicilian productive districts in light of the recent economic and financial crises. Beginning from this concept (which is now widespread in the economy) and linking it to the historical and socio-economic dynamics of the Sicilian context, the meta-districts of Sicily are certainly an interesting case study.

This paper aims to assess the degree of resilience of the various Sicilian districts with particular reference to the group of companies participating in the districts recognized by the Sicilian Region. Therefore, this research intends to illuminate how the member companies of districts respond to the effects of the economic crisis and whether joining the district strengthens their resilience. In particular, following a methodological and historical reconstruction, we focus on the Sicilian production areas – with particular reference to those classified as industrial – beginning from the first years in which the Region was recognized until the recent economic and social crisis. Thus, we will evaluate the different Sicilian districts' resilience and their competitive capacity with a specific focus on the leading enterprises of the districts and the leadership role they exercised during the economic crisis. We see that speaking of competitiveness and resilience means, on one hand, understanding what the factors are that have combined to reduce the vulnerability of a territory and a production system, and on the other, identifying strategies that increase the financing of the same factors that economic theory indicates are crucial to a region's economic growth.

Theoretical framework

The literature on industrial and productive districts is now quite extensive and filled with definitions. However, industrial districts represent a heterogeneous set with regard both to their social base and their production structure, which is particularly evident in a country such as Italy in which this particular form of spatial organization of production is more prevalent than in other countries (Berardi & Iannuzzi, 2012; Paniccia, 1998). Nevertheless, industrial districts have clearly identifiable common features as follows: they are limited areas, and each has a population of manufacturing and services that share business areas that are variously specialized and interconnected (Camuffo & Grandinetti, 2011). In the industrial districts, institutional subjects that support the district's development are at work (Provasi, 2002).

As defined above, the industrial districts do not appear to differ in any way from the clusters defined by Michael Porter (1998) as follows: geographic concentrations of interconnected companies and institutions sharing a particular field of activity. In fact, there is a difference, and it is not insignificant; Porter (1998) makes no reference to the extension of spatial clusters, and there are, therefore, many clusters among his examples that cover the territory of an entire differentiated state, such as the clusters of vine-wine in California, the furniture cluster in North Carolina or the forest products clusters in Sweden (Porter, 1998). Inside the clusters, the concentration process is essentially generated by economic circumstances and the main reference is the enterprise and related industry sector. By all appearances, these production systems are not comparable with traditional Italian industrial districts, which are generally limited to a few and generally small municipalities with an organizational model defined using the local community in which the business population works. In addition, an industrial district is the product of a bottom-up process that involves both the local community and the companies operating in the same territory, and it also requires the presence of a system of standards and shared values and a common level of trust between local actors that interact in this context. In short, the industrial districts form a sub-set of the broader set of clusters defined by Porter (1998).

These considerations are internationally supported through concepts introduced by Alfred Marshall, an economist who studied the late nineteenth-century industrial areas of Sheffield and Lancashire and identified the same elements that make up the term "modern" industrial district, i.e., specific territories, certain productive specializations, populations of businesses and webs of inter-enterprise relationships. In his research, Marshall (1972) focused his attention on the concentration of specialized industries that could rely on "external economies" rather than on the internal organization of big businesses. Marshall's analysis referenced industrial districts by considering their concentration in a defined area, from industries specialized in a single economic activity (mono-sector districts) to those encompassing more economic activities (multi-sector districts) (Bellandi & De Propris, 1982). In the years that followed, Becattini (1990) added a strong interpenetration between the productive and social dimensions – between a business population and a community of people – to these distinguishing elements. The EU factor has great relevance in the theory of industrial districts, as formulated by Marshall and perfected by Becattini and his school, which involves the ability to reduce frictions (transaction costs) in the relations between actors located in the same district (Dei Ottati, 1994). The same factor promotes the dissemination of knowledge in the local context (Camuffo & Grandinetti, 2011) and the formation of the "industrial atmosphere" – using the happy metaphor coined by Marshall (1972). We can then identify a variant of "Marshall's" industrial district, which can easily include a large part of Italian industrial districts (Sforzi, 2003).

For a long time, from the sixties to the first half of the nineties, industrial districts and the vast populations of small and medium enterprises that animated them represented a dynamic component of the Italian economy, responsible to a large extent for the success of the "Made in Italy" manufactured products in the international markets (Becattini, 1998). In the last fifteen years, however, Italy's industrial districts have undergone profound changes and not merely under the pressure of globalization. This process of structural change – which some authors have referred to as the competitive repositioning of Italian industrial districts (Foresti, Guelpa, & Trenti, 2009) – hit the world of recession that began in late 2008 and that resulted in a tremendous tightening of competitive pressures, accelerating the transition and making survival more difficult for companies (Di Berardino & Mauro, 2011).

In line with EU business policies – and in particular with the "Small Business Act" of the European Commission in 2006, which states that SMEs should be supported (even to the extent of including forms of collaboration between companies and institutions with the goal of "networking to grow") – in the last decade, the Sicilian Region has favored the recognition, creation, promotion and support of new combination districts or meta-districts with an effort, perhaps inappropriate, to program the development and aggregation process of Sicilian businesses.

In this sense, and in light of the objects that limit identification of these aggregation districts, the Sicilian Region has sought to foster a vision of the district in terms of a "meta-cluster", which is a structure that was born from the evolution of the district aggregations based on Marshall's meaning or even based on the most advanced models of "business networks". In this view, the definition of the district that is used is similar to that of Porter's industrial clusters (1998) or of a production chain with vertical and/or horizontal displacements in transnational areas, in which the emphasis is on the companies' leaders to respect the 'idea of the district', per Marshall's meaning.

According to the literature (Creti & Bettoni 2001), metadistricts represent production areas of excellence with strong (both existing and potential) ties with the world of research and production innovation. With meta-districts, the aim of the regional institution seems to have been to define areas of manufacturing excellence that represent the poles of development as follows: encouraging technological cooperation between companies in areas with high technological potential, while strengthening companies' competitiveness in local and international markets in centers of technical and scientific research.

The concept of the meta-district begins with the notion that the evolution of systems of production is strongly linked not only to the development of new information technologies but also to the relocation of production, the heightened competition increasingly based on innovation and, in particular, to the industrial application of knowledge. Theoretical and empirical studies from a number of scholars such as, for example, Rullani (2004; 2009), Fortis and Quadrio (2006), Corò and Micelli (2006) have shown that the development of these districts is today related to the development of the knowledge economy, which depends mainly on research, innovation, high-quality human capital, available and efficient "networks" and positive interactions with institutional actors.

In the modern scientific literature, the first criterion for identifying meta-districts is multi-sectoral – not only as a significant link in the supply chain within the areas identified but also as a significant number of services to enterprises (for example, research and experimentation services). The second criterion involves territoriality because if the concept of meta-districts attempts to overcome old ties to create new ones based on new technologies and services necessary for enterprises' competitiveness, it is also true that everything is based on a form of confidence that must give thanks to a relationship of "proximity". Moreover, the new information and communication technologies are not absent from all businesses in the territory. The third criterion involves leadership. In identifying a meta-district, it is essential to ensure the presence of one or more business leaders who can represent the sector and act as a "drag". The final criterion requires that the institutional environment must play a significant role in overcoming barriers related to enterprises' conflicting positions. Based on these elements, the eligible areas within which the presence of district characteristics (strong horizontal structure, a high percentage of outsourcing, close relations of subcontracting, high dissemination of knowledge, etc.) are identified that can enable the modern structures of the "meta-districts" to be achieved.

In contrast to the existing business reality, it seems clear that the Sicilian Region's proposed industrial districts have more in common with the experience of clusters proposed by Michael Porter (or even networks of companies), which makes it easier to identify them in their first application in Sicily. There is in fact no doubt that the efforts of the Sicilian Region to adopt an "industrial" policy and then a legislative instrument to contribute to the creation and subsequent development of hypothetical districts in Sicily is certainly positive but discounts the objective limitation that districts are not created by legislation but are instead also the result of evolutionary processes involving economic, social and cultural (and other) institutions, in addition to the major role played by the regulatory framework (Rullani, 2009; Schilirò, 2010b; Viesti, 2000). We can at most speak of a regulatory model that the various production areas should or could adapt in time.

In line with what has previously been said, Signorini (2000) argued – in referring to the problem of the "creation" of the productive districts by decree – that, in general, districts have sprung up spontaneously and often almost unexpectedly in the evolution of a local artisan tradition to facilitate the maturation of embryonic entrepreneurial skills, to thicken subcontracting relationships, and sometimes in response to the various crises of large local businesses. Furthermore, the birth of the districts is also linked to the development of new businesses and to the beginnings of new productions that aim to compete in the markets and not to "capture" incentives. It is, therefore, difficult to find elements that favor the birth of a district by decree or administrative measures. Thus, a legislative framework, even if useful and properly oriented, cannot constitute a sufficient condition for creating these districts.

Nevertheless, the experience of industrial districts seems, at least, to have played an initial aggregating and supporting role in the Sicilian production system, which perhaps might be even better accompanied and supported in light of recent economic crises. It is significant that the data that from the euphoria of the first application of 23 districts recognized that only 19 remained due to turnover of inputs and lack of rewards.

Following this path in law and practice of industrial clusters and their evolution, the definition of "resilience" seems particularly suited to explain the behavior of the Sicilian productive districts in light of recent economic crises. In the most recent economic literature, the term resilience indeed means the ability of companies and/or regions to adapt their strategies in response to changing economic circumstances that arise from time to time (Christopherson et al., 2010).

More generally, those economic and productive systems affected by shocks may show – over the short or medium term – the following different reactions: a) some manage to absorb the shock and return to their previous growth paths within a relatively short time frame, which is behavior that is "economically resilient"; b) others may not have their balance or paths of economic growth affected at all, indicating that they are, therefore, not vulnerable and "shock-resistant"; c) and, finally, others may appear unable to absorb or react to negative shocks within defined parameters, thus proving to be "non-resilient" (Briguglio, Cordina, Farrugia, & Vella, 2006; Pendall, Foster, & Cowell, 2007; Hassink, 2010).

This ability (which is relevant to any individual or organization) "to deal with and recover from the effect of disturbing action produced by a negative event" (Graziano, 2012, p. 3) is different from the ability to "drag" a system, which otherwise is "the attitude of the same imperturbability" (ibid).

In this sense, the resilience of a region or a production system refers to the ability to reconfigure its industrial, technological and institutional structure and adapt it to the change. If the shock is strong enough, it can alter the behavior of economic agents, changing the composition of the economy and generating new trajectories. Resilience is much higher when a system can respond creatively and flexibly to shocks (Pendall, et al., 2007). Everything depends on the innovative capacity of enterprises, the ability of entrepreneurs to create new business opportunities, the structure of the credit market, the capabilities of institutions to be innovative and the strength of individuals and communities to be able to respond flexibly using innovation.

Inspired by Sheffi (2005), which illustrates some cases of companies that have shown particular abilities with regard to adapting to economic shocks and others that do not have such abilities, it is possible to extend some of the results of these studies to the analysis of the characteristics of local entrepreneurial systems, highlighting, for example, the importance of vertical relationships in chains that are typical of districts.

Finally, Graziano (2012) builds a theoretical framework for describing a territorial system that considers the economic, social and environmental dimensions, as well as later on the major categories of "vulnerability" and "resilience", and is thus able to offer a valuable reading of "resilient" territorial and productive systems. Therefore, a resilient economic, social or environmental system is a system with a diversified and modular structure, with readily available resources and with good strategic adaptability resulting from systemic elements with redundant functions. Graziano's proposed scheme clarifies and highlights the strong relationship between territorial systems, business systems and production in which the vulnerability of enterprises and the vulnerability of the area are two phenomena that are connected with well-determined peculiarities and specificities. Thus, the carrier of a territorial resilient system rests on strengthening the network of interrelations between social, capital and local resources that are available both horizontally (within the same sector) and vertically (featuring interconnections between various levels) and individual strategies, business capabilities and the ability to adapt to shocks.

Methodology

Beginning with the concept of resilience, which is now widespread also in terms of economic and territorial cohesion, this research attempts to evaluate the experience of Sicily's industrial districts, with particular reference to those properly considered "industrial" that are based on an analysis of the internal dynamics and their competitive ability to understand which factors, if any, have helped to reduce the vulnerability of a territory and/or a production system. The subject of this research is thus called the Four Clusters of Sicilian Industry. Thanks to information gathered from both quantitative perspectives (with census data and other aggregated information), and with field surveys, it was possible to reconstruct at least a portion of the dynamics of development and resilience to the recent crisis on the basis of a possible scheme of interpretation. The analysis was completed by collecting and processing the data available in the AIDA database on the main leaders of the districts. The values of turnover and employees are derived from the 2009-2013 period to make a dynamic assessment over the years.

The processing of data correlated the overall economic performances of the four Sicilian productive districts and the performances of the leading enterprises in their respective districts. These data enable a ready comparison between the overall performance of the districts and participating enterprises and the performance of highly internationalized leading enterprises that are export-oriented with a high degree of innovation. This comparison helps us to understand, in contrast to the general data from Sicily, if and how companies participating in the district have benefited from greater resilience than non-participating companies and, finally, whether the leading companies embodied an attractive feature separating it from other companies in the district.

Results

In planning for the implementation of cohesion policy in Sicily, the Sicilian Region has identified the industrial district as a new tool for territorial governance. This choice is related not only to law 140/1999 but also to (financial) law 266/2005 (art. 367-372), since it introduced the legal concept of "productive district" that became a subject with independent legal status.

Regional law 17 December 2004 set up the manufacturing districts. In art. 56, the law states that the Department of Regional Cooperation, Trade, Craft and Fisheries would adopt (by decree) the criteria for recognition of the productive districts, which are interpreted as clusters, such that the same clusters could assume the role of referees for the programming policies and development of the region and, therefore, act as final beneficiaries of EU, state or regional funds. On 1 December 2005, the Department of Regional Cooperation issued a Decree (DA)152 establishing the criteria for identifying and recognizing the procedures for manufacturing districts, and the arrangements for implementing interventions under the Pact of Development District, regulated by art. 5 of the same decree. In particular, art. 2 of the decree defines industrial districts as "industrial clusters characterized by the presence of clusters that carry out similar activities according to a logic of supply chain, vertical or horizontal, and also a set of institutional actors with responsibility and operating in the activity of supporting the local economy". According to regional rules, districts must consist of a cluster of companies engaged in similar activities and having a set of institutional actors (universities, research institutes and higher education, government, etc.). They must present themselves as a horizontal or vertical industry, along with transnational dislocations (i.e., able to guarantee localization and competitive advantages). Moreover, they must have more than 50 enterprises with at least 150 employees; there must be a high degree of integration among these companies (to be documented with supply chains) and there must be a high capacity for technological innovation (production processes, leading companies, educational institutions, etc.). A level of technological innovation is also required, which is proven by their production and/or the presence of leading companies in each sector, as well as by the presence of educational institutions and/or specific documentation centers regarding the local culture of product and labor.

In Sicily, before the Sicily Region Decree recognized the productive districts, ISTAT recognized the presence of only the following two industrial manufacturing districts or SSLs on the island in its 2001 census: the district of Custonaci (TP), within the goods for home sector with 532 companies and 1.355 employees, on one hand, and the District of Sinagra (ME), operating in the textile and apparel sector with 284 companies and 643 employees, on the other. Simultaneously, they identified some areas that with local production systems, such as the ceramics of Caltagirone (CT), the Sea Fisheries District of Mazara del Vallo (TP), the food vegetable District of Pachino (SR), and the technological District "Etna Valley" (CT).

The conclusion of the formal creation of productive districts in Sicily is accomplished by decree 546/12s of 16 March 2007 in which financing 23 industrial clusters is recognized and accepted. Table 1 shows the 23 productive districts recognized by the Region by province and sector.

An analysis of Table 1 and the location of the members of any individual districts shows, first, that the Sicilian Region has favored a territorial demarcation and aggregation rather than sectorial and/or specialized production in attempting to enforce an indicator of continuity between enterprises, except for some cases such as the Red Orange, in which the territorial aggregation, which involves mainly the provinces of Catania and (to a lesser extent) Syracuse, coincides with that of specialization. There are also cases of redundant duplication in areas such as ceramics, wine, recreational boating and (in part) fishing.

The disproportionate number of productive districts recognized that there are 3.448 companies with approximately 43.500 employees, which considers that the National Observatory of the Districts recognizes in its annual report (2014) just 4 districts (fishing, textiles, mechanical and mechatronics). Considering also that in other regions, i.e., "in districts" in Europe such as

Table 1. District production recognized by the Region of Sicily (2007) by province and sector.

Productive districts	Type
Blood Orange (CT)	Agriculture
Ceramics of Caltagirone (CT)	Industrial Craft – Ceramics
Unique Regional Cereals - SWB (EN)	Food Industry
Sicily Eastern Textile Chain (CT)	Industry – Textiles
Sicilian Table Grape - PGI Mazzarone (CT)	Agriculture -Viticoltura
Logistics (PA)	Industry – Logistics
Mechatronics (PA)	Industry – Mechatronics
Nautica Due Mari (ME)	Industry – Nautica
Fishing and Fishing Tourism Siciliae (TP)	Fishing and Tourism
Plastic (SR)	Industry – Chemistry
Fruit and vegetable quality of the Val di Noto (SR)	Agriculture
Sicilian wine (PA)	Agriculture -Viticoltura
Sicilian ceramics (ME)	Industrial Craft – Ceramics
Industrial fishing COSVAP (TP)	Fishing
Etna Valley (CT)	Industry - Hi Tech
Florovivaismo Siciliano (ME)	Agriculture -Floricoltura
Stone Materials Outstanding (TP)	Industrial Craft
Mechanical (SR) Industry - Mechanics	
Pleasure Craft (PA)	IndustryNautica
Horticultural South East Sicily (RG)	Agriculture
Lava Stone (CT)	Industrial Craft
Olive lands of the West Sicily (TP)	Agriculture
Wine in Western Sicily (TP)	Agriculture -Viticoltura

Source: Observatory of Industrial Clusters and SMEs, Sicily (2014)

Veneto, by Census data from ISTAT 2001, there are 22 districts in which 37.784 "Local Manufacturing Units" are operating, there is clearly an inconsistency in the duplication of manufacturing districts in areas that are almost identical and there is a clear fabric weakness in the Sicilian production in comparison with that of the more industrialized regions. This proliferation is neither an expression of dimensional efficiency nor specialization but is instead inspired by other mechanisms related to searching for public funding or political logic and belonging. The large number of districts is unjustified based on the productive dimensions of the entities and their strength in the various markets. Finally, the large number of production areas does not take into account (if not negligible at the moment that partners are identified at the district formation) external economies, i.e., that factor in what the basic economic logic of the companies was when they formed themselves into districts.

Over the years, the Sicilian Region has both recognized additional production areas and confirmed those previously recognized with the first Decree of

Table 2. Productive Districts recognized by the Region of Sicily from 2011 to 2013

Productive districts	Type
Poultry (RG)	Agriculture
Orange of Ribera (AG)	Agriculture
Eda - Eco Domus (AG)	Industry - Construction
The beef food chain (PA)	Agriculture
Ficodindia Calatino South Simeto (CT)	Agriculture
Dairy (RG)	Agriculture
Sicilian Sweet (PA)	Agriculture
Wood and Furnishings (CT)	Craftsmanship
Aluminum and Related Areas (RG)	Industry - Mechanics
Nautica (PA)	Arts - Tourism
Wellness Spa (ME)	Tourism - Health

Source: Observatory of Industrial Clusters and SMEs, Sicily (2014)

Table 3. District production recognized by the Region of Sicily (2014) by province and sector.

Productive districts	Type
Blood Orange (CT)	Agriculture
Unique Regional Cereals – SWB (EN)	Industry – Food
Mechatronics (PA)	Industry – Mechatronics
Beef Food Chain (PA)	Agriculture
Industrial Fishing COSVAP (TP)	Fishing
Etna Valley Catania (CT)	Industry - Hi Tech
Sicilian Florivivalismo (ME)	Agriculture -Floriculture
Outstanding Stone Materials (TP)	Industrial Craft
Mechanics (SR)	Industry - Mechanical
Lava Stone (CT)	Industrial Craft
Poultry (RG)	Agriculture
Eda – Ecodomus (AG)	Industria - Construction
Calatino Ficodindia South Simeto (CT)	Agriculture
Dairy (RG)	Agriculture
Sciliano Sweet (PA)	Agriculture
Wood and Furnishings (CT)	Craftsmanship
Aluminium and related areas (RG)	Industry – Mechanics
Nautica (PA)	Arts - Tourism
Wellness SPA (ME)	Tourism – Health

Source: Observatory of Industrial Clusters and SMEs, Sicily (2014)

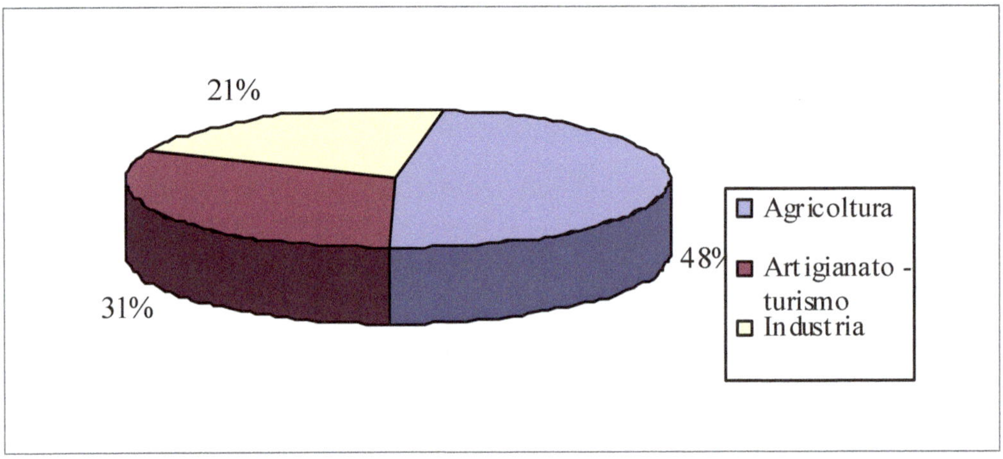

Figure 1. Clusters Sicilian Breakdown by sector.
Source: Authors` own elaboration on the basis of Observatory of Industrial Clusters and SMEs, Sicily (2014)

2007. Decree 611 of 2011 recognized the other 7 (seven) manufacturing districts, and Decree 744 / gab 2012 recognized the Beef Food Chain District, whereas Decree 184/2013 recognized 3 (three) additional districts. Table 2 shows the 10 new productive districts recognized by the Region of Sicily in provinces and sectors from 2011 to 2013.

In recent years, as required by Decree No. 152 in 2005, the Regional Department for Industry verified the existence of indicators of relevance, confirming only 19 industrial clusters. Table 3 shows the 19 productive districts recognized by the Region of Sicily by province and sector up to 2014.

The division of districts by sector, which is depicted in Figure 1 and derived from Table 3, is as follows: Agriculture and Fishing comprise the largest share, at 47% and 9 manufacturing districts, closely followed by Handcrafts and Tourism with a share of 32% with 6 districts and finally the industry with four productive districts with 21%, confirming that the for economic impact of Sicily Agriculture remains important.

Ultimately, there are 10 (ten) productive districts (PD) of industry and crafts recognized by the Sicilian Region. Among these, there are 4 districts in industries excluding construction as follows: Etna Valley (CT), Mechanics (SR), Mechatronics (PA), aluminum (PA). The remaining six districts of production come from crafts, industry or tourism and are as follows: Eda Ecodomus (AG), wood and furnishings (CT), Lapidei Outstanding (PA), Lava Stone (CT) and finally the Wellness Spa (ME). However, Table 4 shows the number of companies involved in each industrial cluster and their territorial distribution by province. A total of 19 companies involved in the production areas at the time of their recognition was 1.958 companies, and the number of people employed at that time amounted to 20.980.

The 10 manufacturing industry, trade and tourism Districts that include 826 companies, some of which are manufacturing companies, service companies and others that engage in marketing the products from the manufacturing districts. In 2015, there were 14,619 employees in the 10 industrial and handicraft districts. It was not included because we consider that number of employees in the Mechanics District.

Since 2008, the ERDF (European Fund for Regional Development) has funded (DDG 2970 del22 / 10/2008) grants, i.e., projects submitted by some of the 23 productive districts recognized in 2007. In particular, the ERDF has financed 12 projects submitted by 11 districts (Productive District Etna Valley has presented two projects, both of which were co-financed) by committing funds equaling a total of € 3.956,400. However, the results have not been satisfactory. Thus, in December

Table 4. District production in Sicily: Number of companies, employees and distribution by province (2014)

Productive Districts	TP	PA	ME	AG	CL	EN	CT	RG	SR	Tot	N. Employees
Blood Orange (CT)		2	2	27			54		19	104	2.033
Unique Regional Cereals– SWB (EN)	1	1	1		1	20	26		3	53	184
Mechatronics (PA)	20	63	3	4	4		4	4	1	103	2.080
Beef Food Chain (PA)		88				30				118	162
Industriale Fishing COSVAP (TP)	85	5		10	1		2		1	104	1.092
Etna Valley Catania (CT)		4	5			1	68	4	2	84	5.111
Sicilian Florivivalism (ME)	1		75		1		13	1		91	n.d.
Outstanding Stone Materials (TP)	44	5	1					12		62	717
Mechanics (SR)					1		1		60	62	n.d.
Lava Stone (CT)							50	1		51	536
Poultry (RG)	1						2	52	6	61	436
Eda – Eco domus (AG)	3	3		139	3		2		1	151	1.711
Calatino Ficodindia South Simeto (CT)					25	18	12			55	260
Dairy (RG)	11	113		2	8			118		252	960
Siciliano Sweet (PA)		42	45	48		17	83	25	34	294	1.234
Wood and Furnishings (CT)							51			51	356
Aluminium and Related Areas (RG)						2	25	97	17	141	1.239
Nautica (PA)	5	50	7	1			4	3		70	317
Wellness SPA (ME)	5	4	21	8			13			51	2.552
Total	176	389	160	239	44	88	410	317	144	1.958	20.980

Source: National Observatory of Italian Districts (2014)

2009, although the Region of Sicily issued a second call concerning the development plans of the supply chain within the ERDF OP 2007/2013 that applied to only 10 Industrial Clusters, it was notable that the undertakings, and in particular the districts recognized by the Region, were not always able to show those investments in design skills and the know-how to incentivize and use it effectively and efficiently.

The results of the empirical analysis refer to four (4) clusters of industry that include Etna Valley (CT), Mechanics (SR), Mechatronics (PA), and Aluminium (PA). Until 2014, there were of 390 companies involved, which employed 11.884 persons. In 2007, the year the productive districts were recognized by the Region, there were 13,447 employees in the three industrial districts (the District of Aluminium had not yet been entered or recognized). These are pre-crisis data, and the employment situation has changed dramatically from 2009 to 2013 as a result of corporate restructuring.

We now consider each of the four districts beginning with Etna Valley Productive district of Catania, which is the most important industry in terms of size, number of employees, turnover, etc. The district Etna Valley is a well-defined technological industry, and its components are bound to one another through a production chain, with dislocations in a vast area of over territorial constraints, through (long) networks of associated companies linked through technological, organizational and functional bases. The business system of the Etna Valley Productive district is characterized by a vertical

Table 5. Industrial districts in Sicily: Number of member companies and employees

Distretti produttivi	2007		2014	
	Tot	Employees	Tot	Employees
Mechatronics (PA)*	94	2.080	103	2.080
Etna Valley Catania (CT)	136	7.916	84	5.111
Mechanics (SR)	94	3.454	62	3.454
Aluminium and Related Areas (RG)**	/	/	141	1.239
Total	324	13.447	390	11.884

* The data of employees are unchanged because the company has employees over the region
** District of Aluminium was recognized in 2014
Source: Observatory Industrial Clusters and SMEs, Sicily (2014)

or horizontal productive chain in the high-tech sector; it included 136 companies operating in the areas of manufacturing and high and medium technology services, with a high density of entrepreneurial enterprises, in some cases, of specialization systems integrated as consortia. The technological center of Etna Valley, which gave birth to the development of the Pact Etna Valley Production District, is the result of a partnership between ST Microeletronics and the University of Catania. The Etna Valley district had approximately 7.916 employees, most of whom are in industries mainly consisting of small businesses and over 3.000 in Microeletronics ST. Today 84 companies are participating in the district, featuring over 5.000 employees. Production revolves around silicon and from this product, the companies of the district have developed many products that are necessary to several production systems in various hi-tech industries. The district is also characterized by a high degree of openness and internationalization, as many of the companies participating in the district are well-positioned in foreign markets. Although the recent economic crisis has reduced both the numbers of companies and numbers of employees, we can certainly say that the Etna Valley district is close to the model of a meta-district that could be organized around a market leader because of its characteristics, including its strong commitment to innovation, its business-university linkages, and its multi-sectorial nature. Finally, the district is active in presenting projects and in obtaining both public and private financing.

The second-ranking Sicilian Productive District in terms of enterprises and employees and in terms of turnover and that also focuses on innovation in the hi-tech sector is the Mechatronics Pin Palermo, which consists of 103 employees compared to 94 at the time of recognition, resulting in a total of 2.080 employees within the entire production chain. The district is characterized by industrial companies performing important functions in the engineering industry, and it also has a presence in the business services sector and ICT, although its manufacturing base consists mainly of micro-enterprises that are unbalanced in traditional sectors. The Mechatronics District not only is represented by companies in the province of Palermo (63%) but also includes companies belonging to the following other provinces in the region: Caltanissetta, Trapani, Catania, Agrigento, Ragusa. The district was promoted by Confindustria Palermo and, together with the University, was born to enhance a highly technological border area, which ranks it highly among the mechanics, auto, electronics and computer science fields. There is a leading enterprise such as *Engineering Ingegneria Informatica* SpA in the field of business *integration*, application outsourcing and infrastructure, and innovative solutions and strategic consulting. Within the manufacturing branch, particularly in Palermo province, the most representative product categories include the following: production of non-ferrous and semi-finished metals, steel casting and, above all, the manufacture of motor vehicles, construction of railway rolling stock and wooden vehicle parts. There is also a significant presence of small and highly competitive firms, thanks to their specialization in particular products such as, for example, components for the *automotive* sector. Although this district is still oriented toward the meta-model district and is active in presenting projects in the region.

The third district is the Mechanics Productive district in Syracuse, which is populated by 62 companies. It is characterized by the presence of some leading companies such as SudProgetti IREM Spa and Spa. Their statistics are not in our possession, and the updated data on employment we consider arbitrarily confirmed. The 2007 data of 3.454 units are found on the official website but with 116 member companies, which compares inexactly to the 94 members in the Sicilian Region. This DP consists largely of companies that produce or are responsible for the maintenance of industrial plants. Moreover, in this PD, there are a good number of companies that provide services to businesses. Although not particularly oriented to innovation, this district has some characteristics similar to the meta-district model (enterprise leaders and multi-sectoral approach). The DP of mechanics has remained active in presenting projects and obtaining funding from the Region.

The last recently recognized manufacturing district is the Productive District of Aluminium and related fields. The District has 141 companies and various institutions and economic and social representatives, with a turnover of approximately EUR 150 million and 1.239 occupied units directly in the field. The District of Aluminium and related fields has its core in Ragusa province, where most of the companies that underwrote the Development Compact District are concentrated, although there are also companies in Siracusa, Catania and Enna provinces. The company that plays a leading role in the District is the *Metra Ragusa Spa*. The production process of the District has a strong vertical and horizontal integration, with a specific concentration of production in the Ragusa province, in which there is a leader at the European level in the field of aluminum profiles, which is the only aluminum alloy foundry in southern Italy, i.e., Metra Ragusa Spa and Ver.all Srl (belonging to the Industrial Group Metra). The chain also consists of several companies that handle the manufacture of accessories and components attached to the manufacture of aluminum frames. Closely linked horizontally are companies that manufacture accessories for windows and doors (hinges, handles, small metal parts, gaskets, etc.), machines for the machining of aluminum profiles, and insulating glass. Even this district is close to the model of meta-district, particularly based on its multi-sectorial nature that is organized around a market leader.

The four industrial districts selected were born around the need to enhance the specificity of the local economic system in which they are inserted and are more than 'mature' structures, which indicates that it is possible to find stable relationships of interdependence between businesses and other entities intertwined with them in the districts as units of an entrepreneurial and local institutional structure that is willing to embark on a path of gradual growth into the model proposed. It consists of more than pilot projects in the construction of a meta-district; instead, it is a real recognition of these districts. Thus, only two of the four are recognized within the National Observatory of Italian Districts, i.e., the Mechanics and the Mechatronics Districts. It is absolutely strange that the District of Etna Valley is missing from the data of the National Observatory because even the ministry on the Catania District was repeatedly the recipient of both public resources and of analysis and evaluation.

A common critical issue to the district companies in Sicily is that they are often simply too small and are often micro-enterprises. Such dimensional problems are also generally related to the use of traditional technologies that are not particularly advanced, which thus leads to a weak propensity for innovation. The ability to build knowledge networks with research centers and universities, incubators of ideas, and science parks is vital in today's knowledge-based economy (Schilirò, 2010 a).

Furthermore, the model of Sicilian meta-districts, in particular, suffers because of the objective difficulties that occur at the system level, due to the many deficiencies in hard and soft infrastructure, inefficiencies in services, gaps and complicated rules in various bureaucracies, the weight of taxation, all of which promote submergence and opacity and can lead to "shadow alliances".

We are in the presence of a dynamic high diversification but with the following thing in common: there

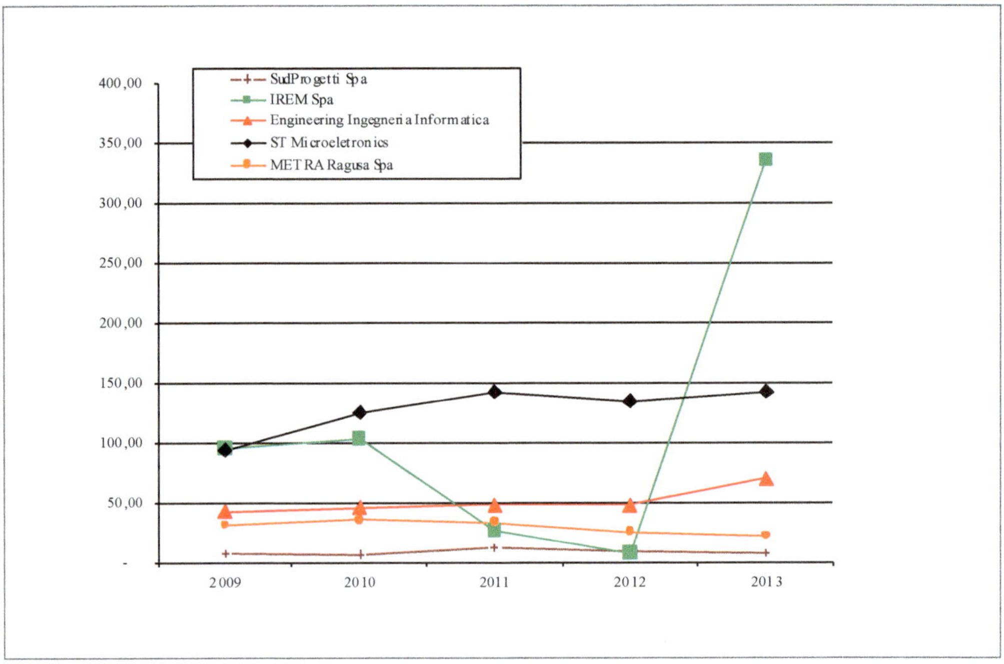

Figure 2. Evolution of revenues from turnover of the leading companies in the Sicilian Production Districts

is no "Sicilian model district" that consists of companies manufacturing products in small amounts and of poor quality for poor markets that are unbranded and that the crisis has greatly worn out over and over during the processes of globalization. Indeed, existing districts tend to differ sharply with regard to other companies outside the meta-districts not only in product endorsements and market but also in industrial organization, the degree of internationalization, the role of sub-contracting in other areas and many other key variables of their history and their current competitive positioning.

The availability of human resources is fundamental to the businesses in the productive districts, given the labor-intensive technologies in almost all the sectors studied. By contrast, the availability of local infrastructure, such as soil equipped for the production plants, is not typically readily available. Indeed, in many cases, there is evidence of enterprises that are newly born outside of areas equipped with adequate infrastructure and have instead used networks of long-haul transport. The vast majority of districts are located in close proximity to major transport networks, mainly motorways.

With regard to the role of the decentralization of production, i.e., products made under subcontracts for companies in other areas, the experience of the four districts is varied. Again, the following different types of districts can be identified: those that arise due to the decentralization of production; those for whom decentralization is an important – but not the only – element in their development; and finally, those for whom decentralization is of limited or no importance. For the Etna Valley district, decentralization is essential. No one ever imagined that high technology products could be produced there before a large company between Italy and France decided not to promote its own production investment in Sicily, creating the conditions for an economy of scale and a positive pole of attraction. The same conditions occurred for mechanics, thanks to productive investments in the petrochemical sector in Syracuse and Augusta. Production also freed the suppliers to establish themselves over the

Table 6. Industrial districts in Sicily: number of employees

	Distretto	2009	2010	2011	2012	2013
Imprese/Occupati						
SudProgetti Spa	Mechanics	24	20	21	19	19
IREM Spa	Mechanics	183	183	250	224	175
Engineering Ingegneria Informatica	Mechatronic	3.597	3.812	3.928	4.065	6.077
ST Microeletronics	High Tech	8.087	8.087	8.658	8.761	9.464
METRA Ragusa Spa	Aluminium	147	131	129	111	110

traditional relations of subcontracting. In these cases, the production and sub-contracted processing are not the elements that gives birth to the district; instead, they have contributed to the birth and beyond. The decentralization of production accompanies quantitative development, but it also happens to work with local entrepreneurs. Finally, there are the cases of Mechatronics Palermo or Aluminium, for which subcontracting was irrelevant.

Now, it is possible to reconstruct the dynamics of development and resilience for the different districts based on t the scheme of interpretation. The values of turnover and employees refer to the 2009-2013 period to make an assessment over the years.

Analyzing data on revenue from the turnover of the five leading industrial districts (two for the machine building sector) (Fig. 2), we note that although there is some volatility registered over the years, at least for the IREM Spa, all enterprises do not suffer terribly or the same through the economic crisis, and some show significant resilience (in terms of turnover and employees) in their respective sectors.

These data seem to be confirmed in the general data on the Sicilian economy, which show that between 2001 and 2011, the proportion of manufacturing in the total number of employees was reduced from 11,4% to 9,2% (from 24,9% to 19,5% in Italy) while sectors in high-tech – and precisely those belonging to the productive districts – have increased their proportion of the total manufacturing sector (from 5,6% to 6,4%), to a level that is higher than the national average (Bank of Italy, Regional economies, 2014).

As for employment, the trend of values is different, with some businesses increasing the number of employees significantly, whereas other companies resized with non-linear trends.

Compared to the regional data of a decrease in employment in the manufacturing sector of more than 10% over the 2009-2013 period, the employees of the leading Sicilian districts seem to respond better to the crisis with a resilience also relevant here. This resilience, although it appears significant in leading companies that feel the economic crisis but react to it, it is thinner than in the other member companies that show data less significant.

Conclusions

The study of the Sicilian productive districts – and particularly the industrial districts – suggests that the regional district system expresses a lack of capacity to react to the shocks generated by the recent economic crisis, which remains incompletely surmounted, except for the leading companies, which for their size, degree of innovation, openness to the outside, propensity to export, industrial relations and networking system, demonstrate that they otherwise hold up to the changes better. However, for these latter companies, values in revenues and employed seem to show a significant resilience to react to economic shocks and to recover along a path of development to pre-crisis values. It is, however, a fact that can help us to imagine effective paths to help the leading companies in regional manufacturing recover and reconstruct, including within the framework of a policy to revitalize the Italian and Sicilian manufacturing sector.

Following the crisis of recent years, companies in the industrial districts also shrank (the data must be considered net of the new district of aluminum), including in terms of the number of employees. However, even these data are to be read ambivalently. It is in fact likely that it is a natural process definition and re-definition of the boundaries and districts of the network system of the meta-districts with the exclusion of subjects that had been involved more for reasons of consistency and quality in the first phase.

It should be noted, also, that as the socio-economic dynamics of the four Sicilian industrial clusters are in many ways similar to those observed in other districts of the South of Italy, this study may involve an issue that is analogous to a difficulty that involves the entire Italian manufacturing system, regardless of its forms, regions and territories.

Ultimately, with regard to the objective of the research, which is to assess whether the productive districts recognized have a resilience to economic shocks and, therefore, may actually be a means of governance for the development of the territory, it should be noted that the results are not particularly comforting. Thus, the results illuminate (except for leading companies) a model of a cohesive, relatively internationalized company that makes some attempts at innovation.

In fact, the research found that the four districts examined are not yet sufficiently 'mature'; although they are well structured in terms of number of companies and number of employees – as required by the relevant regulations. Different causes and arguments might be developed in connection with this empirical evidence, but the main cause is the absence of strong economic and organizational relationships between companies within the manufacturing district. In addition, the lack of a significant regional industrial policy in favor of the productive districts not only refers to financial resources but also to overall policy support and articulated infrastructure, business services, taxation and bureaucracy, and human resources. This is, therefore, not so much about manufacturing districts, but instead (as discussed above) meta-districts or even business networks at present can form the basis for future regional and territorial development projects. Much remains to be undertaken both on the part of individual firms and public institutions to strengthen the entrepreneurial system and their degree of innovation and competitiveness on international markets, in addition to also developing the integration and cooperation processes.

References

Becattini, G. (1990). The Marshallian industrial district as a socio-economic notion. In F. Pyke, F. G. Becattini, & W. Sengenberger (Eds.), *Industrial districts and inter-firm cooperation in Italy* (pp. 37-51). Geneva: International Institute for Labour Studies.

Bellandi, M., & De Propris, L. (1982). *A handbook of industrial districts*. Cheltenham, UK: Edward Elgar Publishing Limited.

Berardi, M., & Iannuzzi, M. (2012). Italian industrial districts: crisis or evolution? *World Review of Entrepreneurship, Management and Sustainable Development,* 8(1), 23–36.

Briguglio, L., Cordina, G., Farrugia, N., & Vella, S. (2006). *Conceptualizing and measuring economic resilience* (Working Paper). Economics Department, University of Malta. Retrieved from https://www.um.edu.mt/islands/publications_of_interest

Camuffo, A., & Grandinetti, R. (2011). Italian industrial districts as cognitive systems: Are they still reproducible? *Entrepreneurship and Regional Development,* 23 (9-10), 815-852.

Christopherson, S., Michie, J. E., & Tyler, P. (2010). Regional resilience: Theoretical and empirical perspectives. *Cambridge Journal of Regions, Economy and Society,* 3(1), 3-10.

Corò, G., & Micelli, S. (2006). *I nuovi distretti produttivi: innovazione, internazionalizzazione e competitività dei territory* [The new production districts: innovation, internationalization and competitiveness of territories]. Venezia: Marsilio.

Cretì, A., & Bettoni, G. (2001). Dai distretti ai metadistretti: una definizione [From the districts to the metadistricts: A definition]. *Liuc Paper,* 96, 1-17.

Dei Ottati, G. (1994). Cooperation and competition in the industrial district as an organization model. *European Planning Studies,* 2(4), 463-483.

Di Berardino, C., & Mauro, G. (2011). Crescita economica e impatto della crisi: il ruolo dei distretti industriali in Italia [Economic growth and impact of the crisis: the role of industrial districts in Italy]. *Economia e Società Regionale,* 112 (1), 92-114.

Foresti, G., Guelpa, F., & Trenti, S. (2009). *Effetto distretto: esiste ancora?* [District effect still exists?]. Milano: Intesa Sanpaolo, Servizio Studi e Ricerch, Collana Ricerche.

Fortis, M., & Quadrio Curzio, A. (a cura di), (2006). *Industria e distretti. Un paradigma di perdurante competitività* [Industry and districts. A paradigm of ongoing competitiveness], Bologna: Il Mulino.

Graziano, P. (2012). Rischio, vulnerabilità e resilienza territoriale [Risk, vulnerability and territorial resilience]. *Quaderni del Dipartimento di Scienze Economiche e Sociali, Serie rossa: Economia*, 87, 1-33.

Hassink, R., (2010). Regional resilience: A promising concept to explain differences in regional economic adaptability? *Cambridge Journal of Regions, Economy and Society*, 3(1), 45-58.

Marshall, A. (1972). *Principles of Economics*. London, UK: MacMillan.

National Observatory of Italian Districts. (2014). Report 2014. Roma: Unioncamere. Retrieved from http://www.osservatoriodistretti.org/rapporto-2014-osservatorio-nazionale-distretti-italiani

Observatory Industrial Clusters and SMEs, Sicily. (2014). *Assessorato delle attivita' produttive* [Department Activities' Productive]. Retrieved from http://pti.regione.sicilia.it/portal/page/portal/PIR_PORTALE/PIR_LaStrutturaRegionale/PIR_AttivitaProduttive/PIR_DipAttivitaProduttive/PIR_Distrettiproduttivi/PIR_Distrettiriconosciuti

Paniccia, I. (1998). One, a hundred, thousands of industrial districts. Organizational variety in local networks of small and medium-sized enterprises. *Organization Studies, 19*(4), 667-699.

Pendall, R., Foster, K. A., & Cowell, M., (2007). Resilience and regions: building understanding of the metaphor (Working Paper No. 12). Macarthur Foundation Research Network on Building Resilient Regions, Institute for Urban and Regional Development, University of California.

Porter, M. (1998). Clusters and the New Economics of Competition. *Harvard Business Review*, 76 (6), 77-90.

Provasi, G. (2002). *Lo sviluppo locale: una nuova frontiera per il non profit* [Local development: A new frontier for the non-profit]., Milano: Franco Angeli.

Rullani, E. (2004). *Economia della conoscenza. Creatività e valore nel capitalismo delle reti* [Knowledge economy. Creativity and value in network capitalism]. Roma: Carocci.

Rullani, E. (2009). Lo sviluppo del territorio: l'evoluzione dei distretti industriali e il nuovo ruolo delle città, Economia Italiana [The development of the territory: The evolution of industrial districts and the new role of cities], *Economia Italiana*, 2, 427-472.

Schilirò, D. (2010a). I Distretti Produttivi in Sicilia. Analisi e proposte per la Competitività, Economia e Società Regionale [The Industrial Clusters in Sicily. Analysis and proposals for the Competitiveness]. *Economia e Società Regionale*, 3, 92-113.

Schilirò, D. (2010b). *Distretti e quarto capitalismo* [Districts and fourth capitalism], Franco Angeli, Milano.

Sforzi, F. (2003). The Tuscan model and recent trends. In G. Becattini, M. Bellandi, G. Dei Ottati, & F. Sforzi (Eds.), *From Industrial Districts to Local Development* (pp. 29-61). Cheltenham: Edward Elgar.

Sforzi, F. (2009). The empirical relevance of industrial districts in Italy. In G. Becattini , M. Bellandi, L. De Propris (Eds.) *A Handbook of Industrial Districts* (pp. 327-342). Cheltenham: Edward Elgar.

Sheffi, Y. (2005). *The Resilient Enterprise: Overcoming Vulnerability for Competitive Advantage*. Cambridge, MA: Mit Press.

Signorini, F. L. (2000). *Lo sviluppo locale: un'indagine della Banca d'Italia sui distretti industriali* [Local development: a survey by the Bank of Italy on industrial districts]. Meridiana Libri, Corigliano Calabro.

Viesti, G. (2000). *Come nascono i distretti industriali* [How they are born the industrial districts]. Bari-Roma: Editori Laterza.

6

The Impact of Corporate Social Responsibility on Firms' Financial Performance in South Africa

Sukanya Chetty[1], Rebekah Naidoo[1], Yudhvir Seetharam[1]

ABSTRACT If Corporate Social Responsibility (CSR) activities are beyond a firm's legal obligations and potentially require a sacrifice in short-term profits, why do firms promote CSR? This question motivates this investigation of the impact of CSR on a firm's Corporate Financial Performance (CFP). This relationship is examined for the period from 2004 to 2013 in South Africa. We assess the short-term impact of CSR announcements on financial returns of firms included in or excluded from the Johannesburg Securities Exchange Socially Responsible Investment Index and determine whether there is a difference in the long-term CFP between these two groups for the entire period. The event study methodology shows that investors were rewarded in 2004 and 2012, when firms entered the index, and were penalized in 2013, when firms exited the index. When using regression analysis, the various industries provide mixed results between CSR and CFP for firms over the long term. Based on these results, we find that CSR activities lead to no significant differences in financial performance.

KEY WORDS: Corporate Social Responsibility, financial markets, South Africa

[1] University of the Witwatersrand - School of Economic and Business Sciences, South Africa

1 Introduction

Corporate Social Responsibility (CSR) can be defined as the treatment of all stakeholders in a responsible and ethical manner (Hopkins, 2003). CSR activities are voluntary actions that go beyond a firm's interests and legal requirements to promote a social good (McWilliams & Siegel, 2001). This gives rise to the following important questions:

> *If CSR activities are beyond a firm's legal obligations and potentially require a sacrifice in short-term profits, why do firms promote CSR? Is the sacrifice of short-term profits compensated by improvement in firms' long-term financial performance? (Choi, Kwak, & Choe, 2010, p. 292)*

While there has been a growing body of global research pertaining to the effect of CSR on Corporate Financial Performance (CFP) since the 1960s, no real consensus has been reached regarding the relationship between CSR and CFP. Wilson (2007) states that developing economies are unable to withstand the high standards of CSR used in its developed counterparts. Heese (2005) and Jamali and Mirshak (2007) support

Correspondence concerning this article should be addressed to: **Yudhvir Seetharam**, University of the Witwatersrand - School of Economic and Business Sciences, 1 Yale Road Braamfontein, Johannesburg, Gauteng 2001, South Africa
E-mail: yudhvir.seetharam@wits.ac.za

this statement, purporting that sustainability practices are not fully evolved in African economies. Due to the inability of emerging African economies to relate to the CSR standards of the rest of the world, few studies have been conducted on the sustainable practices of African firms. However, Baskin (2006) found that South Africa has not only a significant Socially Responsible Investment (SRI) Index among emerging economies but also the most developed CSR outlook in Africa and the Middle East as a result of the domestic pressures of CSR and the influence of corporate governance (Baskin, 2006).

Studies have been conducted with the aim of explaining the relationship between CSR and financial performance in both developed economies such as the United States (US) and Britain and developing economies such as Brazil, Nigeria, Taiwan, Turkey and Indonesia. However, there exists a gap in the literature pertaining to South Africa. The topic of CSR and CFP has been well documented for developed economies (Balabanis, Phillips & Lyall, 1998; Tsoutsoura, 2004) as well as emerging economies (Aras, Aybars & Kutlu, 2009; Crisóstomo, Freire & de Vasconcellos, 2011). However, little research has been conducted in an African context. This study aims to identify whether there is a relationship between CSR and CFP in a South African context. There are two main objectives of this study:

Objective One is to determine the short-term impact of CSR announcements on the financial returns of firms included in or excluded from the Johannesburg Securities Exchange (JSE) Socially Responsible Investment (SRI) Index. The hypotheses pertaining to this objective can be established according to Curran and Moran (2007), as follows:

H_0^1: *Announcements of firms included in or excluded from the JSE SRI Index will be associated with no significant share price changes for those firms*

H_1^1: *Announcements of firms included in the JSE SRI Index will be associated with significant (positive or negative) share price changes for those firms*

Objective Two is to determine whether there is a difference in the long-term financial performance of constituent firms of the JSE SRI Index for the entire period and those that are listed on the JSE All Share Index (ALSI) but are not JSE SRI Index constituents for the entire period. The hypotheses pertaining to this objective can be set up as follows:

H_0^2: *There is no significant difference in financial performance between constituents and non-constituents of the JSE SRI Index.*

H_1^2: *There is a significant difference in financial performance between constituents and non-constituents of the JSE SRI Index.*

Freeman (1984) suggests that corporate decisions involve a trade-off between shareholder value and other stakeholder benefits. Therefore, some scholars believe CSR initiatives deplete shareholder value due to the decrease in profits. Others, such as Bagnoli and Watts (2003), believe CSR initiatives increase financial performance. The mixed results found by previous researchers in international markets may be puzzling to South African researchers and investors, as no real consensus has been reached regarding CSR and financial performance.

This study on the effect of CSR announcements will help determine the short-term impact on capital market performance of firms' entrance into and exit from the JSE SRI Index – whether firms are penalized, rewarded or remain neutral to such announcements – in terms of market-based indicators. As a result, one can gain insight into the impact of CSR on shareholder value as well as investor preferences (Becchetti et al., 2012). Thereafter, the extension of the study provides a long-term view on the performance of firms on the JSE SRI Index relative to firms that are not on the JSE SRI Index but are on the overall index (JSE ALSI). This provides insight into the effects of CSR initiatives on financial performance in terms of accounting-based indicators (Heal, 2008). The results of the study will be beneficial not only to academics focusing on CSR but also to business leaders, managers and investors who are concerned with the impact of CSR on firms' financial performance.

The remainder of the study is structured as follows: Chapter 2 outlines the relevant literature on this particular topic; Chapter 3 describes the methodology, specifically the data collection and the overall research design; Chapter 4 presents a discussion of the obtained results; Chapter 5 provides concluding remarks.

2 Literature review

2.1 Theoretical background

Over the years, the growing importance of CSR for firms has arisen from the pressure various stakeholders place on these firms to engage in additional CSR investments (McWilliams & Siegel, 2000). However, managers across various firms do not share the same attitudes towards these concerns about CSR. On one spectrum, there exists managers who believe that in communicating their better social performance with stakeholders such as investors, consumers, suppliers, bankers and employees, the firm's reputation with these stakeholders may improve (Orlitzky, Schmidt & Rynes, 2003). For example, Spicer (1978) found firms' relationships to improve with bankers and investors if they had a higher level of Corporate Social Performance (CSP), thus allowing these firms to access capital and better contractual terms. Bagnolli and Watts (2003) found that firms with high CSP attracted more socially responsible consumers and experienced improved financial performance. Another reason management may address these concerns is because CSR may serve as a strategy to create and maintain a competitive advantage. By adding value to society, firms realize that they can transcend from doing good to doing better in order to survive and compete in the competitive global market (Lin, Yang & Liou, 2009).

In contrast, some managers find that such CSR activities deplete their profits in the long term and try to resist such initiatives because of this perceived trade-off. Managers who feel that satisfying shareholder interests is a priority and that the primary objective of a business is to make money may render ethical considerations unimportant; therefore, such CSR investments may hurt the financial performance of the business (Friedman, 1970). Ullman (1985) asserts that this negative relationship could result from the inefficient use of resources as firms try to meet the demands of different stakeholders such that the costs incurred from socially responsible actions place these firms at an economic disadvantage.

There is an alternative approach to determining the impact of CSR on a firm's CFP, which is by finding if there is any abnormal financial gain among firms listed on the SRI indices. There has been limited research on the capital market reaction to socially responsible and non-socially responsible activities by corporations. Extant research examines the relationship between positive and negative announcements and changes in stock prices or daily returns. Positive announcements reflect firms that are added to the index, whereas negative announcements reflect firms that have been deleted from the index (Curran & Moran, 2007). Calculating abnormal returns at an announcement date separates the effect of a change in CSR on corporate performance from the reverse causality effect of corporate performance on the CSR of the firm (Becchetti *et al.*, 2012). This is the advantage of investigating the impact of CSR on CFP in financial markets.

From the above, it can be seen that the relationship between CSR and CFP is an important issue for corporate management to consider, and as a result, Preston (1990) suggests that social issues deserve the same attention and rigorous analysis as market factors in determining long-term success.

2.2 Measures of CSR

The lack of consensus regarding CSR measurement has been a problem when attempting to determine the impact of CSR on CFP. In some cases, subjective measures such as surveys by faculty members or students (Heinze, 1976; Moskowitz, 1972) or even reputation indices whereby firms are rated and ranked on the basis of various dimensions of social performance (Balabanis *et al.*, 1998; Preston & O'Bannon, 1997) are used. In other cases, researchers such as Babalola (2012) utilize content analysis, which consists of CSR disclosures as stated in annual reports. In countries in which the above methods are not feasible, CSR indices are more commonly used as a dummy variable in terms of regression analysis, whereby a value of 1 is used when firms are included in the Index and a value of 0 is used when they are not (Crisóstomo *et al.*, 2011; McWilliams & Siegel, 2000; Tsoutsoura, 2004).

Each of the above measures is subject to limitations. Surveys may be subject to bias, as they are based on the researchers' own subjective views. The credibility of the ratings is highly subjective and depends not only on the accuracy of information available to assessors but also on their expertise (Balabanis *et al.*, 1998). Content analysis may be subjective according to the researchers' choice of variables to measure, and firms may not implement their reported actions.

2.3 Measures of financial performance

Similar to CSR measurements, there is a lack of consensus concerning the optimal financial performance measurement instrument to employ. Many researchers utilize accounting measures such as Return on

Equity (ROE), Return on Assets (ROA), Return on Sales (ROS), Return on Capital Employed (ROCE) and Earnings per Share (EPS) (Cochran & Wood, 1984; Waddock & Graves, 1997). Other researchers such as Vance (1975) use market-based measures of financial performance, such as investor returns; others, such as Balabanis *et al.* (1998) and Choi *et al.* (2010), employ a combination of both accounting- and market-based measures. Both accounting- and market-based measures represent different perspectives on financial performance and have different implications.

Accounting-based measures are said to only capture the historical aspects of a firm's financial performance (McGuire, Schneeweis & Hill, 1986). These measures are subject to bias, as they are affected by managerial manipulation as well as by different accounting procedures (Aras et al., 2009). *Market-based measures* focus on a firm's future performance as opposed to past performance; thus, they are less susceptible to managerial manipulation and different accounting procedures (Aras *et al.*, 2009). To account for these shortfalls, this study utilizes both accounting- and market-based measures.

2.4 The JSE SRI Index

The JSE SRI Index serves as an important mechanism for investors to identify good, socially responsible corporations, as well as a benchmark for firms seeking to improve their CSR. The Index was first launched in May 2004 in response to the growing global demand for SRI and was the first CSR Index to be established and owned by an exchange in an emerging economy (Heese, 2005). The main focus of this index is to promote sustainable business practices. Before the inception of the index, South African firms were already actively involved in CSR activity; the origins of SRI in South Africa can be traced back to the early 1990s, when trade unions refused to invest members' contributions in firms that supported the apartheid regime (De Cleene & Sonnenberg, 2004). A more balanced and broader approach was needed to encompass the triple bottom line, which comprises Economic, Social and Governance (ESG) considerations (JSE [Johannesburg Stock Exchange], 2010), resulting in the formation of the JSE SRI Index.

In order for a firm to be considered for the JSE SRI Index, the JSE SRI Index Advisory Committee annually assesses firms based on an array of criteria. The criteria requires firms to be constituents of the FTSE/JSE All Share Index, and they also need to comply with the ESG standards through a number of different indicators that measure corporate policy, practice and reporting (JSE, 2010).

The criteria of the JSE SRI Index is constantly evolving, ensuring that South African sustainability practices are aligned to those of the developed world; this process goes against Wilson (2007), Heese (2005), and Jamali and Mirshak (2007), who state that sustainability practices are not fully evolved in emerging economies, as they are unable to withstand the CSR standards used in developed economies.

2.5 Empirical findings of previous studies

Evidence from a variety of empirical studies concludes that developed and developing economies demonstrate mixed results on the relationship between CSR and CFP.

Curran and Moran (2007) examined the capital market reaction to corporate entry and exit in the UK FTSE4Good Index for the period from 1999 to 2002. The results indicate that the market reacted positively when a firm was added and negatively when firms were excluded from the Index, though these findings were insignificant. Gladysek and Chipeta (2012) considered only the impact on the share returns of firms listing on the South African JSE SRI Index; they also found insignificant abnormal returns for the 2004 to 2009 period. The insignificant findings from both studies suggest that firms do not benefit from a raised share price if they are included in CSR indices. Becchetti *et al.* (2012) conduct their study in a US context and examined the Domini 400 Social Index. They found a significant negative effect on abnormal returns after exit announcements from the Domini 400 Social Index during the 1990 to 2004 sample period. This relationship was present when financial distress shocks and stock market seasonality were controlled for. The results mentioned above are just some of the mixed results attained in this area. A possible reason for the share price not being a clear indicator of the relationship between CSR activities and CFP is because not all SRI indices disclose why firms are added or deleted from their Index (Curran & Moran, 2007). Had there been disclosure, it would have served as a better proxy for CSR.

One must consider the sample size and different measurement approaches and methods when drawing conclusions from the results. Existing techniques involved samples that were too small, in which fewer than 30 firms were considered (Folger & Nutt, 1975), and time periods that were too short (Alexander & Buchholz, 1978). They also relied on content analysis (Abbott & Monsen, 1979) and reputation indices (Folger & Nutt, 1975), which, as mentioned earlier, involves some drawbacks. Lastly, the small sample of CSR firms was compared to control groups of a similar size. These studies failed to find a direct link between CSR and CFP.

Cochran and Wood (1984) improved these existing techniques by increasing the sample size and by using two time periods, large industry-specific control groups, and a key correlate with CSR – asset age – in their model. The average age of corporate assets was found to be highly correlated with a firm's social responsibility ranking. Firms with older assets tend to have lower CSR rankings. Cochran and Wood (1984) reasoned that 'older' firms may be less flexible in adapting to social change, the types of management that older firms attract may be different to those of 'younger' firms, and regulatory constraints may have been less severe in the time period when firms with older assets constructed plants. Overall weak support for a positive relationship between CFP and CSR was found. The exclusion of asset age could explain why no positive relationship was found in earlier studies.

Waddock and Graves (1997) found CSP to be positively related to prior CFP and believed that this finding can be supported by the 'Slack Resource Theory.' This theory asserts that the availability of financial and other (slack) resources to firms as a result of their better financial performance may result in these firms investing in areas related to social domains, such as employee and community relations and the environment (Jensen, 1986). They also found CSP to be positively related to future CFP, providing 'Good Management Theory' as an explanation. This theory asserts that the strong relationship between CSP and good management practice is a result of management paying more attention to CSP domains, which improves relationships with stakeholders and, thus, financial performance (Freeman, 1984).

McWilliams and Siegel (2000) argued that the study by Waddock and Graves (1997) is misspecified, as they failed to control for Research and Development (R&D) intensity. R&D was found to be significantly positively related to financial performance. McWilliams and Siegel (2000) stated that R&D investments lead to knowledge enhancement, resulting in product and process innovation, which enhances a firm's productivity. The inclusion of R&D resulted in a neutral relationship between CSR and financial performance (McWilliams & Siegel, 2000). Aras *et al.* (2009) conducted a study in developing economies and found the same results as McWilliams and Siegel (2000) after controlling for R&D intensity.

Based on the above literature review, it can be seen that there is no real consensus as to the nature of the relationship between CSR and CFP. This could be a result of the incorrect specification of CSR and CFP, as well as the failure to account for key variables that facilitate this relationship. This study will attempt to account for the key variables affecting CSR and CFP.

3 Methodology

3.1 Sampling and data collection

Firms that appear to be most sensitive to social responsibility issues are the firms that are JSE SRI Index compliant. To compare the financial performance of these firms to less socially responsible firms, firms that are not JSE SRI Index compliant but listed on the JSE ALSI will be selected to represent less socially responsible firms; this does not imply that these firms do not engage in CSR. Data for the JSE SRI Index is only available from 2004, which was the year in which the index was launched; hence, the period of the study will run from 2004 to 2013 inclusive, a total of 10 years.

CFP will be measured using accounting- and market-based indicators. The relevant accounting data for each firm considered will be obtained from the McGregorBFA database and computed as an annual value for each year considered. Market-based financial performance will be measured by stock returns. JSE daily closing share prices will be obtained from the McGregorBFA database.

The number of firms examined for the short-term entry announcement event study will range from 40 to 82 for the years from 2004 to 2013. Firms that delisted or had no publicly available information for the period will be excluded. The number of firms examined for the short-term exit announcement event study will range from 1 to 9 for the years 2005 to 2009 and 2011 to 2013. The years 2004 and 2010 will be excluded, as there were no exclusions from the index.

The long-term study focuses on the Financials, Industrials, Consumer Services and Basic Materials industries. The Consumer Goods, Healthcare, Telecommunications and Technology industries will not be represented, as these industries comprise too few firms. The total sample of firms that will be considered is 42.

3.2 Description of overall research design

Regarding objective one, to assess the effect that CSR has on CFP in the short-term, short-term performance will be determined in financial markets by the stock return performance over time, where the event will be the annual announcement of JSE SRI Index constituents. The sample period will be October 2004 to December 2013. A few assumptions must be made before employing the event study methodology (Gladysek & Chipeta, 2012):

- Market agents do not anticipate the announcement.
- No confounding effects during the event window are analyzed.

Daily abnormal share returns will be a proxy for short-term CFP, and the SRI Index will proxy for CSR. The event window will consist of 20 days prior to the announcement date (time T_0) and 20 days following the announcement date. Therefore, the event window will consist of 41 days. This event window is sufficient enough to capture any leakage of information prior to T_0 (Becchetti *et al.*, 2012). It also gives investors enough time to react to the news, as some investors may be latecomers to the announcement (Gladysek & Chipeta, 2012). Logarithmic share returns will be calculated, with expected returns proxied by the JSE SRI Index return. Returns will be computed from 20 trading days prior to the announcement date to 20 trading days after the announcement date (-20, +20). Abnormal returns will then be defined as the difference between the share return and index return. Should the announcement of the SRI constituents have an effect on the market, abnormal returns will change to reflect this new information.

The JSE announces the new constituents of the SRI Index on 26th November each year; hence, the announcement date will be the 26th of November for the years considered in this study. Share returns can be noisy, and thus, abnormal returns will be averaged:

$$AAR_t = \sum \frac{AR_{it}}{N} \quad (1)$$

where AR_{it} is the abnormal return of share i at time t and N is the number of firms in the sample for the given year. The significance of the abnormal returns will be tested with Student's t test.

Objective two investigates the effect of CSR on CFP in the long term. An Ordinary Least Squares (OLS) regression model will be employed to explain the relationship between CSR and CFP:

$$CFP_{it} = \beta_0 + \beta_1 CSP_{it} + \beta_2 Firm\_Size_{it} + \beta_3 Risk_{it} \quad (4)$$

Where

$i = 1 \ldots N$ (*number of firms*)

$CFP = ROA, ROE, EPS$

$CSP = 0 \, or \, 1$

$\text{Firm\_Size} = \ln(Market\,Capitalization)$

$$Risk = \frac{Long-Term\,Debt}{Total\,Assets}$$

For the purposes of this study, CSP will be a proxy for CSR of a particular firm, which is the independent variable. CSP is defined as a dummy variable (0, 1), as no quantifiable measure of the SRI Index exists, nor is information on the ranking of the constituents publically available in South Africa. CSP is *1* if a firm is included in the JSE SRI Index for a given year and *0* if it is not included but listed on the JSE ALSI (McWilliams & Siegel, 2000).

CFP_{it} represents the corporate financial performance of firm *i* in the long term, which is the dependent variable that will be captured by the following effective accounting metrics: Return on Assets (ROA), Return on Equity (ROE) and Earnings per share (EPS). These profitability ratios have been used in numerous empirical studies of this nature to capture corporate financial performance.

Comparisons across firms will be more accurate when using these accounting ratios, as financial leverage and the influences of risk on CFP will be included in the model (Cochran & Wood, 1984). Each financial performance measure will be separately regressed on the independent and additional explanatory variables, such as firm size and risk. These firm- and industry-specific differences must be included, as they have been shown to be related to CFP and CSR in prior empirical research (Ullman 1985).

Burke *et al.* (1986) explains that larger firms attract more attention from external constituents and need to respond more openly to stakeholder demands, which is why they disclose their CSR behavior more often than smaller firms. Perrini *et al.* (2007) provide evidence that larger firms have a tendency to participate more in environmental management practices than small to medium-sized firms, as large firms are more likely to identify relevant stakeholders and meet their specific requirements through various CSR strategies. To control for size, the natural logarithm of market capitalization will be used (Aras *et al.*, 2009).

In order to account for the influence of risk, the ratio of long-term debt to total assets will be used. Previous empirical works have found a significant negative relationship between firm performance and the level of debt. Waddock and Graves (1997) reason that risk must be explained, as management's risk tolerance influences its attitude toward activities that have the potential to elicit savings, incur future and present costs, and build or destroy markets.

R&D intensity must be included to avoid a misspecified model, as it captures the effect of innovative activity on a firm's performance, considering that the various dimensions of CSR can create process and product innovation (McWilliams & Siegel, 2000). Waddock and Graves (1994) find that the differences in R&D intensity across industries have an impact on the performance of these industries. Separating the firms into industries as mentioned above will take these differences in R&D intensity into account. It will also account for differences due to industry-level factors, such as economies of scale and competitive intensity, which must be explained (McWilliams & Siegel, 2000). Industries will be determined in accordance with the Industry Classification Benchmark (ICB), which is the global standard for industry sector analysis that the JSE uses. This study will divide firms into different industries and thereafter run regressions for the firms within each industry. The model will be estimated using E-views.

4 Discussion of results

4.1 Objective one

4.1.1 Entry announcements of the JSE SRI Index

Table 1 displays the descriptive statistics. The standard deviations are relatively low and similar for all years except 2008 and 2013, which exhibit the highest standard deviations. The year 2009, however, exhibited the lowest standard deviation. The years 2008, 2009 and 2013 will be probed further to find possible explanations for these findings.

The announcement date for the SRI Index constituents was the 26th of November 2008, 2009 and 2013. The increased risk in 2008 can be explained by the well-documented global financial crisis of 2008, which peaked around the announcement date that year (Naudè, 2009). Regarding the increased risk for 2013, the leading indicators around November in 2013 deteriorated. The global economic environment continued to improve around this time, suggesting that the sluggishness of the South African economy was caused mainly by domestic circumstances. The minimal risk experienced in 2009 could be justified by the expansion of the mining sector. At the time, sales for the mining sector were flourishing, and the country's diamond-mining industry became the fourth largest in the world. The SRI Index is dominated by this industry, and at this time, there was no labor unrest. Another possible explanation is that the overall construction sector had grown by 7.8% due to infrastructure expenditures for the 2010 Soccer World Cup. This industry is fairly represented in the SRI Index. The extreme minimum and maximum values of 2008 and 2013 are (-0.0392, 0.0305) and (-0.0090, 0.0136), respectively. These values characterize the increased volatility of returns during these periods, when the business cycle was in its trough phase (Gladysek & Chipeta, 2012).

For years 2007 through 2009, mean returns were negative, reflecting the recessionary period. The skewness measures were slightly negative for all years except 2006 and 2009, which showed slight positive skewness. This indicates that our returns are slightly skewed, as opposed to being symmetric in the case of normal distribution. The return distribution appears to be slightly leptokurtic for 2007 and 2010. The other

Table 1. Descriptive Statistics

Descriptive Statistics										
	2004	**2005**	**2006**	**2007**	**2008**	**2009**	**2010**	**2011**	**2012**	**2013**
Mean	0.0010	-0.0001	0.0011	-0.0004	-0.0019	-0.0002	0.0010	0.0003	0.0024	0.0005
Median	0.0009	0.0003	0.0003	0.0002	0.0006	-0.0003	0.0023	0.0011	0.0032	0.0046
Maximum	0.0071	0.0083	0.0118	0.0129	0.0306	0.0060	0.0134	0.0111	0.0137	0.0519
Minimum	-0.0053	-0.0111	-0.0077	-0.0164	-0.0392	-0.0064	-0.0193	-0.0175	-0.0091	-0.0475
Std. Dev.	0.0029	0.0044	0.0049	0.0065	0.0185	0.0028	0.0071	0.0072	0.0061	0.0266
Skewness	-0.1240	-0.1351	0.1908	-0.4863	-0.3728	0.1162	-0.7230	-0.6098	-0.2716	-0.0107
Kurtosis	2.3991	2.6948	2.3590	3.0263	2.2808	2.4977	3.4074	2.8991	2.1353	2.1567
Jarque-Bera	0.7219	0.2838	0.9505	1.6169	1.8333	0.5233	3.8556	2.5585	1.7813	1.2156
Probability	0.6970	0.8677	0.6217	0.4456	0.3999	0.7698	0.1455	0.2783	0.4104	0.5445

years have slightly platykurtic distributions. On this basis, it is evident that returns appear to display some minor non-normality. However, by formally testing the normality assumption of the return distribution with the null hypothesis and jointly testing for skewness and kurtosis (H_0: S=0 and K=3) at the 95% confidence level, the Jarque-Bera probability values are greater than 0.05 for all years, indicating that the null hypothesis, which states that the series is normally distributed, fails to be rejected.

The figures below illustrate the Average Abnormal Rates (AARs) for the entrants to the SRI Index for the years 2004 through 2013. As shown in Figure 1, years 2004 and 2005 had declining AARs just before the announcement date and increase just after the announcement date. Moving to years 2006 and 2007, the AARS showed a sharp increase two days before the announcement date. There was a decrease for a few days after the announcement, before an increase in AARs occurred again. In 2008, there was a sharp decline with an increase just before the announcement date. After the announcement date, there was a slight continuation of the incline before the AARs dropped.

A stationary time series is a series whose properties remain constant over time. Many financial series, such as share prices, appear to be non-stationary, and new statistical issues arise when analyzing non-stationary data. The unit root tests (Augmented Dickey-Fuller (ADF) Phillips-Perron (PP)) and stationarity test (Kwiatkowski-Phillips-Schmidt-Shin (KPSS)) provide sufficient evidence to conclude that the AARs are stationary for firms included in the Index. The results are available upon request.

Figure 2 displays the AARs for 2009 to 2013. Abnormal returns for the years 2009 to 2012 hovered around zero, with 2013 displaying great volatility and the highest positive and negative abnormal returns. The volatility in 2013 could be attributed to economic uncertainty in the country. A possible explanation for this may be South Africa's poor growth in 2013, which was largely due to increased strike activity and its impact on the economy. Before the announcement date, the years 2009 to 2012 displayed decreased AARs, with 2013 displaying a sharp decline and a slight increase. After the announcement date, the same trend was observed, with the years 2009, 2010 and 2012 decreasing and 2013 increasing; however, 2011 showed a slight decline followed by an increase.

The year 2004 experienced minimal declines in AARs. Gladysek & Chipeta (2012) propose the short-lived shareholder interest in the index as an explanation. The years 2008 and 2013 experienced the most significant increases and decreases. Significant results represent daily

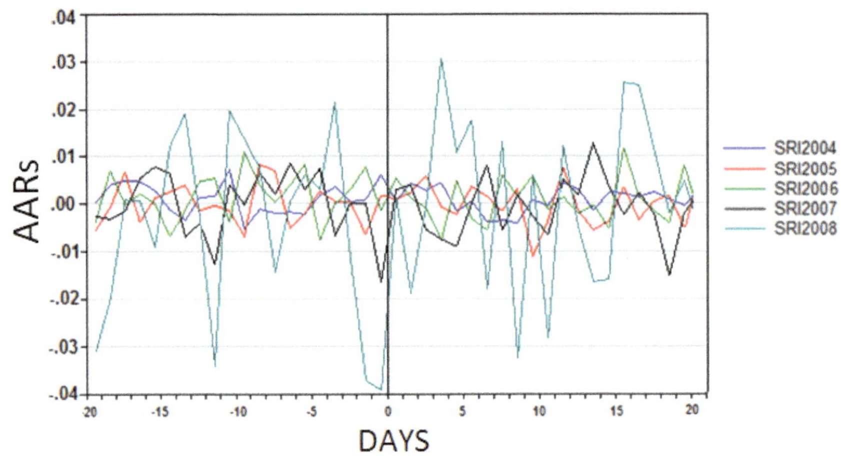

Figure 1. Average Abnormal Returns for the JSE SRI Index for 2004 to 2008

Note: Average abnormal returns observed from 20 days prior the announcement date to 20 days post-announcement date (41-day event window). ARRs are not representative of percentages.

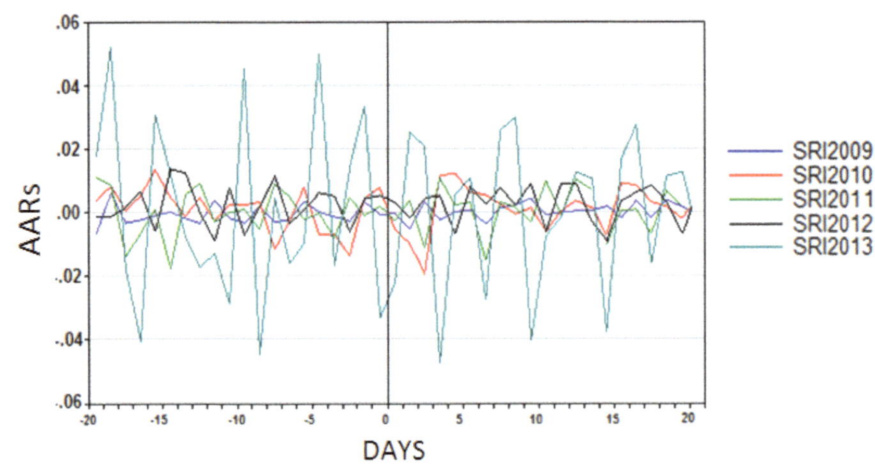

Figure 2. Average Abnormal Returns for the JSE SRI Index for 2009 to 2013

Table 2. Parametric Tests

	Students t Test	
	Statistic	P-value
2004	2.0957	0.0425**
2005	-0.1249	0.9012
2006	1.4279	0.1611
2007	-0.3731	0.7110
2008	-0.6575	0.5146
2009	-0.3944	0.6954
2010	0.9171	0.3646
2011	0.2774	0.7829
2012	2.5451	0.0149**
2013	0.1225	0.9031

Note: *, **, *** indicates significance at 0.01, 0.05 and 0.10, respectively.

AARs, which were greater than 2.5% and less than -2.5% (MacKinlay, 1997). The annual announcement of JSE SRI constituents will be perceived as good news should the daily AARs exceed 2.5%. When AARs are less than -2.5%, the announcement will be perceived as bad news. Therefore, from the figures above, it can be seen that 2008 and 2013 carried both good and bad news.

For the rest of the years studied (2004 to 2007 and 2009 to 2012), the AARs fell within the (-2.5%, +2.5%) limits. This suggests that the market perceives JSE SRI constituent announcements as no news, confirming the findings of Gladysek and Chipeta's (2012) study covering the years 2004 through 2008. The finding of a market reaction in 2008 could be substantiated by the growth of the SRI Index; thus, trading volume had increased. Failure to find a market reaction prior to 2008 and between 2009 and 2012 could reflect that potential investors were still unaware of the index or were falsely advised that an SRI Index will generate a return below that of a general index (Gladysek & Chipeta, 2012). As the years progressed, it is possible that the SRI Index became more widely known, allowing for significant share price movements to be realized around the announcement date. Thus, the results for 2008 and 2013 provide evidence that socially responsible investing is slowly affecting the South African market over time.

Parametric one-sample t tests were run in order to determine the significance of the AARs for the 2004 to 2013 period. Table 2 shows the results for firms included in the index. The AARs for all years except 2004 and 2012 had insignificant p-values. Therefore, based on these results, the null hypothesis that firms that announced their inclusion in the JSE SRI Index are associated with no significant share price changes fails to be rejected at the 95% confidence interval for all years except 2004 and 2012. These two years are significant at the 95% confidence interval and are associated with positive mean values, indicating that the null hypothesis is rejected and that firms that announced their inclusion in the JSE SRI Index are associated with significant positive share price changes. The direction of the AARs was positive for six of the ten years (2004, 2006, 2010, 2011, 2012 and 2013) and insignificant for the other four years; this result may nevertheless suggest that the announcements of firms included in the JSE SRI Index may be associated with positive share price changes for those firms.

4.1.2 Exit announcements of the JSE SRI Index

As shown in Table 3, the years 2008 and 2012 were associated with the highest risk. This result may be due to the poor state of the South African economy at the

Table 3. Descriptive Statistics

Descriptive Statistics								
	2005	**2006**	**2007**	**2008**	**2009**	**2011**	**2012**	**2013**
Mean	0.0004	-0.0006	-0.001913	-0.0003	0.0003	0.0005	-0.0013	-0.0016
Median	-0.0003	-0.0014	0.000283	0.0020	0.0037	-0.0003	-0.0033	-0.0008
Maximum	0.0167	0.0180	0.04793	0.0652	0.0282	0.0281	0.1185	0.0098
Minimum	-0.0158	-0.0205	-0.047373	-0.0732	-0.0291	-0.0248	-0.1430	-0.0152
Std. Dev.	0.0088	0.0104	0.018019	0.0285	0.0127	0.0124	0.0465	0.0059
Skewness	0.0828	0.0264	-0.130365	-0.3260	-0.4492	0.0801	-0.2486	-0.3681
Kurtosis	2.2972	2.3351	3.468121	3.4409	3.0195	2.2789	4.6365	3.3648
Jarque-Bera	0.8906	0.7600	0.490492	1.0582	1.3797	0.9322	4.9972	1.1533
Probability	0.6406	0.6839	0.782512	0.5891	0.5017	0.6274	0.0822	0.5618

time brought about by the global financial crisis of 2008 and the Eurozone debt crisis of 2011, which did not abate by 2012. However, in sharp contrast to our findings for entry announcements, the year 2013 was associated with the lowest risk. For the other years, the standard deviations are relatively similar. The Jarque-Bera probabilities reflect normal distributions for all years except 2012 at the 90% confidence interval. The skewness is minimal, and the kurtosis values are not very far off from 3 for a normal distribution for all years, with the exception of 2012.

As seen in Figure 3, 2005 was associated with an increase in AARs before the announcement date. After the announcement date, the AARs continued to increase before decreasing. The year 2006 exhibited some volatility in AARs. There was an increase before the announcement date, but after the announcement date, there was a sharp decline. The AARs for the years 2007 and 2008 displayed high volatility. For the year 2007, the AARS increased before the announcement date, in contrast to 2008, when there was a decline. However, after the announcement date, the AARs began declining for 2007 but began to increase for 2008.

Figure 4 displays the AARs for 2009, 2011, 2012 and 2013. The AARs for the years 2009, 2011 and 2013 are concentrated around zero, with 2012 displaying large variations. An explanation for these variations could be the vast amount of labor unrest that plagued South Africa in 2012. These unrests originated from the platinum mining sector and spread to other sectors of the economy. An important note to consider is that only one firm exited the Index in 2012, Hulamin (an aluminum-mining firm), which could further explain the variations.

Applying MacKinlay's (1997) definition of significant AARs, the years 2007, 2008 and 2012 experienced the most significant declines and inclines. From Figures 3 and 4, it can be seen that these years carried bad news, displaying decreases greater than 2.5%, and good news, displaying increases greater than 2.5%. The years 2005, 2006, 2009, 2011 and 2013 were perceived as having no news, as they fell within the limits of -2.5% and 2.5%. As explained above, a possible explanation for why the earlier years had no news could be the thin trading volume of the index caused by investors being unaware of the index or under the impression that the JSE SRI Index generates lower returns than general indices, such as the ALSI.

For firms that were excluded from the index, Table 4 shows that the AARs for seven out of eight years have insignificant p-values, implying that these AARs are equal to zero. The year 2013 is significant at the 90%

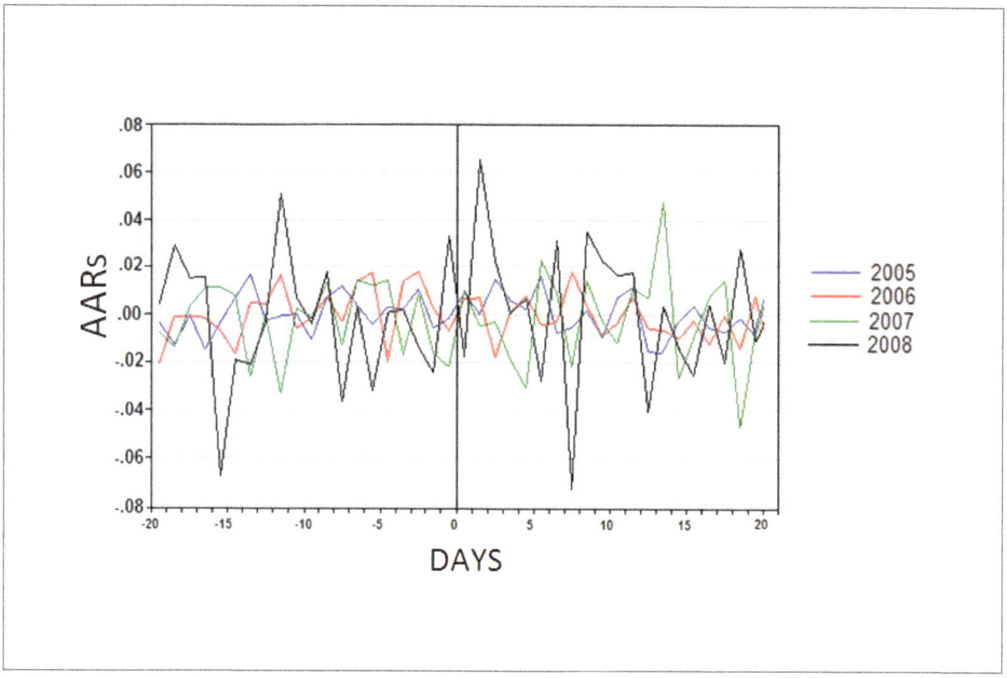

Figure 3. Average Abnormal Returns for the JSE SRI Index for 2005 to 2008

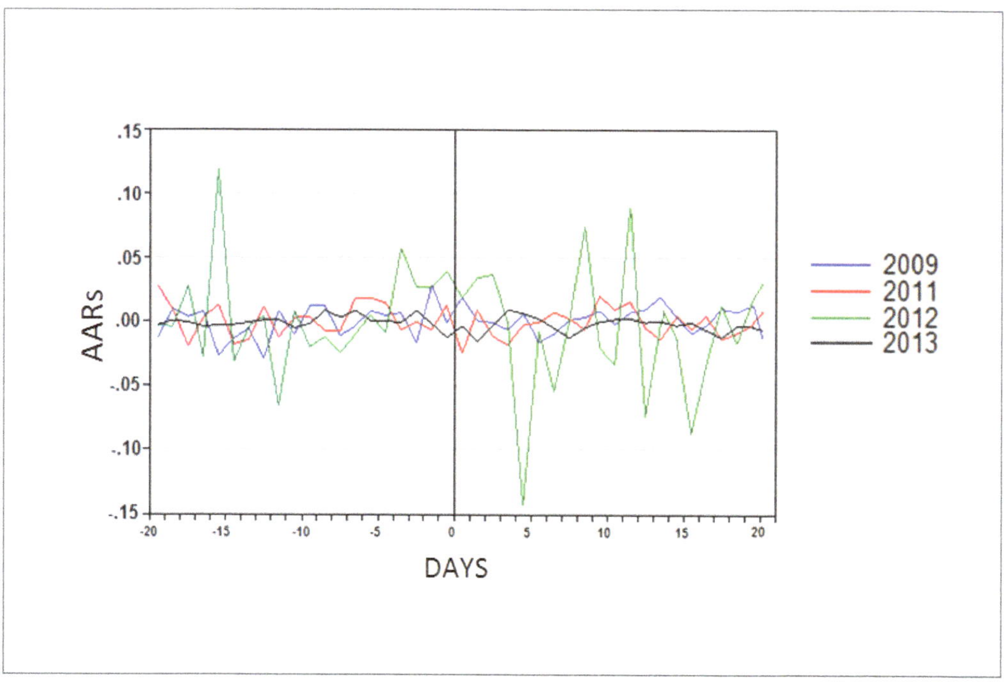

Figure 4. Average Abnormal Returns for the JSE SRI Index for 2009 to 2013

Table 4. Parametric Tests

	Students t Test	
	Statistic	**P-value**
2005	0.2758	0.7841
2006	-0.3657	0.7165
2007	-0.6799	0.5005
2008	-0.0769	0.9391
2009	0.1750	0.8620
2011	0.2369	0.8139
2012	-0.1737	0.8630
2013	-1.7079	0.0954***

Note: *, **, *** indicates significance at 0.01, 0.05 and 0.10, respectively.

confidence interval, suggesting that investors perceive the exclusion of firms from the index as negative information. The direction of the AARs for five of the eight years was negative (2006, 2007, 2008, 2012 and 2013), and although four years showed insignificant AARs, this result nevertheless suggests that the announcements of firms excluded from the JSE SRI Index may be associated with negative share price changes for those firms.

4.2 Objective two

Three financial ratios were used to analyze the financial performance of firms in relation to their social responsibility measures.

The purpose of the regression analysis is to test whether CSR is significantly associated with superior or inferior financial performance within industry groups. The finding of a significant positive relationship may suggest that CSR activities by firms should be increased to produce better implications for firm performance. A leading CSR firm that derives the following benefits highlights why these activities may be characterized by higher financial performance: relationships with stakeholders improve, management of brand and reputation may be more effective, attraction and retention of high-caliber employees may be promoted, and the organization may receive recognition for displaying a high degree of ethical standards (Freeman, 1984; Orlitzky *et al.*, 2003; Waddock & Graves, 1997).

A negative relationship may be explained by the additional costs of undertaking CSR activities that do not enhance or contribute to shareholder value. As a firm becomes more socially responsible, the more difficult it becomes for the firm to increase its economic profits, as it cannot readily engage in projects without assessing their implications for ESG frontiers.

Two possible reasons for why there may be weak support (a neutral effect) for a link between CSP and CFP include the reliability of accounting figures, as some firms manipulate financial statements, and the notion that non-constituents cannot systematically experience weaker performance, as Lee, Faff and Smith (2009) highlight that these firms stand a chance of being liquidated or acquired by market leaders or adjusting their CSR practices in order to maximize their economic profit. Lee *et al.*, (2009) propose an interesting view on why no relationship may exist between CSR and CFP, emphasizing that the financial benefits available to leading CSR firms (in the context of this study, this would refer to JSE SRI constituents) may not be available to lagging CSR firms (non-constituents). However, these lagging CSR firms may have an advantage over leading CSR firms, as they are not constrained by their CSR practices and can thus accept profitable projects that leading CSR firms cannot. These two opposing effects may cancel each other out.

Table 5. Correlation Matrix for the Dependent and Explanatory Variables

Variable	EPS	RISK	ROA	ROE	SIZE	CSR
EPS	1.0000					
RISK	-0.4280	1.0000				
ROA	-0.5289	0.4410	1.0000			
ROE	-0.2863	0.1673	0.1743	1.0000		
SIZE	0.5478	-0.3979	-0.7169	-0.3260	1.0000	
CSR	0.6629	-0.3170	-0.8392	-0.4074	0.9024	1.0000

Table 6. Regressions for CSR and CFP

Variable	Regression 1	Regression 2	Regression 3
	EPS	ROE	ROA
Constant	3608.5610	-6.2569	-35.1603
	(3919.2140)	(76.7390)	(46.5252)
Risk	-791.0636	2.9960	2.0142
	(632.3384)	(12.3813)	(2.0752)
Size	-150.2255	1.3368	10.6044
	(174.8156)	(3.4229)	(7.5065)
CSR	973.5138***	-9.3044	-18.1664**
	(506.6335)	(9.9200)	(6.0143)
F-Statistic	3.7154	0.7322	10.6061
N	14	14	14

Note: *, **, *** indicates significance at 0.01, 0.05 and 0.10, respectively.

4.2.1 Financial Industry

The correlation matrix in Table 5 shows that CSR and ROA are negatively correlated. This finding should not be interpreted as evidence of a causal relationship between CSR and CFP. This result merely indicates that a relationship exists between these two variables of interest in this study. Size and CSR is positively correlated. This relationship is not surprising, as there is a widely held view that corporate responsibility will increase as firm size increases.

From Table 6, Regression 1 indicates that the CSR coefficient is positively related to financial performance and significant at the 90% confidence level. The overall model is significant at the 95% confidence level. This provides evidence that there is a significant difference in financial performance between constituents and non-constituents of the JSE SRI Index. Thus, the null hypothesis is rejected. For every one-unit increase in CSP, ceteris paribus, EPS increases by 973.5138, which suggests that constituents will, on average, ex-

Table 7. Regressions for CSR and CFP

		Regression 1	Regression 2	Regression 3
Industry	**Variable**	**EPS**	**ROE**	**ROA**
Basic Materials	**CSR**	-923.2763	-7.9659	-4.8856
		(1349.7350)	(43.4975)	(27.5579)
Consumer Services	**CSR**	-244.3887	23.8777***	3.6215
		(184.0593)	(10.1479)	(9.5511)
Industrials	**CSR**	79.0387	3.3564	1.6271
		(364.9793)	(12.5981)	(7.3786)

Note: *, **, *** indicates significance at 0.01, 0.05 and 0.10, respectively.

perience better financial performance than non-constituents. This result confirms Chand's (2006) paper, in which a positive association was found when controlling for industry.

Regression 2 suggests that CSP is negatively related to financial performance; however, this result is not significant nor is the model itself. This finding provides empirical evidence in favor of the hypothesis of no significant difference in financial performance between constituents and non-constituents of the JSE SRI Index. The can be interpreted to mean that CSP has a neutral effect on CFP. Similar results were achieved by McWilliams and Siegel (2001), who found this relationship to hold when R&D was accounted for, and Lee *et al.* (2009), who concluded that the ROA and ROE performance measure showed no significant difference between leading CSP and lagging CSP firms.

Regression 3 supports the finding of Ulllman's (1985) study that CSR hurts financial performance. CSR is significantly related to CFP at the 95% confidence level. The model is significant as well. Based on this evidence, the null hypothesis that there is no significant difference in financial performance between constituents and non-constituents of the JSE SRI Index is rejected. For every one-unit increase in CSP, ceteris paribus, ROA will decrease by 18.16635. The findings indicate that on average, constituents of the JSE SRI Index will underperform non-constituents financially by 18.16635.

4.2.2 Basic Materials, Consumer Services and Industrials Industries

The results for the Industrials industry show that size is highly positively correlated to EPS and CSR. Both the Basic Materials and Industrials industries provide empirical evidence supporting the null hypothesis; thus, CSP has a neutral effect on CFP. Although both industries display insignificant results, the CSP coefficients are all positive for the Industrials industry and negative for the Basic Materials industry.

When analyzing the Consumer Services industry, a negative correlation between CSP and EPS is observed. A positive significant relationship is found between CSP and ROE at the 90% confidence interval. CSP is found to have an insignificant relationship with EPS and ROA, emphasizing that JSE SRI Index constituents do not manage their assets more effectively than non-constituents.

5 Conclusion

The results of this study add to the body of literature on CSR and CFP. Very few studies have considered both entry and exit announcements using the JSE SRI Index. This study employs an event study methodology for the short-term and regression analysis for the long-term. The analysis in this study examines short-term shareholder wealth returns around announcement dates and makes a long-term comparison of the operating performance of JSE SRI constituents to that of non-constituents of the index.

The analyses in both parts to the study provide mixed evidence of the relationship between CSR and CFP. The event study methodology shows that investors are not rewarded when firms enter the index, as there are no significant share price movements realized for these firms, confirming the null hypothesis with the exception for the years 2004 and 2012. The findings for 2004 may be attributed to the short-lived enthusiasm for the launch of the index and the finding of significant share price movements in 2012 may be attributed to investors becoming more aware of the index. Investors earned significant positive abnormal returns by investing in the JSE SRI Index around the announcement date in 2004 and 2012. The study of firms exiting the Index indicates that investors were penalized in 2013, as firms experienced significant negative share price changes in this period, thus rejecting the null hypothesis in favor of the alternative hypothesis. Overall, it can de deduced that as the years progressed, the announcement event was considered as good and bad news entering the market.

The analysis over the long term also provides mixed results for CSR and CFP within the different industries. Within a particular industry, it is possible to find significant positive, negative and neutral differences in CFP between constituents and non-constituents of the JSE SRI Index; thus, the relationship between CSP and CFP may be sensitive to the type of CFP measure used. Therefore, it is uncertain whether JSE SRI Index compliance leads to significant differences in financial performance.

Future research could improve the long-term analysis by increasing the sample size of firms under consideration by looking at year-to-year changes as opposed to analyzing firms listed on the indices for the entire ten-year period. Another avenue to consider would be to include asset age in the regression analysis due to its importance, as previously mentioned. If the JSE were more explicit about the relative ranking of the firms on the JSE SRI Index, investors would be provided with a better understanding of CSR and why firms are included in and excluded from the index. This information would allow potential investors to include these considerations in their own investment portfolios.

References

Abbott, W. F., & Monsen, R. J. (1979). On the Measurement of Corporate Social Responsibility: Self-Reported Disclosures as a Method of Measuring Corporate Social Involvement. *Academy of Management Journal*, 22 (3), 501-515.

Alexander, G. J., & Buchholz, R. A. (1978). Corporate Social Responsibility and Stock Market Performance. *Academy of Management Journal*, 21 (3), 479-486.

Aras, G., Aybars, A., & Kutlu, O. (2009). Managing Corporate Performance: Investigating the Relationship between Corporate Social Responsibility and Financial Performance in Emerging Markets. *International Journal of Productivity and Performance Management*, 59 (3), 229-254.

Babalola, Y. A. (2012). The Impact of Corporate Social Responsibility on Firms' Profitability in Nigeria. *European Journal of Economics, Finance and Administrative Sciences*, 45, 39-50.

Bagnoli, M., & Watts, S. G. (2003). Selling to Socially Responsible Consumers: Competition and the Private Provision of Public Goods. *Journal of Economics & Management Strategy*, 12 (3), 419–445.

Balabanis, G., Phillips, H. C., & Lyall, J. (1998).Corporate Social Responsibility and Economic Performance in The Top British Firms: Are They Linked? *European Business Review*, 98 (1), 25-44.

Baskin, J. (2006). Corporate Responsibility in Emerging Markets. *The Journal of Corporate Citizenship*, 24, 29-47.

Becchetti, L., Ciciretti, R., Hasan, I., & Kobeissi, N. (2012). Corporate Social Responsibility and Shareholder's Value. *Journal of Business Research*, 65 (11), 1628–1635.

Burke, L., Logsdon, J. M., Mitchell, W., Reiner, M, & Vogel D. (1986). Corporate Community Involvement in the San Francisco Bay Area. *California Management Review*, 28 (3), 122-141.

Chand, M. (2006). The Relationship between Corporate Social Performance and Corporate Financial Performance: Industry Type as a Boundary Condition. *The Business Review*, 5 (1), 240-245.

Choi, J., Kwak, Y., & Choe, C. (2010). Corporate Social Responsibility and Corporate Financial Performance: Evidence from Korea. *Australian Journal of Management*, 35 (3), 291-311.

Cochran, P. L., & Wood, R. A. (1984). Corporate Social Responsibility and Financial Performance. *Academy of Management Journal*, 27 (1), 42-56.

Crisóstomo, V. L., Freire, F., S., & de Vascincellos, F. C. (2011). Corporate Social Responsibility, Firm Value and Financial Performance in Brazil. *Social Responsibility Journal*, 7 (2), 295-309.

Curran, M. M., & Moran, D. (2007).Impact of the FTSE4Good Index on Firm Price: An Event Study. *Journal of Environmental Management*, 82 (4), 529–537.

De Cleene S., & Sonnenberg, D. (2004). *Socially Responsible Investment in South Africa* (2nd ed.). Johannesburg: African Institute of Corporate Citizenship.

Folger, H. R., & Nutt, F. (1975). A Note on Social Responsibility and Stock Valuation. *Academy of Management Journal*, 18 (1), 155-159.

Freeman, R. E. (1984). *Strategic Management: A Stakeholder Approach.* Boston, MA: Pitman.

Friedman, M. (1970, September 13). The Social Responsibility Of Business Is To Increase Its Profits. *New York Times*, 13, 122–126.

Gladysek, O., & Chipeta, C. (2012).The Impact of Socially Responsible Investment Index Constituent Announcements on Firm Price: Evidence from the JSE. *South African Journal of Economic and Management Sciences*, 15 (4), 429-439.

Heal, G. (2008). *When Principles Pay: Corporate Social Responsibility and the Bottom Line.* New York, NY: Columbia University Press.

Heese, H. (2005). The Development of Socially Responsible Investment in South Africa: Experience and Evolution of SRI in Global Markets. *Development Southern Africa*, 22 (5), 729-739.

Heinze, D. C. (1976). Financial Correlates of a Social Involvement Measure. *Akron Business and Economic Review*, 7 (1), 48-51.

Hopkins, M. (2003). *The Planetary Bargain: Corporate Social Responsibility Matters.* London, UK: Earthscan Publications Ltd.

Jamali, D., & Mirshak, R. (2007). Corporate Social Responsibility (CSR): Theory and Practice in a Developing Country Context. *Journal of Business Ethics*, 72 (3), 243-262.

Jensen, M., C. (1986). The Agency Costs of Free Cash Flow: Corporate Finance and Takeovers. *American Economic Review*, 76 (2), 323-329.

Johannesburg Stock Exchange. (2010). SRI Index Brochure. Retrieved from https://www.jse.co.za/services/market-data/indices/socially-responsible-investment-index

Lee, D. D., Faff, R. W., & Smith, K. (2009). Revisiting the Vexing Question: Does Superior Corporate Social Performance Lead to Improved Financial Performance? *Australian Journal of Management*, 34 (1), 21-50.

Lin, C. H., Yang, H. L., & Liou, D. H. (2009). The Impact of Corporate Social Responsibility on Financial Performance: Evidence from Business in Taiwan. *Technology in Society*, 31 (1), 56–63.

MacKinlay, A. C. (1997). Event Studies in Economics and Finance. *Journal of Economic Literature*, 35 (1), 13-39.

McGuire, J., Schneeweis, T., & Hill, J. (1986). An analysis of alternative measures of strategic performance. *Advances in strategic management*, 4 (2), 127-154.

McWilliams, A., & Siegel, D. (2000). Corporate Social Responsibility and Financial Performance: Correlation or Misspecification? *Strategic Management Journal*, 21 (5) 603-609.

McWilliams, A. & Siegel, D. (2001). Corporate Social Responsibility: A Theory of the Firm Perspective. *The Academy of Management Review*, 26 (1), 117–127.

Moskowitz, M. (1972). Choosing Socially Responsible Stocks. *Business and Society Review*, 1 (1), 71-75.

Naudè, W. (2009). The Financial Crisis of 2008 and the Developing Countries (Discussion Paper No. 2009/01). United Nations University. World Institute for Development Economics Research.

Orlitzky, M., Schmidt, F., & Rynes, S. (2003). Corporate Social and Financial Performance: A Meta-Analysis. *Organization Studies*, 24 (3), 403-441.

Perrini, F., Russo, A., & Tencati, A. (2007). CSR Strategies of SMEs and Large Firms. Evidence from Italy. *Journal of Business Ethics*, 74 (3), 285-300.

Preston, L. E. (1990). Stakeholder Management and Corporate Performance. *Journal of Behavioral Economics*, 19 (4), 361-375.

Preston, L. E., & O'Bannon, D. P. (1997). The Corporate Social-Financial Performance Relationship: A Typology and Analysis. *Business and Society*, 36 (4), 419-429.

Spicer, B. H. (1978). Investors, Corporate Social Performance and Information Disclosure: An Empirical Study. *Accounting Review*, 53 (1), 94-111.

Tsoutsoura, M. (2004). Corporate Social Responsibility and Financial Performance (Working Paper). University of California at Berkeley.

Ullman, A. (1985). Data In Search of a Theory: A Critical Examination of the Relationship among Social Performance, Social Disclosure, and Economic Performance. *Academy of Management Review*, 10 (3), 540–577.

Vance, S. C. (1975). Are Socially Responsible Corporations Good Investment Risks? *Management Review*, 64 (8), 18-24.

Waddock, S. A., & Graves, S. B. (1997). The Corporate Social Performance-Financial Performance Link. *Strategic Management Journal*, 18 (4), 303-319.

Wilson, T. (2007). No, Really – What Are The 'Equator Principles'? *The Institute of Public Affairs Review*, 59 (2), 7-10.

Appendix

The tables below depict the correlation matrices and regression results for the Basic Materials, Consumer Services and Industrials industries.

Basic Materials Industry

Table A1. Correlation Matrix for the Dependent and Explanatory Variables

Variable	EPS	ROA	ROE	RISK	SIZE	CSR
EPS	1					
ROA	0.792253	1				
ROE	0.799943	0.994396	1			
RISK	-0.15004	-0.10499	-0.137	1		
SIZE	0.560989	0.164708	0.170279	0.088631	1	
CSR	0.116712	0.014035	0.007743	0.298992	0.576056	1

Table A2. Regressions for CSR and CFP

Variable	Regression 1	Regression 2	Regression 3
	EPS	**ROE**	**ROA**
Constant	-11243.5300	-79.6600	-44.7631
	6133.7420	197.6701	125.2343
Risk	-1751.2320	-43.5070	-20.7053
	3965.2670	127.7873	80.9599
Size	538.9705***	4.4637	2.6935
	270.0136	8.7016	5.5129
CSR	-923.2763	-7.9659	-4.8856
	1349.7350	43.4975	27.5579
F-Statistic	1.5256	0.1406	0.1121
N	11	11	11

Note: *, **, *** indicates significance at 0.01, 0.05 and 0.10, respectively.

Consumer Services Industry

Table A3. Correlation Matrix for the Dependent and Explanatory Variables

Variable	EPS	ROA	ROE	SIZE	RISK	CSR
EPS	1					
ROA	-0.66214	1				
ROE	-0.60698	0.512261	1			
SIZE	0.372829	-0.48496	-0.20033	1		
RISK	0.10573	0.163541	-0.35875	0.309039	1	
CSR	-0.40445	0.099984	0.598215	0.094794	0.095371	1

Table A4. Regressions for CSR and CFP

Variable	Regression 1	Regression 2	Regression 3
	EPS	ROE	ROA
Constant	-1628.5620	86.7379	179.6028***
	1773.8090	97.7968	92.0459
Risk	91.9238	-105.1854	74.4162
	1464.1900	80.7263	75.9793
Size	89.7842	-2.1517	-6.9899
	77.1960	4.2561	4.0058
CSR	-244.3887	23.8777	3.6215
	184.0593	10.1479	9.5511
F-Statistic	1.0058	2.4588	1.1208
N	10	10	10

Note: *, **, *** indicates significance at 0.01, 0.05 and 0.10, respectively.

Industrials Industry

Table A5. Correlation Matrix for the Dependent and Explanatory Variables

Variable	EPS	ROA	ROE	SIZE	RISK	CSR
EPS	1					
ROA	-0.22628	1				
ROE	0.856996	-0.01885	1			
SIZE	0.832758	-0.4051	0.577952	1		
RISK	0.057592	0.212974	-0.16315	-0.23428	1	
CSR	0.583434	-0.26054	0.511223	0.738481	-0.43153	1

Table A6. Regressions for CSR and CFP

Variable	Regression 1	Regression 2	Regression 3
	EPS	ROE	ROA
Constant	-4827.7810	-42.6659	43.9632
	2500.2940	86.3037	50.5470
Risk	1006.7690	1.8041	6.5510
	1072.9520	37.0355	21.6913
Size	230.2608	2.5149	-1.5155
	116.4330	4.0190	2.3539
CSR	79.0387	3.3564	1.6271
	364.9793	12.5981	7.3786
F-Statistic	3.2503	0.5390	0.2375
N	7	7	7

Note: *, **, *** indicates significance at 0.01, 0.05 and 0.10, respectively.

7

Transnational Business as a Manifestation of the Integration of the Global Economy and a Driving Force of its Development

Svetlana S. Morkovina[1]; Alexandr S. Natsubidze[2]; Margarita S. Irizepova[3]; Nikolai G. Sinyavsky[4,5]; Vladimir V. Chashchin[6]

ABSTRACT

The purpose of this article is to determine the significance of transnational business in the development of the global economic system, to present perspectives on its further functioning and distribution in the global economy, and to develop recommendations for state regulation of entrepreneurship in developing countries for the purposes of attracting transnational business and stimulating the internationalization of domestic business.

To achieve this purpose, the authors use statistical information combined with several methods: substantiation of mathematical expressions "by contradiction", structural analysis, classical methods of analyzing economic effectiveness, comparative analysis, problem and SWOT-analysis, systemic analysis, modeling of the current state of (and perspectives on) the development of economic systems, and formalization.

The authors reach the conclusion that transnational business is a manifestation and driving force of the development of the modern global economy and that maximization of the economic growth of the global economy in the long-term requires the creation of favorable conditions for further development of transnational business.

Transnational business plays an important role in the development of the global economic system. Perspectives on the further functioning and distribution of transnational business in the global economy are connected to the development of integration processes and the realization of a free trade policy. To overcome threats to the development of transnational business, the authors of this study offer recommendations for state regulation of business in developing countries for the purpose of attracting transnational business and stimulating the internationalization of domestic business, and a special model is developed.

KEY WORDS: transnational business, integration of the global economy, driving force of development, developed countries, developing countries

---

[1]Voronezh State University of Forestry Engineering named after G.F. Morozov, Russia; [2]Moscow International Academy, Russia; [3]Volgograd State University, Russia; [4]Volgograd State Agricultural University, Russia; [5]Financial University under the Government of the Russian Federation, Russia; [6]Ural State Institute of Stock Market, Russia

Introduction

Transnational business emerged from the influence of integration processes that shaped the global economy in the late 19th and early 20th centuries. This initiated a rapid acceleration of the development of the global economic system due to the movement of capital from the developed countries, which usually have an excess of financial resources, to the developing countries, which are known to have deficits and an urgent need for investment resources.

Correspondence concerning this article should be addressed to: Alexandr S. Natsubidze, Moscow Institute of State and Corporate Management, Russia, 107023, Moscow, 21 Elektrozavodskaya St., Apt. 21 E-mail: sciencescience108@yahoo.com

When transnational businesses appeared in developing countries, they established production facilities, which provided new jobs for the local population and stimulated local purchasing ability, the development of entrepreneurship, and economic growth. This reflects the ability of transnational business to stimulate development in countries that need it but cannot independently close the gap that exists between them and developed countries.

During the modern stage of development of the global economy, transnational business became an inextricable part of the global economic system and one of its most important members, as it represents large business structures through which dialogue between the governments of various countries and business as a whole is conducted. Transnational corporations pursue their own interests, which, as the accumulated experience of transnational business shows, coincide largely with the global goals of economic development.

The unique capability of transnational business to revive the economies of developing countries by activating business activities, combined with its inclination for solving global economic problems (particularly problems of disproportionate economic growth in the global economy) makes it not only one of the most notable players in international economic relations but also one of the most promising mechanisms of improving the modern global economy.

Thus, the study of transnational business and its role in the development of the global economy is highly topical and is, accordingly, the focus of this article. The authors of this study propose the hypothesis that transnational business is a driving force behind the development of the modern global economy. Thus, to maximize the economic growth of the global economy in the long-term, it is necessary to create favorable conditions for the further development of transnational business.

The purpose of this research is to verify this hypothesis, determine the meaning of transnational business in the development of the global economic system, determine perspectives on its further functioning and distribution in the global economy, and develop recommendations for state regulation of business in developing countries for the purpose of attracting transnational business and stimulating the internationalization of domestic business.

Literature review

The consequences of the globalization of the world economy; the notions, senses, and factors at play in the integration of processes in the modern global economic system; the role of international organizations in regulating these processes; the phenomena of regionalization and polarization of the global economy within the process of integration; and the causes of the possible future disintegration of the global economy – all these issues are explored in the works of such authors as (Burhan, Sidek, Kurniawan, & Mohamad, 2015; Capello & Perucca, 2015; Gozgor, 2015; Lauder & Brown, 2015). Globalization has led to the growth of economic systems and their close cooperation (Egbetunde & Akinlo, 2015). International organizations coordinate this process and provide support for underdeveloped countries, with the goal of unifying the global economic system (Vasin & Gamidullaeva, 2015). However, there are still significant differences in the levels of economic development of countries around the world, which may be a reason for the disintegration of the global economy in the future (Lee, Lee, & Chang, 2015).

Issues related to the specifics of economic growth in the modern global economy, the drivers of economic development, ways of overcoming crisis phenomena in the global economy, analysis of possibilities and perspectives related to further global economic growth, and determination of the most important factors that stimulate and hinder the achievement of the strategic development goals of global economic systems – these topics are studied in the works of such scholars as (González-Pernía &,Peña-Legazkue, 2015; Leonida, Maimone Ansaldo Patti, Marini, & Navarra, 2015; Odhiambo, 2015; Pogosov, 2015; Popkova, Yurev, Stepicheva, & Denisov, 2015; Sarracino & Bartolini, 2015; Zeira & Zoabi, 2015). In today's globalizing environment, crisis phenomena that may have begun in one economic system can spread throughout the whole world (Choi & Shin, 2015). Countries can overcome global crises only by uniting their efforts (Lee & Oh, 2015). Despite the universality of strategic interests, most countries continue to seek their own goals of economic development, which hinders the development of the global economic system as a whole (Castiglione, Infante, & Smirnova, 2015).

Manifestations of the internationalization of business under the conditions of the integration and globalization of the world economy, the conditions necessary for the movement of production factors within the global economic system under the influence of the market mechanism, and internal stimuli that can improve the economic effectiveness of the organization of production and maximization of profit are examined in multiple studies by contemporary authors, including works by (Debrulle & Maes, 2015; Guillotin & Mangematin, 2015; Monteiro & Meneses, 2015; Purkayastha, Manolova, & Edelman, 2015). Under the conditions of integration and globalization of the world economy, the internationalization of business activities is ongoing. In this setting, both local and national business enters the international level (Ginting, 2014). In today's globalizing world, under the influence of market mechanisms and internal stimuli, production factors move within the global economic system (Eisend & Schmidt, 2014) to increase the economic effectiveness of production and maximize profit (Ahmad, 2014).

Many authors have studied various aspects of the manifestation of transnational business and its further distribution in the global economic system; its role in business development, overcoming the gaps between developing countries, and reducing disproportionate economic growth in the modern global economy; the specifics of the work of transnational corporations; and issues of state regulation of transnational business activities. Such authors include (Bagwell, 2015; Delteil, 2014; Lan, 2015; Thauer, 2015). Transnational business plays an important role in the development of business, as it provides access to new sales markets and cheaper resources, which increases the effectiveness of business (Eberlein, Abbott, Black, Meidinger, & Wood, 2014). Transnational business also contributes to overcoming the gaps between developing countries and to reducing disproportionate economic growth in the modern global economy by means of developing trade and business – and by moving resources into developed countries and capital into developing ones (Porter, 2014). State regulation of the activities of transnational corporations is performed at present and is aimed at the protection of internal markets (Lee, Ryu, & Kang, 2014).

The large volume of materials on this topic creates a strong theoretical base, but it does not mean there is no need for new research. Issues relating to the ability of transnational business to be a driving force behind the development of the global economy are of high scientific and practical interest, as are the possibilities of realizing such an economic policy in developing countries. This would produce the maximum advantages from the functioning of transnational business, making this research both necessary and important.

Method

To achieve its stated goal, this work uses general scientific methods of research: induction, deduction, and synthesis. Determining the meaning of transnational business in the development of the global economic system requires research in two key directions. First, it is advisable to substantiate the necessity of transnational corporations in the development of the global economy.

For this, the authors use both analysis of statistical information and evidence of mathematical expressions "by contradiction", within which – on the basis of the basic laws of logic and the principle of double negation – the possibility of eliminating transnational business from the structure of elements of the global GDP is determined.

Second, there is a need to determine the level of economic effectiveness of the functioning of transnational business. For this, the authors use the method of structural analysis, classical methods of analysis of economic effectiveness, and the method of comparative analysis. These are used to compare the levels of economic effectiveness of the activities of transnational business and national business, through comparison of the resources used, efficiency of production, and contribution to global GDP.

To determine perspectives on the further functioning of transnational business and its distribution in the global economy, the authors of this study use the method of problem and SWOT-analysis, with the help of which the advantages and disadvantages of transnational business – compared to national business – as well as possibilities of and threats to the development of transnational corporations in the short-term are determined.

To determine the causal relations involved in realizing the recommendations developed here regarding state regulation of business in developing countries for the purpose of attracting transnational business and stimulating the internationalization of domestic business, this work uses systemic analysis, modeling of the current situation, perspectives on the development of economic systems, and the method of formalization.

Results

According to official statistics provided by the international organization UNCTAD in 2015, transnational business creates approximately 10% of global employment (Fig. 1), more than 40% of global production (Fig. 2), almost 60% of direct foreign investments (Fig. 3, 4), and 80% of global innovation production (Fig. 5).

Analysis of statistical information, presented graphically in Fig. 1-5, shows that transnational business has been playing an important role in the functioning and development of the global economy in recent decades. To determine the need for transnational corporations in the development of the global economy, let us build a mathematical model of the formation of the global GDP.

According to the official UNCTAD statistics for 2014, 70% of global GDP is based on the manufacture of standard products, and 30% is based on the manufacture of innovative products, 80% of which are manufactured by transnational business and 20% by national business. On the basis of the above, it is possible to create a structural and logical model of the formation of global GDP, as follows:

$$GDPworld=0.7UP+0.3(0.8TB+0.2NB) \quad (1)$$

where GDPworld – global GDP;
UP – products that are not innovative;
TB – transnational business;
NB – national business.

On the basis of existing statistical information, let us insert values into this model and produce the following equation: 77,302=54,111UP+18,552TB+4,638NB. Let us suppose that transnational business contributes greatly to the development of the global economy and formation of the global GDP. Then, TB≈0.

In this case, the equation has the following form: 77,302=54,111UP+4,638NB. While the values of various sides of this equation are not equal and differ from each other (77,302>58,749), this contradicts the initial supposition of the insignificance of transnational business' contribution to the formation of the global GDP and proves that it is indeed an important component of the development of the global economy, according to the 2014 data.

To determine the level of economic effectiveness of transnational business, let us determine the structure of innovative products. To develop innovative technologies and purchase equipment necessary for the manufacture of innovative products, investments are necessary. Innovative products are manufactured by employees who represent the human resources of enterprises. Consequently, in its general form, the model of manufacture of innovative products could be presented in the following way:

$$HR*IR=IP \quad (2)$$

where HR – human resources;
IR – investment resources;
IP – innovative products.

According to the UNCTAD statistics for 2014, 10% of global human resources are concentrated in transnational business, which, in turn, accumulates 60% of global investment resources and manufactures 80% of global innovative products. This allows a mathematical presentation of the contribution of transnational business to the manufacture of innovative products, as follows: 0.1HR*0.6IR=0.8IP.

Then, the contribution of national business to the manufacture of innovative products will have the following form: 0.9HR*0.4IR=0.2IP. To evaluate effectiveness, let us use such economic indicators as labor efficiency (determined as the ratio of manufactured innovative products to the human resources used) and capital intensity of production (calculated as the ratio of investment resources used for the manufacture of innovative products).

The labor efficiency of transnational business during the manufacture of innovative products is calculated as follows: 0.8IP/0.1HR=0.8 $ million/person. The labor efficiency of national business during the manufacture of innovative products is calculated as follows: 0.2IP/0.8HR=$0.25 million/person. It is obvious that $0.8 million/person> $0.25 million/person, which proves that labor efficiency is higher in the sphere of transnational business.

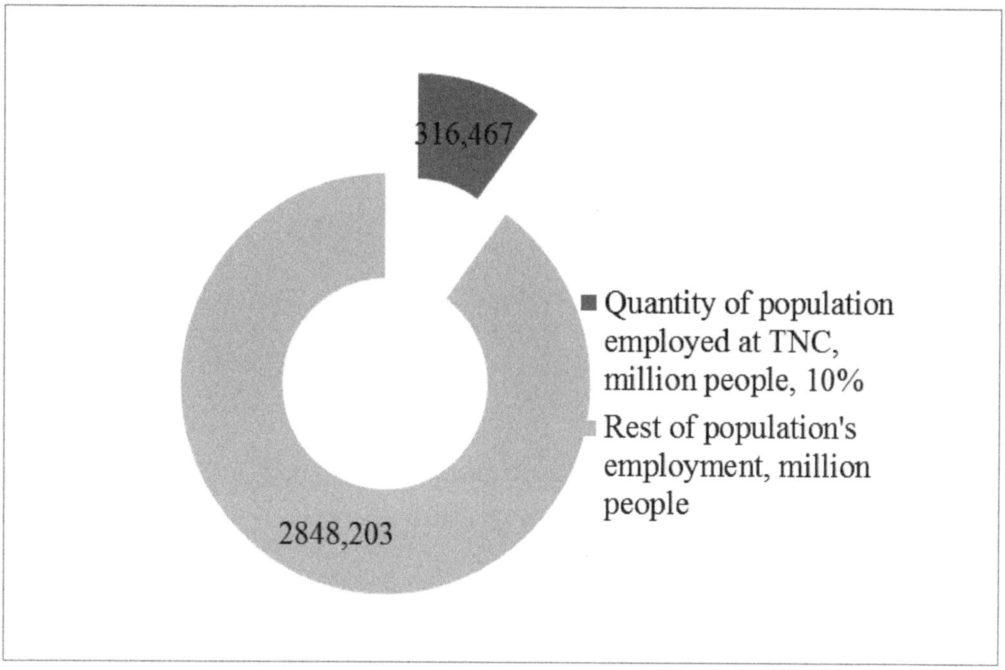

Figure 1. Structure of global employment in 2014
Source: United Nations Conference on Trade and Development, 2015.

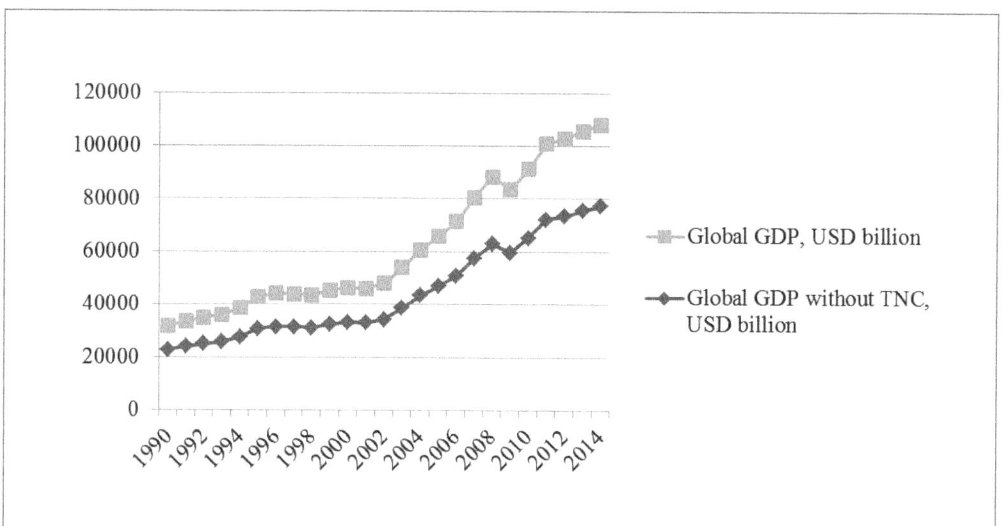

Figure 2. Statistics of global GDP with and without TNC in 1990-2014
Source: KNOEMA, 2016.

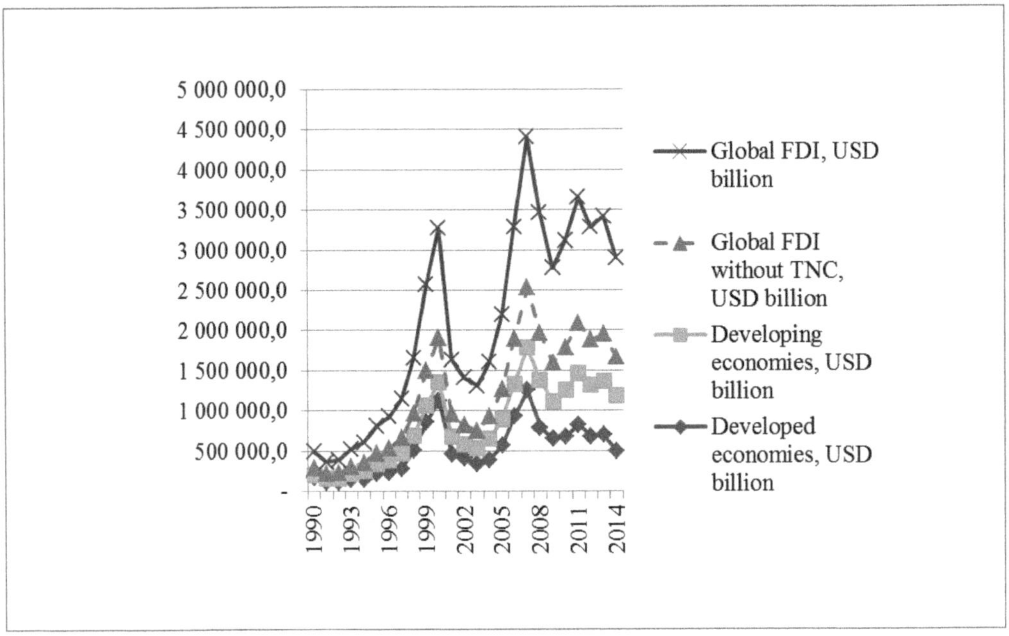

Figure 3. Statistics on global direct foreign investments in 1990-2014
Source: United Nations Conference on Trade and Development, 2016.

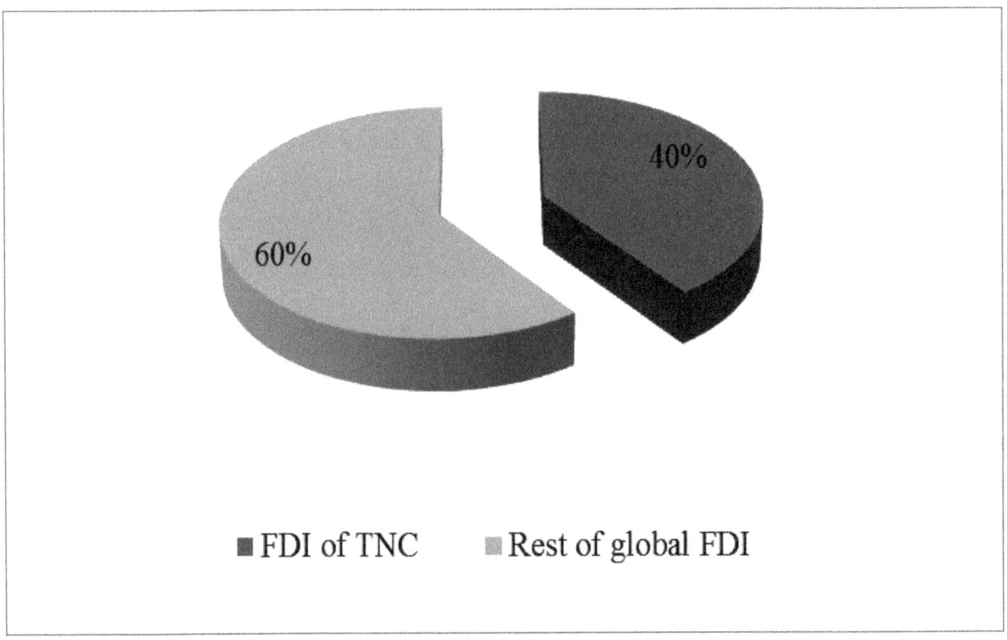

Figure 4. Structure of global direct investments in 2014
Source: United Nations Conference on Trade and Development, 2016

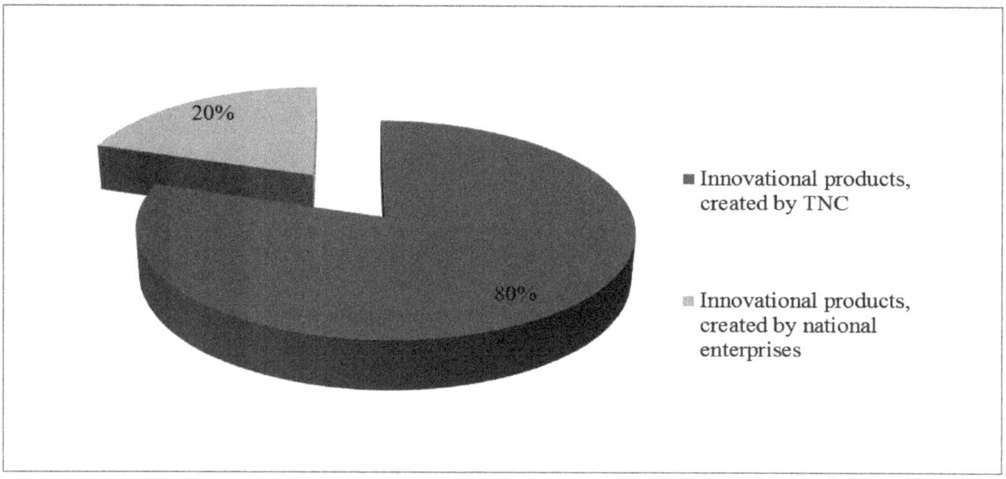

Figure 5. Structure of global innovative production in 2014
Source: United Nations Conference on Trade and Development, 2015

Table 2. SWOT-analysis of development of transnational business

Advantages of transnational business (S)	Disadvantages of transnational business (W)
high effectiveness of production	striving for minimization of taxes
high innovative activity	inclination toward monopolization of markets
high mobility of production	ecological irresponsibility
stimulation of global production	increased risks to business
Perspectives on development of transnational business (O)	Threats to development of transnational business (T)
development of integration processes in the global economy	tendency for disintegration of the global economy
weakening of customs barriers within policy of free trade	strengthening of customs barriers within policy of protectionism

The capital intensity of manufacturing innovative products in the sphere of transnational business is calculated as follows: 0.6IR/0.8IP=$0.75 million. In other words, to manufacture innovative products that cost $1 million, transnational corporations need $0.75 million in investment resources. The capital intensity of manufacturing innovative products in the sphere of national business is calculated as follows: 0.4IR/0.2IP=$2 million. In other words, to manufacture innovative products that cost $1 million, national corporations need $2 million in investment resources.

In comparing these values, it is clear that $2 million>$0.75 million, which reflects the lower capital intensity and higher effectiveness of transnational business' manufacture of innovative products. It should be noted that despite its high effectiveness and important role in the development of the global economy, transnational business often faces obstacles.

Transnational business possesses many advantages compared to national business: highly effective production, significant innovative activity due to the presence of necessary resources, high mobility of production due to the lack of a fixed connection to a specific territory, and stimulation of global production.

At the same time, there are drawbacks to transnational business. These are related to its goal of mini-

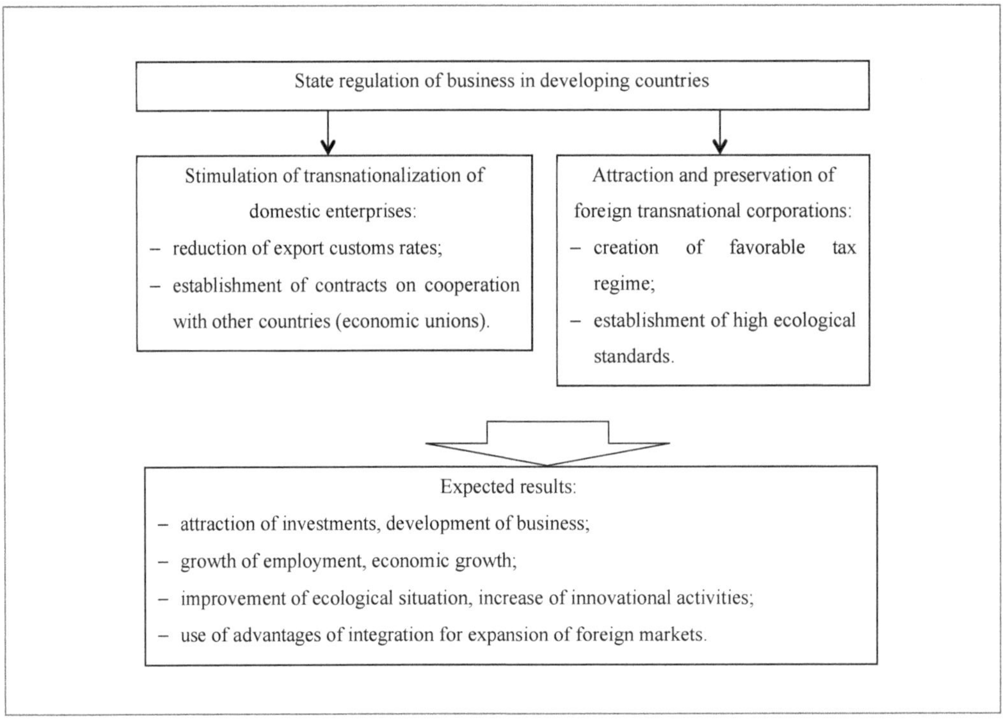

Figure 6. Model of development of transnational business as a result of realization of the proposed measures for state regulation of business in developing countries

mizing the taxes it pays, its inclination to monopolize markets, its transfer of ecologically dangerous production into developing countries, and the increase in business risks due to the probability of transnational corporations' leaving countries with unfavorable situations, which can lead to crisis phenomena in these countries' economies.

The results of SWOT-analysis of the development of transnational business are shown in Table 1. As seen in Table 1, perspectives on the further functioning and distribution of transnational business in the global economy are related to the development of integration processes and realization of the policy of free trade. In the case of the opposite tendency – disintegration of the global economy – it is possible to wait for a reduction in transnational business. A threat to its development is posed by the strengthening of customs barriers within the policy of protectionism.

As the recent global financial crisis showed, under conditions of instability, the governments of various countries are interested in the preservation of domestic production and may use tools to protect national business, which may disadvantage the interests of transnational corporations. Announcements from a range of territories regarding their wish to leave various associations – of which they are now members – show the high probability of the disintegration of the global economy in the near future.

To reduce the above threats, some possible recommendations for state regulation of business in developing countries – for the purpose of attracting transnational business and stimulating the internationalization of domestic entrepreneurship – can be offered: reduction in export custom rates, establishment of contracts regarding cooperation with other countries (economic unions), creation of favorable tax regimes, and establishment of high ecological standards. The causal relations involved in the realization of these recommendations and the development of transnational business are shown in Fig. 6.

Conclusion

As a result of this research, the proposed hypothesis was proven, and it was substantiated that transnational business is a manifestation and driving force of the development of the modern global economy. Maximizing the economic growth of the global economy in the long-term requires the creation of favorable conditions for further development of transnational business.

Transnational business plays an important role in the development of the global economic system: it provides approximately 10% of global employment, more than 40% of global production, almost 60% of direct foreign investments, and 80% of global innovative production.

The use of mathematical tools showed that the capital intensity with which transnational business manufactures innovative products is much lower than that of national business, and labor efficiency in the sphere of transnational business is also much lower, which proves its high effectiveness.

Perspectives on the further functioning and distribution of transnational business in the global economy are related to the development of integration processes and realization of the policy of free trade. To overcome threats to the development of transnational business, the authors of this study offer recommendations for state regulation of business in developing countries for the purpose of attracting transnational business and stimulating the internationalization of domestic entrepreneurship.

These recommendations are reflected in the proprietary model of the development of transnational business as a result of the realization of the proposed measures of state regulation of business in developing countries, within which two directions of state economic policy are offered: stimulation of transnationalization of domestic enterprises and attraction and preservation of foreign transnational corporations.

Realization of this model will lead to increased investments, development of business, higher employment, economic growth, improvement of the ecological situation, increased innovative activity, and the use of the advantages of integration for the expansion of foreign markets. It should be noted that this model is oriented toward developing countries – however, developed countries are equally interested in the development of transnational business and attracting transnational corporations.

This is why determining the possible directions of state regulation of business in developed countries (for the purpose of stimulating the transnationalization of domestic enterprises) and attracting and preserving foreign transnational corporations have major scientific and practical significance and are interesting avenues for further research in this sphere.

The theory of transnationalization of entrepreneurial activities may receive further development due to the expansion of integration processes in the global economy. This requires the development of theoretical and methodological provisions regarding the creation of a corresponding institutional environment that stimulates the development of transnational business.

References

Ahmad, S. Z. (2014). Small and medium enterprises' internationalisation and business strategy: Some evidence from firms located in an emerging market. *Journal of Asia Business Studies, 8*(2), 168-186.

Bagwell, S. (2015). Transnational entrepreneurship amongst Vietnamese businesses in London. *Journal of Ethnic and Migration Studies, 41*(2), 329-349.

Burhan, N. A. S., Sidek, A.H., Kurniawan, Y., Mohamad, M. R. (2015). Has globalization triggered collective impact of national intelligence on economic growth? *Intelligence, 48, 152-161.*

Capello, R., Perucca, G. (2015). Openness to globalization and regional growth patterns in CEE countries: From the EU accession to the economic crisis. *Journal of Common Market Studies, 53*(2), 218-236.

Castiglione, C., Infante, D., & Smirnova, J. (2015). Environment and economic growth: is the rule of law the go-between? The case of high-income countries. *Energy, Sustainability and Society, 5*(26). doi:10.1186/s13705-015-0054-8.

Choi, K. H., Shin, S. (2015). Population aging, economic growth, and the social transmission of human capital: An analysis with an overlapping generations model. *Economic Modelling, 50*, 138-147.

Debrulle, J., Maes, J. (2015). Start-ups' internationalization: The impact of business owners' management experience, start-up experience and professional network on export intensity. *European Management Review, 12*(3), 171-187.

Delteil, V. (2014). Domestic labor regulation and foreign business influence: The case of the Guangdong transnational capitalism. In X. Richet, V. Delteil, & P. Dieuaide (Eds.), Strategies of multinational corporations and social regulations. European and Asian Perspectives (pp. 219-240). Berlin: Springer Verlag.

Eberlein, B., Abbott, K. W., Black, J., Meidinger, E., Wood, S. (2014). Transnational business governance interactions: Conceptualization and framework for analysis. *Regulation and Governance, 8*(1), 1-21.

Egbetunde, T., Akinlo, A. E. (2015). Financial globalization and economic growth in Sub-Saharan Africa: Evidence from panel cointegration tests. *African Development Review, 27*(3), 187-198.

Eisend, M., Schmidt, S. (2014). The influence of knowledge-based resources and business scholars' internationalization strategies on research performance. *Research Policy, 43*(1), 48-59.

Ginting, G. (2014). Proposed conceptual model internationalization of small medium industries (SMIs) in Indonesia: The relationship between entreprenurial orientation, network capital, degree of internationalization and business performance. *Asian Social Science, 10*(19), 220-229.

González-Pernía, J. L., Peña-Legazkue, I. (2015). Export-oriented entrepreneurship and regional economic growth. *Small Business Economics, 45*(3), 505-522.

Gozgor, G. (2015). Causal relation between economic growth and domestic credit in the economic globalization: Evidence from the Hatemi-J's test. *The Journal of International Trade and Economic Development, 24*(3), 395-408.

Guillotin, B., & Mangematin, V. (2015). Internationalization Strategies of Business Schools: How Flat Is the World? *Thunderbird International Business Review, 57*(5), 343-357.

Knoema. (2016). World GDP 1980-2014. Retrieved from http://knoema.ru/tbocwag/gdp-by-country-1980-2014?country=Мир

Lan, S. (2015). Transnational business and family strategies among Chinese/Nigerian couples in Guangzhou and Lagos. *Asian Anthropology, 14*(2), 133-149.

Lauder, H., & Brown, P. (2015). Economic globalisation, skill formation and development. In S. McGrath, Q. Gu (Eds.), Routledge Handbook of International Education and Development (pp. 303-312). London, UK: Routlege.

Lee, J. Y., Ryu, S., & Kang, J. (2014). Transnational HR network learning in Korean business groups and the performance of their subsidiaries. *The International Journal of Human Resource Management, 25*(4), 588-608.

Lee, C. C., Lee, C. C., Chang, C. P. (2015). Globalization, economic growth and institutional development in China. *Global Economic Review, 44*(1), 31-63.

Lee, S., Oh, D. W. (2015). Economic growth and the environment in China: Empirical evidence using prefecture level data. *China Economic Review, 36*, 73-85.

Leonida, L., Maimone Ansaldo Patti, D., Marini, A., Navarra, P. (2015). Political competition and economic growth: A test of two tales. *Economics Letters, 135*, 96-99.

Monteiro, R., Meneses, R. (2015). The relevance of business diplomacy in internationalisation processes: An empirical study. *International Journal of Business and Globalisation, 15*(1), 20-44.

Odhiambo, N. M. (2015). Government expenditure and economic growth in South Africa: An empirical investigation. *Atlantic Economic Journal, 43*(3), 393-406.

Pogosov, I. A. (2015). Factors of long-term economic growth: Scientific and technical progress and capital intensity of production. *Studies on Russian Economic Development, 26*(5), 423-433.

Popkova, E. G., Yurev, V., Stepicheva, O., Denisov, N. (2015). Transformation and concentration of intellectual capital as a factor of economic growth in the modern economy. *Regional and Sectoral Economic Studies, 15*(1), 53-60.

Porter, T. (2014). Technical systems and the architecture of transnational business governance interactions. *Regulation and Governance, 8*(1), 110-125.

Purkayastha, S., Manolova, T. S., & Edelman, L. F. (2015). Business group effects on the innovation-internationalization relationship: Evidence from the Indian Pharmaceutical Sector. In L. Tihanyi, E.

R. Banalieva , T. M. Devinney , T. Pedersen (Eds.), *Emerging economies and multinational enterprises (Advances in International Management, Vol. 28, pp. 379-402).* Bingley, UK: Emerald Group Publishing Limited.

Sarracino, F., Bartolini, S. (2015). The dark side of Chinese growth: Declining social capital and well-being in times of economic boom. *World Development, 74,* 333-351.

Thauer, C. R. (2015). In need of meta-governance: Business networks of transnational governance. *Israel Law Review, 48*(2), 189-218.

United Nations Conference on Trade and Development. (2015). Transnational Corporations Statistics (2015). Retrieved from http://unctad.org/en/Pages/DIAE/Transnational-Corporations-Statistics.aspx

United Nations Conference on Trade and Development. (2016). FDI inflows, by region and economy, 1990-2014 Retrieved from http://unctad.org/en/Pages/DIAE/World%20Investment%20Report/Annex-Tables.aspx

Vasin, S. M., Gamidullaeva, L. A. (2015). Methodical approach and tools to improve the efficiency of managing of the innovation potential in the context of economic globalization. *Review of European Studies, 7*(3), 124-139.

Zeira, J., Zoabi, H. (2015). Economic growth and sector dynamics. *European Economic Review, 79,* 1-15.

An empirical approach to marketing innovation in small and medium retailers: an application to the Spanish sector

Natalia Medrano[1], Cristina Olarte-Pascual[1]

ABSTRACT

Although numerous studies explore innovation, most of them focus on technological innovations. It is currently difficult to focus exclusively on products and processes when discussing innovation because new ideas can transform any part of an organization's value chain. Indeed, marketing innovation is essential for small and medium firms and its study is extremely important given the current lack of empirical evidence. Furthermore, the retail sector in Spain plays a significant role in the country's economy due to its contribution to gross domestic product and employment and to its role in the growth of cities and regions. In this context, the present study analyzes the determinants of marketing innovation practices of small and medium retailers and the relationships among the four types of innovation (product, process, organizational and marketing) to improve our understanding of marketing innovations in the retail sector. This study uses secondary data on innovation activity for Spanish companies in the years 2010-2012. Logistic regression models are estimated, and the results show that the introduction of new marketing methods has a positive impact on the propensity to engage in all other types of innovation (product, process and organizational). Furthermore, all of these methods positively impact the propensity to introduce marketing innovations. This study concludes with insights that can help managers to direct innovation processes in their companies and assist public administrators in the promotion of marketing innovations among small and medium retailers.

KEY WORDS: marketing innovation, non-technological innovations, retail, SME

[1]Universidad de La Rioja, Spain

Introduction

Innovation is considered a decisive factor in wealth creation and a fundamental process for company competitiveness. Because of its importance, innovation has been analyzed from various perspectives (e.g., Cooke, 2005; Crossan & Apaydin, 2010; Porter, 1998), leading to multiple definitions and typologies (e.g., Armbruster, Bikfalvi, Kinkel, & Lay, 2008; Becheikh, Landry, & Amara, 2006; Francis & Bessant, 2005; Garcia & Calantone, 2002; Oke, 2007; Rowley, Baregheh, & Sambrook, 2011; Schumpeter, 2012). Most of the numerous studies on innovation focus on technological innovations. However, it is currently difficult to limit

Correspondence concerning this article should be addressed to: Natalia Medrano Sáez, Edificio Quintiliano, C/ La Cigüeña 60, 26006 Logroño, La Rioja, Spain. E-mail: natalia.medrano@unirioja.es

the discussion of innovation to product and process innovations because new ideas can transform any part of an organization's value chain. For this reason, the definition proposed by the OECD/Eurostat (2005) in the Oslo Manual, which is recognized as an international reference, identifies four areas of innovation: product, process, organizational and marketing.

The lack of empirical evidence in the literature on the impact of marketing innovations – despite the fact that their effects differ from those of innovations in areas such as products and processes – is noteworthy. Additionally, marketing methods and tools play important roles in the evolution of industries (e.g., Bhaskaran, 2006; Chen, 2006; Rammer, Czarnitzki, & Spielkamp, 2009; Schubert, 2010).

Spanish public policy has placed particular importance on supporting small and medium enterprises (SMEs) because these firms are the backbone of industry. Moreover, marketing innovation is essential for small firms to transform products into profit (Soltani, Azadi, Hosseini, Witlox, & Passel, 2015). The tendency to engage in marketing innovation depends on the activities of an enterprise, and differences between the manufacturing and service sectors are significant (Medrano & Olarte-Pascual, 2016). Companies in the service sector are more likely than those in the manufacturing sector to innovate in the areas of promotion, placement and price. Within the service sector, studies of the Spanish retail sector are important due to the significant contributions retail businesses make to Spanish GDP and employment. Furthermore, the retail sector is key to the growth of cities and regions (Medrano, Olarte-Pascual, Pelegrín-Borondo, & Sierra-Murillo, 2016). Taking into account the context in which small and medium retailers currently operate, as well as all of the public business programs launched to encourage firm innovation, an improved understanding of this situation is needed to create effective public policies for each type of business.

Thus, the objective of this paper is to understand marketing innovation and its determinants among small and medium retailers based on data from the Technological Innovation Panel (PITEC). More precisely, this study investigates (1) the factors influencing the four types of innovation (product, process, organizational and marketing) and (2) the relationships between marketing innovation and the other types of innovation.

This paper, which focuses on marketing innovation, is organized as follows: first, the concept of marketing innovation and its repercussions in the literature are discussed. Second, the sample and methodology employed are described. Finally, the results and conclusions of the study are presented.

Theoretical framework and hypotheses

The first studies of innovation focused on product innovation in the manufacturing context. Although the literature on innovation is abundant, most of it refers to product and process innovations, which are called technological innovations. Certain studies have attempted to relate technological and organizational innovation (e.g., Brown & Duguid, 1991; Brown, 2002; Djellal & Gallouj, 1999; Kishore & McLean, 2002; Tether et al., 2002). However, non-technological innovations – i.e., marketing and organizational innovations – have generally been neglected in the literature.

Marketing innovation is defined as the "implementation of a new marketing method involving significant changes in product design and/or packaging, product placement, product promoting or pricing" (OECD/Eurostat, 2005, p. 49). However, there was a significant change to the definition of innovation in the 2005 Oslo Manual. Previously, technological product and process innovations were defined as the two types of innovation considered in the measurement of innovation. In the third edition of the Oslo Manual, two other types of innovation were added at the same level as technological innovation: marketing innovation and organizational innovation.

According to Wang (2015), three main streams of marketing innovation studies are found in the literature. The first stream discusses the competitive advantages that can be achieved through marketing innovation. The second addresses the relationships between marketing innovations and the other innovation types. Finally, the third stream attempts to understand the characteristics of firms that adopt marketing innovations.

From the competitive advantage perspective, authors usually view marketing innovation as a type of incremental innovation (Grewal & Tansuhaj, 2001; Naidoo, 2010) that enables small and medium companies to successfully compete with large businesses (Bhaskaran, 2006; O'Dwyer, Gilmore, & Carson,

2009a, 2009b; Rammer et al., 2009). Therefore, this research focuses on marketing innovation in small and medium enterprises. Furthermore, Bhaskaran (2006) and Rammer et al. (2009) note that small and medium enterprises, especially those in low- and mid-tech industries, may be more willing to engage in potentially less costly marketing innovations than in technological innovations. Hence, marketing innovation is more important for small and medium retailers.

Relationships between marketing innovation and the other innovation types

According to Walker (2004), innovation activities are thought to influence each other and thus need to be implemented in conjunction with each other. The disputed relationship between technological innovation and marketing innovation centers on whether they are complements or substitutes; according to Kijek (2013), it is quite intuitive that the introduction of a new process or product calls for changes in marketing strategies. For instance, a new product line often requires changes in packaging and sales channels. Lewis and Wackowski (2006) provide an example from the tobacco industry, in which the introduction of flavored cigarettes was intensively supported by marketing innovations. However, other authors argue that marketing innovations do more than merely support technological innovations (Bhaskaran, 2006 and Rammer et al., 2009). Following this reasoning, Schubert (2010) maintains that marketing innovations are, on average, complements – rather than substitutes – for technological innovations but notes that this relationship is sensitive to external and internal factors, such firm size and technological opportunities. However, this author argues that marketing innovations make product and process innovations more successful. Furthermore, Walker (2008) concludes that organizational, marketing and service (or product) innovations are interrelated in public organizations. In a study of manufacturing firms in Turkey, positive relationships were shown between organizational innovation and process innovation, organizational innovation and marketing innovation, process innovation and product innovation, and marketing innovation and product innovation (Gunday, Ulusoy, Kilic, & Alpkan, 2011). Additionally, Soltani et al. (2015) show that although there is no direct cause-and-effect relationship between organizational and production innovation, both of these innovation types are influenced by marketing innovation.

Considering the existing literature on the relationships between marketing innovation and the other types of innovation, the following hypotheses are formulated:

H1. Marketing innovation in small and medium retailers is positively associated with product innovation.

H2. Marketing innovation in small and medium retailers is positively associated with process innovation.

H3. Marketing innovation in small and medium retailers is positively associated with organizational innovation.

Features of firms that adopt marketing innovations

In addition to researching interactions among innovation types since the official inclusion of other forms of innovation in the Oslo Manual, researchers have begun to examine the relation between marketing innovation and various other aspects of firms, such as size (e.g., Geldes & Felzensztein, 2013; Halpern, 2010; Moreira, Silva, Simões & Sousa, 2012), R&D expenditure (e.g., T. Kijek, 2013; Moreira et al., 2012), personnel training (e.g., Geldes & Felzensztein, 2013; Kijek, 2013; Moreira, Silva, Simões, & Sousa, 2012), export activities (e.g., Geldes & Felzensztein, 2013; Medrano & Olarte-Pascual, 2016), class of company and cooperation (e.g., Geldes & Felzensztein, 2013), market share (e.g., Camisón & Villar-López, 2014; Schubert, 2010; Shergill & Nargundkar, 2005), market concentration (e.g., Schubert, 2010), and group membership (e.g., Medrano & Olarte-Pascual, 2016; Schubert, 2010), among other firm characteristics.

Several recent analyses of technological and marketing innovations not only focus on the direct relationship between these two types of innovation but also address the impact of technological innovation activities on the propensity to innovate in marketing (Kijek, Lisowski, & Starzyńska, 2013; Moreira at al., 2012). Kijek (2013) finds that product innovations influence the decision to introduce marketing innovations; however, there is little support for the view that

Table 1. Research technical specifications

Scope	Small and medium Spanish companies
Sample size	Retailers 463; Other sectors 5,511
Region of study	Spain
Information compilation system	Self-administered postal questionnaire
Organization responsible for the questionnaire	National Statistics Institute
Reference period	2010-2012
Statistical programs	SPSS 15.0, STATA SE 10.0

process innovations induce marketing innovations. In Spain, enterprises that conduct product, process or organizational innovations are more likely to innovate in marketing (Medrano & Olarte-Pascual, 2016). The findings of Soltani et al. (2015) for small food industries show that when product and organizational innovations increase, marketing innovation also increases. Hence, the following hypotheses are formulated for small and medium retailers:

H4. Small and medium retailers that conduct product innovations are more likely to innovate in marketing.

H5. Small and medium retailers that conduct process innovations are more likely to innovate in marketing.

H6. Small and medium retailers that conduct organizational innovations are more likely to innovate in marketing.

Research methods

Survey

Data from PITEC are used to conduct this study. This database follows the methodological guidance provided by the OECD in the Oslo Manual using two periodically published sources: the Innovation in Companies Survey of Spanish firms and the Statistics on R&D Activities database. The technical characteristics of this study are shown in table 1. The data include 5,974 small and medium companies, of which 463 companies are in the retail sector and the remaining 5,511 companies are in other sectors.

Statistical methods

To determine whether there is a multicollinearity problem, this study considers the tolerance and variance inflation factor (VIF). A tolerance smaller than 0.20 and/or a VIF of 5 or higher indicate a multicollinearity problem (O'Brien, 2007).

Considering the two aims of the study, the analysis is divided into two parts. In the first part, the probability that firms engage in each kind of innovation (product, process, organization and marketing) is examined to verify the relationship between marketing innovation and the other types of innovation. Logistic regression is selected because it adapts to all types of independent variables (metric and non-metric) and does not require multivariate normality (Hair, Black, Babin, Anderson, & Tatham, 2006). The dependent variable in each model is binary (coded 0 if the company does not innovate and 1 if the company innovates), and the independent variables in the four models are the other types of innovation and the following firm characteristics: belonging to a business group, percentage of women employed, company market (local, national, EU or other), training, public financing, and company class (private, private with <10% foreign capital, private with 10% to 50% foreign capital, private with >50% foreign capital). Additionally, for each dependent variable, the marginal effects are estimated. In the second part of this study, the probability that firms conduct each kind of marketing innovation is estimated using the same method (that is, using four binary logistic regressions) to verify the determinants of the four types of marketing innovation.

Table 2. Number of small and medium companies that innovate in the retail and other sectors

	Retail		Other Sectors	
Types of innovations	Innovate	%	Innovate	%
General				
Marketing	125	27	1560	28
Design	57	12	916	17
Pricing	50	11	544	10
Promotion	76	16	851	15
Placement	73	16	722	13
Product	114	25	2291	42
Process	121	26	2281	41
Organizational	155	33	2185	40
Total Companies	463	100	5511	100

Table 3. Multicollinearity diagnosis indexes for independent variables

Independent Variables	**Tolerance**	**VIF**
Marketing	0.775	1.289
Product	0.719	1.390
Process	0.767	1.303
Organization	0.761	1.312
Group	0.972	1.028
Employment_women	0.963	1.037
Local Market	0.784	1.275
National Market	0.583	1.713
EU Market	0.665	1.503
Other Country Markets	0.840	1.189
Training	0.915	1.091
Public_Finan (Local)	0.849	1.176
Public_Finan (National)	0.921	1.084
Public_Finan (EU)	0.734	1.361
Company Class	0.775	1.289

Results and discussion

The database provides a sample of 463 companies, with just over one-quarter (27%) reporting that they implemented marketing innovation activities (table 2). However, the data show the importance of the retail sector because this sector does not exhibit the same average behavior as other sectors. In other sectors, marketing innovation is the least frequently implemented innovation of the four types of innovation. In contrast, our analysis of the retail sector shows that marketing

Table 4. Logistic regression for types of innovation in small and medium retailers

	Innovations							
Variables	Marketing		Product		Process		Organization	
	B	dy/dx	β	dy/dx	β	dy/dx	B	dy/dx
Innovations								
Marketing			1.56***	0.28	0.99***	0.19	2.19***	0.48
Product	1.54***	0.28			0.23	0.04	0.29	0.06
Process	1.00***	0.17	0.27	0.04			0.94***	0.21
Organization	2.20***	0.40	0.27	0.04	0.91***	0.16		
Firm Characteristics								
Group	0.09	0.01	-0.21	-0.03	0.34	0.05	0.49*	0.10
Employment_women	0.01*	0.00	0.00	0.00	-0.00	-0.00	-0.00	-0.00
Market								
Local Market	-0.73	-0.13	1.64	0.14	0.97	0.12	-0.17	-0.03
National Market	0.65	0.08	1.19*	0.13	1.07**	0.14	-0.40	-0.09
EU Market	-0.67*	-0.11	0.79**	0.10	0.09	0.01	0.82**	0.16
Other Country Markets	0.82***	0.12	-0.20	-0.02	-0.54*	-0.09	-0.25	-0.05
Training	0.32	0.05	0.43	0.07	3.08***	0.64	0.70	0.16
Public_Finan (Local)	-0.95	-0.11	1.23**	0.24	0.99*	0.21	1.76***	0.41
Public_Finan (National)	-0.00	-0.00	2.63***	0.56	0.75	0.15	-0.00	-0.00
Public_Finan (EU)	-2.90**	-0.18	2.50**	0.54	2.05	0.46	0.60	0.13
Company Class								
Private	0.24	0.03	-0.76**	-0.13	0.54	0.08	0.23	0.04
Private (<10% Foreign Capital)	1.69*	0.36	-1.03	-0.11	-1.95	-0.18	-0.33	-0.06
Private (10% to 50% Foreign Capital)	-2.02	-0.16	2.34**	0.51	1.13	0.24	-0.35	-0.06
Pseudo-R2	46.5		39.7		34.6		40.6	
% Correct Predictions	81.2		81.4		78.8		79.7	

Note: *Statistically significant at the 0.1 level, **statistically significant at the 0.05 level, ***statistically significant at the 0.01 level.

innovation ranks second behind organizational innovation. Differences in terms of the importance assigned to different types of marketing innovation are also observed. Design innovation is the most important, on average, in other sectors, whereas promotion and placement are the most frequently conducted activities in the retail sector.

When all independent variables are included in the analysis, table 3 shows that none has a tolerance less than 0.70 and there is no VIF higher than 2. In conclusion, multicollinearity is not an issue in this study.

Table 4 presents the estimation results of the logistic regressions for the four types of innovation in small and medium retailers. First, the results show that the introduction of new marketing methods has a positive impact on the propensity to conduct all other types of innovations (product, process and organizational). Thus, H1, H2 and H3 are supported. Second, the results show that introducing new product, process and organizational methods has a positive impact on the propensity to conduct marketing innovations, confirming the results obtained by Wang (2015). These results also support

Table 5. Logistic regression for types of marketing innovation in small and medium retailers

	Marketing Innovations							
Variables	Design		Pricing		Promotion		Placement	
	B	dy/dx	β	dy/dx	B	dy/dx	B	dy/dx
Innovations								
Design			0.61	0.02	0.39	0.02	1.45***	0.13
Pricing	0.47	0.02			2.33***	0.31	0.64	0.04
Promotion	0.35	0.01	2.26***	0.19			3.23***	0.44
Placement	1.53***	0.11	0.68	0.03	3.28***	0.48		
Product	1.75***	0.12	-0.01	-0.00	-0.06	-0.00	0.58	0.03
Process	0.88**	0.04	0.57	0.02	0.54	0.03	-0.09	-0.00
Organization	0.92**	0.04	1.24***	0.06	1.13***	0.08	1.09***	0.07
Firm Characteristics								
Group	0.29	0.01	0.13	0.00	-0.05	-0.00	-0.36	-0.01
Employment_women	0.01	0.00	0.01	0.00	0.00	0.00	-0.00	-0.00
Market								
Local Market	-1.90***	-0.18	0.67	0.02	-0.94	-0.08	1.54	0.04
National Market	0.12	0.00	0.41	0.01	-0.25	-0.01	1.57*	0.05
EU Market	1.09**	0.04	-1.06**	-0.04	-0.08	-0.00	-0.68	-0.04
Other Country Markets	0.11	0.00	-0.04	-0.00	0.15	0.00	0.95**	0.05
Training	-1.13	-0.03	0.75	0.04	-0.04	-0.00	0.00	0.00
Public_Finan (Local)	0.56	0.03	-1.54*	-0.03	-0.87	-0.03	0.25	0.01
Public_Finan (National)	-0.06	-0.00	0.04	0.00	0.38	0.02	0.28	0.01
Public_Finan (EU)	(omitted)		1.29	0.09	(omitted)		1.01	0.08
Company Class								
Private	-0.11	-0.00	-0.04	-0.00	1.24**	0.05	-1.17**	-0.09
Private (<10% Foreign Capital)	1.49	0.12	1.55	0.12	2.37**	0.35	(omitted)	
Private (10% to 50% Foreign Capital)	(omitted)		0.62	0.03	0.28	0.01	-1.11	-0.03
Pseudo-R2	46.8		46.2		62.3		59.8	
% Correct Predictions	89.2		90.5		91.1		89.8	

Note: *Statistically significant at the 0.1 level, **statistically significant at the 0.05 level, ***statistically significant at the 0.01 level.

Soltani et al. (2015) because there are significant positive cause-and-effect relationships between product and organizational innovations and marketing innovations in the studied firms. This result is also consistent with Kijek (2013), who establishes that product innovations influence the decision to introduce marketing innovations, suggesting a complementary relationship and a positive impact of product innovation on marketing innovation. However, this result conflicts with the results of Geldes and Felzensztein (2013), who find a statistically significant negative relation between marketing and product innovation in the agribusiness sector.

For the specific case of marketing innovation in small and medium retailers, statistically significant positive relations are obtained for the employment of women, other country markets and private companies (<10% foreign capital) and negative relations are obtained for the EU market and EU public financing. For product innovations, positive relations with the EU market and public financing are obtained, with negative relations for private companies (<10% foreign capital). With regard to process innovations, statistically significant positive relations are obtained for the national market, training and local public financing, with a negative relation for other country markets. Kijek et al. (2013) also find evidence that expenditures on training positively affect the implementation of marketing innovations in enterprises. However, in this case, the statistically significant positive relation is with process innovation rather than marketing innovation. Additionally, among small and medium retailers, organizational innovations have a statistically significant positive relation with the EU market, local public financing and group membership.

Table 5 presents the estimation results of the logistic regressions for four types of marketing innovation in small and medium retailers. Model 1 considers the percentage of firms that introduced design innovation as the response variable; models 2, 3 and 4 consider the same thing for pricing, promotion and placement innovation, respectively.

The results show that the introduction of new organizational methods has a positive impact on the propensity of small and medium retailers to engage in all types of marketing innovations. Thus, H6 is supported for all types of marketing innovations, confirming the results of Soltani et al. (2015). However, the introduction of new products or processes has a significant positive impact only on the propensity to conduct design innovation. The effects on the implementation of changes in sales channels, pricing methods and promotion are insignificant. Thus, H4 and H5 are only partially supported. The results partially support the finding of both Kijek (2013) and Medrano and Olarte-Pascual (2016) that the introduction of new products has a positive impact on the propensity to engage in all types of marketing innovation. Soltani et al. (2015) show that when product innovation increases, marketing innovation also increases. Thus, for small and medium retailers, the introduction of new products induces changes only in design innovation.

For the specific case of design innovation, a statistically significant positive relation with the EU market is observed, whereas the relation with the local market is negative. For pricing innovation, negative relations with the EU market and public financing (local) are observed. For promotion innovation, statistically significant positive relations with private companies and private companies (<10% foreign capital) are obtained. Additionally, placement innovation has a statistically significant positive relation with the national market and training and a negative relation with private companies.

Conclusions

In the modern world, it is undeniable that globalization, stronger competition, increasingly stringent and segmented demand, rapid technological evolution and increasingly shorter life cycles have led to substantial growth in the relevance of innovation as a key factor in achieving leverage in the market. These obvious changes in both society and consumer behavior render previously appropriate models unsuitable in current conditions, and the marketing discipline – like practical and scientific expertise – is not exempt from these changes. In the current scenario, small and medium retailers are losing customers every day; these stores eventually close, and over time, cities slowly lose their cultural and economic vibrancy (Medrano et al., 2016).

In this context, the present study analyzes the determinants of the marketing innovation practices of small and medium retailers and the relationships among the four types of innovation (product, process, organizational and marketing) in order to better understand marketing innovation in the retail sector.

The first result shows that marketing innovation is the second-most frequently implemented innovation by small and medium retailers, whereas in other sectors, marketing innovation is the least frequently implemented innovation of the four types of innovation. This result indicates the importance of marketing innovation in the retail sector and is consistent with Bhaskaran (2006) and Rammer et al. (2009), who note that small and medium enterprises, especially those in low- and mid-tech industries, may be more willing to engage in marketing innovation, which can be less costly than technological innovation.

The second result shows that the introduction of new marketing methods among small and medium retailers has a positive impact on the propensity to conduct all other types of innovation (product, process and organizational). However, introducing other types of innovation does not have the same impact. All other innovation types positively impact the propensity to introduce marketing innovations, albeit not of all types. We also conclude that product, process and organizational innovations present different determinants and different inter-relations among the different types of innovations.

The last result shows that the introduction of new organizational methods has a positive impact on the propensity of small and medium retailers to conduct all types of marketing innovation (design, pricing, promotion and placement). However, the introduction of new products or processes only has a positive impact on the propensity to conduct design innovations. Thus, we conclude that the determinants of marketing innovation differ among the four types of marketing innovation in the retail sector.

In conclusion, it is important to highlight that the included types of innovation (marketing, organizational, process and products), as well as the various types of marketing innovation (design, pricing, promotion and placement), have different determinants, and the relationships among the different types of innovations vary. These results confirm the findings of Rammer et al. (2009), Mothe and Nguyen-Thi (2012), Mothe and Thi (2010) and Geldes and Felzensztein (2013). There is a need for further study of individual firms and their inter-relations across different economic and territorial sectors (Crossan & Apaydin, 2010).

These results can help managers and public administrators to undertake actions that promote innovation. According to Medrano and Olarte-Pascual (2016), the tendency to engage in marketing innovation depends on the activity of an enterprise, and the differences between the manufacturing sector and the service sector are significant. Furthermore, Bhaskaran (2006) and Rammer et al. (2009) note that small and medium enterprises, especially those in low- and mid-tech industries, might be more willing to engage in marketing innovation, which might be less costly than technological innovation. Hence, marketing innovation becomes more important for small and medium retailers.

This paper cannot be concluded without noting the limitations of the study. The first limitation stems from the use of a pre-prepared database (PITEC). It was not possible to work with all the suitable variables or to measure the "marketing innovation" variable in a more appropriate manner. Additionally, the models presented in this paper exhibit acceptable overall significance of the parameters and high percentages of correct predictions. The adjustments of the pseudo-R^2 models were between 34.6% and 62.3%. These adjustments were expected because most of our variables are qualitative.

These limitations open up various paths for further research. First, it would be interesting to analyze a longer time span using panel data, as Guisado González and Coca Pérez (2015) recommend. In addition, this study could be extended by breaking down the "market" variable more precisely. The "other countries" variable in this paper covers a very wide range of countries with vastly different cultures and thus it would be interesting to look more deeply into this aspect. Finally, research into the concept of "marketing innovation" remains interesting because it is not clear what companies mean by "marketing innovation". To this end, it might be a good idea to develop an ad hoc measuring system that would allow us to understand occurrences in marketing more fully through the possibilities offered by new technologies with a multitude of new systems for customer relations.

References

Armbruster, H., Bikfalvi, A., Kinkel, S., & Lay, G. (2008). Organizational innovation: The challenge of measuring non-technical innovation in large-scale surveys. *Technovation*, 28(10), 644-657. doi:10.1016/j.technovation.2008.03.003

Becheikh, N., Landry, R., & Amara, N. (2006). Lessons from innovation empirical studies in the manufacturing sector: A systematic review of the literature from 1993–2003. *Technovation*, 26(5), 644-664.

Bhaskaran, S. (2006). Incremental innovation and business performance: Small and medium-size food enterprises in a concentrated industry environment. *Journal of Small Business Management*, 44(1), 64-80. doi:10.1111/j.1540-627X.2006.00154.x

Brown, J. S. (2002). Research that reinvents the corporation. *Harvard Business Review*, 80(8), 105-114.

Brown, J. S., & Duguid, P. (1991). Organizational learning and communities-of-practice: Toward a unified view of working, learning, and innovation. *Organization Science*, 2(1), 40-57. doi:10.1287/orsc.2.1.40

Camisón, C., & Villar-López, A. (2014). Organizational innovation as an enabler of technological innovation capabilities and firm performance. *Journal of Business Research*, 67(1), 2891-2902. doi:10.1016/j.jbusres.2012.06.004

Chen, Y. (2006). Marketing innovation. *Journal of Economics and Management Strategy*, 15(1), 101-123. doi:10.1111/j.1530-9134.2006.00093.x

Cooke, P. (2005). Regionally asymmetric knowledge capabilities and open innovation. Exploring 'Globalisation 2' - A new model of industry organization. *Research Policy*, 34(8), 1128-1149. doi:10.1016/j.respol.2004.12.005

Crossan, M. M., & Apaydin, M. (2010). A multi-dimensional framework of organizational innovation: A systematic review of the literature. *Journal of Management Studies*, 47(6), 1154-1191. doi:10.1111/j.1467-6486.2009.00880.x

Djellal, F., & Gallouj, F. (1999). Services and the search for relevant innovation indicators: A review of national and international surveys. *Science and Public Policy*, 26(4), 218-232. doi:10.3152/147154399781782400

Francis, D., & Bessant, J. (2005). Targeting innovation and implications for capability development. *Technovation*, 25(3), 171-183. doi:10.1016/j.technovation.2004.03.004

Garcia, R., & Calantone, R. (2002). A critical look at technological innovation typology and innovativeness terminology: A literature review. *Journal of Product Innovation Management*, 19(2), 110-132. doi:10.1111/1540-5885.1920110

Geldes, C., & Felzensztein, C. (2013). Marketing innovations in the agribusiness sector. *Academia Revista Latinoamericana de Administración*, 26(1), 108-138. doi:10.1108/ARLA-05-2013-0042

Grewal, R., & Tansuhaj, P. (2001). Building organizational capabilities for managing economic crisis: The role of market orientation and strategic flexibility. *Journal of Marketing*, 65(2), 67-80. doi:10.1509/jmkg.65.2.67.18259

Guisado González, M., & Coca Pérez, J. L. (2015). Complementarity between different types of innovation: An oasis in the middle of the desert. *Esic Market* 152, 46(3), 9-56.

Gunday, G., Ulusoy, G., Kilic, K., & Alpkan, L. (2011). Effects of innovation types on firm performance. *International Journal of Production Economics*, 133(2), 662-676. doi:10.1016/j.ijpe.2011.05.014

Hair, J. F., Black, W. C., Babin, B. J., Anderson, R. E., & Tatham, R. L. (2006). *Multivariate data analysis* (6th ed.). Upper Saddle River, NJ: Pearson Prentice-Hall.

Halpern, N. (2010). Marketing innovation: Sources, capabilities and consequences at airports in Europe's peripheral areas. *Journal of Air Transport Management*, 16(2), 52-58. doi:10.1016/j.jairtraman.2009.10.002

Kijek, A., Lisowski, M., & Starzyńska, W. (2013). Innovation Activity of the Polish Manufacturing Enterprises. *International Advances in Economic Research*, 19(1), 33-43. doi:10.1007/s11294-012-9387-7

Kijek, T. (2013). An empirical analysis of the relationship between technological and marketing innovations : A Case of Polish manufacturing firms. *Acta Scientiarum Polonorum. Oeconomia*, 12(2), 15-25.

Kishore, R., & McLean, E. R. (2002). The next generation enterprise: A CIO perspective on the vision, its impacts, and implementation challenges. *Information Systems Frontiers*, 4(1), 121-138. doi:10.1023/A:1015303109679

Lewis, M. J., & Wackowski, O. (2006). Dealing with an innovative industry: A look at flavored cigarettes promoted by mainstream brands. *American Journal of Public Health*, 96(2), 244-251. doi:10.2105/AJPH.2004.061200

Medrano, N., & Olarte-Pascual, C. (2016). The effects of the crisis on marketing innovation: An application for Spain. *Journal of Business & Industrial Marketing*, 31(3), 404–417. doi:10.1108/JBIM-02-2013-0048

Medrano, N., Olarte-Pascual, C., Pelegrín-Borondo, J., & Sierra-Murillo, Y. (2016). Consumer behavior in shopping streets: The importance of the salesperson's professional personal attention. *Frontiers in Psychology*, 7. doi:10.3389/fpsyg.2016.00125

Moreira, J., Silva, M. J., Simões, J., & Sousa, G. (2012). Drivers of marketing innovation in portuguese firms. *Amfiteatru Economics*, 14(31), 195-206.

Mothe, C., & Nguyen Thi, T. U. (2012). Non-technological and technological innovations: Do services differ from manufacturing? An empirical analysis of Luxembourg firms. *International Journal of Technology Management*, 57(4), 227-244. doi:10.1504/IJTM.2012.045544

Mothe, C., & Nguyen Thi, T. U. (2010). The link between non-technological innovations and technological innovation. *European Journal of Innovation Management*, 13(3), 313-332. doi:10.1108/14601061011060148

Naidoo, V. (2010). Firm survival through a crisis: The influence of market orientation, marketing innovation and business strategy. *Industrial Marketing Management*, 39(8), 1311-1320. doi:10.1016/j.indmarman.2010.02.005

O'Brien, R. M. (2007). A caution regarding rules of thumb for variance inflation factors. *Quality and Quantity*, 41(5), 673-690. doi:10.1007/s11135-006-9018-6

O'Dwyer, M., Gilmore, A., & Carson, D. (2009a). Innovative marketing in SMEs. *European Journal of Marketing*, 43(1-2), 46-61. doi:10.1108/03090560910923238

O'Dwyer, M., Gilmore, A., & Carson, D. (2009b). Innovative marketing in SMEs: A theoretical framework. *European Business Review*, 21(6), 504-515. doi:10.1108/09555340910998805

OECD/Eurostat. (2005). Oslo Manual: Guidelines for collecting and interpreting innovation data (3rd ed.). Paris: OECD Publishing. Available from http://www.oecd-ilibrary.org/science-and-technology/oslo-manual_9789264013100-en Oke, A. (2007). Innovation types and innovation management practices in service companies. *International Journal of Operations & Production Management*, 27(6), 564-587. doi:10.1108/01443570710750268

Porter, M. E. (1998). Clusters and the new economics of competition. Harvard Business Review, 76(6), 77-90. Rammer, C., Czarnitzki, D., & Spielkamp, A. (2009). Innovation success of non-R&D-performers: Substituting technology by management in SMEs. *Small Business Economics*, 33(1), 35-58. doi:10.1007/s11187-009-9185-7

Rowley, J., Baregheh, A., & Sambrook, S. (2011). Towards an innovation-type mapping tool. *Management Decision*, 49(1), 73-86. doi:10.1108/00251741111094446

Schubert, T. (2010). Marketing and organisational innovations in entrepreneurial innovation processes and their relation to market structure and firm characteristics. *Review of Industrial Organization*, 36(2), 189-212. doi:10.1007/s11151-010-9243-y

Schumpeter, J. A. (2012). *The theory of economic development. An inquiry into profits, capital, credit, interest, and the business cycle* (16th ed.). New Brunswick, NJ: Transaction Publishers.

Shergill, G. S., & Nargundkar, R. (2005). Market orientation, marketing innovation as performance drivers. *Journal of Global Marketing*, 19(1), 27-47. doi:10.1300/J042v19n01_03

Soltani, S., Azadi, H., Hosseini, S. J. F., Witlox, F., & Passel, Van Passel, S. (2015). Marketing innovation in rural small food industries in Iran. *Journal of Food Products Marketing*, 21(5), 533-551. doi:10.1080/10454446.2015.1041196

Tether, B., Miles, I., Blind, K., Hipp, C., de Liso, N., & Cainelli, G. (2002). *Innovation in the service sector: Analysis of data collected under the Community Innovation Survey* (CIS-2). Manchester, UK: The University of Manchester & UMIST.

Walker, R. M. (2004). *Innovation and organisational performance: Evidence and a research agenda* (Research Paper No. 002). Advanced Institute of Management. doi:10.2139/ssrn.1306909

Walker, R. M. (2008). An empirical evaluation of innovation types and organizational and environmental characteristics: Towards a configuration framework. *Journal of Public Administration Research and Theory*, 18(4), 591-615. doi:10.1093/jopart/mum026

Wang, S. (2015). *What motivates marketing innovation and whether marketing innovation varies across industry sectors* (Postdoctoral thesis, Telfer School of Management, University of Ottawa). Retrieved from https://www.ruor.uottawa.ca/bitstream/10393/33008/1/Wang_Shu_2015_Thesis.pdf

Acknowledgements

This work was funded by the Cátedra de Comercio of Universidad de La Rioja.

9

Regional Innovation Development as a Feature of Competitiveness in the XXI Century

Irina S. Zinovyeva[1], Yuri A. Kozenko[2], Kirill B. Gerasimov[3], Yulia I. Dubova[4], Margarita S. Irizepova[2]

ABSTRACT The authors of this paper hypothesize that one of the most significant features of regional competitiveness in the global economy is innovation development and that through innovation application, underdeveloped regions can reduce the gap between them and leading regions and can in turn surpass leading regions. The purpose of the article is to verify this hypothesis, to determine the role and significance of innovation development in the provision of regional competitiveness and to identify ways to increase the competitiveness of underdeveloped regions through innovation application. The methodological basis of the research is comprised of a specially developed proprietary methodology for the evaluation of regional competitiveness and a modified factor analysis methodology for the determination of factors of regional economic growth using the "economic miracle" case for various regions. Through this study, the authors validate the proposed hypothesis and conclude that innovation development critically shapes regional competitiveness by determining the quality of economic growth. The proposed model for increasing regional competitiveness on the basis of innovation development presents new opportunities to increase the competitiveness of underdeveloped regions through innovation application.

KEY WORDS: innovation development, regional economies, competitiveness

---

[1] Voronezh State University of Forestry and Technologies named after G.F. Morozov, Russia; [2] Volgograd State University, Russia; [3] Samara National Research University, Russia; [4] Volgograd State Technical University, Russia

Introduction

In the XXI century, competition has risen to a whole new level. Currently, not only specific enterprises but also entire countries compete with one another. They compete for access to resources – human, material, and capital – for sales markets of manufactured products, for investments into the development of regional businesses, etc. This competition is global in nature, and thus, neighboring countries presenting similar peculiarities form regions that are subjects of global competition and that act on behalf of all countries that form them.

The most competitive regions become leaders in the global economy. They form coalitions and initiate strong relations with investors, further strengthening their competitiveness. These regions develop dynamically and boast strong quality of life

Correspondence concerning this article should be addressed to:
Kirill B. Gerasimov, Samara National Research University; 34 Moscow HWY, Samara, 443086, Russian Federation.
E-mail: 270580@bk.ru

standards, and this in turn attracts highly qualified specialists from the entire world and leads to the accumulation of significant intellectual capital in these regions.

Meanwhile, regions that are less competitive struggle to become suppliers of raw materials and centers for the sale of products to leading regions. Presented no opportunities for development, underdeveloped regions stagnate and lose their competitiveness. As a result of low living standards, the most qualified specialists who offer the most intellectual capital form migration flows and gradually leave these regions (Popkova, Yurev, Stepicheva, & Denisov, 2015).

Despite the obvious advantages of leadership in the global economy, the most competitive regions are not interested in having other regions lag behind, as high levels of differentiation in regional economic development lead to the growth of global tensions, crisis phenomena, violations of economic ties, uncontrolled migration from underdeveloped to developed regions, etc.

This is why not only underdeveloped regions but also leading regions are interested in aligning levels of economic development across regions. This will require increasing the competitiveness of underdeveloped regions. This article presents the scientific hypothesis that one of the most significant factors affecting regional competitiveness in the global economy is innovation development and that through innovation application, underdeveloped regions can close the existing gap and surpass leading regions. The purpose of this article is to verify the presented hypothesis, to determine the role and meaning of innovation development for regional competitiveness and to identify ways to increase to competitiveness of underdeveloped regions through innovation application.

Literature review

The theoretical basis of the present study lies in the works of modern scientists focused on regional economies. An analysis of previous studies published in this discipline shows that several works have been published on regional development, including studies by (Li, Cheng, & Wu, 2016; Malikov, Sharipova, Kharisov, Sunaeva, & Mukhametova, 2015; Zarubin, Tkhakushinov, Kuizheva, Nekrasova, & Ovsyannikova, 2015; Zinovyeva, 2015). A regional economy is the economic system of a specific region within a national economy (Meléndez, Borges-Mendez, Visser, & Rosofsky, 2015). The study of regional economic development is necessary for the successful planning of territorial economic organization (Solodilova, Malikov, & Grishin, 2015). Under current economic conditions, regions can be independent subjects acting in national and international markets (Tsathlanova, Idzhilova, & Erdnieva, 2015).

Scientific studies have focused on principles and facets of global competition. Such works include (Cerna & Chou, 2014; Choi, 2013; Demedts, 2015; Docquier & Machado, 2016; (Hartmann, 2014; Kim & Urpelainen, 2015; Miyagiwa & Sato, 2014; Sung, 2015). Through the internationalization of economic relations, global competition has evolved over recent decades (Demedts, 2015) as enterprises, regions, and countries have struggled to access resources and sales markets of manufactured products at the international scale (Hartmann, 2014). Such global competition is rooted in limited resources and sales markets (Miyagiwa & Sato, 2014). As new members become involved in international trade, global competition continues to grow.

An important collection of these studies focuses on regional competitiveness in the global economy. Such works include (Guerrero, Urbano, & Fayolle, 2014; Huggins, Izushi, Prokop, Thompson, 2014; Kamalova & Polovkina, 2014; Komarova, Zjablova, & Denmukhametov, 2014; Ženka, Novotný, & Csank, 2014) The competitiveness of a region in the global economy is determined based on its capacities to provide high living standards (Gallyamova, 2014), to attract investment resources (, and to effectively use the economic potential of the region for the manufacturing of goods and services (Kirshin & Kuzminov, 2014).

Issues of regional innovation development have recently been studied in the following works: (Kropelnytska & Vusyatytska, 2015; Makkonen & Inkinen, 2015; Ng, Kanagasundram, Wong, & Chandran, 2015; Sadyrtdinov, Korablev, & Vladimirova, 2015; Salamonsen, 2015; Schwerdtner, Siebert, Busse, & Freisinger, 2015; Yakovleva, Azarova, & Titova, 2015). Regional innovation development is the most important condition for regional global competitiveness (Za-

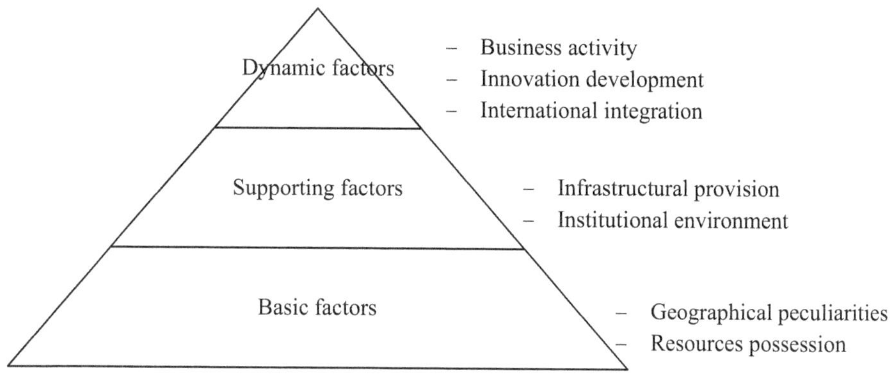

Figure 1. Pyramid of factors of regional competitiveness

rubin & Tkhakushinov, 2014). Regional innovation development involves the development of process, organizational, or technological innovations (Vaz, de Noronha Vaz, Galindo, & Nijkamp, 2014) and their application in production activities of the enterprises of a region for the generation of innovation products (Baimbetova, 2013).

However, despite the numerous studies conducted in the sphere of regional development, most are fragmented and focus on specific features of regional competitiveness. There is currently no scientific proof of the existence of a causal relationship between various factors and levels of regional competitiveness. There is also no theoretical or methodological basis for increased regional competitiveness, creating the necessity to conduct further research in this area. This paper addresses these gaps.

Method

The following scientific methods are applied: induction, deduction, analysis, synthesis, and formalization. The methodological basis of the present study is also related to special methods of scientific research used in the sphere of economic theory.

In particular, this work uses a specially developed proprietary methodology for the evaluation of regional competitiveness. The international productive specialization of a region determines its targeted markets and competitiveness factors as follows (Fisher, Perekrestova, & Lomakina, Irizepova, 2014):

- natural, climatic, geographic, and ecological features of a region;
- the possession of resources (natural resources – cheap and available raw materials, human resources – cheap or high-quality human resources, capital resources – accessibility of financial sources, i.e., credit and investment, resources);
- regional business activities;
- development of infrastructural provisions of business activities and correspondence to international norms and standards;
- quality and development of regional institutional environments;
- levels of international integration and regional cooperation, which determines levels of involvement in global economic processes occurring in the global economy; and
- levels of regional innovation development.

Table 1. Methods of evaluation of regional competitiveness

Factors of regional competitiveness	Indicators of regional competitiveness		Indicator weights
	Model region	This region	
		Basic factors	
Geographical peculiarities	1.00	GP	0.3
Resources possession	1.00	RP	0.7
Index of base (IB)	1.00	IB=(GP*0.3+RP*0.7)/2	-
		Supporting factors	
Infrastructural provision	1.00	IP	0.5
Institutional environment	1.00	IE	0.5
Support index (SI)	1.00	SI=(IP*0.5+IE*0.5)/2	-
		Dynamic factors	
Business activity	1.00	BA	0.3
Innovation development	1.00	ID	0.5
International integration	1.00	II	0.2
Index of dynamics (ID)	1.00	ID=(BA*0,3+ID**0.5+II*0.2)/3	-
Integral indicator of regional competitiveness (CI)	1.00	CI=(BA+IP+ID)/3	-

The stated features of regional competitiveness can be grouped in the following way:

- basic factors: geographic peculiarities and resources;
- supporting factors: infrastructural provisions and institutional environments; and
- dynamic factors: business activities, innovation development, and international integration.

This grouping of factors is determined by regional management opportunities. Factors form a pyramid composed of basic factors that form initial peculiarities of a given region. In the middle of the pyramid, there are supporting factors that create a basis for regional development. The top of the pyramid includes dynamic factors that are the most active and flexible (Fig. 1).

According to the given classification, factors are added to the table. The method for evaluating regional competitiveness involves comparing indicators of regional competitiveness on given factors with values of the modeled region. Consolidated indices are calculated as groups of factors (basis, support and dynamics indexes) based on the arithmetic average of the product of weighted factor values.

As a result, the integral indicator of regional competitiveness is calculated as the arithmetical average of all indices (Table 1). The retrieved integral indicator of regional competitiveness is compared to the value for the modeled region and constitutes a certain percentage of this value, allowing one to identify differences between regions.

The methodology is advantageous in its universality for determining the competitiveness of various regions, for comparing retrieved values, for conducting simple calculations, and for the quick receipt of evaluation results. The methodology is slightly limited

Table 2. Summary of regional competitiveness factors

Factors of regional competitiveness	Place as to region	Duration of influence	Power of influence	Manageability of influence	Type of caused effect
		Basic factors			
Geographical peculiarities	internal	long-term	low	uncontrolled	simple effect
Resources possession	Internal	long-term	medium	poorly controlled	multiplication effect
		Supporting factors			
Infrastructural provision	internal	mid-term	high	highly controlled	multiplication effect
Institutional environment	internal	mid-term	high	highly controlled	multiplication effect
		Dynamic factors			
Business activities	internal	short-term	medium	poorly controlled	simple effect
Innovation development	internal	short-term	high	moderately controlled	synergetic effect
International integration	internal/external	short-term	low	moderately controlled	multiplication effect

in its use of expert evaluations for assigning values to indicators, ascribing a certain degree of subjectivity to the final results.

The method also involves using a modified factor analysis approach for determining factors of regional economic growth based on the "economic miracle" case for various regions. Based on expert evaluations, the values of regional competitiveness factors in provisioning "economic miracle" conditions for each region are determined and assigned values of 1 (the smallest contribution) to 10 (the largest contribution).

Results

Factors of regional competitiveness differ on various attributes: by region, the duration of effects, the power of effects, the manageability of effects, and types of effects creating peculiarities (Table 2). Table 2 shows that all factors relate to each region, and only the factor of international integration is partially external, as it concerns the involvement of international representatives. Effects (determining the speed of effect changes) last over the long term for basic factors, over the medium term for supporting factors and over the short term for dynamic factors.

The influence of geographic factors is the least significant, while the influence of institutional, infrastructural, and innovation factors is the most significant. Resource and business factors are poorly controlled, while geographical factors are uncontrolled. Innovation development and international integration are of average manageability, and infrastructural and institutional factors are highly manageable.

Geographic and business factors have simple effects, meaning that their effects do not extend beyond the limits of this sphere of the economy. Resource, infrastructural, institutional, and integra-

Table 3. Summary of factors of "economic miracle" of various regions

Factors of regional competitiveness	Japanese miracle	Chinese miracle	Italian miracle
	Basic factors		
Geographic peculiarities	1	1	3
Resources possession	2	2	1
	Supporting factors		
Infrastructural provision	3	4	3
Institutional environment	4	3	4
	Dynamic factors		
Business activities	4	3	4
Innovation development	5	5	5
International integration	4	4	3

Note: Adapted from (Testa, 2015; Tillack, 2015; Yang & Zhao, 2015)

tion factors have multiple effects, meaning that their effects are felt in other spheres of the economy. Only innovation factors have synergetic effects, meaning that they can qualitatively influence the entire economic system of a given region, highlighting their importance.

Let us conduct a factor analysis of "economic miracle" conditions for various regions using the cases of Japan, China, and Italy (Table 3). From the results of our factor analysis, it is possible to conclude that the factor contributing most to the economic growth of various regions is innovation development. This was determined by assigning weights to various indicators while evaluating regional competitiveness.

The Japanese economic miracle involved a historical phenomenon of record growth in the Japanese economy that began in the mid-1950s and that lasted until the oil crisis of 1973. Annual economic growth during this economic miracle period amounted to almost 10%, and rates were the highest among the most developed countries of the period. The "miracle" was spurred by low taxes and by the intensive scientific development of new technologies in Japan, which did not reach Japan before World War II due to isolation policies imposed by authorities.

The Chinese economic miracle involved a period of economic reform in China lasting from 1978-1997, when the gross domestic product of the country grew 5.7-fold and 9.6% annually. GDP grew at a record speed every 7.5 years. The Italian economic miracle involved a period of rapid domestic economic growth occurring from the mid-1950s to the mid-1970s. During this period, the economy of the country evolved from agrarian to industrial and into one of the most heavily industrialized economies in the world, rendering the country a global leader. This economic growth was rooted in the widespread modernization of production.

This proves that innovation development is one of the most important features of regional competitiveness. Therefore, increasing the competitiveness of underdeveloped regions requires innovation application. Let us conduct an evaluation of the competitiveness of the Eastern European, Asian, and African regions using the proposed methodology (Table 4).

Table 4 shows that the Eastern European region keeps pace with the North American region on basic indicators but is less strong with respect to supporting and dynamic factors. The integral indicator of the competitiveness of the Eastern European region is

Table 4. The results of the competitiveness evaluation

Factors of regional competitiveness	Indicators of regional competitiveness			
	North American region ("model")	East European region	Asian region	African region
	Basic factors			
Geographical peculiarities	1.00	1.00	0.40	0.30
Resources possession	1.00	1.00	0.60	0.50
Base index (BI)	1.00	1.00	0.27	0.22
	Supporting factors			
Infrastructural provision	1.00	0.30	0.60	0.20
Institutional environment	1.00	0.30	0.40	0.10
Index of support (IS)	1.00	0.30	0.50	0.15
	Dynamic factors			
Business activity	1.00	0.50	0.50	0.10
Innovation development	1.00	0.40	0.60	0.10
International integration	1.00	0.90	0.70	0.80
Index of dynamics (ID)	1.00	0.18	0.20	0.08
Integral indicator of regional competitiveness (CI)	1.00	0.49	0.32	0.15

valued at 0.49. Rather, its competitiveness value is half that of the global leader

The Asian and African regions are substantially weaker than the North American region on all factors. Integral competitiveness indicators of 0.32 and 0.15, respectively, were found. That is, the global leader's competitiveness is three times stronger that of the Asian region and seven times stronger than that of the African region. The following factors hinder innovation development in underdeveloped regions most:

- limited scientific and educational development;
- underdeveloped patent systems and complex innovation copyright registration systems;
- limited connections between science and business;
- lacking investment resources for the implementation of innovational projects;
- weak state support for enterprise innovation activities; and
- high-risk components of innovation projects due to the unpredictability of economic conditions.

The following are presented as ways to address such problems and to create conditions for innovation development in underdeveloped regions:

- develop innovation business infrastructure;
- create strong institutional bases for the creation and application of innovations in processes of production;
- increase the investment attractiveness of given regions;
- encourage state facilitation of enterprise innovation activities; and
- forge strong relations between scientific and business sectors.

As a way to direct underdeveloped regions onto innovative paths of development, this research proposes

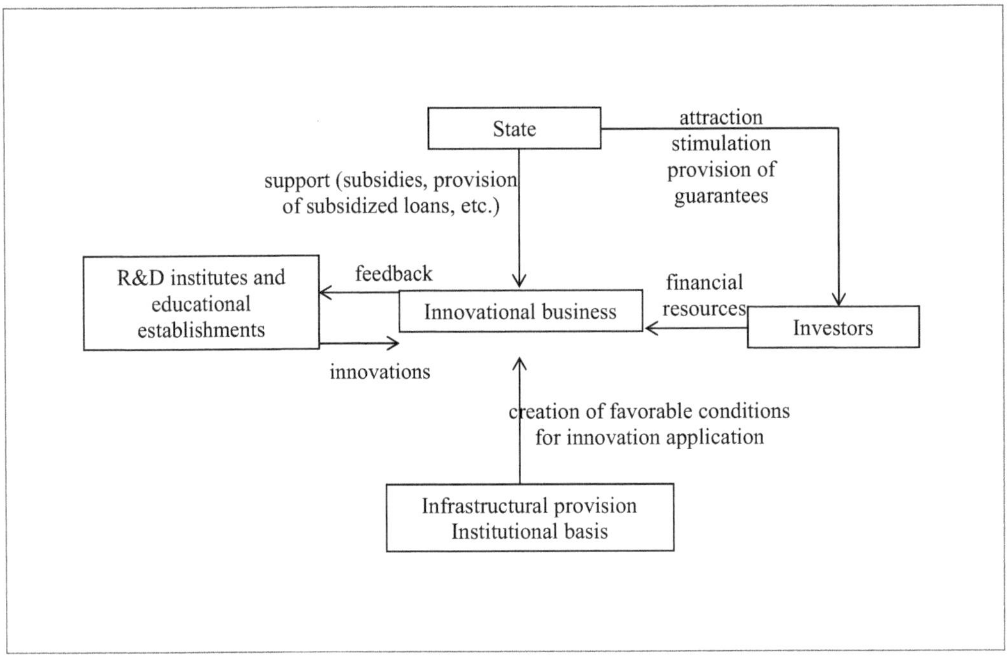

Figure 2. Model of increasing regional competitiveness on the basis of innovation development

using the developed model to boost regional competitiveness via innovation development, in turn allowing for the application of our recommendations (Fig. 2).

Fig. 2 shows that the majority of the increase in regional competitiveness on the basis of innovation development is attributable to innovation entrepreneurship, which is actively supported by states and investors, closely related to R&D institutes and educational establishments, and offers necessary infrastructural provisions and strong institutional bases from which to create favorable conditions for innovation application.

Conclusion

Through the present study, the proposed hypothesis was proven. It was determined that one of the most significant factors shaping regional competitiveness in the global economy is its degree of innovation development and that through innovation application, underdeveloped regions can reduce the gap with and even surpass leading regions, as proven through the experiences of countries experiencing "economic miracles."

It is thus possible to conclude that innovation development occupies an important place in the provision of regional competitiveness, as it determines the quality of economic growth. The proposed model for increasing regional competitiveness on the basis of innovation development broadens opportunities to increase the competitiveness of underdeveloped regions through innovation application.

It should be noted that when applying the proposed model, it is necessary to pay special attention to the management of risks related primarily to the realization of innovational projects; to long periods of investment returns; to the unpredictability of results; and to opposition to business, societal, and state innovations, which are manifestations of inclinations towards traditions and toward the preservation of stability.

Despite the universality of the proposed methodology in evaluating regional competitiveness and its representation in quantitative form, the method is limited by subjectivities that reduce the precision of research results generated. Future research conducted in this area should thus involve the development of fully objective methodologies for the evaluation of regional competitiveness on the basis of specific statistical indicators.

It should be noted that under conditions of global regional competition, constant development is needed to preserve positioning in global markets. While global leaders are presented with ample opportunities for innovation application and creation, this does not mean that other regions cannot improve their positioning in the global economy. Innovations are key to reducing the gap between developed and developing countries and to balancing the global economy.

References

Baimbetova, A. A. (2013). Innovations as a major factor in the socio-economic development of Kazakhstan in the global competition. *World Applied Sciences Journal, 27*, 24-27.

Cerna, L., Chou, M. H. (2014). The regional dimension in the global competition for talent: Lessons from framing the European Scientific Visa and Blue Card. *Journal of European Public Policy, 21*(1), 76-95.

Choi, Y. J. (2013). The Global Financial Crisis Revisited: Competition and Regulation. *Global Economic Review, 42*(4), 362-381.

Demedts, V. (2015). Which future for competition in the global trade system: Competition chapters in FTAs. *Journal of World Trade, 49*(3), 407-436.

Docquier, F., & Machado, J. (2016). Global competition for attracting talents and the world economy. *World Economy, 39*(4), 530-542.

Fisher O. V., Perekrestova L. V., & Lomakina T. P. Irizepova, M. S. (2014). Оценка эффективности налогового стимулирования инновационной деятельности в России [Evaluation of effectiveness of tax stimulation of innovational activities in Russia]. Налоги *и* налогообложение *[Taxes and taxation], 2*(103), 156-173.

Gallyamova, D. (2014). Cluster policy as a tool of regional economics competitiveness improvement. *Economic Annals-XXI, 3-4*(1), 12-15.

Guerrero, M., Urbano, D., & Fayolle, A. (2016). Entrepreneurial activity and regional competitiveness: evidence from European entrepreneurial universities. *The Journal of Technology Transfer, 41*(1), 105-131.

Hartmann, E. (2014). The fetish of global competition. *Capital and Class, 38*(1), 184-196.

Huggins, R., Izushi, H., Prokop, D., & Thompson, P. (2014). Regionalna konkurentnost, gospodarski rast i faze razvoja [Regional competitiveness, Economic growth and stages of development]. *Zbornik Radova Ekonomskog Fakultet au Rijeci, 32*(2), 255-283.

Kamalova, A. A., & Polovkina, E. A. (2014). Regional aspect of value added use in assessing competitiveness of economic districts. *Mediterranean Journal of Social Sciences, 5*(24), 24-27

Kim, S. E., & Urpelainen, J. (2015). Rising regional powers meet the global leader: A strategic analysis of influence competition. *International Political Science Review, 36*(2), 214-234.

Kirshin, I. A., & Kuzminov, S. V. (2014). Evaluation method development for regional economies competitiveness. *Mediterranean Journal of Social Sciences, 5*(18), 159-164.

Komarova, V. N., Zjablova, O. V., & Denmukhametov, R. R. (2014). An infrastructure factor in regional competitiveness. *Mediterranean Journal of Social Sciences, 2*(1), 355-360.

Kropelnytska, S., Vusyatytska, M. (2015). Institutional and financial support for regional innovation development based on cluster approach. *Economic Annals-XXI, 3-4*(2), 37-40.

Li, Z., Cheng, J., & Wu, Q. (2016). Analyzing regional economic development patterns in a fast developing province of China through geographically weighted principal component analysis. *Letters in Spatial and Resource Sciences, 9*(3), 233-245.

Makkonen, T., Inkinen, T. (2015). Geographical and temporal variation of regional development and innovation in Finland. *Fennia, 193*(1), 134-147.

Malikov, R. I., Sharipova, I. M., Kharisov, V. I., Sunaeva, G. G., & Mukhametova, D. D. (2015). Development of assessment tools for economic activity of regional business. *Mediterranean Journal of Social Sciences, 6*(5), 434-444.

Meléndez, E., Borges-Mendez, R., Visser, M. A., & Rosofsky, A. (2015). The restructured landscape of economic development: Challenges and opportunities for regional workforce development collaborations. *Economic Development Quarterly, 29*(2), 150-166.

Miyagiwa, K., Sato, Y. (2014). Free entry and regulatory competition in a global economy. *Journal of Public Economics, 118*, 1-14.

Ng, B. K., Kanagasundram, T., Wong, C. Y., Chandran, V. G. R. (2015). Innovation for inclusive development in Southeast Asia: The roles of regional coordination mechanisms. *Pacific Review, 29*(4), 573-602.

Popkova, E. G., Yurev, V., Stepicheva, O., Denisov, N. (2015). Transformation and concentration of intellectual capital as a factor of economic growth in the modern economy. *Regional and Sectoral Economic Studies, 15*(1), 53-60.

Sadyrtdinov, R. R., Korablev, M. M., Vladimirova, S. A. (2015). Regional innovation system development: Comparative analysis of the Republic of Tatarstan and Volga Federal District Regions. *Mediterranean Journal of Social Sciences, 6*(1), 317-321.

Salamonsen, K. (2015). The effects of exogenous shocks on the development of regional innovation systems. *European Planning Studies, 23*(9), 1770-1795.

Schwerdtner, W., Siebert, R., Busse, M., & Freisinger, U. B. (2015). Regional open innovation roadmapping: A new framework for innovation-based regional development. *Sustainability, 7*(3), 2301-2321.

Solodilova, N. Z., Malikov, R. I., & Grishin, K. Y. (2015). Potential for development and limitations of regional business environment. *Economy of Region, 42*(2), 137-148.

Sung, T. K. (2015). The creative economy in global competition. *Technological Forecasting and Social Change, 96*, 89-91.

Testa, C. (2015). La nuova Italia del Miracolo Economico: 'Un disco per l'estate' mezzo secolo fa [The new Italy of economic miracle: "A drive for summer" half a century ago]. *Forum Italicum, 49*(2), 674-676.

Tillack, P. (2015). Concrete abstractions: Gotô meisei's hapless danchi dwellers and Japan's economic miracle. *Positions, 23*(2), 231-257.

Tsathlanova, T. T., Idzhilova, D. V., & Erdnieva, E. V. (2015). The problem-oriented analysis of regional cluster policy development in the Russian Federation. *Mediterranean Journal of Social Sciences, 6*(4), 333-339.

Vaz, E., de Noronha Vaz, T., Galindo, P.V., & Nijkamp, P. (2014). Modelling innovation support systems for regional development - analysis of cluster structures in innovation in Portugal. *Entrepreneurship and Regional Development, 26*(1-2), 23-46.

Yakovleva, E. A., Azarova, N. A., Titova, E. V. (2015). Innovation as a vector of regional economic development and a necessary condition for the progress of the world economy. *Asian Social Science, 11*(20), 90-96.

Yang, H., Zhao, D. (2015). Performance legitimacy, state autonomy and China's economic miracle. *Journal of Contemporary China, 24*(91), 64-82.

Zarubin, V. I., Tkhakushinov, E. K. (2014). Management of innovation development system of regional economic: Project approach. *World Applied Sciences Journal, 30*(2), 191-194.

Zarubin, V. I., Tkhakushinov, E. K., Kuizheva, S. K., Nekrasova, S. O., & Ovsyannikova, T. A. (2015). Conceptual specific of project management of regional economy development. *Asian Social Science, 11*(14), 306-313.

Ženka, J., Novotný, J., & Csank, P. (2014). Regional competitiveness in Central European Countries: In search of a useful conceptual framework. *European Planning Studies, 22*(1), 164-183.

Zinovyeva, A. A. (2015). The development of regional management by smoothing of spatial polarization. *Asian Social Science, 11*(11), 253-258.

10

Time-Varying Linkages of Economic Activities in China and the Stock Markets in ASEAN-5

Kee Tuan Teng[1], Siew Hwa Yen[2], Soo Y. Chua[2], Hooi Hooi Lean[2]

ABSTRACT

This study attempts to investigate the evolution of dynamic linkages and volatility spillover between the five countries of the Association of Southeast Asian Nations (ASEAN-5) stock markets and China's economic activities. By using the movements and structural breaks of the time-varying correlation and Granger causality test, a suitable destination for equity portfolio diversification can be determined among the studied markets. This study covers monthly data from January 1991 to March 2015. The DCC-MGARCH model shows that the studied countries are time-varying correlated, while the structural break observed by Bai and Perron test coincided with major economic shocks, policy changes and the establishment of regional trade policies. The VAR model Granger causality test observed no volatility spillover from Chinese economic activities to the ASEAN-5 stock markets, except for Malaysia and the Philippines. However, the ASEAN-5 stock markets' volatility exerts a significant influence on China's economy, except for Singapore's stock market volatility. This study reveals that ASEAN-5 has gradually became the preferred destination for diversifying equity portfolios for investors in China.

KEY WORDS: ASEAN, China, financial integration, volatility spillover

[1]Tunku Abdul Rahman University College, Malaysia; [2]Universiti Sains Malaysia, Malaysia

1 Introduction

Over the past two decades, China has played a growing and significant role in global trade. By 2011, China became either the largest or second-largest trading partner to 78 countries, which accounted for almost 55 per cent of the global GDP. These countries include all major global economies — the EU, the U.S., the Association of Southeast Asian Nations (ASEAN), Japan and India.[1]

Correspondence concerning this article should be addressed to: **Hooi Hooi Lean,** Universiti Sains Malaysia - Economics Program. School of Social Sciences Universiti Sains Malaysia USM Penang 11800, Malaysia E-mail: hooilean@usm.my

Although China claimed to be immune from crises in Asia, particularly the Asian Financial crisis, the late 2007 financial crisis that originated in the U.S. has an apparent impact on the future prospects of Asian economies, including China. The Chinese GDP growth rate plunged from 14.2% in 2007 to 9.6% in 2008, and it has not experienced a double-digit growth rate since then. This condition has a varying impact on various industries and its trading partners as a reduction in investments and infrastructure spending causes downward pressure for China's demand. This has been a major concern for ASEAN-5 investors; the impact of China's economic slowdown could be felt around the world.[2] It is also important to note that China has experienced miraculous economic growth without any recessions since the last trough in December 1989.[3] As an emerging economy, investors may also speculate about the possibility that volatility in the ASEAN-5 stock markets could be transmitted to China's economy.

As such, it is appropriate for us to look at the dynamic cross-country volatility transmission across ASEAN-5 stock markets with China's economic movements. This study examines the time-varying cross-country correlation movements between the ASEAN-5 stock markets and the economic activities in China using the Dynamic Conditional Correlation Multivariate GARCH (DCC-MGARCH) model (Engle, 2002). We identify the structural breaks dates in the time-paths of the dynamic conditional correlation using the Bai and Perron (2003) multiple structural break test. This procedure could detect sudden changes in the nature of the cross-market co-movement. This study also explores the possibility of stock portfolio diversification among the studied markets using the Granger causality, which is based on the vector autoregression (VAR) model, to capture the direction of the time-varying volatility transmission. One should note that cross-country linkages are gaining importance to investors and policy makers. It would be insightful to assess the changing direction of the volatility spillover among the relevant countries with the rise of China in the global economic context.

This paper contributes to the existing literature by addressing the chicken-and-egg paradox that existed in the relationship between stock market volatility and economic movement volatility. This study also attempts to fill the gap in investigating the interaction between emerging economies caused by the ASEAN-5 stock market performance and Chinese economic growth in a time-varying manner and provides some noteworthy insights into the aspect of the volatility spillover direction across stock markets and economic activity movements in a multi-country context. We hope that our findings may shed some light on international asset diversification and management in ASEAN-5 and China, serving as a constructive guide to investors in determining the appropriate portfolio channel for equity market diversification.

The remainder of this study is structured as follows: Section 2 examines the portfolio diversification literature, and Section 3 presents the methodology and describes the data. The results are reported in Section 4, and the last section concludes the study.

2 Literature Review

Studies in the international diversification of assets have generated interest among academics and investors in ASEAN-5 because the ASEAN-5 stock markets are becoming more financially integrated over time (Candelon, Piplack, & Straetmans, 2008; Lim, 2009; Majid et al., 2009; Plummer & Click, 2005). It is vital to understand the concept of portfolio management prior to the discussion on the allocation of assets in international markets.

The modern portfolio theory was proposed by Markowitz (1952). According to this theory, risk-averse investors optimize the return on their investments by diversifying the portfolio of assets with negative correlations. This means that low and negative correlations among assets will offer gains in diversification (Hassan & Naka, 1996; Laopodis, 2005). High correlations, high volatility spillover and highly synchronized movements among the stock markets implied limited opportunity for risk diversification among the correlated and synchronized assets (Bekaert & Harvey, 1997). However, the rise in correlation among financial markets does not necessarily increase volatility in the domestic market (Bekaert & Harvey, 1997). It may be concluded that a high level of market integration reduces the possibility of risk sharing in the asset portfolio among these markets.

One should note that market integration shows a dynamic trend and changes over time (Gupta and Donleavy, 2009). The level of interdependency between countries changes gradually over time with trade and financial liberalization, the formation and implementation of regional trade arrangements, and information technology breakthroughs (Guillaumin, 2009; Harvey, 2000; Hooy & Goh, 2010; Laopodis, 2005). Aside from this, a regime change in the financial market of an emerging economy is prone to stimulation by the rise of market integration between countries (Bekaert & Harvey, 2002).

The diversification of assets is, in fact, a risk management method that intends to minimize the risk of the selected portfolio while maximizing the return of the portfolio (Vo & Daly, 2005). This can be done by combining a broad selection of investments with different levels of risk within a portfolio. To optimize portfolio investment, investors are advised to invest in various markets, in different industries, and in different regional blocks because the risk exposure tends to vary regionally. This implies that investors should aim to diversify in markets with low correlation. Even if the correlation rises over time and the value of the correlation is still relatively small over time, it is still possible to gain risk-adjusted returns by diversifying in that market (Bekaert, Harvey, & Lumsdaine, 2002; Forbes & Rigobon, 2002; Gupta and Donleavy, 2009).

Investors can benefit by diversifying their portfolio of assets internationally over time, but Kasa (1992) highlighted that previous studies may generate spurious conclusions based on the benefits gained from international diversification if researchers refer solely to the correlation. According to Kasa (1992), countries that share a common stochastic movement will increase their overall portfolio risk by diversifying into equities among these markets. Hence, financial markets that share a common stochastic trend are said to be cointegrated or financially integrated, which implies that the benefits of international diversification are limited in the long run (Laopodis, 2005). Nevertheless, a rational investor should not totally rule out cointegrated assets from the choices when diversifying his portfolio because there is still space for short-run gains in these cointegrated markets (Marashdeh, 2006; Masih & Masih, 1999; Syriopoulos, 2011). Benefits gained in the short run by international investors are possible by taking advantage of arbitrage mispricing that occurs in financial markets because the law of one price does not hold in the short run (Marashdeh, 2006; Syriopoulos, 2011). This point is especially practical when cointegration occurred among countries with low correlation (Phengpis & Swanson, 2006).

The existence of a low correlation between cointegrated economies potentially limits the benefits of assets portfolio diversification between these markets in the long run, but the opportunity for gains in the short run still exists (Bekaert & Harvey, 1997). If the two integrated financial markets are less correlated during a financial crisis, the collapse of the stock market in the first country will not cause the stock market in another country to collapse, as well. Hence, the portfolio diversification by the first country into the other country will help minimize the total losses during a financial crisis in the first country.

Several methods have been used to assess the potential gains in international portfolio diversification, namely, the bivariate and multivariate correlation in a GARCH framework, the cointegration analysis, VAR, VECM, Granger causality and cycle synchronization based on the stock market turning points (Guillaumin, 2009; Huang, Yang, & Hu, 2000; Pagan and Harding, 2002; Sohel Azad, 2009; Syriopoulos, 2011; Vo & Daly, 2005). These procedures can be used to assess the possibility of international portfolio diversification for the long and short horizon. It is hypothesized that if two stock markets are cointegrated, the gains from diversifying in these two markets are limited in the long horizon (Candelon et al., 2008; Sohel Azad, 2009). However, the possibility for risk sharing among these markets in the short horizon still exists. The short horizon portfolio diversification can be assessed through the VECM and Granger causality (Gilmore & McManus, 2002).

3 Data and Methodology

Data Description

The sample period in this study ranges from January 1991 to March 2015. The economic activity index for China is shown by China's industrial production index (CH). The stock markets indices for the ASEAN-5 are the Jakarta Stock Exchange composite stock price index (JSE), the Kuala Lumpur Stock Exchange composite price index (KLCI), the Philippines Stock Exchange composite price index (PSE), the Straits Times Stock Exchange index of Singapore (SSI) and the Bangkok Stock Exchange price index (THSE).[4] As a standard procedure, the order of integration for the indices is determined using the augmented Dickey–Fuller (ADF) unit root test. The results confirmed that all series are I(1).[5] Hence, all indices are expressed as the natural logarithm at first difference, which studies the return of the series or the growth rate of the index.[6]

A set of diagnostic procedures is conducted on the return series to ensure that the correct residuals are obtained from the series before further testing on the DCC-MGARCH model. These tests are to confirm the suitability of using the GARCH model on the return series. Table 1 shows that the mean growth rate of

Table 1. Descriptive Statistics (January 1991-March 2015)

	CH	JSE	KLCI	PSE	SSI	THSE
Mean (%)	-0.02%	0.87%	0.45%	0.86%	0.45%	0.30%
Std. Dev. (%)	3.63%	7.43%	6.42%	7.28%	5.36%	8.25%
Skewness	-0.4713	-1.0388	0.1899	0.3531	-0.0937	-0.2187
Excess Kurtosis	9.4996***	3.2744***	4.8376***	5.5854***	2.6660***	2.0196***
Jarque-Bera	1104.963***	182.3368***	285.4978***	384.3072***	86.60244***	51.77549***
Q(12)	111.955***	37.3921***	66.4097***	3.9402 (1)**	26.4219***	13.3635
ARCH, Q2(12)	91.3329***	76.2439***	270.257***	8.44705 (2)*	59.3143***	126.425***
ADF (Level)	-0.3871(3)	2.6211(1)	0.6335(2)	2.6120(0)	0.9663(0)	0.3284(0)
ADF (1st dif)	-16.35623(2)***	-7.3230(2)***	-9.3173(1)***	-16.0728(0)***	-14.7203(0)***	-16.5551(0)***

Notes: Lag length is given in parentheses. ***, **, * indicate significance at 1%, 5% and 10%, respectively. For the ADF test, MAXLAG = 14,
Automatic is based on SIC.

China's industrial production index was negative but almost close to zero for China. The standard deviation for economic activity in China was below 5.5 percent, which implies that the risk of economic turbulence was low in China, indicating a stable economy over time. China's industrial production index displayed negative skewness and positive excess kurtosis, which indicates a leptokurtic distribution.

The ASEAN-5 stock markets' average market return and risk are shown by the mean and standard deviations of the monthly return series, respectively. The ASEAN-5 stock markets have higher volatility with moderate returns compared to economic movements in China. This implies that ASEAN-5 stock markets could have high inherent risk. Most stock returns in this study show negative skewness except for Malaysia and the Philippines. This suggests a high probability of positive returns in Malaysian and Philippines' stock market investment. All ASEAN-5 stock market returns had a leptokurtic distribution, which implies that the stock markets may generate either very large or very small future returns. This is shown by the positive excess kurtosis implicating high volatility in these stock markets' investments.

The Jarque-Bera test statistics strongly reject the hypothesis of normality, which implies that all return series are not normally distributed. The Engle (1982) ARCH test rejects the null hypothesis of no ARCH effects for all stock return series. The results justified the choice of the GARCH model. The autocorrelation patterns in the return series was examined using the Ljung-Box test. The Q statistics test results are significant at lag 12 for all series except for the stock market index for the Philippines at lag 1. The stock market index for Thailand is insignificant for Q statistics. The first order autocorrelations are low; hence, the first-order autoregressive process, AR(1), needs to be included in the mean equation of the GARCH (1,1) model (Arouri & Nguyen, 2009; Hamilton & Gang, 1996).[7]

3.1 Dynamic Conditional Correlation - Multivariate Generalized Autoregressive Conditional Heteroscedasticity Model

Unlike the previous studies that focus on interactions between stock markets, this paper employs the DCC-MGARCH model to evaluate the volatility and co-volatility dynamics across multiple countries' stock markets and Chinese economic activities. One of the key advantages of this model is the number of parameters generated in the dynamic structures of the conditional correlation, and the covariance matrices reduced as the model dimensions increased. This overcomes the main weaknesses of other MGARCH models (Engle, 2000). Hence, this multivariate model is superior to other methods and produces the most accurate estimators (Engle, 2000).

The DCC-MGARCH model is used in this study to evaluate changes in economic interdependency as it can capture the degree of volatility correlation changes between two countries in a time-varying manner. The extent of market integration is indicated by the time-varying conditional correlation (dynamic conditional correlation), whereas its trend can be gauged by the patterns of conditional correlation movements. Markets are said to become more integrated when conditional correlations increase over time (Yu, Fung, & Tam, 2010). Conditional correlations can also infer whether two economies are decoupling or recoupling over time. For example, two economies are viewed as decoupling when the conditional correlation falls over time. A high conditional correlation between two stock markets can also indicate less opportunity for diversification.

The DCC-MGARCH model (Engle, 2002) generates the volatility correlation between two markets either directly through its conditional variance or indirectly through its conditional covariances. The conditional covariances generated show the time-variant cross-market volatility correlation or the dynamic conditional correlation.

The DCC-MGARCH model is a dynamic model with the time-varying means, variances and covariances of the n return series, $r_{i,t}$ for country i at time t with the equations as follows:

$$r_{i,t} = \mu_{i,t} + \varepsilon_{i,t} \quad \varepsilon_{i,t} \middle| \Psi_{t-1} \sim N(0, H_t) \qquad (3.1)$$

where Ψ_{t-1} is the set of information available at times t-1 that contains at least $\{r_{i,t-1}, r_{i,t-2}, \ldots\}$.

Each individual country's return series follows an autoregressive process (Arouri and Nguyen, 2009; Hamilton and Gang, 1996). The conditional mean equation of the return series for country i is written as $\mu_{i,t} = \lambda_0 + \lambda_1 r_{i,t-1}$, where λ_0 is a constant term, and λ_1 is the coefficient of the lagged return for each market.

The conditional variance-covariance matrix for the DCC-MGARCH model is written as $H_t = D_t R_t D_t$, where H_t is also denoted as the conditional correlation estimator, R_t of the DCC model is a (n x n) time-varying conditional correlation matrix, and the conditional variance must be unity, while D_t is a (n x n) diagonal matrix of time-varying standard deviations of the returns in the mean equation from the univariate GARCH (1, 1) model.[8]

D_t for a multivariate model is expressed as $D_t = diag\left(\sqrt{h_{1,t}}, \ldots, \sqrt{h_{n,t}}\right)$ with $h_{i,t} = \tau_i + \alpha_i \varepsilon^2_{i,t-1} + \beta_i h_{i,t-1}$, where τ_i is a constant term for the conditional variance equation for country i, α_i is the ARCH effect of the return series, while β_i is the GARCH effect of the return series. A positive coefficient of β_i implies volatility clustering and persistence in positive changes in stock market indices. A sum of α_i and β_i that is less than 1 indicates the stationarity of the GARCH model and shows that the volatility shock is time-decaying and mean-reverting (Bollerslev, 1986).[9] The R_t matrix contains the coefficients of the conditional correlation, which is given as $R_t = diag(Q_t)^{-1} Q_t diag(Q_t)^{-1}$, where Q_t is a (n x n) conditional covariance matrix that is a symmetric and positive definite, given by $Q_t = \left(1 - \alpha_{dcc} + \beta_{dcc}\right)\bar{Q} + \alpha_{dcc}\left(\varepsilon_{t-1}\varepsilon'_{t-1}\right) + \beta_{dcc} Q_{t-1}$, where $\bar{Q}$ denotes the unconditional covariances of the standardized errors matrix, which is a (n x n) symmetric positive definite matrix, and $\varepsilon_t = (\varepsilon_{1,t}, \ldots, \varepsilon_{n,t})'$ is the standardized residual terms.[10] If (α_{dcc} + β_{dcc}) < 1, the model is mean reverting, but when (α_{dcc} + β_{dcc}) = 1, the model is said to be integrated.

Engel (2002) suggested the estimation of the time-varying conditional correlations ($q_{ij,t}$) for any two return series included in R_t by the following GARCH (1, 1) process.

$$q_{ij,t} = \bar{\rho}_{ij} + \alpha_{dcc}(\varepsilon_{i,t-1}\varepsilon_{j,t-1} - \bar{\rho}_{ij}) + \beta_{dcc}(q_{ij,t-1} - \bar{\rho}_{ij}) \qquad (3.2)$$

where $\bar{\rho}_{ij}$ is the unconditional correlation between $\varepsilon_{i,t}$ and $\varepsilon_{j,t}$, and $\bar{q}_{ij,t}$ is the mean value of $q_{ij,t}$. The average variance is unity and the conditional correlation estimator is. $\rho_{ij,t} = \frac{q_{ij,t}}{\sqrt{q_{ii,t} q_{jj,t}}}$ Hence, $\rho_{ij,t}$ for the DCC (1, 1) can be rewritten as follows:

$$\rho_{ij,t} = \frac{(1-\alpha_{dcc}-\beta_{dcc})\bar{q}_{ij} + \alpha_{dcc}\varepsilon_{i,t-1}\varepsilon_{j,t-1} + \beta_{dcc} q_{ij,t-1}}{\sqrt{(1-\alpha_{dcc}-\beta_{dcc})\bar{q}_{ii} + \alpha_{dcc}\varepsilon^2_{i,t-1} + \beta_{dcc} q_{ii,t-1})(1-\alpha_{dcc}-\beta_{dcc})\bar{q}_{jj} + \alpha_{dcc}\varepsilon^2_{j,t-1} + \beta_{dcc} q_{jj,t-1})}} \qquad (3.3)$$

The significance of α_{dcc} and β_{dcc} implies that the estimators obtained in the DCC-MGARCH are dynamic and time-varying. α_{dcc} measures the short-run volatility impact, which means that the persistency of the standardized residuals from the previous period. β_{dcc} measures the lingering effect of a shock impact on the conditional correlations, which is the persistence of the conditional correlation process.

In this paper, the conditional correlation between the stock return series of country *i* and the industrial growth rate series of country *j* at time *t* is referred to as $[R_{t,}]_{ij} = \rho_{ij,t}$, where $\rho_{ij,t}$ indicates the direction and strength of the correlation and measures the degree of covariance between two indices in relation to the market's individual variances (Savva, 2009). A positive $\rho_{ij,t}$ implies that the correlation between the return series is rising and moving in the same direction and vice versa.

DCC-MGARCH Log Likelihood Estimation

This study uses the Quasi-maximum likelihood (QML) estimation proposed by Bollerslev and Wooldridge (1992) for the estimation of the DCC-MGARCH model.[11] The log-likelihood of the H_t estimator can be written in the following forms:

$$\mathrm{L} = -\frac{1}{2}\sum_{t=1}^{T}\left(n\log(2\pi)+\log\left|H_t\right|+r_{i,t}^{'}H_t^{-1}r_{i,t}\right) \tag{3.4}$$

The log-likelihood function consists of the volatility component, and correlation component can be expressed as $L\ (\theta,\Phi)=L_v(\theta)+L_c(\theta,\Phi)$, where θ is the parameter for D_t and Φ is the additional parameter in R_t. The volatility component function can be written as

$$L_v(\theta)=-\frac{1}{2}\sum_{t}\left(n\log(2\pi)+\log\left|D_t\right|^2+r_{i,t}^{'}D_t^{-2}r_{i,t}\right), \tag{3.5}$$

while the correlation component is written as

$$L_c(\theta,\Phi)=-\frac{1}{2}\sum_{t}(\log\left|R_t\right|+\varepsilon_t^{'}R_t^{-1}\varepsilon_t-\varepsilon_t^{'}\varepsilon_t) \tag{3.6}$$

Two-Stage Estimation of the DCC-MGARCH Model

The DCC-MGARCH model estimation uses a two-stage procedure. Under acceptable uniformity conditions, the second stage's consistency is dependent on the first stage's consistency. The univariate GARCH (1,1) model for each return series in the multivariate system is estimated in the first stage. Standardized residuals are obtained by maximizing the likelihood, $\hat{\theta}=\arg\max\{L_v(\theta)\}$. The generated standardized residuals from stage 1 are then used to estimate the DCC parameters in stage 2 using the following equation:. $\max_{\Phi}\{L_c(\hat{\theta},\Phi)\}$

3.2 Bai and Perron Multiple Structural Break Test

The BP multiple structural break test is applied to statistically investigate any structural changes that may have occurred in the conditional correlations between the ASEAN-5 stock return volatilities and the growth rate of economic movements in China. The actual economic event that coincided with the observed structural break dates explained the changes in the dynamic linkages between the pairs of countries.

The DCC series generated by the DCC-MGARCH model step 2 is used to detect the structural changes occurring naturally by employing the Bai and Perron (BP) (2003) multiple structural break test. It is not realistic to date only certain economic events and apply it to all pairs of countries in this study because each possible combination pair of countries may then face different economic events, which will impact them either as individual nations or jointly. In view of this, the conventional structural break test, such as the Chow structural break test, is not applicable in this study. The reason is that this test needs to set the structural break dates to test the significance of the events' impacts on the markets linkages. On the other hand, the Gregory and Hansen (1996) cointegration test with structural breaks is not applied in this research because it can only capture one break in the intercept and/or slope coefficient in the cointegrating relationships. The regime switching method is another commonly used approach in dating structural breaks, but it is relatively less powerful than the BP method (Bai & Perron, 2003).

The Bai and Perron (BP) multiple structural break test has been adopted to estimate the number of break dates that happened naturally in the conditional correlations (Arouri & Nguyen, 2009; Nguyen & Bellalah, 2008).[12] It is vital to identify the date of the structural changes in the financial market, which is induced by the advancement in market integration (Bekaert & Harvey, 2002). This study followed the approach of Bekaert et al. (2002), which allows the structural break dates to narrate what is actually happening in the markets.

According to this method, the structural changes occurring naturally in the dynamic conditional correlation series at time t are denoted as $y_t = \eta_j x_t + \varepsilon_t$, where $t = T_{j-1}+1,\ldots,T_j$ ($j = 1,\ldots, m+1$), η_j is the coefficient of the covariate vectors, and x_t. ε_t is the error term at time t. The model is estimated by minimizing the sum of squared residuals (SSR) to find an unknown number of breaks (m) in the model. The estimated break points $(\hat{T}_1,\ldots,\hat{T}_m) = \arg\min_{T_1,\ldots,T_m} S_T(T_1,\ldots,T_m)$ obtain global minimizers for the SSR, where $S_T(T_1,\ldots,T_m)$ denotes the resulting SSR. The null hypothesis of no structural breaks is tested against an alternative hypothesis of an unknown number of breaks with the upper bound of m in the model. Normally, m is set as 5 for empirical studies, which means 5 is the maximum number of breaks allowed in the model. The selection of the optimal number of breaks is based on the minimum value of the Bayesian Information Criterion (BIC).

3.3 Vector Autoregression Model - Granger Causality Tests

The two-step estimation allows this study to utilize the conditional variances generated in step 1 to more accurately reveal the direction of the volatility spillover among the ASEAN-5 stock markets and Chinese economic activities. This strategy differs from previous studies because the estimation is based on the stocks' return to determine the volatility spillover effect.[13] The results of the direction of spillover among the studied countries will aid the ASEAN-5 and investors in China in determining the direction of the investment portfolio.

Causality tests can be used to locate the direction of the volatility transmission and the degree to which one economy's stock market or economic volatility impacts other markets or volatilities (Gupta & Guidi, 2012; Huang et al., 2000; Savva, 2009). Before conducting the Granger Causality test, the stationarity properties and a cointegration relationship among the conditional variances for the countries selected in this study need to be confirmed.[14]

The conditional variance generated by the DCC-MGARCH model from the first stage is used to examine the volatility spillover from one economy to another. Following the standard procedures, the integration properties of the series need to be confirmed prior to conducting the cointegration and causality tests. The unreported unit root test results show that all the conditional variances in the models are I(0).[15] Hence, VAR model is a suitable model for capturing the short-run dynamic adjustment and reveals the direction of causality.

Rejection of the null hypothesis using the Wald χ^2 statistic implies that the excluded variable Granger causes the dependent variable, which means that the history of the excluded variable does help predicting the future values of the dependent variable.

4 Empirical Findings

4.1 Empirical Results of the DCC-MGARCH Model and its Diagnostic Tests

Prior to estimation of the DCC-MGARCH model, the Tse (2000) Lagrange Multiplier (LM) test was employed to confirm the existence of dynamic properties of the conditional correlation series generated by the constant conditional correlation MGARCH model to avoid model misspecification. The Tse (2000) test statistic strongly rejects the null hypothesis of constant correlation against dynamic correlation at the one percent level. This implies the presence of dynamic properties in the correlation series for all pairs of countries selected in this study.[16] Thus, we can proceed with the estimation of the DCC-MGARCH model based on the return series of each market.

4.2 ASEAN-5 Stock Market Volatility and China Industrial Production Volatility

The univariate GARCH parameters, which are estimated from step 1 of the DCC-MGARCH model, are reported in Table 2. The impact of the previous disturbances on the conditional variance denoted by the ARCH coefficient (α) is significant for all selected countries in this study. All GARCH coefficients (β) are highly significant, which implied persistency in the positive changes in the volatility of the stock index except for China. The sum of ($\alpha + \beta$) are all less than one for the ASEAN-5 stock markets as well as for China's economic performance, which indicates the persistence of disturbance over time.

The robust tests for the model standard residual are provided in Table 2. The Ljung-Box test on the standardized residuals (Q) was insignificant for most of the series except for JSE. The squared standardized residual (Q^2) statistic was insignificant for all series.

Table 2. DCC-MGARCH Step 1 Estimation Results for Full Sample (January 1991-March 2015)

	JSE	KLCI	PSE	SSI	THSE	CH
Mean Equation: AR(1) model:						
Constant: λ_0	0.0119***	0.0068***	0.0133***	0.0063*	0.0110***	-0.0012
AR (1): λ_1	0.2012***	0.0920	0.1300	0.1735**	0.0664	-0.2790
Variance Equation: GARCH (1, 1) model:						
Constant: τ_i	0.0005***	0.9421	2.2897	1.4216*	0.0006**	4.1442***
ARCH: α_i	0.1358**	0.2622***	0.1973*	0.1097***	0.3237***	0.7413**
GARCH: β_i	0.7599***	0.7366***	0.7744***	0.8342***	0.5962***	-0.0122
$\alpha_i + \beta_i$	0.9611	0.9988	0.9717	0.9439	0.9200	0.7291
Robust Tests for model standardized residuals:						
Q (1)	3.8589**	1.3578	1.5834	24.9791 (18)	0.0045	1.1068
$Q^2(1)$	0.7241	0.3589	0.4313	0.9115	0.4923	0.0761
Skewness	-0.7509***	0.2983***	0.0120***	-0.1661***	0.1611***	0.4311***
Excess Kurtosis	2.8942***	1.7682***	1.9825***	1.185***	1.4112***	8.0630***
Jarque-Bera	128.9100****	42.2260***	47.6610***	18.3800***	25.4050***	797.2900***

Remarks: Lag length: Automatic is based on SIC, MAXLAG = 14. Lag length is given in parentheses. ***, **, * indicate significance at 1%, 5% and 10%, respectively. UniGARCH for the A5-US model will be used as a comparison reference for all models. Only minor and insignificant differences exist in the results for all models.

The statistically insignificant results of these two tests indicate the absence of serial correlation and ARCH-effects in the conditional means and variances. The results of these two tests justified the employment of the DCC-GARCH specification for the selected countries, thus passing the misspecification tests.

Table 2 also reports the diagnostics of the standardized residuals. The skewness is positive for most stock return indices except for JSE and SSI. CH showed a high excess kurtosis of more than three. Thus, the level of risk for CH is low as the past returns yield a leptokurtic distribution.[17] The JB test for normality strongly rejected the null hypothesis, which means that the indices do not follow a normal distribution. Hence, this suggests that the excess kurtosis in the residuals of the return indices were not fully eliminated by the conditionally normal GARCH process. Consequently, the diagnostics test justified the use of QML procedures in the estimation of the DCC-MGARCH model.

Conditional Volatilities

The monthly volatility of the ASEAN-5 stock markets and the industrial production growth rate for China, as measured by the conditional variances, are depicted in Figure 1. The volatility clustering in 1994 for JSE, KLCI, PSE and THSE can be explained by the aftermath effect of the unification of the exchange rate regime and the abolishment of exchange controls on the current account transactions in China. The volatility of stock returns in ASEAN-5 appeared to be affected most by

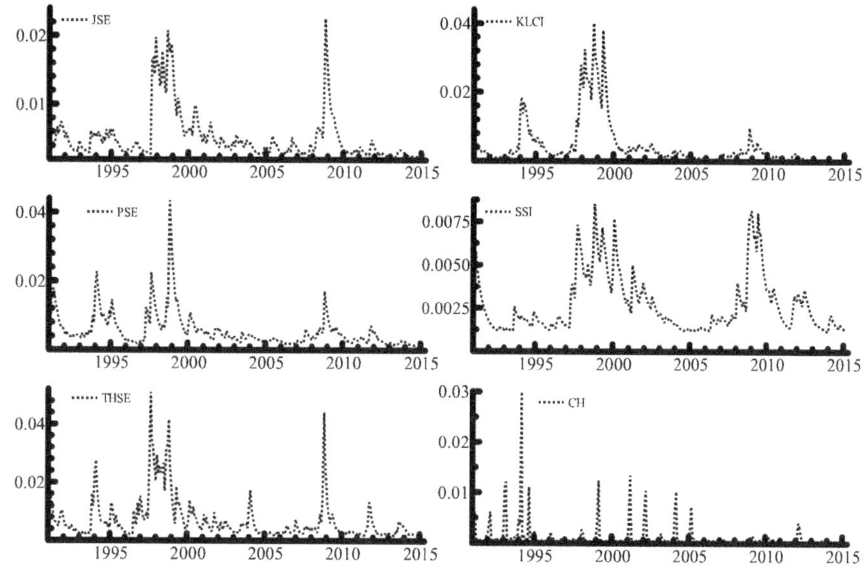

Figure 1. Conditional Variances of Stock Return for ASEAN-5 and Industrial Production Growth Rate for China

the Asian financial crisis from July 1997 until 2000, as shown in Figure 1, while the Chinese economy remained relatively calm and stable with only a sudden spike in 1999. The ASEAN-5 stock market conditional variances displayed a downward trend during the crisis period. However, during the subprime crisis, the ASEAN-5 stock return movements displayed a sudden surge in 2009, except in Malaysia. The stock return volatility in Singapore was more persistent during the occurrence of the subprime crisis compared to other ASEAN-5 stock return volatilities. The most noticeable feature from Figure 1 is the tendency for the volatility to cluster. The figures for the conditional variance for the ASEAN-5 stock returns suggest the existence of ARCH-GARCH effects.

The plot for China's industrial production growth rate was consistently volatile throughout the sample, especially at the beginning of the sample period. The Chinese economy was more volatile and surged to a peak between the late 1990s and 2005. After 2006, the volatility in the industrial production growth rate in China began to stabilize with very small clustering. There is a small surge in early 2012. The graphs in Figure 1 served as indicators of the presence of ARCH-GARCH effects.

4.3 The DCC-MGARCH - Time-Varying Patterns for ASEAN-5 Stock Markets with the Chinese Economic Activities

Table 3 reports the time-varying co-movement between the ASEAN-5 stock markets with the economic movements in China. The DCC-α and DCC-β are significant, which imply that ASEAN-5 stock returns with the industrial production growth rate for China were highly dynamic and time varying. The DCC-β indicates the high persistence in the dynamic conditional correlation of stock returns of ASEAN-5 with China's economic activities. The sum of the DCC-α and DCC-β are less than one, which indicates that the conditional correlations in the models are not constant over time, as reported in Table 3.

Table 3. DCC-MGARCH Step 2 Estimation Results for Full Sample (January 1991-March 2015)

α_{dcc}	β_{dcc}	$\alpha_{dcc} + \beta_{dcc}$
0.0291***	0.8610***	0.8900

Remarks: ***, **, * indicate significance at 1%, 5% and 10%, respectively

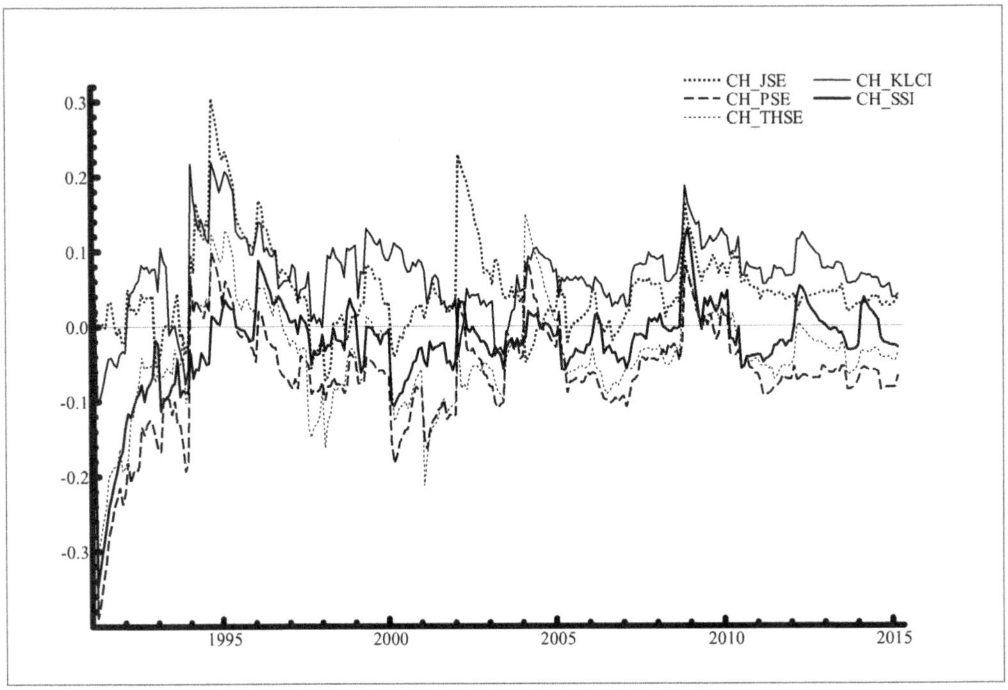

Figure 2. Dynamic Conditional Correlation between Stock Markets in ASEAN-5 and China's Economic Activities

To have a better picture of inter-regional correlation among ASEAN-5 stock markets with economic performance for China, the plots for their time-varying conditional correlations are illustrated in Figure 2. The DCCs were maintained at a level below 0.3 during the study period. At the beginning of the study period until 1994, most of the DCCs remained at a negative level, which implies that the ASEAN-5 stock markets and Chinese economies activities were inversely related. However, the DCC was increasing during pre-1994. However, in the post-1994 period, the DCC remained stable around the magnitude of +/− 0.1 level with a slight downward trend. The trend remained relatively stable between the ASEAN-5 stock markets and Chinese economic activities with a sudden surge and fall. However, after 2009, there was a sudden change in the DCC movement to a sliding trend. Both the ASEAN-5 stock markets and Chinese economies activities move in opposite directions. This implies that if there were any slump in the ASEAN-5 stock markets, Chinese economic activities will continue to grow. On the other hand, even with a downturn in the Chinese economy, the stock markets in ASEAN-5 could still perform well. This reveals that the ASEAN-5 stock markets were suitable destinations for investors in China to diversify their financial portfolio for hedging purposes.

Table 4. Bai and Perron Structural Break Dates for the Conditional Correlations

JSE-CH	KLCI-CH	PSE-CH	SSI-CH	THSE-CH
Jul-94	**Jul-94**	**Jul-94**	**Jul-94**	**Jul-94**
Feb-98		Feb-98	Jan-99	Feb-98
	Feb-01	Jan-02		Jun-03
	Mar-07	Sep-10	Sep-07	

To summarize, from the analysis of the time variant correlation, the estimated conditional correlations between stock markets and economic activities were relatively low with a few peaks and plunges. A weak correlation of below 30% between these two regions shows that they were less integrated. To further confirm the observed movements of DCC in Figure 2, it is necessary to identify the possible structural changes that occurred during that time to determine the actual structural break dates. To achieve this, the BP multiple structural break test was adopted.

4.4 Perspective of Structural Change

The source of structural change that happened in the conditional correlation among ASEAN-5 countries and China in July 1994 may have come from China because China's growth rate series fluctuated between 20% and −20% with a volatility of 3% (see Figure 1), while the return series of the ASEAN-5 stock markets were relatively stable, with volatility below 2.5% for that time period. The detected date could be the aftermath effect of the unification of the exchange rate regime in China and the abolishment of the exchange controls on the current-account transactions that took place in April 1994. The move to full current account convertibility and the realization of the RMB convertibility under the current account was achieved in late 1996 (McKinnon and Schnabl, 2009).18 The success in this area stabilized the real economic growth in China while promoting a bilateral currency exchange between ASEAN and China. This economic event will impact ASEAN-5 and China concurrently.

The break dates on February 1998 and January 1999 for the conditional correlation between the ASEAN-5 stock market with the Chinese economic growth, except KLCI-CH, can be justified by a series of financial reform measures taken by the ASEAN-5 government to revive the economy after the adverse effects of the Asian financial crisis.

The break dates observed on February 2001 and January 2002 for KLCI-CH and PSE-CH may be related to the dot-com bubble, which occurred during the stock market meltdown in 2000-2002. September 2000 is the starting point of the slump, where the internet boom was at its peak and the NASDAQ index was over 5000 points (Yu, 2004). This devastating stock market crash swirled in the impacted economies for approximately two years. The internet bubble in China expanded until the market became overheated during the meltdown of the internet bubble in the U.S. because the spillover of the U.S. internet boom to China was slower than the internet burst in the U.S. (Girardin & Liu, 2007).

The break date between THSE-CH occurred in June 2003 coincided with the signing of the China-Thailand Free Trade Area (FTA) that took effect in October 2003. This agricultural goods agreement is an "early harvest agreement" with the aim to encourage the bilateral agricultural trade and enhance the welfare of the two nations.

The two breaks, in March and September-2007 for KLCI-CH and SSI-CH, could be due to either the direct or indirect impact of the U.S. subprime mortgage crisis, which coincided with the U.S. recession (December 2007- June 2009). A similar result was observed in Lean and Teng (2013). As for the detected date, September 2010 for PSE-CH could correspond with the European sovereign debt crisis, which started at the end of 2009 and intensified beginning in early 2010.

Table 5. VAR Granger Causality Tests for Conditional Variances

Short Run Causality Direction	CH
JSE	J→C***
KLCI	K↔C***
PSE	P ↔C ***
SSI	
THSE	T→C**

Remarks: ***, **, * indicate significance at 1%, 5% and 10%, respectively. Null hypothesis: The excluded variable does not Granger-cause the dependent variable. The best lag selection is automatic based on lag length criteria (AIC). For the full sample, the best lag is 12.

Overall, the BP multiple structural break dates show that some of the breaks corresponded with the events in the countries, and some are related to global or regional events. This indicates that the countries examined experienced not only cross-country spillover effects but also the spillover effect from external shocks that affect both countries' correlation. Hence, it is worthwhile to further analyze the direction of the cross-country spillover effects between the ASEAN-5 stock market volatility and the Chinese economic activity volatility. This is important because the results will show whether the Chinese economic activity volatility influences the ASEAN-5 stock markets or vice versa. The findings will aid investors in deciding their future investment directions for portfolios.

4.5 Volatility Spillover between ASEAN-5 Stock Markets and China's Economic Activities

During the period of study, the Chinese economic activities were Granger-caused by the ASEAN-5 stock markets except for the Singapore stock return volatility. However, the influence of China's economic movements on ASEAN-5 stock markets' volatility was insignificant over the period of study except with regard to Malaysia and the Philippines' stock markets. The findings of this study are consistent with Valadkhani and Chen (2014), who found that the stock volatility of one country or region does influence the economic volatilities in another country or region. Similar conclusions were observed in studies by Schwert (1989; 1990), Hamilton and Gang (1996) and Ibrahim (2010). However, Tiwari et al. (2015) did not observe any bilateral causality between the stock market and economic activity, which contradict the findings of this paper.

Over the short term, fluctuations in Chinese economic activities only impacted Malaysia and the Philippines' stock volatilities. Hence, only Malaysia and the Philippines' stock markets displayed a bilateral causality relationship with Chinese economic activities. This implies that Malaysia and the Philippines' stock markets were more vulnerable to external economic shocks compared to other ASEAN-5 stock markets. This finding supports Tsouma's (2009) conclusion that the growth of the industrial production index influences stock returns in the emerging market.

As a conclusion, Singapore is a preferred destination for investors in China to diversify their asset portfolio and vice versa.

5 Conclusion

The purpose of this study is to explore the dynamic linkages between Chinese economic movement and ASEAN-5 stock markets using the time-variant framework and Granger causality tests. The aim is *to identify the direction of the volatility spillover among the studied markets.* This study also intends to detect the structural break dates observed between the ASEAN-5 stock markets and the Chinese economy, which are related to important facts and economic events. Last, the study attempts to review the equity diversification portfolio destination of China with ASEAN-5. Taken together, this study aims to uncover the possible deepening in the future regional economic integration in Asia.

The dynamic linkages between the ASEAN-5 stock markets with the economic conditions in China show that both regions were still weakly correlated between January 1991 and March 2015. These results imply that stock market movements in ASEAN-5 were not really being affected by the economic conditions in China. Another important finding is that the DCC between ASEAN-5 and China dropped noticeably during the Asian financial crisis, the collapse of the internet bubble and the subprime crisis. The observed dates from the BP multiple structural break test further supports the observation in DCC movements. Most of the observed dates coincided with China's economic reforms, together with the FTAs' conclusion and some major economic crises (1997 Asian financial crisis, collapse of the internet bubble, the subprime crisis and the European sovereign debt crisis). Another observation from this study is that shocks emanating from Chinese economic movements had no influential effects on ASEAN-5 stock markets volatilities except with regard to Malaysia and the Philippines, whereas China's economy was influenced by the volatility of ASEAN-5 stock markets except Singapore.

Overall, this study concluded that the stock volatility of ASEAN-5 with the economic activities in China still remained at a very low level, and diversion among these regions was observed during times of financial turbulence. The results based on the DCC-MGARCH model have confirmed the conjecture that ASEAN-5 had gradually stood out as a preferred destination for the international portfolio diversification for Chinese investors, except for Malaysia and the Philippines. On the other hand, China has become the preferred portfolio diversification area for investors in Singapore to diversify their investment portfolio.

The empirical findings also support the idea that ASEAN-5 governments should implement suitable economic policies and monitor the financial development that has been taking place in China. Combined with prudent portfolio diversification management, this would help minimize volatility in the financial portfolio. Policy makers should also attract the participation of large foreign institutional investors into the ASEAN-5 stock markets, especially those with relatively low correlation with ASEAN-5 stock markets and those that are less volatile or do not coincide with any financial crisis in the ASEAN-5 stock markets such as China. All these suggestions should be favorable in cushioning stock market volatility and improving market discipline in the ASEAN-5 stock markets.

These findings offered important implications for investors, portfolio managers, policymakers, and leaders in ASEAN and China. Hence, it is wise for ASEAN leaders to pursue market-based integration with China rather than an institutional-based integration. It is also not recommended for ASEAN to push forward with economic integration with the Eurozone due to its current debt crisis.

References:

Arouri, M. H., & Nguyen, D. K. (2009). Time-varying characteristics of cross-market linkages with empirical application to Gulf stock markets. *Managerial Finance, 36*(1), 57-70.

Bai, J. & Perron, P. (2003). Computation and analysis of multiple structural change models. *Journal of Applied Econometrics, 18*(1), 1-22.

Bekaert, G. & Harvey, C. R. (1997). Emerging equity market volatility. *Journal of Financial Economics, 43(*1), 29–77.

Bekaert, G. & Harvey, C. R. (2002). Research in emerging markets finance: Looking to the future. *Emerging Markets Review, 3*(4), 429-448.

Bekaert, G., Harvey, C. R., & Lumsdaine, R. L. (2002). Dating the integration of world equity markets. *Journal of Financial Economics, 65*(2), 203-247.

Berben, R. P. & Jansen, W. J. (2005). Comovement in international equity markets: A sectoral view. *Journal of International Money and Finance, 24*(5), 832-857.

Bollerslev, T. & Wooldridge, J. (1992). Quasi-maximum likelihood estimation and inference in dynamic models with time-varying covariances. *Econometric Reviews, 11*(2), 143-172.

Bollerslev, T. (1986). Generalized autoregressive conditional heteroskedasticity. *Journal of Econometrics, 31*(3), 307-327.

Candelon, B., Piplack, J., & Straetmans, S. (2008). On measuring synchronization of bulls and bears: The case of East Asia. *Journal of Banking & Finance, 32*(6), 1022-1035.

Engle, R. F. (1982). Autoregressive conditional heteroskedasticity with estimates of the variance of UK inflation. *Econometrica, 50*(4), 987–1008.

Engle, R. F. (2002). Dynamic conditional correlation - a simple class of multivariate GARCH models. *Journal of Business and Economic Statistics, 20*(3), 339-350.

Forbes, K. J. & Rigobon, R. (2002). No contagion, only interdependence: measuring stock market co-movements. *Journal of Finance, 57*(5), 2223–2261.

Gilmore, C. G., & McManus, G. M. (2002). International portfolio diversification: US and Central European equity markets. *Emerging Markets Review, 3*(1), 69-83.

Girardin, E., & Liu, Z. (2007). The financial integration of China: New evidence on temporally aggregated data for the A-share market. *China Economic Review, 18*(3), 354-371.

Goetzmann, W. N., Li, L., & Geert Rouwenhorst, K. (2001). Long-term global market correlations (Working Paper No. 8612). National Bureau of Economic Research. Retrieved from http://www.nber.org/papers/w8612

Gregory, A. W. & Hansen, B. E. (1996). Tests for cointegration in models with regime and trend shifts. *Oxford Bulletin of Economics and Statistics, 58*(3), 555-560.

Guillaumin, C. (2009). Financial integration in East Asia: evidence from panel unit root and panel cointegration tests. *Journal of Asian Economics, 20*(3), 314-326.

Gupta, R. & Donleavy, G. D. (2009). Benefits of diversifying investments into emerging markets with time-varying correlations: An Australian perspective. *Journal of Multinational Financial Management, 19*(2), 160-177.

Gupta, R., & Guidi, F. (2012). Cointegration relationship and time varying co-movements among Indian and Asian developed stock markets. *International Review of Financial Analysis, 21*, 10-22.

Hamilton, J. D., & Gang, L. (1996). Stock market volatility and the business cycle. *Journal of Applied Econometrics, 11*(5), 573-593.

Harvey, C. R. (2000). Drivers of expected returns in international markets. *Emerging Markets Quarterly, 4*(3), 32-48.

Hassan, M. K. & Naka, A. (1996). Short-run and long-run dynamic linkages among international stock markets. *International Review of Economics & Finance, 5*(4), 387-405.

Hooy, C. W. & Goh, K. L. (2010). Exposure to the world and trading-bloc risks: A multivariate capital asset pricing model, *Research in International Business and Finance, 24*(2), 206-222.

Huang, B. N., Yang, C. W., & Hu, J. W. S. (2000). Causality and cointegration of stock markets among the United States, Japan and the South China Growth Triangle. *International Review of Financial Analysis, 9*(3), 281-297.

Ibrahim, M. H. (2010). An empirical analysis of real activity and stock returns in an emerging market. *Economic Analysis and Policy, 40*(2), 263-271.

Jones, C. P., Walker, M. D., & Wilson, J. W. (2004). Analyzing stock market volatility using extreme day measures. *Journal of Financial Research, 27*(4), 585-601.

Johnson, R. & Soenen, L. (2003). Economic integration and stock market comovement in the Americas. *Journal of Multinational Financial Management, 13*(1), 85-100.

Kasa, K. (1992). Common stochastic trends in international stock markets. *Journal of Monetary Economics, 29*(1), 95-124.

Laopodis, N. T. (2005). Portfolio diversification benefits within Europe: Implications for the US investor. *International Review of Financial Analysis, 14*(4), 455-476.

Lean, H. H., & Teng, K. T. (2013). Integration of world leaders and emerging powers into the Malaysian stock market: A DCC-MGARCH approach. *Economic Modelling, 32*, 333-342.

Lim, L. K. (2009). Convergence and interdependence between ASEAN-5 stock markets. *Mathematics and Computers in Simulation, 79*(9), 2957-2966.

Lucey, B. M., & Muckley, C. (2011). Robust global stock market interdependencies. *International Review of Financial Analysis, 20*(4), 215-224.

Majid, M. S. A., Meera, A. K. M., Omar, M. A., & Aziz, H. A. (2009). Dynamic linkages among ASEAN-5 emerging stock markets. *International Journal of Emerging Markets, 4*(2), 160-184.

Marashdeh, H.A. (2006). Financial integration of the MENA emerging stock markets (Unpublished doctoral dissertation). University of Wollongong, Wollongong, Australia.

Markowitz, H. (1952). Portfolio selection. *The Journal of Finance, 7*(1), 77-91.

Masih, A. M. M., & Masih, R. (1999). Are Asian stock market fluctuations due mainly to intra-regional contagion effects? Evidence based on Asian emerging stock markets. *Pacific-Basin Finance Journal, 7*(3-4), 251-282.

McKinnon, R. & Schnabl, G. (2009). China's financial conundrum and global imbalances (Working Paper No. 277). Bank for International Settlements. Retrieved from http://www.bis.org/publ/work277.pdf

National Bureau of Statistics of China (2012, February 22). Statistical Communiqué on the 2011 National Economic and Social Development. Retrieved from http://www.stats.gov.cn/english/NewsEvents/201202/t20120222_26575.html

Nguyen, D. K. & Bellalah, M. (2008). Stock market liberalization, structural breaks and dynamic changes in emerging market volatility. *Review of Accounting and Finance, 7*(4), 396-411.

Pagan, A. R. & Harding, D. (2002). Dissecting the cycle: a methodological investigation. *Journal of Monetary Economics,* 49(2), 365-381.

Phengpis, C. & Swanson, P. E. (2006). Portfolio diversification effects of trading blocs: The Case of NAFTA. *Journal of Multinational Financial Management, 16*(3), 315-331.

Plummer, M. G. & Click, R. W. (2005). Bond market development and integration in ASEAN. *International Journal of Finance & Economics, 10*(2), 133-142.

Savva, C. (2009). International stock markets interactions and conditional correlations. *Journal of International Financial Markets, Institutions & Money, 19*(4), 645-661.

Schwert, G. W. (1989). Business cycles, financial crises, and stock volatility. *Carnegie-Rochester Conference Series on Public Policy, 31*(1), 83-125.

Schwert, G. W. (1990). Stock returns and real activity: A century of evidence. *Journal of Finance, 45*(4), 1237-1257.

Sohel Azad, A. S. M. (2009). Efficiency, cointegration and contagion in equity markets: Evidence from China, Japan and South Korea. *Asian Economic Journal, 23*(1), 93-118.

Syriopoulos, T. (2011). Financial integration and portfolio investments to emerging Balkan equity markets. *Journal of Multinational Financial Management, 21*(1), 40-54.

Teräsvirta, T. (2006). An introduction to univariate GARCH models (Working Paper No. 646). Stockholm School of Economics. Department of Economic Statistics.

Tiwari, A. K., Mutascu, M. I., Albulescu, C. T., & Kyophilavong, P. (2015). Frequency domain causality analysis of stock market and economic activity in India. *International Review of Economics & Finance, 39*, 224-238.

Tse, Y. K. (2000). A test for constant correlations in a multivariate GARCH model. *Journal of Econometrics, 98*(1), 107-127.

Tsouma, E., 2009. Stock returns and economic activity in mature and emerging markets. *The Quarterly Review of Economics and Finance, 49*(2), 668-685.

Valadkhani, A., & Chen, G. S. (2014). An empirical analysis of the US stock market and output growth volatility spillover effects on three Anglo-Saxon countries. *International Review of Applied Economics, 28*(3) 323-335

Vo, V. X., & Daly, K. J. (2005). European equity markets integration - implications for US investors. *Research in International Business and Finance, 19*(1), 155-170.

Yu, I. W., Fung, K. P., & Tam, C. S. (2010). Assessing financial market integration in Asia - Equity markets. *Journal of Banking & Finance, 34*(12), 2874-2885.

Yu, T. S. (2004). Can East Asia rise again. In C. Wiemer & H. Cao (Eds.), *Asian economic cooperation in the new Millennium: China's economic presence* (Vol. 1, pp. 197-211). Singapore: World Scientific Publishing.

Endnotes

1 *National Bureau of Statistics of China (2012, February 22)*

2 *ASEAN-5 consists of five nations: Indonesia, Malaysia, Singapore, Thailand and the Philippines.*

3 *Detailed sourced from Economic Cycle Research Institute, available at http://www.businesscycle.com/ecri-business-cycles/international-business-cycle-dates-chronologies*

4 *All indices are extracted from DataStream. The indices are denominated in local currency to avoid the impact of the exchange rate volatility on the stock market linkages. The intention of this study is to analyse the stock market linkages that happened naturally among countries without being affected by the fluctuation of exchange rates (Berben & Jansen, 2005; Goetzmann, Li, & Geert Rouwenhorst, 2001; Johnson & Soenen, 2003; Lucey & Muckley, 2011; Plummer & Click, 2005). All indices are seasonally adjusted using the Census X-12 filter. Four multivariate models are formed to discuss the interdependency between the ASEAN-5 stock markets and Chinese economic condition.*

5 *The results are available upon request.*

6 *The growth rate of the IPI is used to measure the relative degree of fluctuation in economic activities.*

7 *Most studies typically assume that the errors of the return series either follow an AR(1) or the first order moving average, MA(1) process. The results are available upon request.*

8 *Rt of the DCC model is different from the CCC model as Rt of the CCC model is time-invariant.*

9 *The time-decaying and mean-reverting GARCH model means that the conditional variance does not persist over time but slowly moves toward the long-run mean level at the rate recommended by the sum of* α_i *and* β_i.

10 *Positive covariance implies that the tested variables are strongly linked and move in the same direction and vice versa.*

11 *QML is maximum likelihood with a robust variance-covariance estimator.*

12 *The conditional correlation is generated from the DCC-MGARCH model discussed in the previous section.*

13 *It is not advisable to model the return series as independent and identically distributed over time because the return series are actually interdependent with the increase of data frequencies (Teräsvirta, 2006). This makes volatility a better measure for stock market risk compared to stock market returns and the standard deviation of stock returns (Jones, Walker, & Wilson, 2004)*

14 *The Granger causality test is performed using EVIEWS 7.*

15 *The results are available upon request.*

16 *ASEAN-5 and the reference country are tested as a group of six countries.*

17 *Investors who wish to avoid large, erratic swings in portfolio returns may wish to structure their investments to produce a leptokurtic distribution.*

18 *By December 1, 1996, China had formally fulfilled the International Monetary Fund's Article 8 from the Agreement on International Currencies and Funds on current account convertibility.*

11

Fiscal Austerity Versus Growth in Croatia

Marinko Škare[1], Romina Prziklas Druzeta[1]

ABSTRACT

The role of fiscal austerity has been questioned for centuries, but a rapidly increasing deficit along with the financial crisis in 2007/2008 influenced a renewed debate on the economics of austerity. This paper analyzes the role of austerity versus the role of economic growth. It also attempts to highlight the role of the theoretical context of austerity policy and the economic history lesson learned during the transition from the Bretton Woods model to Washington's consensus.

Despite numerous studies and polarized debate, no consensus on the implementation of fiscal austerity has been achieved because this complex subject has not been the subject of a sufficient methodological exploration. Emphasis should be placed on defining the methodology of austerity and gathering statistical data to influence the implementation of social transfer policies. In addition, it is necessary not only to take a hybrid approach to fiscal and monetary policy but also to adopt economic laws and quantitative economic relationships. The benchmarking country used in this paper is Croatia. The outcome of this research can serve as the basis for future decision-making and research.

KEY WORDS: fiscal austerity; economic growth; business cycles; macroeconomic adjustments

[1] Juraj Dobrila University of Pula - Faculty of economics and Tourism "Dr. Mijo Mirkovic", Croatia

Introduction

The concept of "fiscal austerity" and its adjustment has attracted considerable attention in recent years. This focus on fiscal austerity is of particular importance, especially in transitional countries affected by declining GDP, decreasing wages and social protections, increasing inequality, balance-of-payments difficulties, and a sharply declining aggregate demand. The EU's authority over new Member States includes the authority to monitor national fiscal policies to impose new rules. Governments expected to avoid creating deficits and to reduce their public debt to a "sustainable level". National governments' primary economic goals—to achieve long-term prosperity and to maintain employment that contributes to long-term economic growth—were sacrificed to achieve a balanced budget and to reduce the national debt. Different countries have followed are different paths to austerity. Although international debates usually focus on issue affecting the PIGS countries (Portugal, Ireland, Greece, Spain), the UK, Germany and major economies such as the USA, Japan, and France (which enjoy a higher fiscal capacity, exercise political sovereignty and use a world currency), this paper's benchmark country is Croatia. This paper analyzes the role of austerity versus the role of economic growth. It also attempts to highlight the role of the theoretical context of austerity policy and the economic history lesson learned during the transi-

Correspondence concerning this article should be addressed to: **Marinko Škare** Juraj Dobrila University of Pula - Faculty of economics and Tourism "Dr. Mijo Mirkovic" Preradoviceva 1/1 Pula Istarska zupanija 52100 Croatia.
E-mail: mskare@unipu.hr

tion from the from Bretton Woods model to Washington's consensus. Despite numerous studies responding to the issues of whether governments should adopt austerity despite their weak economies and whether balanced budgets can ensure sustainable economic growth, because these complex issues have not been the subjects of a sufficient methodological exploration, there is no consensus—only a polarized debate.

The dramatically negative experiences of the PIIGS countries' European debt crisis and the vulnerability of the Croatian economy indicate the need for a methodological investigation to determine whether there are other forms of adjustment that focus on employment growth and prosperity. To achieve the moderate scenario of a "Goldilocks economy", it is necessary to build an optimal model of economic growth and to forecast that model based on knowledge of economic rules and quantitative economic relationships. In this way, crises and economic cycles can be foreseen and managed. Thus, just as in Keynes's proposal that depending on the period of an economy's business cycle, the implementation of austerity should be emphasized (Keynes, 1936). In addition, it is necessary to require a hybrid approach to fiscal and monetary policy. To ensure sustainable growth in light of the budget deficit, it is of the utmost importance to implement appropriate redistributive policies based on the macroeconomic indicators that reflect societies' well being. In the 21st-century context in which human relationships are becoming increasingly complex, scholars and scientists must reconsider the position of human beings in the contexts of new technologies, science, global economics, social relations and future prospects. Consequently, a multidisciplinary approach is always required (Sharma, 2013). The outcome of this research could affect transitional countries' immediate decision-making related to the implementation of social policies. It could also serve as the basis for further research. Its implications, limitations and directions for further research are offered. This paper is structured into four sections. Section I analyzes the theoretical context of austerity policy and the lessons of economic history. Section II provides background research. Section III analyzes austerity versus growth using the example of Croatia. Section IV presents concluding remarks and policy recommendations.

The theoretical framework of austerity policy versus economic growth

The phenomenon of austerity economics has been the subject of scientific research for centuries. According to Konzelman (2012), no general agreement has emerged from the polarized debate about the economics of austerity about what austerity is, when it should be applied or in whose interest it is presumed to operate. Austerity measures therefore include some combination of public expenditure reductions and increased taxes. The aim of economic austerity is to reduce a country's deficit—i.e., the difference the government's revenues and expenses. The economics of reaffirming austerity and the economics of the deficit-financing problem were greatly influenced by the emergence of the Industrial Revolution in the mid-18th and 19th centuries, WWI (1914-1918), WWII (1939-1945) and the global financial crisis of 2007-2008. Early debates on austerity economics focused on the role of facilitating the financing of national emergencies, such as wars and national defense. With capitalism's evolution, the debate has shifted toward the state's expectations and the use of public debt. More specifically, the turbulent economic events of the 1970s produced a change in economic theory and policy. The transition from the Bretton Woods model to the Washington consensus, along with the incorporation of monetarism into government policy, imposed radical changes and prompted the adoption of new rules. Although the Washington consensus was primarily designed as a development model for Latin American countries and did not deliver the expected results—inequality of both income and wealth distribution increased along with poverty, economic and financial crises—subsequently it was applied as the development model for the post-communist transition economies of Central and Eastern Europe that were confronted by with structural problems associated with de-industrialization, slow economic growth, declining productivity and the like during the transition process. A new economic turn has occurred under the influence of several factors.

The 1973 oil crisis and drastic increase in oil prices caused worldwide inflation, lower production and decreased employment decline). Furthermore, Bretton Woods collapsed; the era of fixed exchange rates ended after 1971, when United States President Richard Nixon suspended the full convertibility of the American dollar into gold at a fixed parity established by Bretton Woods; an imbalance of payments emerged, increasing concerns about "overheating" of the economy when accounting for inflation in exchange for full employment; and there was a crisis of capital accumulation and a very low level of profit in the real economy. With the advent of stagflation, stagnated help from Western countries, a strong inflow of private capital, and the growth of deficits, Keynes's interventionist theory that saved the American economy from collapse during the Great Depression of 1929-1933 through a policy of full employment, economic growth, stabilization of the international environment, and the welfare state began to evaporate. With the end of the "golden years" of 1950-1969, national economies' dynamism and efficiency did not come to life for more than 20 years. In the late 1970s, advocates of neoliberalism entered the world stage, including University of Chicago economists (led by Milton Friedman), the conservative government of Margaret Thatcher and the Republican administration of President Ronald Reagan. With the appearance of neoliberal policy and "market fundamentalism" to increase profits, measures were established to reduce workers' real wages and social rights, market deregulation begin. That deregulation included the liberalization and privatization of economic enterprises and even of the public sphere (railroads, electricity, water supplies, education, health, etc.), a reduction of public consumption (particularly in health, educational and social institutions), a reduction on taxes on capital and assets, and in increase of the consumption tax, which ultimately shifted the tax burden from capital to citizens and thus increased inequality and poverty.

Actual growth factors stimulated by multinational corporations have contributed to the erosion of the role of nation states, which through a lack of internal dynamics neglected their own technological capabilities and industrialization (Sharma, 2002).

South Korea and the "East Asian Tigers" have demonstrated a level of self-sufficiency with minimal reliance on commercial loans and have invested in education and their own technology: thanks to the efficiency of their governments, they have successfully achieved growth. By abandoning protectionism and interventionism (although it is important to note that developed countries have retained protectionist measures to succeed in industrializing and developing their national economies), the impact of global institutions has dramatically strengthened. Those institutions include the "troika" of the European Union (EU), the European Central Bank, and the International Monetary Fund, which have worked to develop countries through structural adjustment programs. The fate of national economies has become significantly dependent on decisions made at the centers of financial power and in various international organizations. Ensuring economic and social stability required the state to play a more active role, but neoliberalism advocated a free market in which the state budget would play a reduced role in redistribution of income and so on. Opposing the power of transnational corporations was difficult with weakened trade unions and workers suffering from a degraded status. As the 80s brought new obligations to neoliberal politics, debts increased and under the "curtain" of stabilization, a shift in the policy's focus been justified by not only aggregate demand for economies with productive capacity but also the use of monetary policy to fight inflation. From the 1980s onwards, theory and policy looked to pre-Keynesian ideas such as the "Treasury view", which plunged the economy into an even greater depression. Growing public debt has renewed interest in the economics of austerity. According to Konzelmann (2012), austerity has become a policy objective rather than a policy whose objective is macroeconomic stabilization. The 1990s were marked by an increase in world production accompanied by inflationary pressures and many developing countries' failure to service their debts. Furthermore, the prolonged period of expansion described as the "Great Moderation" (a period of stable global inflation, high global growth and low interest rates), which was built on an unsustainable growth model, preceded both the global financial crisis (2007-2008) and the debt crisis. According to Minsky (1992) and his financial instability hypothesis, during periods of prolonged prosperity financial institutions invest more in riskier assets, which boomerang in the end, causing the system to experience even greater instability and vulnerability. In 2010, a dramatic European debt crisis was kicked off by the economic collapse of the PIIGS (Portugal, Iceland,

Ireland, Greece, Spain) countries and the impending collapse of the European Monetary Union. The global financial crisis that began in 2007 in the United States, the European debt crisis that culminated in 2010 and the general crisis of 21st-century capitalism have theoretically revived Keynes and Marx and have prompted new discussions between state interventionists and those committed to the idea of market liberalism. Despite numerous studies, no heterodox model that could serve as an economic panacea has been found. The financial crisis has been reflected in high fiscal deficits, increasing debt, and a decline in aggregate demand and production, all of which have had a negative impact on employment and have deepened both inequality and poverty, especially in transitional countries that are confronted by structural problems. To simultaneously reduce both fiscal deficits and the public debt, governments have shifted their policy from fiscal stimulus to austerity. However, according to Alfred Calcagno (2012), if slow growth or recession is caused by insufficient demand, a new round of fiscal tightening will further depress economic activity. As a result, governments will reduce tax revenues and increase social expenditures without guarantee that fiscal balances will improve. In the infancy of the global financial and economic crisis, the Croatian economy—which has been confronted by structural problems since the transition—was affected. Although the transitional countries have functioned completely differently from the developed economies, primarily due to business-cycle fluctuations (developed economies have time series of a few hundred years) because of the escape of capital, decision-making systems etc., global trade liberalization and deregulation has substantially affected small, open countries such as Croatia. Because the current policy goal is to restrain the public debt and inflation and to comply with European Union rules (i.e., the budget deficit must not exceed 3% of GDP and the public debt must not exceed 60%) despite high unemployment, inequality, poverty, economic contractions and economic vulnerability, there is a question of how to turn toward full employment and long-term economic prosperity. According to Zaman et al. (2014), the government officials and policy makers should reopen the debate about pro-poor-growth policies pursuant to which wealth trickles down to the poor.

The neoliberal model that advocates austerity even in weak economies and despite the diversity of the national economies that are simultaneously adopting austerity has become questionable in both Europe and the United States.

Fiscal austerity problems in review

Recently, the literature on fiscal austerity and fiscal adjustment has attracted considerable attention. However, studies and research lead to transversal views.

The focus on austerity is of particular importance in transitional countries because the costs of transition are reflected in GDP contraction; balance-of-payment difficulties; falling wages, employment, and social protection; and increasing inequality and social insecurity, especially for those at the bottom of the scale. Therefore, a frequently mentioned issue in recent studies is "Should governments adopt austerity despite their weak economies or can balancing the budget ensure sustainable economic growth"?

Konzelmann (2012) has reviewed the historical experience of how the world economy has attempted to address austerity and macroeconomic imbalances and has concluded that the economics of austerity cannot be meaningfully separated from austerity's social and political context. The author supports Keynes's idea of the impact of business cycles on the application of austerity, that is, on the use of deficit spending to stimulate economic growth and employment during a prolonged recession. Given the current course of austerity policy, Konzelmann questions why a government would pursue an austerity policy in the context of economic recession when there is no economic basis for austerity and persistent macroeconomic imbalances threaten to further destabilize the global economy. She finds an answer in the political and economic impact of liberalized global financial markets. Specifically, Konzelman notes that under neoliberalism, fiscal policy is guided by the interests of the wealthy and the private-sector financial elite. According to her, the demand for austerity measures proves that a national government can manage its deficits and repay its debts, thus demonstrating that austerity is not a policy aimed at macroeconomic stabilization: austerity itself is the target policy. She concludes that if economic austerity continues to undermine macroeconomic performance, financial markets are unlikely to support the affected countries. What is missing from the ongoing debates about austerity is recognition not only that stimulus/incentive is not the only alternative to austerity policy but also that reducing the public debt and the deficit can be achieved by reducing public spending and by increasing tax revenues. Simultaneously, she stresses that future public spending can be divided into current and capital spending, which have significantly different macroeconomic effects.

According to Blyth (2013), austerity is a form of voluntary deflation in which the economy is adjusted by reducing wages, prices and public spending to restore competitiveness, which is (supposedly) best achieved by cutting the state's budget, debts and deficits. Blyth criticizes austerity as an economic policy and notes that the austerity measures proposed to ensure the stability of the Eurozone countries have done exactly the opposite. As an example, he cites the PIIGS (Portugal, Ireland, Italy, Greece, Spain) countries, which implemented austerity measures in response to the 2008 financial crisis, believing that economic growth would return if they slashed their budgets and reduced their debt. However, that scenario was nowhere close to accurate. According to Blyth, austerity is a dangerous idea because it ignores increasing inequality (people at the bottom of the scale, who most often cure debt with more debt, tend to be the most affected), the paradox of saving (i.e., if everybody saves money at the same time, there will be no investment-stimulating spending) and different externalities. Furthermore, he states that the budget deficit follows business cycles, which are cyclical—not secular. Observing the crisis period in the United States, European Union and Eastern Europe reveals that the crisis was generated by the private sector but it was paid for by the public sector. He concludes that in the future, financial repression and high taxes on top earners will become a part of the landscape. We will be forced to solve our debt problems in this way because austerity simply does not work.

Papadimitriou and Hannsgen (2012), in a paper researching how the Eurozone countries have fared under austerity, note that austerity is the wrong policy at the wrong time. They conclude that austerity has brought pain, not relief, to the Eurozone. Austerity has resulted in slow growth, rising unemployment, declining aggregate demand and falling profits. The authors support Keynes's argument that the right time for austerity is during a boom, not a slump; they also make proposals. Their general approach is to propose tax cuts that primarily benefit the wealthy, which would help to loosen fiscal policy for little social purpose rather than a macroeconomic one. They support increased programmatic spending aimed at solving key problems, along with tax cuts and transfers to individuals and families with the highest needs and lowest saving rates. They hope that a large proportion of the new spending would be used in ways that increase employment.

According to Ogujiuba and Ehigiamusoe (2014), the government should reduce wasteful non-development-related spending financed by domestic and foreign borrowing and instead should allocate more resources for developing the education, health, and infrastructure sectors of the economy.

In his book "Bad Samaritans", Chang (2008) notes that the emphasis on fiscal restraint is the central theme of neoliberal macroeconomic policy. He notes that Southern Korea, which was a "sorry country" during the 1960s, is now one of the wealthiest countries in the world. Its progress is the result of a mixture of market incentives and government administration. Chang also states that although neoliberal founders will attribute Korea's success to the belief that Korea adopted a neoliberal economic development strategy (a free market, low inflation, private enterprise, free trade, and foreign investments) during the "miracle years" between the 1960s and the 1980s, the reality is significantly different. Korea based its development on new industries selected by the government in consultation with the private sector, using customs protection, subsidies and other forms of state support. The government owned all of the banks and therefore could direct business loans. If private companies were not doing well, the government felt free to restore state-owned companies, which it would often restructure or resell. The government also protected heavy industries with tariffs and subsidies. However, tariff protection and subsidies were not used to protect industries from international competition but to buy time to absorb new technologies and establish new organizational skills until industries could compete on the world market. In conclusion, the author states that the "Korean miracle" was based on correcting the market through interventionist policy. The contribution of "Bad Samaritans" is to argue that that neoliberal policy propagated by the "Bad Samaritans" who promote an ethos of "do as we say, not as we did" can be very harmful to economic growth and development.

Chang's (2011) book "23 Things They Don't Tell You About Capitalism" argues that the huge budget deficits created by the crisis will force governments to significantly reduce public investments and welfare entitlements, negatively affecting economic growth, poverty and social stability—possibly for decades. He concludes that this catastrophe was ultimately created by the free-market ideology that has ruled the world since the 1980s. Although, he emphasizes that being critical of free-market ideology is not the same as being anti-capitalism. His criticism is of a particular version of capitalism—free-market capitalism—that has dominated the world for three decades.

According to Calcagno (2012), austerity policies are based not only on an incorrect diagnosis of the nature and depth of the crisis but also on an erroneous view of economic mechanisms. A strategy of cutting education, research and infrastructure investments will deliver neither growth nor competitiveness. The implicit identification of fiscal tightening with fiscal consolidation shows the deficiency of the macroeconomic approach. The author notes that if slow growth or recession is due to insufficient demand, a new round of fiscal tightening will further depress economic activity that will reduce tax revenues and increase social expenditures with no guarantee that fiscal balance will be restored. Additionally, by deepening the recession, larger parts of the financial system may need government support, which would cause fiscal accounts to become dramatically disoriented. Thus, he concludes that governments that criticize "living above their means" often forget that government expenditure and revenues are linked. Furthermore, he notes that only a recovery in growth, with nominal GDP expanding at rates higher than interest rates in the medium and long terms will abate debt-to-GDP ratios. Such growth can result from coordinated supportive policies, which may include changes in the level and composition of public income and expenditures and a better distribution of income and credit that would expand fiscal multipliers and the purchasing power of low- and medium-income groups with a high propensity to consume. His analysis highlights that fiscal tightening has become almost a universal recommendation, despite countries' different structures and levels of development. For instance, high fiscal deficits and rapidly growing debt ratios resulted from the crisis, but only in developed economies: in most developing and transition economies, the debt-to-GDP ratio resumed its downward trend following recovered growth and in many cases, the terms of trade resulted in new gains. He follows recent studies (UNCTAD 2011, Box, 3.2.) which found that expansionary fiscal policy has a positive and significant effect on the level of economic activity, spending multipliers are larger than tax-cut multipliers, and tax cuts benefiting lower-income households have a stronger effect than tax cuts benefiting high-income households. Another recent study from (International Monetary Fund [IMF], 2012) admits that fiscal adjustment may have a substantial impact on activity because fiscal multipliers may be quite large during a recession, when the traditional crowding-out argument is less applicable. In conclusion, fiscal austerity and wage compression have become part of the problem, not the solution. Moreover, there are enough instruments available to pursue pro-growth policies, including, e.g., monetary policy, income policies and instruments, including specific structural and institutional reforms that are better suited to national goals. Monetary policy can still be better targeted, which means that less attention should be paid to the global amount of money than to who gets the money and how they use it. In addition, income policy may be used to stimulate domestic demand. Income policies aimed at reversing the declining trend in the wage share of national income may prove a decisive stimulus to demand and restart growth. For many households, debt is the only way to maintain or increase consumption. This article also follows Aglietta's (2012) critique, according to which the solution for Eurozone countries will come not from additional fiscal tightening or dismantling the welfare state but instead from deeper fiscal and financial integration and a cooperative approach to economic rebalancing. Calcagno concludes that it is most important for deficit countries to avoid self-defeating austerity and to find a way to stimulate their economies; surplus economies must contribute by leading the expansionary response to the global crisis. Therefore, according to the author, structural reforms cannot substitute for supportive macroeconomic policies to recover economic growth because they may not deliver the expected result.

Constantinos and Nellis (2013) provide a critical assessment of austerity measures that are being implemented in crisis-stricken countries of the Eurozone; in particular, they discuss the implications of internal devaluation for the Greek economy. They challenge theoretical underpinnings and the expected impact of Greece's pursuit of an internal devaluation policy under an austerity framework forced on the country by the so-called "troika" (the European Central Bank (ECB), the European Commission (EC), and the International Monetary Fund (IMF)). In their opinion, austerity measures should be relaxed. The contractionary effects of fiscal policy should be eased and refocused on reducing unemployment by channeling public-sector spending toward viable, socially desirable investment projects. There is also a need for centrally managed European fiscal policy to effectively transfer resources between richer and poorer regions, thus insulating member states from undesirable economic shocks. Their proposals to fundamentally reform regional and industrial policies and to have the European Investment Bank immediately introduce a major program of investments—particularly in the most crisis-stricken economies of Europe's southern region—by issuing euro bonds. This type of program will provide the leeway required for Europe's distressed Southern economies and help them slowly return to the path to recovery. Finally, they make a strong argument that the troika must immediately reconsider the enforcement of fiscal austerity and fiscal consolidation measures. They suggest an alternative economic approach aimed at emancipating the Greek economy from the crisis of the current economic system. This approach should seek to accomplish the following goals: (a) to renegotiate Greece's existing loan agreement with the troika; (b) to establish an employment creation agenda through "employer of last resort" schemes; (c) to reconstruct and transform the existing banking system; and (d) to adopt a more flexible, more appropriate approach to the implementation of austerity and internal devaluation.

Arestis and Pelagidis (2010) note that the "post-Great Recession"-era policy has finally prevailed globally, especially around Europe; the UK and similar countries might find it even harder to administer an export-led policy medication to their economies. In Europe in particular, the near absence of a stimulus has indeed brought the Eurozone close to dissolution. According to the authors, the problem is that embarking on austerity increases risk of dreaded outcomes in Europe, including negative growth in gross domestic product, sovereign default, political instability and shuttered capital markets. Such outcomes make bank failures more likely, not less. They note that it is easier to understand the embrace of austerity in a political context. Namely, the emphasis on austerity has emerged even in countries with strong balance sheets despite the fact that one of history's most well-known lessons is that in times of recession, fiscal stimulus is the best medicine. They explain phenomena with the following facts; if state budgets are restricted, sovereign bond prices will rise, rescuing imperiled banks. In that way, moribund interbank lending will be resuscitated and government borrowing costs will decline. In another way, it is obvious that European politicians are incapable of directing stimuli towards productive public investment and the public continues to reject tax increases to cover the future deficits that would create a stimulus today. According to the author, the government should support postsecondary education, investment in clean energy, new transportation infrastructures and so on. Otherwise, austerity mania will hit us very hard.

According to Škare (2013), an important aspect of fiscal austerity dates from approximately 375 BC, as seen in Kautilya's papers. Škare states that Kautilya opposed any strict fiscal policy measure, recognizing the negative effects of fiscal austerity—including generating both negative business cycles and "deficit fetishists"—that are clearly implied in his remarks. According to Škare, fiscal austerity is a road to economic distress because it ruins personal wealth and the power of consumption-generating business cycles. The author stresses that Philips's theory (1962) of economy as a science attempts to explain how the system works. In that paper, he notes that production activities are the main imperative when creating wealth and therefore, banks and economic policy makers should work on defining an interest rate that will reflect a reasonable rate of profit and risk. With respect to Kautilya's critique, he notes that Kautilya was aware of the market's negative consequences, for example, the legacy of tax and tax policy (higher taxes lead to lower consumption, lower production, and therefore, higher unemployment and economic cycles). Accordingly, Kautilya had no intention of using tax policy for income (re) distribution. His idea was to limit profit margins in the market (by taxing extra profit) while either limiting or protecting markets that generate an unfair income distribution.

Furthermore, Škare (2010; a) shares the opinion and legacy of A.W. Philips (1962) that none of the economic policies designed and adopted without the knowledge of quantitative economic relationships between the three most important economic variables (unemployment/ inflation /output) can be considered effective and appropriate economic policy. Otherwise, the knowledge of such quantitative relations could be used to design a set of monetary and fiscal policies with the able to ensure a sustainable, long-term combination of unemployment, inflation and growth. One way to confirm this approach is to conduct an historical examination of economic crises; for example, over the last 200 years, the United States has experienced more than 47 of them. The author states that world economies reacted differently to the economic crisis, although the budget deficit, social rights and strong state intervention can be reduced under a common denominator. According to the author, the budget stabilization that becomes the exclusive goal during a crisis actually deepens and prolongs the crisis. Furthermore, Škare (2010; b) analyzes how a bad exchange rate policy and the 1993 stabilization program placed Croatia found itself in the steel embrace of the golden triangle. Because of Croatia's exchange rate and credit policy, its current monetary policy is limited and it cannot perform its appropriate role in times of crisis. Therefore, fiscal policy alone cannot be the solution—i.e., cutting the budget is neither the key issue nor a possible solution. According to the author, "cutting " aggregate consumption would lead to a further decline in production and would generate a vicious circle of poverty. The rationalization of public finances is a necessary but not a sufficient condition for economic growth. Unemployment/ inflation/output are the only three variables that simultaneously act as policy objectives and instruments of economic policy, and knowledge of their quantitative relationship is essential to understanding how the system works. In conclusion, Škare believes it necessary to perform fiscal consolidation in a manner that has a positive effect on employment and production.

Antonakakis and Collins (2014) examine the impact of fiscal austerity on suicide in Greece. The responsiveness of suicide to fiscal austerity is established as a means of providing policy guidance on the extent of suicidal behavior associated with different fiscal austerity measures.

Branas et al. (2015) also discuss the health effects of fiscal austerity. More specifically, they analyze the impact of fiscal austerity and prosperity events on suicide in Greece using a 30-year interrupted time-series analysis and suggest that the consideration of future austerity measures should give greater weight to unintended mental health consequences and the public messaging of austerity policies and related events.

Despite numerous studies, this complex topic has not been the subject of a sufficient methodological exploration. Due to the lack of methodological implementation and statistical data, it is not surprising that there is no consensus on the application of austerity policy.

Data and analysis

The financial turmoil of 2007/2008 affected many countries, especially EU and transitional countries, but the roots of the structural difficulties and fiscal unsustainability confronting national economies were in place long before the world crisis.

Aristovnik and Berčić (2007) state that in the early stage of transition, the need for major fiscal reforms was generally underestimated. According to them, the need to rapidly privatize and "get the state out of the economy" were emphasized, unlike more recent practices, which have admitted the need for an entirely new system, new fiscal institutions, new skills, technical knowledge and political capital.

In most of the transitional countries, including Croatia, spillover of the financial crisis into the real sector has resulted in recession. The effects of the national economy's primary problems are evident in movements in the dynamics of the real GDP growth rate, the structure of demand, and trends in both unemployment and central government finance (see Tab below). The extreme growth of public deficits and debt called into question the sustainability of public finance.

Table 1. Annual percentage growth rate of GDP in Croatia, 2001-2013

	2001	2002	2003	2004	2005	2006	2007	2008	2009	2010	2011	2012	2013
GDP growth (annual) %	3.7	4.9	5.4	4.1	4.3	4.9	5.1	2.1	-6.9	-2.3	-0.2	-1.9	-1.0

Note: Adapted from "GDP growth (annual %)", by The World Bank (2014g). Retrieved from http://data.worldbank.org/indicator/NY.GDP.MKTP.KD.ZG

Table 2. Structure of demand in Croatia, 2000, 2012 (% of GDP)

	2000	2012
Household final consumption expenditure	62	60
General government final consumption expenditure	21	20
Gross capital formation	20	19
Export of goods and services	37	42
Imports of goods and services	40	41
Gross savings	19	19

Note: Adapted from "World Development Indicators: Structure and Demand", by The World Bank (2014a). Retrieved from http://wdi.worldbank.org/table/4.8

To reduce the negative effects of these economic developments, an immediate economic-policy response was requested. The direction of economic policy was greatly influenced by Croatia's accession to the EU on July 1, 2013, because of newly imposed restrictions known as convergence criteria. The burden of adjusting the Washington consensus and adopting new convergence criteria mostly fell onto the labor market and income redistribution. Specifically, by applying the policy of "fiscal austerity" or "sharp cuts" to public finances, economic actors have refocused the objectives of economic policy from increased domestic production, competitiveness, and employment to solving the problems of the budget deficit and public debt, which had negative effects on welfare. The main instrument of economic policy becomes fiscal consolidation, whereas monetary policy is neutral and procyclical. The effects of this "austerity experiment" are questionable given increasing unemployment, the decline in aggregate demand, increasing public debt and the lack of revenue to repay that debt (See Tab below). We begin our analysis with the effects of the primary problems in Croatia's economy, to determine whether fiscal austerity contributes to Croatia's economic growth.

Results

Structural imbalances are reflected in the decline in annual percentage growth rate of GDP recorded by Croatia records since the beginning of its transition. The first half of the decade 1991-2000 showed a decrease in economic activity caused by war, destruction and the transition to a market economy (along with the disintegration of the Eastern European market and the beginning of the disintegration of the common Yugoslav market). The second part of the decade 2001-2010 (see Table 1) marked a new development cycle with growth that continued until 2009 and the financial crisis, after which we see a contraction of growth.

As noted by Mendonca (2014), the European crisis presents a structural dimension that has been developing for years and has gained momentum primarily from an inability to respond in a timely way to the factors that caused the shocks.

It is important to emphasize that the pre-2009 economic growth was built on an unsustainable growth model based on household consumption rather than investment spending, thus creating the foundation for the crisis. These negative developments are interpreted in the Table 2.

Table 3. Gross investment in fixed assets by technical composition, 2000, 2011, 2012

	Equipment (%)	Construction works (%)	Other (%)
2000	4.6	52.3	6.1
2011	37.06	52.15	10.79
2012	38.26	50.61	11.13

Note: Adapted from "Statistical yearbook of Croatia 2002", by Croatian Bureau of Statistics (2002). Retrieved from www.dzs.hr/Hrv_Eng/ljetopis/2002/sljh2002.pdf; "Statistical yearbook of Croatia 2013", by Croatian Bureau of Statistics (2013). Retrieved from www.dzs.hr/Hrv_Eng/ljetopis/2013/sljh2013.pdf; "Statistical yearbook of Croatia 2014, by Croatian Bureau of Statistics (2014). Retrieved from www.dzs.hr/Hrv_Eng/ljetopis/2014/sljh2014.pdf

Table 4. Unemployment rates (%) 2005-2013

Countries	2005	2006	2007	2008	2009	2010	2011	2012	2013
EU-28	9.0	8.2	7.2	7.0	9.0	9.6	9.6	10.4	10.8
Euro area (EA-18)	9.1	8.4	7.5	7.6	9.5	10.1	10.1	11.3	12.0
Bulgaria	10.1	9.0	6.9	5.6	6.8	10.3	11.3	12.3	13.0
Czech Republic	7.9	7.1	5.3	4.4	6.7	7.3	6.7	7.0	7.0
Croatia	12.8	11.4	9.6	8.4	9.1	11.8	13.5	15.9	17.2
Romania	7.2	7.3	6.4	5.8	6.9	7.3	7.4	7.0	7.3
Slovakia	16.4	13.5	11.2	9.6	12.1	14.5	13.7	14.0	14.2
Slovenia	6.5	6.0	4.9	4.4	5.9	7.3	8.2	8.9	10.1
Hungary	7.2	7.5	7.4	7.8	10.0	11.2	10.9	10.9	10.2
Poland	17.9	13.9	9.6	7.1	8.1	9.7	9.7	10.1	10.3

Note: Adapted from "Unemployment rate by sex and age groups - annual average, %" by Eurostat (2015). Retrieved from http://appsso.eurostat.ec.europa.eu/nui/show.do?dataset=une_rt_a&lang=en

The policy advanced by the creators of the Washington consensus has ensured liberalization and deregulation of the capital markets, resulting in increased foreign borrowing and significant credit expansion. Most of the spending in 2000 and 2012 was directed at household consumption typically financed by foreign borrowing—62% and 60%, respectively—whereas the lowest percentage—19%—was directed at gross savings. The effect of the recession is primarily reflected by the decline in household consumption expenditures (62% in 2000; 60% in 2012) and government consumption expenditures (21% in 2000, 20% in 2012). The inability of even the private sector to generate aggregate demand is confirmed by the data regarding share in gross savings. Indeed, households have a higher propensity during recessions to save than to invest. Gross capital formation (19% in 2000, 19% in 2012) primarily includes investments in roads, railways, buildings and so on, which ultimately do not create additional value (see Table 3).

The table shows that in 2000 and 2011-2012, the largest share of gross investment in fixed-assets construction works was 52.3% in 2000, 52.15% in 2011, and 50.61% in 2012, whereas there was a significantly lower proportion of investment in equipment with only 41.6% in 2000, 37.06% in 2011 and 38.26% in

Table 5. Central government finances, revenues and expenses, 2000, 2012 (% of GDP)

	Revenue 2000	Revenue 2012	Expense 2000	Expense 2012
Croatia	35.3	33.9	38.7	36.6

Note: Adapted from "World Development Indicators: Central government finances", by The World Bank (2014b). Retrieved from http://wdi.worldbank.org/table/4.12

Table 6. Structure of central government expenses, 2000

Countries	Goods and services (% of expenses)	Compensation of employees	Interest payments	Subsidies and other transfers	Other expenses
Croatia	24	26	4	43	3

Note: Adapted from "World Development Indicators: Central government expenditure", by The World Bank (2014c). Retrieved from http://wdi.worldbank.org/table/4.13

2012. To achieve a "big push", it is necessary to initially begin to develop investment projects and to invest in equipment that will not only create new added value but also influence the growth of exports. As noted above, the burden of adjusting to the Washington consensus and adopting EU rules mostly affected the labor market and the redistribution of income, as indicated by the Table 4.

Most countries in the observed period before the financial crisis (2005-2008) note a decrease in unemployment; following the financial crisis of 2008, however, the massive contraction of credits, reduced imports, and reduced demand for exports negatively affected both production and employment, as confirmed by the experiences of Poland, Romania, Hungary and so on. Low agricultural productivity, low industrial productivity (i.e., deindustrialization), technological backwardness and the neglect of innovations, and negative investment trends related to capital expenditures have resulted in an increase in Croatia's for unemployment rate between 2008-2013; in 2013, Croatia reported the highest unemployment rate (17.2%) among not only the observed transition countries but also the EU countries overall. This decline in production and employment has resulted in even higher borrowing and lower revenues than expenses, as indicated by the Table 5.

This table shows that in 2000 and 2012, Croatia recorded higher expenses than revenues. Unlike in 2000, in 2012 the percentage of revenue decreased from 35.3% to 33.9%, although the table shows that expenses declined from 38.7% to 36.6%. Croatia's lack of sufficient revenue to ensure the sustainability of its public debt has created a demand for austerity. The tables below show that Croatia spends the most on current, short-term expenditures, namely, subsidies and other transfers that clearly cannot be the subject of long-term financing considering that they are most often settled by increased borrowing.

Accordingly, in 2000, the largest portion of Croatia's expenditures was attributable to subsidies and other transfers at 43% and the smallest portion was attributable to interest payments at 4% and other expenses at 3%.

The largest share of Croatia's expenditures in 2012 was attributable to subsidies and other transfers at 54% and the smallest share was attributable to interest payments at 7% and other expenses at 5%. As opposed to the situation in 2000, in 2012 the share of goods and services declined from 24% to 8%, earmarks for interest payments increased from 4% to 7%, and subsidies and other transfers increased from 43% to 54%, once again indicating the problem of public debt financing. The following table indicates the structure of the Croatian government's revenues.

Table 7. Structure of central government expenses, 2012

Countries	Goods and services (% of expenses)	Compensation of employees	Interest payments	Subsidies and other transfers	Other expenses
Croatia	8	26	7	54	5

Note: Adapted from "World Development Indicators: Central government expenditure", by The World Bank (2014c). Retrieved from http://wdi.worldbank.org/table/4.13

Table 8. Central government revenues, 2000, 2012

	Taxes on income, profits and capital gains (% of revenue)	Taxes on goods and services (% of revenue)	Taxes on international trade (% of revenue)	Other taxes (% of revenue)	Social contributions (% of revenue)	Grants and other revenue
2000	9	46	6	1	32	5
2012	8	47	2	1	34	9

Note: Adapted from "World Development Indicators: Central government revenues", by The World Bank (2014d). Retrieved from http://wdi.worldbank.org/table/4.14

Table 9. Structure of output in Croatia, 2000, 2012

	Agriculture (%)	Industry (%)	Manufacturing (%)	Services (%)
2000	6	29	18	64
2012	4	27	14	68

Note: Adapted from "World Development Indicators: Structure of output", by The World Bank (2014e). Retrieved from http://wdi.worldbank.org/table/4.2

The revenue side primarily reflects shortfalls in income tax and taxes on international trade, which increases social contributions, grants and other revenue.

The earnings model based on industrialization, exports, savings and investments has been replaced by a model based on imports and deindustrialization, as indicated by the Table 9.

This table shows that from 2000-2012 agriculture, industry, and manufacturing showed a decreasing trend, whereas services are the only sector that showed an increasing trend. The structure of investment and output reveals an unsustainable path to economic growth and development. More specifically, deindustrialization, technological backwardness, and directing investment policy towards infrastructure development and services instead of capital expenditures (education, health, development centers) created the basis for increased public debt (see Table 10).

The continuous growth of Croatia's deficit caused an increase in public debt: by 2013, it reached 67.4%. The table shows that public debt is a matter of concern not only because of its amount but also because of the dynamics of its movement (i.e., the growth rate of total public debt was higher than the growth rate of GDP). Croatia's long-term deficit also indicates structural problems with the national economy. More specifical-

Table 10. Budget deficit and public debt in Croatia, 2007-2013

	2007	2008	2009	2010	2011	2012	2013
Public debt (% of GDP)	33.3	30.0	36.6	45.0	52.0	55.9	67.1
Deficit (% of GDP)	-1.9	-1.9	-5.4	-6.4	-7.8	-5	-4.9

Note: Adapted from "World Development Indicators: Structure of demand", by The World Bank (2014a). Retrieved from http://wdi.worldbank.org/table/4.8

Table 11. Budget deficit of selected countries, 2012

Countries	Cash surplus deficit (% of GDP)
Czech Republic	-2.5
Germany	0.1
Slovenia	-3.6
Spain	-9.0
Portugal	-7.0
Italy	-3.1
Greece	-9.4
UK	-5.8
USA	-7.5

Note: Adapted from "Cash surplus deficit (%of GDP)", by The World Bank (2014f). Retrieved from http://data.worldbank.org/indicator/GC.BAL.CASH.GD.ZS

ly, negative economic developments in Croatia—especially after 1994—have a strong hold over Croatia's economic policy, which aimed to stabilize prices and exchange rates rather than to spur development. Croatia's exchange rate policy changed the structure of the economy: the import sector became dominant, resulting in both debt growth and deficit growth in Croatia's current account balance. It is important to emphasize, however, that Croatia's exchange rate policy was not the only cause of its economic problems. Very important are the structure of deficit and deficit financing. From the table below, it is clear that other countries experience high rates of deficit compared to their to GDP; however, the manner in which the country finances its deficit and the purpose of the country's public debt are both important.

The strongest world economies—for example, the United States and the U.K.—finance economic recovery by growing their deficits, whereas the EU countries takes the opposite approach, i.e., they prioritize the fight against deficits. Significantly, in most transition countries, the financial crisis and declining GDP, not structural adjustments, have affected declining deficits due to lower imports.

Discussion

During the debt crisis, most of the European countries affected, including Croatia, implemented fiscal discipline policies to reduce debts. Most commonly, however, measures that intended to achieve reduced debt and an economic recovery resulted in increased debt and increased unemployment (Table 12). Promotion of the

Table 12. Economic effects of austerity

	2012	2013
Budget deficit (% of GDP)	-5	-4.9
Public debt (% GDP)	55.9	67.1
Real GDP growth rate	-1.9	-1.0
Unemployment rate (% GDP)	15.9	17.2

Note: Adapted from "World Development Indicators: Structure of demand", by The World Bank (2014a). Retrieved from http://wdi.worldbank.org/table/4.8; "GDP growth (annual %)", by The World Bank (2014g). Retrieved from http://data.worldbank.org/indicator/NY.GDP.MKTP.KD.ZG; "Unemployment rate by sex and age groups - annual average, %" by Eurostat (2015). Retrieved from http://appsso.eurostat.ec.europa.eu/nui/show.do?dataset=une_rt_a&lang=en

The vast majority of the factors implicated by austerity are not included in these indicators.

"sharp cuts" policy—i.e., a policy in which the main instrument of economic policy is fiscal consolidation, whereas monetary policy is neutral and pro-cyclical—has created negative effects. Those negative effects have been particularly severe with respect to employment and citizens' standard of living, most notably for citizens who are at the bottom "of the scale." Therefore, we must ask what has happened to the goal of reduced unemployment and increased prosperity. According to Bejaković (2013), a significant number of Croatians suffer from difficult social conditions and lack adequate access to public goods and services. With increased unemployment and budgetary problems, we can expect further deterioration of social conditions.

Indeed, Croatia has one of the highest unemployment rates in the EU. Given the dynamics of movement and the amount of public debt, it is important to note the importance of rationalizing—not necessarily reducing—public spending. The funds freed by rationalization can be used for active employment policy measures, co-signing loan obligations, improving general liquidity, etc. Based on an analysis of macroeconomic indicators, it can be concluded that the objectives of increasing domestic production and economic growth are mutually transversal with the aim of solving budget deficits by applying austerity policy. If we reach the bottom of the business cycle by reducing wages, we will not see an increase in employment, national income, exports and competitiveness, as demonstrated in the previous tables. Instead, we will see a decrease in economic growth. Therefore, this author supports Keynes's idea of the impact of business cycles on the application of austerity. In translated terms, austerity can have both positive and negative effect on the economy depending on the business cycle. To avoid repeating the negative experience of the PIGS countries, Croatia—like South Korea—needs to create a macroeconomic environment based on industrialization, production and employment, thus solving the deficit problem. As noted by Radulescu and Druica (2014), in today's world of financial and economic turmoil, labor is a key resource that (in their opinion) is considered to have relatively high education and training levels and a strong scientific base. The above referenced steps will result in higher wages and productivity, which is important for economic growth. Blažević (2013) notes that from the public policy perspective, the minimum wage is an attractive tool because it carries strong political symbolism without requiring increased public expenditures. She concludes, however, that most empirical studies find that the minimum wages has effects that are both negative and self-interested.

When an economic policy experiences radical changes, its objectives must be redefined.

Conclusion

Mainstream economic theory and neoliberal economic policy were called into question after the global financial crisis highlighted their limitations. No consensus on the implementation of fiscal austerity has been achieved because despite numerous studies, this complex topic is not been the subject of sufficient methodological exploration. Emphasis should be placed on defining the methodology of austerity and gathering statistical data to influence the implementation of social transfer policies. In addition, it is necessary to adopt a hybrid approach to fiscal and monetary policy that comprehends both economic laws and quantitative economic relations. The outcome of this research should affect the transitional countries' immediate decision-making related to the implementation of social policies. It can serve also as a basis for further research. Implications, limitations, and directions for further research are offered.

References

Aglietta, M. (2012). Zone Euro, *Eclatement ou Federation*. Paris: Michalon.

Antonakakis, N. and Collins, A. (2014). The impact of fiscal austerity on suicide: on the empirics of a modern Greek tragedy. *Social Science and Medicine Journal,* 112, 39-50.

Arestis, P., Pelagidis T. (2010). Absurd Austerity Policies in Europe. *Challenge,* 53 (6), 54-61.

Aristovnik, A., Berčić, B. (2007). Fiscal Sustainability in Selected Transition Countries. (MPRA, No.122). University Library of Munich, Germany.

Bejaković, P. (2013). The importance of social transfers in reducing poverty in Croatia. Economic Research, [Special Issue], 103-116.

Blažević, S. (2013), Is employment decreasing due to minimum wage increase? Economic Research, 26 (1), 69-100.

Blyth, M. (2013). *Austerity; The history of a dangerous idea.* Oxford, UK: Oxford University Press.

Branas, C. C., Kastanaki, A. E., Michalodimitrakis, M., Tzougas, J., Kranioti, E. F., Theodorakis, P. N., Carr, B.G., & Wiebe, D. J. (2015). The Impact of Economic austerity and prosperity events on suicide in Greece: A30-Year Interrupted Time-Series- Analysis. Health Policy, 5 (1), (n.d.) DOI:10.1136/bmjopen-2014-005619.

Calcagno, A. (2012). Can austerity work? *Review of Keynesian Economics,* [Inaugural Issue], 24-36.

Constantinos, A. , Nellis, J. G. (2013). Challenging the Raison d'etre of Internal Devaluation in the Context of the Greek Economy. *Panoeconomicus,* 60 (6), 813-836.

Chang, H. J. (2011). *23 Things they don't tell you about capitalism.* London, UK: Penguin Group.

Chang, H. J., (2008). *Bad Samaritans. The Myth of Free Trade and the Secret History of Capitalism.* New York, NY: Bloomsbury Press.

Croatian Bureau of Statistics (2002). Statistical yearbook of Croatia 2002. Retrieved from http:// www.dzs.hr/Hrv_Eng/ljetopis/2002/sljh2002.pdf

Croatian Bureau of Statistics (2013). Statistical yearbook of Croatia 2013. Retrieved from http:// www.dzs.hr/Hrv_Eng/ljetopis/2013/sljh2013.pdf

Croatian Bureau of Statistics (2014). Statistical yearbook of Croatia 2014. Retrieved from http:// www.dzs.hr/Hrv_Eng/ljetopis/2014/sljh2014.pdf

International Monetary Fund (2012). *Fiscal Monitor (April 2012). Balancing, Fiscal Policy Risks.* Retrieved from http://www.imf.org/external/pubs/ft/fm/2012/01/pdf/fm1201.pdf

Keynes, J. M. (1936), *The General Theory of Employment, Interest and Money.* London, UK: MacMillan.

Konzelmann, S. J. (2012). The Economics of Austerity (Working Paper). Centre for Business Research. Retrieved from http://eprints.bbk.ac.uk/5867

Minksy, H. P. (1992). The financial instability hypothesis (Working Paper No. 74). The Jerome Levy Economics Institute of Bard College.

Mendonca, A. (2014). The European Crisis and Global Economy Dynamics: Continental Enlargement versus Atlantic Opening. *Panoeconomicus,* 61 (5), 543-569.

Ogujiuba, K. K., Ehigiamusoe, K. (2014). Capital Budget Implementation in Nigeria: Evidence from the 2012 Capital Budget. *Contemporary Economics,* 8 (3), 243-348.

Papadimitriou, D.B.., Hannsgen, G (2012). A Brief Guide to the US stimulus and Austerity Debates, One-Pager/No. 35.

Phillips, A.W. (1962). Employment, Inflation and Growth. *Economica,* 29 (113), 1-16.

Radulescu, M., Druica, E. (2014). The impact of fiscal policy on foreign direct investments. Empiric evidence from Romania, *Economic Research,* 27 (1), 86-106.

Sharma, S. (2002). *Economics does Matter: About Economics and Economists,* Mikrorad, Zagreb.

Sharma, S. (2013). Making the Social World: A retrospect. *Economic Research,* 26 (1), 243-256.

Škare, M. (2013). The missing link: From Kautilya s The Arthashastra to modern economics. *The Journal of Philosophical economics*, 6 (2), 2-31.

Škare, M. (2010a). Can there be a golden "triangle" of internal equilibrium? *Journal of Policy Modeling*, 32 (4), 562-573.

Škare, M.(2010b). Hrvatska u „Čeljusti" zlatnog trokuta [Croatia in the Golden triangle trap]. *Economics*, 1 (17), 79-100.

UNCTAD (2011). Trade and development report. Retrieved from http://unctad.org/en/Docs/tdr2011_en.pdf

The World Bank (2014a). World Development Indicators: Structure of demand. Retrieved from http://wdi.worldbank.org/table/4.8

The World Bank (2014b). World Development Indicators: Central government finances. Retrieved from http://wdi.worldbank.org/table/4.12

The World Bank (2014c). World Development Indicators: Central government expenditure. Retrieved from http://wdi.worldbank.org/table/4.13

The World Bank (2014d). World Development Indicators: Central government revenues. Retrieved from http://wdi.worldbank.org/table/4.14

The World Bank (2014e). World Development Indicators: Structure of output. Retrieved from http://wdi.worldbank.org/table/4.2

The World Bank (2014f). Cash surplus deficit (%of GDP). Retrieved from http://data.worldbank.org/indicator/GC.BAL.CASH.GD.ZS

The World Bank (2014g). GDP growth (annual %). Retrieved from http://data.worldbank.org/indicator/NY.GDP.MKTP.KD.ZG

The World Bank (2012). World Development Indicators 2012. Retrieved from http://data.worldbank.org/sites/default/files/wdi-2012-ebook.pdf

Eurostat (2014a). General Government Gross Debt. Retrieved from http://epp.eurostat.ec.europa.eu/tgm/table.do?tab=table&init=1&language=en&pcode=tsdde410&plugin=1

Eurostat (2014b). General Government Gross Deficit/Surplus. Retrieved from
http://epp.eurostat.ec.europa.eu/tgm/table.do?tab=table&init=1&language=en&pcode=tec00127&plugin=1

Eurostat (2015). Unemployment rate by sex and age groups - annual average, %. Retrieved from http://appsso.eurostat.ec.europa.eu/nui/show.do?dataset=une_rt_a&lang=en

Zaman, K., Khilji, B. A., Awan, U., Ali, G., Naseem, I. (2014). Measuring pro poor sectoral analysis for Pakistan: trickle down? *Economic Research*, 27 (1), 713-728.

12

Unification of Economic Systems in the Global Economy: Barriers and Preconditions

Svetlana G. Vokina[1], Yulia S. Zima[2], Nikolai G. Sinyavsky[3, 4], Vadim Meshkov[5], Aleksandra V. Sultanova[6]

ABSTRACT

The purpose of the article is to determine barriers and preconditions for reducing the differences in the level of development in the global economy's countries and to develop recommendations for solving the problem of the global economy's economic systems unification.

In order to determine the gap between developed and developing countries, the authors use the comparative analysis method. In order to determine possibilities, problems, perspectives, and threats to overcoming the gap by developing countries, the authors use the SWOT-analysis method. For studying the global economy's economic development disproportions, this research uses specially developed proprietary analysis of gap depth in economic development.

As a result of the analysis, the authors determined that the level of economic development of the most developed countries exceeds the level of developing countries by more than four times. This reflects a huge gap depth and a high level of differentiation for countries in the global economy.

The authors conclude that barriers of unification of economic systems in the global economy are primarily related to socio-political factors. Preconditions to reducing the difference in level of economic development for countries in the global economy are predetermined by the influence of globalization and international integration of economic systems.

KEY WORDS: Problem of Unification, Economic System, Global Economy, Economic Development Disproportions

[1] Plekhanov Russian University of Economics, Russia; [2] Rostov State Economic University, Russia; [3] Volgograd State Agricultural University, Russia; [4] Financial University under the Government of the Russian Federation, Russia; [5] Perm Institute of Economics and Finance, Russia; [6] Samara State Technical University, Russia

Introduction

It is difficult to overestimate the actuality of the studying the problem of unification of economic system. The global economy's change in polarity after the breakup of the Soviet Union increased the gap between Northern American and Central European developed countries and the rest of the world, i.e., a large group of African and post-Soviet developing countries.

Among developing countries, there are many economic systems that develop very quickly and create separate categories of countries, including NIC, BRICS, etc. They cannot be considered to be developed countries yet, but in the near future they can reach this

Correspondence concerning this article should be addressed to: **Svetlana G. Vokina**, Department of Information Technology of Plekhanov Russian University of Economics, 36 Stremyanny Ln., Moscow 117997, Russia. E-mail: svetlana-voki@rambler.ru

level or even exceed it. These countries are the most perspective players in the system of modern international economic relations, and their economic state is the most predictable.

At a first glance, it may seem that such structure of the global economy is normal. In macro-economic research, the system that is built according to the pyramid principle (with a massive foundation from the least secured groups of the population at the bottom, a narrower middle part comprised of a population with medium welfare, and small top represented by the elite of a society with the highest level of income) is, as a rule, considered to be the model.

Stability of the macro-economic pyramid is ensured by means of low socio-economic mobility of population and high level of securing a social position with various categories of economic subjects. However, on a global scale, social lift works faster because with the reduction of living standards, citizens of the least developed countries strive into developed countries, which strengthens migration flows.

As a result, developing countries lose their most valuable human resources, which required state budget assets to develop. This loss reduces their capability for economic development. On the other hand, developed countries receive a lot of refugees without money and knowledge of the language, which increases the size of the population of marginal groups and reduces the population's living standards.

The concept of economic development does not presume reducing the developed countries' living standards, which will lead to stagnation of the global economy, but increase of living standards in developing countries for overcoming the gap between these categories of countries and achieving relatively even global economic growth. On the one hand, developed countries are interested in keeping their competitive positions and preserving their advantage of an elite position in the global economy. On the other hand, mass migration negatively influences their economic development and motivates them to support developing countries.

Despite the gravity of the global economic system's situation and the necessity for a solution, which all members of international economy realize, there are no working methods for overcoming the growing gap between developed and developing countries. The purpose of this article is to determine barriers and preconditions to reducing the differences in the level of economic development in the global economy's countries and to develop recommendations for solving the problem of the global economy's economic systems unification.

Literature review

Many modern authors have studied and researched the issue of the global economy's economic disparity by analyzing economic systems' existing vectors and growth poles; determining the global economy's causes and consequences of unequal development; and comparing the economic systems' possibilities and conditions for development (Bhanumurthy & Singh, 2013; Bozkurt, Erdem, & Eroılu, 2015; Caporale & Spagnolo, 2012). The disproportions of economic development are a difference between the rate of economic growth and living standards in various countries (Gehringer, 2014). They emerge due to different geographical conditions and cultural traditions, a difference in methods of economic activities, and various approaches to conducting business, etc. (Jahfer & Inoue, 2014). These disproportions negatively influence the most and the least developed countries (Al Mamun & Sohag, 2015). There are ongoing studies analyzing the possibility for increasing the rate of economic growth and its qualitative transformation by reducing the expansion of exhaustible resources, and shutting down ecologically unsafe industrial produced, developed, and manufactured innovative products and services (González-Pernía & Peña-Legazkue, 2015; Leonida, Patti, Marini, & Navarra, 2015; Odhiambo, 2015; Pogosov, 2015; Popkova, Yurev, Stepicheva, & Denisov, 2015b; Bartolini & Sarracino, 2015; Zeira & Zoabi, 2015; etc.).

Economic growth is one of the most important indicators of an economic system's development (Choi & Shin, 2015). It reflects the volume of national production in dynamics and comparison with other countries of the world (Lee & Oh, 2015). Economic growth is a method for overcoming the gap of the least economically developed countries (Castiglione, Infante, & Smirnova, 2015)

Additionally, there is current research into the reasons for developed countries' domination in the global economic system; evolution of their formation, moving forces, and conditions of their development today; peculiarities of state management, social specifics, and character of business activities and innovational activities; and the role of developed countries in activities of international organizations and efforts to reduce the gap between them and developing countries (Chechina & Sultanova, 2016; Fan, Cui, Li, & Zhu, 2015; Gevorkyan & Semmler, 2015; Kandil, 2016; Sekine, 2015 etc.). In the modern global economy, the most developed countries are in Western Europe and the USA (Tsenkov, 2015) because their population's have the greatest inclination for implementating innovations and a high regard for the entrepreneurial spirit (Anderson, Sutherland, Severe, 2015).

Oddly, state management in the most developed countries stimulates free competition, which is considered to be a source of economic growth and development (Popkova, Abramov, & Chechina, 2015a).

There is also research into the possibilities of developing countries' economic growth; reasons and perspectives of overcoming the gap between them; structure of their economic systems; level of their involvement in integration and globalizing processes in modern global economy; the relationship between state and business structures; methods for attracting investments; and approaches to diversifying an economy (Chen & Chen, 2015; Dowlah, 2015; Dögl & Behnam, 2015; Kuruppu & Willie, 2015; Regmi, 2015). Many developing countries possess huge natural and human resources, which creates conditions for their successful development (Sarmiento Espinel, Silva Arias & Van Gameren, 2015). However, the level of entrepreneurial and innovational activity in these countries is rather low (Dube & Sivakumar, 2015). The state strives to realize protectionist policies and monopolize the economy in these countries (Jeníček & Grofová, 2015).

Nevertheless, despite large interest in the problem of unification of economic systems in the global economy, its solution has not yet been found. This leaves a space for further research in this sphere that should not be theoretical, but rather applicable in nature. This research should also be aimed at searching for mechanisms to reduce the level of differentiation of economic development of various countries in the global economy and develop perspective models for activating developing countries' economic growth.

Method

In order to determine the gap between developed and developing countries, this paper uses the comparative analysis method. For determining possibilities, problems, perspectives, and threats to developing countries' overcoming the gap, the SWOT-analysis method is used. For studying the global economy's economic development disproportions, this research uses a specially developed proprietary method of analysis of gap depth in economic development.

Within this method, several of the most typical systems for each of three categories of countries (in this article, three countries of each category was selected in order to stay within the limits of the scientific article) are selected, and the most significant indicators of their economic development are viewed:

- growth rate of national GDP;
- structure of GDP;
- volume of investments into the economy;
- share of innovational products in structure of national production; and
- migration flows (number of emigrant and immigrants).

It is assumed that these indicators show the difference between developed and developing countries, and these indicators are accessible as reflected in international statistical data.

The selected methods are used to classify countries in the international economy. It is acknowledged that developed countries have a post-industrial GDP structure (domination of the service sphere), low rate of GDP growth, substantial volume of investments into the economy, high rate of innovational products, and positive migration flow (number of immigrants is higher than the number of emigrants).

Developing countries are characterized by industrial GDP structure (domination of industry), high growth rates of GDP, low share of innovational products, and positive migration flow (number of emigrants is larger than the number of immigrants). Large volumes of investments into the economy characterize the leading developing countries, and the underdeveloped countries are characterized by zero volume or even outflow of investments.

In the process of analysis of statistical information in the current state and dynamics of the given indicators, regularities peculiar for each of the selected category of countries are determined. On the basis of these regularities, the system of scales for three categories of countries is developed.

After that, the received values in scales are compared, and the ratio of the largest value to the smallest one is found, and depth of the gap between countries as to all indicators is determined. Finally, the economic disproportion index (EDI) is calculated as an average of all the indicators. Correspondingly, the larger the index means the stronger the level of disproportion of economic development of the global economy's countries.

Results

Using the developed proprietary method to study gap depth in economic development of developed as well as quickly and slowly developing countries, we will look at the developed countries of the USA, Norway, and Sweden; India, China, and the United Arab Emirates for the quickly developing countries; and Brazil, Russia, and South Africa for the slowly developing countries, which lag behind the most. These countries are selected based on their ranking of prosperity in the world in 2014 (Legatum Institute, 2015). Results of analysis of economic development of the selected countries are given in Tables 1-3.

Based on the data of Tables 1-3, it is possible to conclude that the highest rate of economic growth, more than 4% per year, is peculiar for quickly developing countries, which helped determine their name. Developed countries show an average national GDP rate of growth at 1.2% - 4% per year. The slowly developing countries, which lag behind, show the smallest rate of growth at less than 1.2% per year.

In developed countries, the service sphere accounts for 65% - 80% and determines their international production specialization, while quickly developing countries specialize in industrial production and their share of service sector accounts for 30%-45%. The slowly developing countries, which lag behind, have increased their volume in the service sphere, but still cannot reach the level of developed countries.

Developed countries have the largest investment attractiveness, and the volume of investments into these countries constitutes more than $700 billion. For example, in the USA, this indicator was $2,000 billion in 2014. Developing countries are ranked second for investment attractiveness, and they receive $300-700 billion of investments annually. Underdeveloped countries pose less interest for investors and, as a result, this leads to a $300 billion per year level of investments into these countries.

Share of innovational products in the structure of GDP of developed countries is the largest and constitutes more than 15%; in quickly developing countries it constitutes 4-10%; and it is less than 4% in underdeveloped countries. Developed countries received more than 10,000 immigrants annually, and less than 4,000 people emigrated. Quickly developing countries received 4,000-10,000 people annually, and more than 10,000 people emigrated.

This is due to the fact that quick level of development predetermines increase of birth rate of population, which leads to overpopulation. In underdeveloped countries, incoming migration flow constitutes less than 4,000 people annually, and outgoing flow comprised of 4,000-10,000 people. Based on this data, a combined table is compiled that reflects gap depth between different categories of countries for viewed indicators, (Table 4).

Calculation of economic disproportion index for the global economy in 2014 looks as follows: EDI=(4+5+7+7+3+3)/6=4. The received value of index shows that the level of economic development of the most developed countries exceeds the level of underdeveloped countries by more than four times. It shows huge gap depth and a high level of differentiation of the global economy's countries. The gap between developed and developing countries is shown in Table 5. The most important barriers of unification of economic systems in the global economy are the following:

- deep socio-cultural development, leading to different attitudes to business, different levels of perceiving innovations, etc.;
- orientation at overcoming the development path for the purpose of achieving the level of developed countries instead of searching for its own innovational economic development path;
- lack of investments for realizing innovational projects; and
- lack of stimuli for developing national production due to a policy of protectionism and low level of competition in a relatively closed national economy.

Table 1. Analysis of economic development of developed countries

Indicators	Developed countries		
	USA	Norway	Switzerland
Growth rate of national GDP, %	2.4	1.8	1.3
Share of industry/Share of service sphere in GDP	20/80=0.25	20/75=0.26	34/65=0.52
Volume of investments into economy, $ billion	2,093	63	307
Share of innovational products in structure of national production, %	35	14	12
Number of immigrants, thousand people	45	0.7	9
Number of emigrants, thousand people	3	0.2	3

Source: Adapted from "Ranking of countries as to the rates of growth of GDP in 2014" by NoNews (2015). Retrieved from http://non-ews.co/directory/lists/countries/gdp-temp; "Ranking of countries as to volume of direct foreign investments in 2014", by Yes!travel (2015). Retrieved from http://www.yestravel.ru/world/rating/stock_of_direct_foreign_investment_at_home_rank_order/

Table 2. Analysis of economic development of quickly developing countries

Indicators	Quickly developing countries		
	India	China	UAE
Growth rate of national GDP, %	5.6	7.4	4.3
Share of industry/Share of service sphere in GDP	30/50=0.60	45/45=1.00	60/40=1.50
Volume of investments into economy, $ billion	96	759	44
Share of innovational products in structure of national production, %	5	20	7
Number of immigrants, thousand people	5	0.8	8
Number of emigrants, thousand people	14	10	0.1

Source: Adapted from "Ranking of countries as to the rates of growth of GDP in 2014" by NoNews (2015). Retrieved from http://non-ews.co/directory/lists/countries/gdp-temp; "Ranking of countries as to volume of direct foreign investments in 2014", by Yes!travel (2015). Retrieved from http://www.yestravel.ru/world/rating/stock_of_direct_foreign_investment_at_home_rank_order/

Table 3. Analysis of economic development of underdeveloped countries

Indicators	Underdeveloped countries		
	Brazil	Russia	South Africa
Growth rate of national GDP, %	0.3	0.5	1.4
Share of industry/Share of service sphere in GDP	30/65=0.46	30/60=0.46	25/65=0.38
Volume of investments into economy, $ billion	248	272	93
Share of innovational products in structure of national production, %	4	3	2
Number of immigrants, thousand people	0.6	11	2
Number of emigrants, thousand people	1.7	11	0.7

Source: Adapted from "Ranking of countries as to the rates of growth of GDP in 2014" by NoNews (2015). Retrieved from http://non-ews.co/directory/lists/countries/gdp-temp; "Ranking of countries as to volume of direct foreign investments in 2014", by Yes!travel (2015). Retrieved from http://www.yestravel.ru/world/rating/stock_of_direct_foreign_investment_at_home_rank_order/

Table 4. Combined table for determining the gap between levels of economic development of countries from different categories

Indicators	Countries			Gap
	Developed	Quickly developing	Underdeveloped	
Growth rate of national GDP, %	1.2-4	>4	<1.2	4
Share of industry/Share of service sphere in GDP	0.25-0.37	0.50-1.00	0.38-0.49	5
Volume of investments into economy, $ billion	>700	300-700	<300	7
Share of innovational products in structure of national production, %	>15	4-15	<4	7
Number of immigrants, thousand people	>10	4-10	<4	3
Number of emigrants, thousand people	<4	>10	4-10	3

Source: Adapted from "Ranking of countries as to the rates of growth of GDP in 2014" by NoNews (2015). Retrieved from http://nonews.co/directory/lists/countries/gdp-temp; "Ranking of countries as to volume of direct foreign investments in 2014", by Yes!travel (2015). Retrieved from http://www.yestravel.ru/world/rating/stock_of_direct_foreign_investment_at_home_rank_order/

Table 5. Gap between developed and developing countries

Criterion of comparison	Developed countries	Developing countries
Leading sphere of economy	Service sphere	Industry
Role in industrial production process	Development of production, creation of technologies, production management	Direct manufacture of industrial products
Production factors based on an economy's functioning	Human capital, investment resources, entrepreneurial capability	Cheap workforce, cheap and abundant natural resources
Level of development of institutional and infrastructural basis	Advanced institutions and infrastructure	Underdeveloped institutions and infrastruce
Level of investment attractiveness of an economy	High level of investment attractiveness of an economy	Low level of investment attractiveness of an economy

Preconditions for reducing the level of economic development differentiation of the global economy's countries are the following:

- reduction of socio-cultural differences and transition to the policy of free-trading in the process of globalization;
- announcement of the course for building an innovation-oriented economy in developing countries; and
- strengthening capital flow from developed countries into developing ones under the influence of integration processes in the global economy.

Recommendations for solving the issue of unification of economic systems in the global economy are the following:

- development of the population's competencies through changing the existing educational pro-

Table 6. SWOT-analysis results for overcoming developing countries' underperformance

Capabilities of developing countries in the sphere of economic growth	**Problems of economic growth of developing countries**
Availability of accessible natural resources	Society's inadaptability for market conditions of economy
Cheap workforce	Lack of investment resources
Unexhausted potential for development	Low-competitive business environment
Perspectives of overcoming the developing countries' underperformance	Threats to overcoming developing countries' underperformance
Social changes under the influence of globalization of the world economy	Termination of social adaptation due to reducing process integration
Attraction of investments by means of creating a favorable investment climate	Inefficiency of measures to increase investment attractiveness
Development of business as a result of state support	Without support and market stimuli, business will not develop

grams and under the conditions of an innovation-oriented market economy;

- stimulation of development of innovational business through a simplified system of business registration, financial accounting and state financing for creating innovational startups; and
- creation of a favorable tax regime and provision of state guarantees for investors to attract foreign investments in order to realize innovational projects in developing countries.

Table 6. shows how the SWOT-analysis results demonstrate the developing countries' underperformance and how they can overcome it by realizing the given tendencies

Conclusion

As a result of comparative analysis of economic development of developed countries, quickly developing countries, and underdeveloped countries, it was determined that the countries' level of development in the various categories differs by four times, which demonstrates a high differentiation of economic systems in the global economy.

The gap between developed and developing countries consists in their differences in their roles in the production process. Developed countries create technologies and produce management. On the other hand, developing countries are involved in the direct manufacture of industrial production and, as a result, take ecological risks and environmental losses by placing hazardous industries on the territory.

The developed countries' economy functions thanks to human capital, investment resources, and business capabilities; whereas, developing countries' economy is based on a cheap workforce and natural resources. Moreover, the developed countries have advanced institutions and infrastructure as well as are attractive for investments but developing countries are not as attractive for investments.

Barriers for unification of economic systems in the global economy are primarily caused by socio-political factors. The influence of globalization and the international integration of economic systems will help reduce the differentiation of the level of economic development of the global economy's countries. In order to resolve the issue of economic systems unification in the global economy, developing countries must activate their market processes, stimulate business development, and attract foreign investments.

As the results of the SWOT-analysis in overcoming the developing countries' underperforance demonstrate, the most important means of solving the problem of the global economy's economic systems unification is to institute effective state policies and develop their internal potential to create and grow innovative businesses.

The conducted research's results are limited by the reviewed criteria and countries selected for comparative analysis in the various categories, which could be a reason for not determining all of the peculiarities for developed, quickly developing, and underdeveloped countries. Further research may be developed by conducting a more complex and systemic analysis of the disproportions of the global economy's development.

References

Al Mamun, M., & Sohag, K. (2015). Revisiting the dynamic effect of foreign direct investment on economic growth in LDCs. *International Journal of Economic Policy in Emerging Economies, 8*(2), 97-118.

Anderson, J., Sutherland, D., & Severe, S. (2015). An event study of home and host country patent generation in Chinese MNEs undertaking strategic asset acquisitions in developed markets. *International Business Review, 24*(5), 758-771.

Bartolini, S., Sarracino, F. (2015). The dark side of Chinese growth: Declining social capital and well-being in times of economic boom. *World Development, 74*, 333-351.

Bhanumurthy, N.R., & Singh, P. (2013). Financial sector development and economic growth in Indian states. *International Journal of Economic Policy in Emerging Economies, 6*(1), 47-63.

Bozkurt, Ö.G., Erdem, C., & Eroılu, I. (2015). Identifying the factors affecting the economic growth of oil-producing countries. *International Journal of Trade and Global Markets, 8*(2), 97-111.

Caporale, G.M., & Spagnolo, N. (2012). Stock market, economic growth and EU accession: Evidence from three CEECs. *International Journal of Monetary Economics and Finance, 5*(2), 183-191.

Castiglione, C., Infante, D., & Smirnova, J. (2015). Environment and economic growth: Is the rule of law the go-between? The case of high-income countries. *Energy, Sustainability and Society, 5*(26). doi:10.1186/s13705-015-0054-8.

Chechina, O. S., & Sultanova, A. V. (2016). Human Capital as a Key Factor of Economic Growth in Crisis. *European Research Studies Journal, 19*(2), 71-78.

Chen, J.-H., & Chen, Y. (2015). New industry creation in less developed countries - the case of the Taiwanese flat panel display industry. *Innovation: Management, Policy and Practice, 17*(2), 250-265.

Choi, K.-H., & Shin, S. (2015). Population aging, economic growth, and the social transmission of human capital: An analysis with an overlapping generations model. *Economic Modelling, 50*, 138-147.

Dowlah, C. (2015). International trade, competitive advantage and developing economies: How less developed countries are capturing global markets. Taylor and Francis Inc.

Dögl, C., & Behnam, M. (2015). Environmentally sustainable development through stakeholder engagement in developed and emerging countries. *Business Strategy and the Environment, 24*(6), 583-600.

Dube, O. P., & Sivakumar, M. (2015). Global environmental change and vulnerability of least developed countries to extreme events: Editorial on the special issue. *Weather and Climate Extremes, 7*, 2-7.

Fan, D., Cui, L., Li, Y., & Zhu, C.J. (2015). Localized learning by emerging multinational enterprises in developed host countries: A fuzzy-set analysis of Chinese foreign direct investment in Australia. *International Business Review, 25*(1), 187-203.

Gehringer, A. (2014). Financial liberalisation, financial development and productivity growth: An overview. *International Journal of Monetary Economics and Finance, 7*(1), 40-65.

Gevorkyan, A., & Semmler, W. (2016). Macroeconomic variables and the sovereign risk premia in EMU, non-EMU EU, and developed countries. *Empirica, 43*(1), 1-35.

González-Pernía, J. L., Peña-Legazkue, I. (2015). Export-oriented entrepreneurship and regional economic growth. *Small Business Economics, 45*(3), 505-522.

Jahfer, A., & Inoue, T. (2014). Financial development, foreign direct investment and economic growth in

Sri Lanka. *International Journal of Economic Policy in Emerging Economies,* 7(1), 77-93.

Jeníček, V., & Grofová, Š. (2015). Least developed countries – the case of Burundi. *Agricultural Economics, 61*(5), 234-247.

Kandil, M. (2016). On the relationship between public and private spending in developing and developed countries. *The Journal of International Trade and Economic Development, 25*(2), 165-191.

Kuruppu, N., & Willie, R. (2015). Barriers to reducing climate enhanced disaster risks in least developed country-small islands through anticipatory adaptation. *Weather and Climate Extremes, 7,* 72-83.

Lee, S., & Oh, D.-W. (2015). Economic growth and the environment in China: Empirical evidence using prefecture level data. *China Economic Review, 36,* 870, 73-85.

Legatum Institute (2015). The 2014 Legatum Prosperity Index (2015). Available from http://media.prosperity.com/2014/pdf/publications/PI2014Brochure_WEB.pdf

Leonida, L., Maimone Ansaldo Patti, D., Marini, A., Navarra, P. (2015). Political competition and economic growth: A test of two tales. *Economics Letters, 135,* 96-99.-99.

NoNews (2015). Ranking of countries as to the rates of growth of GDP in 2014. Retrieved from http://nonews.co/directory/lists/countries/gdp-temp

Odhiambo, N. M. (2015). Government expenditure and economic growth in South Africa: An empirical envestigation. *Atlantic Economic Journal, 43*(3), 393-406.

Pogosov, I.A. (2015). Factors of long-term economic growth: Scientific and technical progress and capital intensity of production. *Studies on Russian Economic Development, 26*(5), 423-433.

Popkova, E. G. Chechina, O. S., & Sultanova, A. V. (2016). Structural and Logical Model of Contemporary Global Economic System. European Research Studies Journal, 19(2), 218-227.

Popkova, E. G., Yurev, V., Stepicheva, O., & Denisov, N. (2015b). Transformation and concentration of intellectual capital as a factor of economic growth in the modern economy. *Regional and Sectoral Economic Studies, 15*(1), 53-60.

Regmi, K. D. (2015). The influence of supranational organizations on educational programme planning in the least developed countries: The case of Nepal. *Prospects, 45*(4), 501-514.

Sarmiento Espinel, J. A., Silva Arias, A. C., Van Gameren, E. (2015). Quality differences of higher education and its determinants in a less-developed country. *Journal of Higher Education Policy and Management, 37*(2), 204-221.

Sekine, A. (2015). Effects of mineral-commodity price shocks on monetary policy in developed countries. *Applied Economics, 47*(31), 3332-3346.

Tsenkov, V. (2015). Crisis influences between developed and developing capital markets – The case of Central and Eastern European countries. *Ikonomicheski Izsledvania, 24*(3), 71-107.

Yes!travel (2015). Ranking of countries as to volume of direct foreign investments in 2014. Retrived from http://www.yestravel.ru/world/rating/stock_of_direct_foreign_investment_at_home_rank_order/

Zeira, J., & Zoabi, H. (2015). Economic growth and sector dynamics. *European Economic Review, 79,* 1-15.

13

Valuation of Contractual Assets Using Statistical Simulation

Jan Vlachý[1]

ABSTRACT This paper develops a dynamic option-based model for the valuation of rental and other similarly structured lease contracts under the conditions of uncertainty that is then solved by statistical simulation (Monte Carlo). The motivation, research background and methodology of the paper follow up on a previously published general firm-theoretical approach by the author, who takes an interdisciplinary approach to apply the model in this particular context. It is shown that due to the path dependency of the problem, Monte Carlo is an appropriate and practical tool for analyzing embedded options, incident in most rental and lease relationships, and can be used as a major determinant of their value. In addition to its basic valuation function, exploitable for business acquisition or lease contracting purposes, this Monte Carlo model is very well disposed for various microeconomic analyses. Accordingly, we demonstrate the particular impacts and sensitivities of contractual party-specific, as well as environmental, factors including parties' transaction costs, information asymmetry and enforceability of legal claims.

KEY WORDS: intangibles valuation, rental contracts, embedded options

[1]Czech Technical University in Prague - Masaryk Institute of Advanced Studies, Czech Republic

Introduction

Value-based methods for assessing tangible investments are familiar tools for most decision-makers, constituting a fundamental part of management education and are extensively used for key components of the strategic management process, such as capital budgeting. The essential principles of the discounted cash-flow model have been in the public domain and in regular use by practitioners for at least the last one hundred years (Fischer, 1907; Rubinstein, 2006; Williams, 1938).

Correspondence concerning this article should be addressed to: **Jan Vlachý,** Czech Technical University in Prague - Masaryk Institute of Advanced Studies, Kolejní 2637/2a, Praha 6, 160 00, Czech Republic. E-mail: jan.vlachy@cvut.cz

More recently, many researchers have expressed that, besides tangible assets, the value of any business may be strongly determined by intangibles (Blair & Wallman, 2001; Daum, 2001; Lev, 2001; Saaty, 2009) These generally constitute various rights, opportunities and obligations that can substantially enhance and/or diminish the value of a company when compared to the balance of its assets and liabilities, and they may include diverse items, ranging from licenses and brands to specific business skills and market share (Corrado, Hulten, & Sichel, 2005; Kogut and Zander, 1992; Ortiz, 2006; Wang, Wang, & Liang, 2014).

Vlachý (2009) embraced the topic within the framework of a comprehensive firm-theoretical model (Table 1) with direct couplings to existing valuation tools based on contemporary financial theory that uses real options.

Table 1. Value-Based Model of the Firm (Vlachý, 2009)

1. Tangible Assets		scarce goods under ownership control
2. Contractual Assets	2.1 Rights on Tangible Assets	sale, purchase, lease, rent, options...
	2.2 Rights on Product of Human Capital	employee, authorship, consultancy...
	2.3 Rights on Opportunities	patents, trademarks, licenses, quotas...
3. Strategy		combination of Tangible and Contractual Assets and their use

Vlachý (2010), preceded by Vlachý and Vlachý (2008), has developed this valuation concept for the particular case of contractual assets, i.e., any value, positive or negative, constituted by an outstanding contract, explicit or implicit, between a company and any other party. Such a contract may be concluded either within the firm (e.g., with its employees) or outside of the firm (e.g., with its suppliers, customers, or the state). At the same time, the form of the contract may be either explicit (i.e., formally concluded between counterparties) or implied (i.e., arising from pertaining legislation, standards, custom etc.). Furthermore, Vlachý (2010) has shown that embedded options may substantially impact the contract's value and also determine the precedent negotiating strategy.

This paper focuses on the valuation of contractual assets originated from long-term lease contracts (and, thus, a particular type of rights on tangible assets, as per classification 2.1 in Table 1). Conceptually, it follows up on that by Vlachý and Vlachý (2008), who analyzed contractual situations based on combinations of simple buy-and-sell contracts and their characteristics, analytically deriving closed-form solutions for their valuations. The present problem is much more challenging, however, as it includes an intertemporal structure of path-dependent options, which do not allow generalized closed-form solutions, and the analysis in special cases would typically be too complex to be practicable (Geske, 1979; Wilmott, 2006).

Financial economics describes any right, including the right or opportunity to abandon a commitment, as an option. In contrast to financial options, which are typically conceived as negotiable securities (Hull, 2012), embedded options constitute inseparable components of either financial or real contracts (Davidson & Levin, 2014; Kling, Russ, & Schmeiser, 2006; Moore, 2001). These defining attributes notwithstanding, options may materially impact such contracts' values and, in some special cases, this difference (i.e., option value) can be observed empirically (Giaccotto, Goldberg, & Hedge, 2007; Mitchell, 1991; Myers, 1977).

This paper takes a similar approach, not only focusing on application in commercial rental agreements but also, by analogy, on the assessment of lease situations in general. Its goal is to develop and analyze an option-based model of rental lease valuation and contracting. We shall emphasize their value drivers stemming from termination clauses and transaction costs, which constitute a characteristic feature of contracts in the industry (Goddard & Marcum, 2012) and, as demonstrated by Fisher and Ciochetti (2007), determine their commercial characteristics. In contrast to Vlachý and Vlachý (2008) and Vlachý (2010), the valuation model uses numerical (Monte Carlo) simulations, which constitutes a considerably more universal approach than closed-form solutions of stochastic differential equations (Breton & Ben-Ameur, 2005).

The paper is organized as follows: First, the various contractual situations will be described and analyzed within the framework of single-step payoff functions. A dynamic intertemporal valuation model is then developed. Finally, selected simulation results will be discussed, illustrating how the model can bring useful insights into the nature of particular rental-contract value drivers.

1. Analyzing the Contractual Terms

We assume two contracting parties, the seller of a service (i.e., lessor), designated S, and its buyer (tenant), designated B. The contract will be stipulated at a market-corresponding fixed price P (rental rate, in monetary unit per sqm).

From the point of view of the seller, the future value of the contract V_S will be contingent on the future market rental rate p as in (1):

$$V_S = P - p. \quad (1)$$

If the buyer has an option to terminate a contract (or, alternatively, its compliance is effectively unenforceable, which will be discussed in more detail in Part 3.3), the seller becomes an issuer of a call option as in (2). This equation clearly constitutes a position with overall negative time value, and the contract would be unacceptable to a rational seller, unless an up-front premium were charged:

$$V_S = \min\{P - p; 0\}. \quad (2)$$

In contrast to financial options, it is not customary to charge up-front premiums for embedded options. Other conditions must, therefore, provide for an equilibrium that could lead to negotiable terms. The equilibrium may be conceivably influenced by several factors in real-world tenancy agreements.

Apparently, the seller can simply charge the buyer an above-market rental rate $R > P$ to compensate for the option value. Assuming no additional constraints, such a solution becomes highly unstable, however, because the buyer has an incentive to terminate as soon as possible (i.e., virtually immediately) and renegotiate at the market price P.

The buyer must therefore be incentivized to retain tenancy, which can be achieved by stipulating a penalty clause on termination F (an income of the lessor) or with the existence of other transaction costs relating to premises change C_B. For these terms to provide a stable solution, it is essential to meet the condition (3):

$$F + C_B \geq R - P. \quad (3)$$

Such a constraint also allows for solutions at the market price, i.e., $R = P$; however, these are trivial because it suffices to set a prohibitively high F, and effectively make the contract irrevocable (provided the penalty is enforceable).

The value of the contract with an embedded termination right may, thus, ensue solely from a termination penalty F, or from its combination with an adjusted rental rate $R > P$, both of which are summarily described by (4). This is similar to a short position in an instrument that financial market practitioners usually call a cancellable forward or Boston option (Kat, 1994; Rawls & Smithson, 1989)

$$V_S = \min\{R - p; F\}, \text{ assuming } R \geq P \text{ and } F \geq R - P. \quad (4)$$

In either case, the buyer's and seller's positions are symmetric, i.e., $V_B = - V_S$. This simple equilibrium characteristic, where both parties are expected to settle at an initial expected value of the contract equal to zero (for a comprehensive review of various approaches leading to this assumption, see Chow, McAleer and Sequeira (2000)) ceases to hold once transaction and opportunity costs of termination (e.g., moving, cleanup, refurbishment, commissions, vacancy) are taken into account.

For generalization, we shall allow for transaction costs borne by the buyer C_B, as well as by the seller C_S. This results in contract value according to (5) from the point of view of the seller, (6) from the point of view of the buyer, both of which are illustrated in Figure 1.

$$V_S = \min\{R - p; F + C_B\} - D, \text{ where } D = C_B + C_S \text{ for } p < (R - F - C_B), \text{ else } D = 0, \text{ assuming } R \geq P \text{ and } F + C_B \geq R - P; \quad (5)$$

$$V_B = \max\{p - R; - F - C_B\}. \quad (6)$$

The technical term D contained in the sum (5) represents a cash-or-nothing binary (digital) call option (Rubinstein & Reiner, 1991).

Wherever $V_B \neq - V_S$, as in (5) as opposed to (6), the two different values do not constitute an equilibrium. In case of $V_S < - V_B$, whenever $C_B + C_S > 0$, the negotiation turns into a negative-sum game. This is a crucial finding because using conventional game-theoretical criteria (Vega-Redondo, 2003) and assuming transactional costs of moving are positive, rational contractors would be expected to generally avoid agreements including termination options.

That such agreements are being negotiated in practice and that they actually constitute the majority of

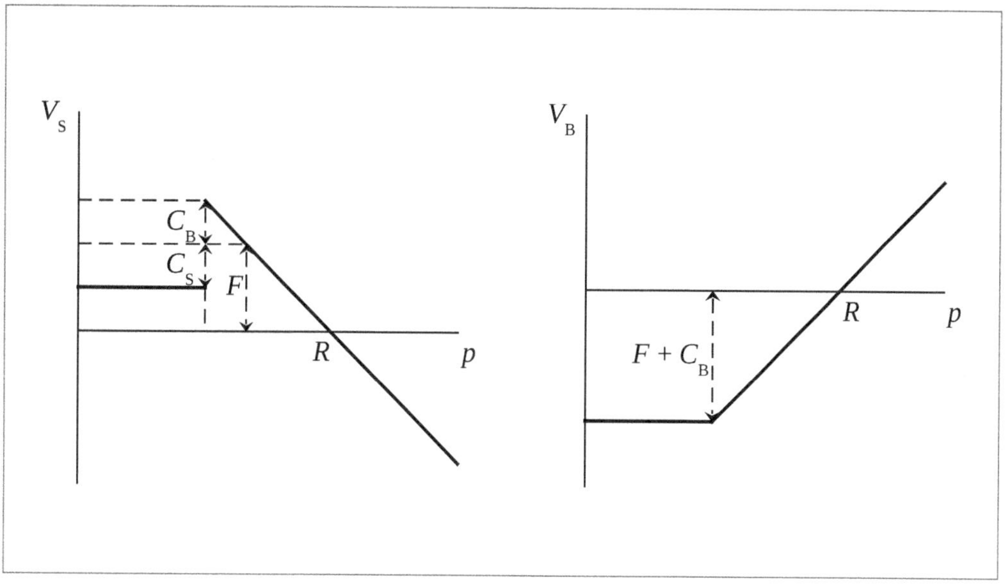

Figure 1. Seller's and Buyer's Payoff Functions.

long-term rental contracts, can only be explained by the fact that various market inefficiencies let sellers generate sufficient margins to sustain business in a primarily demand-driven market (this market feature is investigated in detail by Kholdy and Sohrabian (2008) and Baum (2009)). In other words, lessors will end rental contracts that, on a stand-alone basis, have negative value while still retaining positive value on their development projects.

Actual pricing will thus be based primarily on the assessment of V_B, rather than V_S, whereby C_S becomes irrelevant. However, this pricing structure would have an impact if the preponderance of sellers with high transaction costs were to to push down the benchmark rates P for contracts without termination options; this would be characteristic in a market with very high vacancy rates, as shown by Sivitanides (1997).

2. Developing a Multi-Period Valuation Model

A regular rental contract is usually long term, with potential termination risk arising during its duration, contingent on the temporal development of the market rental rate as well as on the contractual covenants. Any realistic model has to take an intertemporal view, which results in valuation situations composed of compound options.

Despite the existence of analytical solutions for particular types of compound options (Geske, 1979), it is much more efficient and universal to adopt a numerical approach. Discrete numerical analysis methods for the valuation of options can be divided into two fundamental categories. One is based on the simple and elegant backward-induction lattice model introduced by Cox, Ross and Rubinstein (1979), Rendleman and Barter (1979), and Sharpe (1978), which in absolute usage terms, is currently the preferred method for evaluating miscellaneous types of options, including real and embedded (Mun, 2012; Reuter & Tong, 2007).

The alternative, which is used in this study, exploits statistical simulation (Monte Carlo). This technique, initially developed during World War II (Metropolis & Ulam, 1949), and long common for miscellaneous applications in areas ranging from Neurology to Technology to Natural Sciences (Fishman, 1996), was initially proposed for option valuation by Boyle (1977). It has not gained much acceptance for the val-

Table 2. Contractual Terms as a Function of Rental Rate Volatility.

σ	5%	10%	20%	30%	40%	50%
φ = π (t=10)	4%	8%	17%	25%	33%	42%
φ = π (t=20)	6%	12%	25%	37%	49%	61%
φ = π (t=30)	7%	15%	30%	44%	58%	72%

Table 3. Price Premium as a Function of Rental Rate Volatility Assuming Fixed Penalty.

φ		20%			30%	
σ	10%	20%	30%	20%	30%	40%
π (t=10)	4%	15%	27%	11%	23%	36%
π (t=20)	9%	27%	48%	21%	42%	66%
π (t=30)	12%	35%	64%	29%	57%	88%

uation of most financial options, with the exception of certain types of path-dependent exotic options (Wilmott, 2006), primarily because of its relatively high computing-power demands, it has a strong potential for solving particular real-option problems and path-dependent embedded options (Charnes, 2012; Mun, 2006; Onimus, 2011).

The present simulation model is designed as follows: A contract is negotiated for *n* periods (years) at the price (rental rate) *R*, with the buyer holding an option to terminate at any discrete time step of the simulation Δt. If and when the option is exercised, the buyer pays the seller the amount *F*, bears an additional cost C_B, and the seller bears a cost C_S; a new rental agreement is then contracted at the price r_t, derived from the current market price p_t and original premium π, stated as a percentage of the rental price commensurate with (9). Exercise (termination) by the tenant is contingent on the criterion (7), in accordance with (6):

$$p_t < R - F - C_B. \quad (7)$$

The market price p_t is generated as an opportune stochastic process. The simulations in Part 3 will assume its log-normal Brownian diffusion described by (8), where μ represents the price's expected periodical trend, σ its standard deviation (volatility), and ε a random value with normalized normal distribution.

$$p_{t+\Delta t} = p_t \exp\left[\left(\mu - \sigma^2/2\right)\Delta t + \sigma\varepsilon\sqrt{\Delta t}\,\right]. \quad (8)$$

To generalize the results, the rental premium π, termination penalty ϕ and transaction costs χ_B, χ_S are each standardized as percentage values of the rental price *R*, using the parameters as in (9), (10), (11) and (12).

$$\pi = R / P - 1; \quad (9)$$

$$\phi = F / R; \quad (10)$$

$$\chi_B = C_B / R; \quad (11)$$

$$\chi_S = C_S / R. \quad (12)$$

Thus, the actual rate *R* becomes irrelevant (i.e., can be perceived as unit). Furthermore, the initial contracting constraint (3) may be restated as (13):

$$\phi + \chi_B \geq \pi / (\pi + 1). \quad (13)$$

Table 4. Contractual Terms ($\varphi = \pi$) as Functions of Buyer's Transaction Costs (σ = 25%).

χB	0%	10%	20%	30%	40%	50%	60%
$\varphi = \pi$ (t=10)	20%	17%	14%	11%	8%	5%	3%
$\varphi = \pi$ (t=20)	30%	27%	23%	19%	16%	12%	9%
$\varphi = \pi$ (t=30)	37%	33%	29%	25%	21%	17%	13%

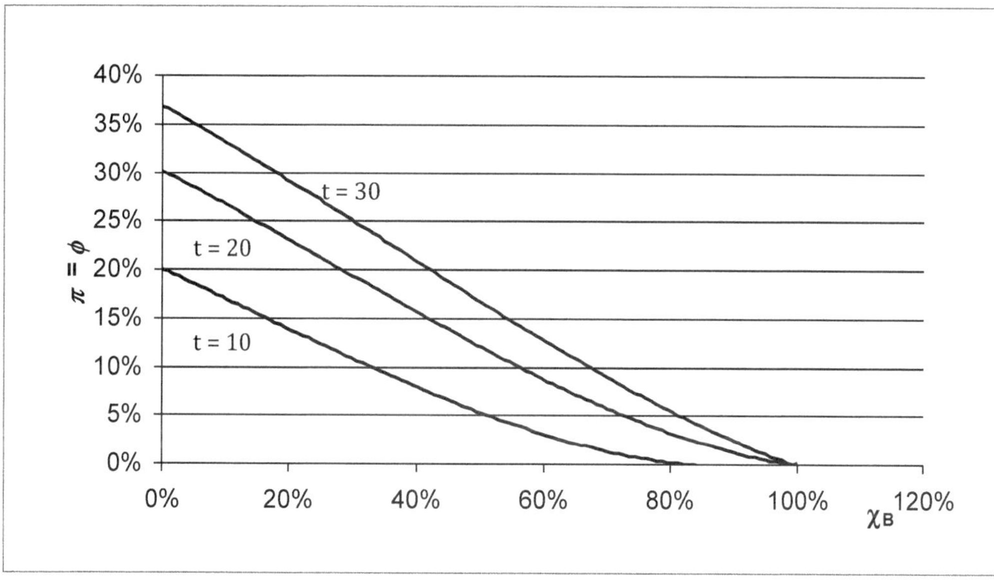

Figure 2. Contractual Terms ($\varphi = \pi$) as Functions of Buyer's Transaction Costs (σ = 25%).

3. Discussion of Assorted Model Solutions

The model can be utilized for diverse value-based analyses. Moreover, for example, facilitating actual contracting or providing valuation data for M&A transactions, it may also serve to quantify the various sensitivities arising from relevant contractual and market terms. An illustration of this approach will be given herein, complementing the essential findings in Part 2 and offering a better insight into some of the key value drivers for rental agreements.

In each case, the mean discounted value of the simulation $^*V$ is benchmarked against the *NPV* (Net Present Value) of rental incomes, contracted for a lease with the equivalent time horizon $n\ \Delta t$ at the current market price $p_0 = P$ with no termination rights (V_{BENCH}). Equilibrium of particular contracted terms is then derived by numerically iterating $^*V \rightarrow V_{BENCH}$.

Results have been calculated for contractual maturities of $n = \{10; 20; 30\}$ (years) and the discount rate r = 5%, with no price trend anticipated (μ = 0). All simulations have been performed using Crystal Ball simulation software (for details on its characteristics see, e.g., Charnes, 2012; Harris, 2014), set at 10,000 experimental runs.

3.1. Price Premium and Termination Penalty as Functions of Price Volatility

The first set of simulations omits transaction costs and seeks various cases of contracting equilibrium. One apparently reasonable strategy is setting the termination penalty equal to the price premium, which incidentally meets criterion (13). This means deriving the function $\phi = \pi = f(\sigma)$ while leaving the other parameters unchanged at $\chi_B = 0$, $\chi_S = 0$.

The results in Table 2 suggest that, interestingly, there is a linear relationship between $\phi = \pi$ and σ, whose slope is solely determined by the contract's duration and converging toward perpetuity. This seems to suggest a useful contracting heuristic. Unfortunately, situations with high price volatility and/or long contract durations then result in very high levels of termination penalties (higher, for example, than 50% of the annual rent), which may not be commercially viable, and might even be legally or practically unenforceable, as discussed in more detail in Part 3.3.

Alternatively, it is possible to set a fixed termination penalty and investigate the related equilibrium price premium. This mitigates the risk of the penalty not being enforceable, however, as shown in Table 3, it may lead to unstable solutions (highlighted in *italics*) due to the tenant's immediate incentive to terminate, as they do not meet the criterion $\phi > \pi / (\pi + 1)$, i.e., the applicable special case of (13).

3.2. Impact of Transaction Costs

Formulas (4) and (5) indicate that the seller's transaction costs do not impact termination; they only reduce the seller's payoff on termination. On the other hand, the buyer's transaction costs diminish his inclination to terminate, but, in contrast to the termination penalty, do not increase the seller's payoff on termination. In a buyer's market, it is only the tenant's transaction costs and the termination penalty that influence the terms of the contract.

These will now be examined using a reasonable volatility assumption (Kanak & Tien, 2000) of $\sigma = 25\%$ and, again, setting $\phi = \pi$. We derive the function $\phi = \pi = f(\chi_B)$.

The results in Table 4 and Figure 2 show that increasing transaction costs χ_B borne by the tenant markedly decrease the premium and termination penalty levels that the lessor will be able to charge for the option to terminate, i.e., offer a more competitive contract (intuitively, all results converge toward zero when it becomes prohibitive for the tenant to terminate).

One of the interesting conclusions of this simulation that can be further investigated in game-theoretical settings, relates to the fact that the lessor may be in a position to discriminate between different tenants based on the recognition of their disparate transaction costs. On the other hand, tenants can improve their negotiating position by inflating lessors' expectations in this respect.

3.3. Impact of Imperfect Enforcement

As detailed by Farnsworth (1970), Mattei (1995), Miller (2004) and García (2012), different jurisdictions take diverse approaches in respect to penalty clauses and each may result in particular constraints as concerns their actual enforceability.

Summarily, common law tends to render penalty clauses unenforceable in deference to the just compensation principle, which essentially means that the clause may not serve to coerce the defaulting promisor into avoiding contractual breach, but a liquidated damages clause is deemed acceptable, provided it is deemed to represent a genuine pre-estimate of damages. On the other hand, civil law generally permits sanctions, but judges may be allowed or required to moderate contract penalties which are deemed grossly excessive. In addition to such specifics, the net costs of enforcement (including opportunity costs) may make some claims dormant, not to mention judicial environments that simply do not guarantee credible recovery (Aboal, Noya, & Rius, 2014).

With regard to the present model, any effect made by these factors bears on the expected values of ϕ, χ_S and χ_B, respectively (even though χ_S does not directly impact contracting decisions, it affects the value of the lessor's assets). Furthermore, parties' expectations may differ in this respect, for example, when one is domestic (and, thus, presumably more realistic) and the other one is foreign.

The model clearly shows that a decrease in expected termination penalty recovery will result in either higher lease premiums (i.e., increased effective rental rates), or, in case they would exceed criterion (13), a reluctance to conclude long-term contracts.

Conclusions

In this paper, we have developed and applied a dynamic model for the valuation of rental and similar contracts that is based on appropriate payoff functions. Statistical simulation has been shown to be a flexible time- and cost-efficient method for solving the model. In addition to its straightforward application for quantitative support in contracting or M&A situations, a microeconomic approach has been suggested because it facilitates a proper understanding of market dynamics and value-driver sensitivities.

We have thus shown how termination rights become less valuable as a result of tenants' transaction costs on the one hand and more valuable with increasing market volatility on the other hand. Lessors' transaction costs are irrelevant from the contracting point of view, but they are important in terms of assessing the value of the contract for that party. In addition to other factors, actual negotiation results will be affected by the lessor's capability to correctly estimate the tenant's transaction costs. The lessor may also be able to effectively discriminate between tenants due to information asymmetry characteristics.

The findings of this paper are both methodological as well as theoretical. On the one hand, empirical-data calibration and parametrical adjustments can turn the model into a management tool suitable for valuation or negotiation support. On the other hand, further research opportunities include, for example, using outputs of the model for a game-theoretic analysis of rental contract negotiation as well as for implicit parametrization in macroeconomic studies.

References:

Aboal, D., Noya, N., & Rius, A. (2014). Contract enforcement and investment: A systematic review of the evidence. *World Development, 64*, 322-338.

Baum, A. (2009). *Commercial Real Estate Investment.* New York, NY: Taylor & Francis.

Boyle, P. P. (1977). Options: A Monte Carlo approach. *Journal of Financial Economics, 4*(3), 323-338.

Blair, M. M., & Wallman, S. M. H. (2001). *Unseen wealth: Report of the brookings task force on intangibles.* Washington DC: Brookings Institution Press.

Breton, M., & Ben-Ameur, H. (2005). *Numerical methods in finance*, New York, NY: Springer.

Charnes, J.M. (2012). *Financial modeling with oracle crystal ball and excel.* (2nd ed.). Hoboken, NJ: John Wiley & Sons.

Chow, Y. F., McAleer, M., & Sequeira, J. M. (2000). Pricing of forward and futures contracts. *Journal of Economic Surveys, 14*(2), 215-253.

Corrado, C., Hulten, C., & Sichel, D. (2005). Measuring capital and technology: An expanded framework. In C. Corrado, J. Haltiwanger & D. Sichel (Eds.), *Measuring capital in the new economy.* National Bureau of Economic Research, Studies in income and wealth (Vol.65, pp. 11-45). Chicago, IL: University of Chicago Press.

Cox, J. C., Ross, S. A., & Rubinstein, M. (1979). Option pricing: A simplified approach. *Journal of Financial Economics, 7*(3), 229-263.

Daum, J. (2001, July 26). How accounting gets more radical in measuring what really matters to investors. The New Economy Analyst Report. Available from http://juergendaum.com/news/07_26_2001.htm

Davidson, A., & Levin, A. (2014). *Mortgage valuation models: embedded options, risk and uncertainty.* Oxford, UK: Oxford University Press.

Farnsworth, E. A. (1970). Legal remedies for breach of contract. *Columbia Law Review, 70*(7), 1145-1216.

Fischer, I. (1907). *The rate of interest: Its nature, determination and relation to economic phenomena.* New York, NY: Macmillan.

Fisher, L. M., & Ciochetti, B. A. (2007). Determinants of the terms and performance of office leases. (Working Paper No. 133). Real Estate Research Institute. Retrieved from http://www.reri.org/research/article_pdf/wp133.pdf

Fishman, G. S. (1996). *Monte Carlo: concepts, algorithms, and applications.* New York, NY: Springer.

García, I. M. (2012). Enforcement of penalty clauses in civil and common law: A puzzle to be solved by the contracting parties. *European Journal of Legal Studies, 5*(1), 98-123.

Geske, R. (1979). The valuation of compound options. *Journal of Financial Economics, 7*(1), 63-81.

Giaccotto, C., Goldberg, G. M., & Hedge, S. P. (2007). The value of embedded real options: Evidence from consumer automobile lease contracts. *Journal of Finance, 42*(1), 411-445.

Goddard, G. J., & Marcum, B. (2012). *Real estate investment.* Berlin: Springer.

Harris, M. (2014). *Inside the Crystal Ball: How to make and use forecasts.* Hoboken, NJ: John Wiley.

Hull, J. C. (2012). *Options, futures and other derivatives* (8th ed.). New Jersey, NJ: Prentice Hall.

Kanak, P., & Tien, F. S. (2000). Implied volatility in the U.K. Commercial property market: Empirical evidence based on transaction data. *The Journal of Real Estate Finance and Economics, 20*(1), 5-24.

Kat, H. M. (1994). Contingent premium options. *Journal of Derivatives, 1*(4), 44-55.

Kholdy, S., & Sohrabian, A. (2008). Capital gain expectations and efficiency in the real estate markets. *Journal of Business & Economics Research, 6*(4), 43-52.

Kling, A., Russ, J., & Schmeiser, H. (2006). Analysis of embedded options in individual pension schemes in Germany. *The Geneva Risk and Insurance Review, 31*(1), 43-60.

Kogut, B., & Zander, U. (1992). Knowledge of the firm, combinative capabilities and the replication of technology. *Organization Science, 3*(3), 383-397.

Lev, B. (2001). *Intangibles: Management, measurement, and reporting.* Washington, DC: Brookings Institution Press.

Mattei, U. (1995). The comparative law and economics of penalty clauses in contracts. *American Journal of Comparative Law, 43*(3), 427-444.

Metropolis, N., & Ulam, S. (1949). The Monte Carlo method. *Journal of the American Statistical Association, 44*(247), 335-341.

Miller, L. (2004). Penalty clauses in England and France: A comparative study. *International and Comparative Law Quarterly, 53*(1), 79-106.

Mitchell, K. (1991). The call, sinking fund, and term to maturity features of corporate bonds: An empirical investigation. *Journal of Financial and Quantitative Analysis, 26*(2), 201-222.

Moore, W. T. (2001). *Real options and option-embedded securities.* New York, NY: John Wiley & Sons.

Mun, J. (2006). *Modeling risk: Applying Monte Carlo simulation, real options analysis, forecasting and optimization techniques.* Hoboken, NJ: John Wiley & Sons.

Mun, J. (2012). *Real options analysis: Tools and techniques for valuing strategic investments and decisions.* Hoboken, NJ: John Wiley & Sons.

Myers, S. C. (1977). Determinants of corporate borrowing. *Journal of Financial Economics, 5*(2), 147-175.

Onimus, J. C. (2011). *Assessing the economic value of venture capital contracts: An option pricing approach.* Wiesbaden: Springer Science.

Ortiz, M. A. A. (2006). Intellectual capital (intangible assets) valuation considering the context. *Journal of Business & Economics Research, 4*(9), 35-42.

Rawls, S. W., & Smithson, C. W. (1989). The evolution of risk management products. *Journal of Applied Corporate Finance, 1*(4), 18-26.

Rubinstein, M., & Reiner, E. (1991). Unscrambling the binary code. *Risk, 4*(9), 75-83.

Rendleman, R. J., & Barter, B. J. (1979): Two state option pricing, *Journal of Finance, 34*(5), 1092-1110.

Reuer, J. J., Tong, T. W. (2007). How Do Real Options Matter? Empirical Research on Strategic Investments and Firm Performance. In J. J. Reuer, T. W. Tong (ed.), Real Options Theory (Advances in Strategic Management, Vol. 24, pp. 145-173). Oxford, UK: JAI Press.

Rubinstein, M. (2006). *A history of the theory of investments.* Hoboken, NJ: John Wiley & Sons.

Saaty, T. L., Sagir, M. (2009). Extending the measurement of tangibles to intangibles. *International Journal of Information Technology & Decision Making, 8*(1), 7-27.

Sharpe, W. F. (1978). *Investments.* Englewood Cliffs, NY: Prentice-Hall.

Sivitanides, P. S. (1997). The rent adjustment process and the structural vacancy rate in the commercial real estate market. *Journal of Real Estate Research, 13*(2), 195-210.

Vega-Redondo, F. (2003). *Economics and the theory of games.* Cambridge, UK: Cambridge University Press.

Vlachý, J. (2009). Strategie podniku a finanční teorie [Corporate Strategy and Financial Theory]. *Politická ekonomie, 57*(2), 147-162.

Vlachý, J. (2010). Assessing and negotiating commercial contracts. *The Romanian Economic Journal, 13*(37), 143-163.

Vlachý, J. (2008). The effect of cancellation rights on the value of contracts. *European Financial and Accounting Journal, 3*(2), 51-69.

Wang, Z., Wang, N., & Liang, H. (2014). Knowledge sharing, intellectual capital and firm performance. *Management Decision, 52*(2), 230-258.

Williams, J. B. (1938). *Theory of investment value.* Cambridge, MA: Harvard University Press.

Wilmott, P. (2006). *Paul Wilmott on Quantitative Finance* (2nd ed.). Hoboken, NJ: John Wiley and Sons.

14

Implications of Unprofitable Horizontal Mergers: A Positive External Effect Does Not Suffice To Clear A Merger!

Oliver Budzinski[1], Jürgen-Peter Kretschmer[2]

ABSTRACT Standard analysis of mergers in oligopolies along the lines of the popular Farrell-Shapiro Framework (FSF) relies, regarding its policy conclusions, on the assumption that rational agents will only propose privately profitable mergers. If this assumption were held, a positive external effect of a proposed merger would represent a sufficient condition to allow the merger. However, the empirical picture on mergers and acquisitions reveals a significant share of unprofitable mergers, and economic theory, moreover, demonstrates that privately unprofitable mergers can be the result of rational action. Therefore, we drop this restrictive assumption and allow for unprofitable mergers to occur. This exerts a considerable impact on merger policy conclusions: while several insights of the original analysis are corroborated (e.g., efficiency defense), a positive external effect does not represent a sufficient condition for the allowance of a merger any longer. Applying such a rule would cause a considerable amount of false decisions.

KEY WORDS: mergers & acquisitions, oligopoly theory, horizontal merger policy, profitability of mergers, antitrust

[1] Ilmenau University of Technology, Institute of Economics, Germany; [2] Federal Cartel Office, Germany

1. Introduction

The framework for analyzing horizontal mergers introduced by *Farrell* and *Shapiro* (1990) has become very popular in industrial and business economics. In the context of the so-called 'more-economic approach to competition policy' (*Neven*, 2006), this framework additionally enjoys an increasing importance for empirical and policy analyses of horizontal mergers and, consequently, also for the self-assessment of business companies considering a merger project. One of the most distinctive characteristics of the Farrell-Shapiro framework (FSF) is the conceptual differentiation between an 'internal effect' (on the merging companies) and an 'external effect' (on the competitors of the merging companies and on the consumers). This allows for a clarified interpretation of an 'efficiency defense': the total welfare of a horizontal merger is positive if the positive internal effect overcompensates for a negative external effect. Furthermore, any horizontal merger entailing a positive external effect is deemed to be welfare enhancing (*Farrell* & *Shapiro* 1990; 1991). This policy conclusion is rooted in a crucial assump-

Correspondence concerning this article should be addressed to: **Oliver Budzinski**, Ilmenau University of Technology, Institute of Economics, Ehrenbergstraße 29, D-98693 Ilmenau, Germany
E-mail: oliver.budzinski@tu-ilmenau.de

tion: because rational enterprises will only engage in a merger if the combination increases the profitability of the merged entity compared to the non-merged companies, *Farrell* and *Shapiro* (1990; 1991) assume that only profitable mergers will occur (the increase in profits might either be a result of efficiencies, for instance, synergy effects or economies of scale, or a result of market power), i.e., the internal effect of rational mergers is always positive. In doing so, they find themselves in line with the majority of industrial economics analyses of horizontal mergers.

Although the limitation to profitable mergers on the grounds of the rationality assumption appears to be straightforward, the empirical picture differs significantly. According to the vast majority of empirical studies on merger profitability, a considerable share of horizontal mergers fails to enhance profitability ex post (section 2). Moreover, it can be argued that unprofitable mergers might well be undertaken by rational agents (section 2). Therefore, we re-configure the FSF by introducing the possibility of unprofitable mergers occurring (section 3). Against this background, we review the policy conclusions given by *Farrell* and *Shapiro* (section 4). While we support some of their recommendations, we also find cases in which the disregard of unprofitable mergers impedes a welfare-maximizing merger policy.

2. (Un-)Profitability of Mergers

The comprehensive empirical literature on the profitability of mergers is typically classified into two methodological approaches: first, the 'success' of a merger is evaluated against the background of data from balance sheets pre- and post-merger, so-called outcome studies. These studies generally identify a significant share of mergers that decrease profits as well as profitability post-merger. Depending on the analyzed timeframe and the included industries, the ratio of unprofitable mergers lies between 25 and 50 percent (*Gugler* et al., 2003; *Kaplan* & *Weisbach,* 1992; *Pautler* 2003; *Ravenscraft* & *Scherer,* 1987; *Röller*, Stennek, & Verboven, 2006; *Tichy,* 2001). This share tends to increase with the transaction volume of the merger. *Gugler* et al. (2003) find that only approximately 30 percent succeeded in improving both profits and sales compared to a control group of non-merging companies. Furthermore, indication exists that internal growth performs systematically better than external growth through M&A activity (*Dickerson, Gibson, & Tsakalotos,* 1997). Second, so-called event studies analyze stock market reactions to merger announcements. The underlying idea is that capital markets reflect the profitability changes in the course of mergers and acquisitions through the evolution of (abnormal) stock returns. While studies that restrict themselves to a short window of time around the announcement generally find a large share of value-increasing mergers, those that employ a longer window of time - in particular, extending to several years post-merger - show a wide distribution of results with a generally negative mean tendency (*Andrade, Mitchell, & Stafford,* 2001; *Pautler,* 2003; *Rau* & *Vermaelen,* 1998; *Röller* et al., 2006; *Tichy,* 2001).

Each of these studies may be criticized on methodological grounds (e.g., *Beigi* & *Budzinski* 2013), and their results are far from being homogeneous or mutually congruent. However, irrespective of the diversity of methods and irrespective of the respectively derived share of unprofitable mergers, the empirical picture clearly shows that unprofitable mergers do occur and do not represent a rare or negligible exception. This alone justifies including the possibility of unprofitable mergers in policy-relevant modeling. Does it, however, really contradict the model assumptions? In the FSF, it is assumed that *rational* enterprises engage only in profitable mergers. In principle, this offers scope for irrational (unprofitable) mergers. However, it seems *a priori* dissatisfying to label all unprofitable mergers 'irrational'. Therefore, the question arises whether rational agents might engage in unprofitable mergers. Therefore, why do unprofitable mergers occur?

First, principal-agent problems between owners and managers can promote unprofitable mergers (*Firth,* 1980; *Jensen,* 1986). Rational managers will maximize their individual utility. Elements of the respective utility functions might include income, power, prestige, publicity or career opportunities - factors that depend more upon the size and growth of the company than on profitability (*Jensen,* 1986; *Tichy,* 2001). The literature refers to concepts like empire building (*Shleifer* & *Vishny,* 1988; *Trautwein,* 1990), hubris (*Roll,* 1986), or free cash (*Jensen,* 1986; *Bruner,* 1988). Second, consultants may also be self-interested and, therefore, promote unprofitable mergers because creating a merger can be more profitable for consultants than preventing a merger. Moreover, post-merger re-organization represents a lucrative follow-up business. Obviously, rational consultants will not promote unprofitable mergers if they can be made responsible for this ex post (negative reputation effects). However, in combination with imperfect ex ante information, it may be difficult and ambiguous to identify the reasons of failure in ex post evaluation. Why, for instance, did the Daimler-Chrysler merger fail? Was it wrong from the beginning or due to bad policy post-merger or even external, unpredictable market circumstances (e.g., the unexpected decline of the SUV-segment in the U.S.)? Thus, rational consultants might expect to escape without reputation damage, in particular if the assessment is a close call (i.e., a merger project is on the brink of profitability). An unambiguously unprofitable merger, however, can hardly be explained along these lines. In these two cases, resulting mergers might not be rational from an enterprise point of view, but they are, nevertheless, the result of individually rational agents acting within organizations (with normal control problems). Consequently, ex ante unprofitable merger projects are conducted as a result of rational individual action.

Third, preemptive and defensive mergers might occur (*Fridolfsson* & *Stennek*, 2005). Company A might decide to merge with company B despite a lack of profitability of this combination to prevent B from merging with C (building of a powerful competitor) - an alternative that would be even worse for company A. Similarly, a merger might be done to prevent a hostile takeover of any merging party by C (white knight mergers). Although unprofitable in absolute terms, preemptive and defensive mergers might represent the less unprofitable choice for a specific enterprise. Thus, an unprofitable merger is rationally undertaken.

Fourth, mergers and especially merger waves are explained with psychological phenomena, such as herd behavior (merging because everyone else merges), information cascades, and framing effects, etc. It is debatable whether such phenomena belong to rational behavior. While advanced concepts of rationality - referring to human cognitive and mental processes and their limits - would include them (Budzinski, 2003; Kahneman, 2003a; 2003b), these modes of behavior might well fall outside more traditional concepts of rationality.

In summary, empirical evidence shows that unprofitable mergers occur with considerable frequency, and theoretical explanations note that rational agents have incentives to engage in unprofitable mergers. Therefore, merger policy cannot rely on a positive internal effect, i.e., that any proposed merger increases the profits of the merged entity compared to the single enterprises, either through (procompetitive) efficiency gains or through (anticompetitive) exploitation of market power. Sound merger policy decisions thus require consideration of the frequent occurrence of unprofitable mergers with a negative internal effect. To demonstrate the implications of this, we now address the FSF in more detail.

3. Unprofitable Mergers in the Farrell-Shapiro Framework

3.1 The Farrell-Shapiro Framework

Farrell and *Shapiro* (1990) use a model of Cournot oligopoly with homogenous goods. Inverse demand is given by $p(X)$, where X is the total industry output, p is the price, and $p'(X)<0$. The number of firms is exogenous and given by n, which rules out the entry of new firms. *Farrell* and *Shapiro* (1990) consider only the entry of new firms that behave oligopolistically. The entry by and existence of price-taking fringe firms is, however, not ruled out by the model framework. In this case, $p(X)$ can be interpreted as the residual demand curve facing the oligopolists.

Firm i's output and cost functions are given by x_i and $c^i(x_i)$, respectively, and $c_x^i(x_i)$ denotes firm i's marginal cost. Total industry output is therefore given by $X=\sum_{i=1}^{n} x_i$, and $y_i=\sum_{j\neq i} x_j = X - x_i$ summarizes the aggregated output of all firms other than firm i.

In the Cournot equilibrium, every firm i maximizes its profits, $\pi^i(x_i,y_i)=p(x_i+y_i)x_i-c^i(x_i)$, over its output x_i, given its rivals' output y_i. The solution is an output vector $(x_1,\ldots,x_n)$, such that the first-order condition,

$$\frac{\partial \pi^i}{\partial x_i}=p(X)+x_i p'(X)-c_x^i(x_i)=0, \quad i=1,\ldots,n, \tag{1}$$

holds for all n firms, whereas the existence and stability of a Cournot equilibrium requires the fulfillment of two weak assumptions on a given range:

(a) Each firm's reaction curve – which is given by (1) – slopes downward. This is equivalent with the requirement that firm i's marginal revenue is lowered by an increase in rivals' output (*Novshek*, 1985), i.e.

$$p'(x_i + y_i) + x_i p''(x_i + y_i) < 0. \tag{2}$$

(b) Firm i's residual demand curve intersects its marginal cost curve from above. Equivalently,

$$c^i_{xx}(x_i) > p'(X). \tag{3}$$

The slope of firm i's reaction schedule can be derived from equation (1): $\frac{dx_i}{dy_i} = R_i$, where $-1 < R_i < 0$ because of (2) and (3). This means that firm i reduces its output if the other firms jointly expand their production. However, firm i contracts its output by less. Converting the slope of the reaction curve gives:

$$dx_i = -\lambda_i dX, \tag{4}$$

where $\lambda_i = -\frac{R_i}{1+R_i} > 0$ under the conditions given by (2) and (3), which measures firm i's "output response to changes in industry output" (*Werden*, 1991).

This results in the effect of an exogenous output change of firm 1 on the total industry output, which is given by the "Lemma" (*Farrell & Shapiro*, 1990) *Consider an exogenous change in firm 1's output, and let the other firms' output adjust to re-establish a Cournot equilibrium among themselves. If firms' reaction curves slope downward (condition* [2]*), and if the stability condition* [3] *holds, then aggregate output moves in the same direction as firm 1's output, but by less.* That is: $1 > \frac{dX}{dx_1} > 0$.

To analyze the effect of a horizontal merger on total output, the cost function of the merged entity M, $c^M(\cdot)$, must be compared with the cost functions of the merging firms ("insiders"). The central result is given in proposition 1, whereby "*M* must enjoy *substantially* lower marginal costs than did its constituent firms, if price is to fall", and industry output increases, respectively (*Farrell & Shapiro*, 1990). The larger the pre-merger market shares of the constituent firms were, the larger must be this cost reduction. It is therefore not unreasonable to expect a reduction in total output as a result of a merger.

The following consideration of the total welfare effects contains the crucial assumption that proposed mergers are privately profitable, i.e., the change in the insiders' (I) total profits is positive ($\Delta\pi^I > 0$). Under this central assumption, a merger will raise welfare if it has a positive external effect on consumers and the nonparticipant firms ("outsiders") jointly (*Farrell & Shapiro*, 1990).

The sign of the external effect is determined by considering the reaction of the outsiders O with respect to an output change of the insiders. This allows the determination of the total effect on outsiders' profits π^O and consumer surplus CS. The change in equilibrium output by the insiders, ΔX_I, can be treated as exogenous because "consumers care only about the net effect on aggregate output, ΔX, and [...] rivals care only about the change in equilibrium output by the merging ('insider') firms, ΔX_I, not about what caused that change" (*Farrell & Shapiro*, 1990). The total change in insiders' output ΔX_I is considered as the integral of infinitesimal changes dX_I. First, the external effect is determined due to an infinitesimal merger, and the total external effect is the integral of the effects of these infinitesimal mergers. The latter are given by

$$dW - d\pi^I = \underbrace{\left(\sum_{i \in O} \lambda_i x_i - X_I\right)}_{\equiv \eta} \times p'(X)\, dX. \tag{5}$$

Given the reasons that determine the change in insiders' output, it is particularly important to consider the case of an output reduction. Converting η into market shares, i.e., $s_i = \frac{x_i}{X}$, the external effect is positive if the sum of the outsiders' market shares – weighted by their reaction parameters – is larger than the insiders' market shares, i.e., $\sum_{i \in O} \lambda_i s_i > s_I$ (see proposition 4 of *Farrell* and *Shapiro*, 1990).

To determine the total external effect, it must be shown that this condition is fulfilled along a "path" given by ΔX_I. Hence, "the net externality is a weighted integral of η along a path from $X_I^{initial}$ to X_I^{final}" (*Farrell & Shapiro*, 1990):

$$\Delta W - \Delta\pi^I = \int_{X_I^{final}}^{X_I^{initial}} \eta(X)\left[-p'(X)\right] \frac{dX}{dX_I}\, dX_I. \tag{6}$$

The lower and upper bound of the integral are given by X_I^{final} and $X_I^{initial}$, respectively, because the insider output falls from $X_I^{initial}$ to X_I^{final}.

In proposition 5 (*Farrell* & *Shapiro*, 1990), sufficient conditions are given for an increase of η as X_I falls. If these conditions are fulfilled, it follows for $\eta \geq 0$ before a merger that an output reducing and profitable merger results in an increase in total welfare. Therefore, any proposed merger that is aligned with a positive external effect should be allowed. If the external effect of a merger is negative, the reverse does not apply automatically, and the positive change in insiders' profits can offset the negative external effect. These conclusions are based on the presumption that mergers are only proposed if they are privately profitable, i.e., $\Delta\pi^I > 0$. The case of unprofitable mergers is explicitly ruled out of the analysis (*Farrell* & *Shapiro*, 1990).

3.2 Extensions and Modifications

This section gives a brief literature-based overview of models that modify and enhance the FSF. In regards to the aim of this paper, we particularly focus on whether the profitability assumption becomes modified. *Barros* and *Cabral* (1994) apply the FSF to mergers in open economies. They uphold the assumption that only profitable mergers are proposed and introduce merger control authorities. If consumers and producers are located in different countries, different objective functions of an international merger authority and national authorities and the resulting welfare implications are analyzed. *Levin* (1990) analyses the effects of mergers of a fraction of firms in markets where the outsiders are restricted to behaving à la Cournot, whereas the insiders (i.e., merging firms) are not. The results supplement the ones of *Farrell* and *Shapiro* (1990). Concerning welfare analysis, the focus lies on profitable mergers. Any proposed merger of a fraction of firms with no more than 50 percent of the premerger market share causes welfare to rise. Additionally, in a Cournot setting, *Hennessy* (2000) regards mergers of a small fraction of firms. He contrasts the view that these mergers are motivated by cost efficiencies instead of enhancing market power. In doing so, he refers to special industry demand curves that allow the occurrence of welfare-reducing mergers because of their private profitability even without cost efficiencies.

Verboven (1995) compares the results of the static Cournot model of *Farrell* and *Shapiro* (1990) with a model of quantity-setting firms that behave collusively. Assuming a linear demand function, the insiders' maximum allowable market share in the case of an output-decreasing capital transfer is higher than with *Farrell* and *Shapiro* (1990). However, this comparison also considers only privately profitable mergers. *Spector* (2003) allows for market entries in the FSF and analyses profitable mergers according to a consumer welfare standard. If mergers fail to generate synergies or economies of scale (not induced by fixed costs), then consumers are harmed, i.e., prices are higher, irrespective of entry conditions. *Brueckner* and *Spiller* (1991) consider airline networks (hub-and-spoke networks), which are characterized by economies of density and costs of complementarities. Competition on parts of these networks generates negative externalities on markets outside the competitive parts. As a result, mergers on the competitive parts can have net positive gains in consumer surplus, which leads them to the reconsideration of antitrust policy in not focusing attention on the parts where market power may increase. They do not, however, explicitly consider unprofitable mergers in evaluating the overall welfare effect.

Nilssen and *Sørgard* (1998) regard sequential merger decisions of disjoint groups of firms and their intertemporal dependence. Most important with respect to our analysis is the strategic motive, which reflects the effect of one merger on possible future merger decisions by rival firms, and its implications for policy conclusions. Concerning unprofitable mergers, the strategic motive explains these in expectation of future mergers, which will have a positive feedback for the first. While the policy conclusions are derived by explicitly referring to and reconsidering the argumentation of the FSF, the analysis of *Nilssen* and *Sørgard* (1998) is distinct to ours in that they refer to the possible intertemporal dependences of merger decisions and the effects on the evaluation of welfare effects. Our analysis focuses on the effects of introducing unprofitable mergers and the implications on assessment decisions for these based on the FSF.

Fridolfsson (2007) analyses endogenous merger formation. In this setup, firms have strong incentives to engage in anti- rather than procompetitive mergers. One reason is that firms pre-empt being an outsider of procompetitive mergers, which would have a negative external effect on them. The lack of pursuing procompetitive mergers, which would result in an output-increase, is the benefit (i.e., external effect) that outsiders gain from anticompetitive mergers. As a policy conclusion, *Fridolfsson* (2007) regards the assessment of the relevant alternatives to a proposed merger, which may be another merger rather than the original market structure. However, this approach focuses on an endogenous explanation of the formation of unprofitable mergers, whereas we analyze the effects of unprofitable mergers (however motivated) in the FSF.

Cheung (1992) addresses the problem of an automatic inference from the proposition of mergers on the creation of a minimal level of required cost savings because of the profitability assumption. Because output-increasing mergers can reduce welfare, *Cheung* (1992) shows – by means of a simple numerical example – that these mergers have an incentive to underestimate cost savings to imitate output-reducing mergers. The application of *Farrell* and *Shapiro*'s externality condition does not handle this problem because proposed mergers are assumed to be privately profitable, and the fulfillment of the externality condition indicates a welfare-improving merger. As a result, some welfare-reducing mergers are allowed. He provides his policy conclusions by either obtaining more precise information or by banning all output-reducing mergers. Cheung's numerical example fits as a special case of our more general treatment of the problem.

Two specifically interesting papers address an often-neglected subcase of the FSF. When mergers are privately not profitable (wherefore they are not done) but desirable from a total welfare perspective, then according to *Faulí-Oller* (2002) and *Dragone*, Lambertini and Mantovani(2006) subsidizing the unwilling-to-merge firms becomes the welfare-optimal merger policy in a couple of very specific cases. However, note that both *Faulí-Oller* (2002) and *Dragone* et al. (2006) restrict their analyses to very specific cases – declining industries and industries with plenty of competitors plus insignificant fixed costs, respectively. We will address this issue more closely in our more general framework in section 4.

3.3 *Introducing Unprofitable Mergers*

We now introduce the consideration of unprofitable mergers in the FSF. Derived from the analysis in section 3.1, we consider the case of an output-reducing merger, i.e., $\Delta X_I < 0$. It emerges from proposition 1 that this case is very reasonable because an increase in output requires substantially lower marginal costs of the merged entity compared to its constituent firms. As *Farrell* and *Shapiro* (1990, p. 111) note, "[m]ergers differ enormously in the extent to which productive assets can usefully be recombined". The authors permit possible relationships between the merged entity's cost function and the cost functions of its constituent firms, but they explicitly refer to changes that follow anticompetitive motivations, rationalization or synergies. Wherewith, it is implicitly assumed that the change in costs is positive (because the authors primarily consider output-reducing mergers, it is implicitly assumed that this positive change in costs is not big enough). Because no *a priori* assumptions on the merged entity's cost function are made – except the ones given by conditions (2) and (3) – negative movements of costs due to a merger are not ruled out.

If the assumption of privately profitable mergers is removed, two important conclusions can be drawn: First, it is permitted that a change in costs due to a merger was misjudged, is unexpected, or was intentional. Hence, we include both the cases of merger projects that appear profitable ex ante but turn out to be unprofitable ex post (failures in post-merger management, imperfect information, etc.) and of such that are already ex ante unprofitable but are conducted due to agency problems or preemptive and defensive strategies (managerial or consultancy interests, preemptive and defensive mergers; see section 2). We treat both cases in the same way because from a competition policy perspective, it is effects that matter and not motives: for merger control, it is only relevant if the *effects* of a merger lead to a negative internal effect and not whether this was *intentional*. Second, this need not mean that mergers lead to losses; merely the *change* in insiders' profits – after the merger combined in the merged entity – is now permitted to be negative. Furthermore, third, this also includes cases of self-interested managers with personal gains from unprofitable mergers (see section 2). While the gains for the managers represent a welfare increase that needs to be deducted from the losses for the shareholders in the case of an unprofitable merger, it appears very unlikely and a far-stretch to assume that these personal gains for a few individuals may outweigh total unprofitabil-

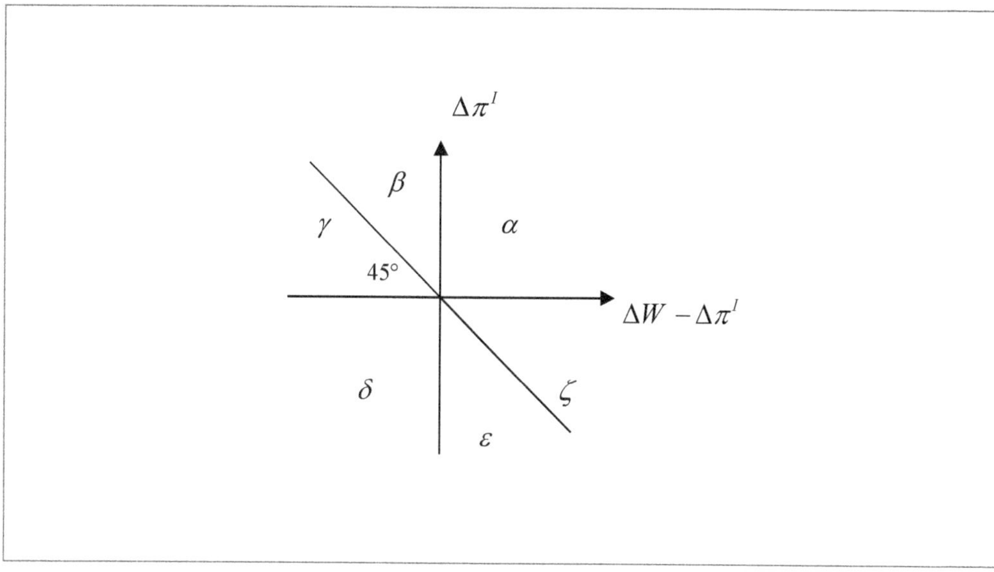

Figure 1. Welfare Effects of Horizontal Mergers (modified version from Farrell and Shapiro's (1990)

ity of a merger. Therefore, we do not explicitly model the manager gains-effect in the following.

Otherwise, the framework of *Farrell* and *Shapiro* (1990) is maintained and now used to permit the possibility of unprofitable mergers, i.e., $\Delta\pi^I < 0$. Given the reasons that determine the change in insiders' output, we focus on output-reducing mergers, i.e., $\Delta X_I < 0$. This is most plausible if it is assumed that a negative change in insiders' profits is the result of disadvantageous cost changes.

Again, the case of an infinitesimal merger is considered first. The external effect is given by (5). After converting η into market shares, i.e., $\sum_{i\in O}\lambda_i s_i - s_I$, the reasoning is thus analogous to the one given in proposition 4. A small reduction in insiders' output has a net negative welfare effect on outsiders and consumers if and only if the sum of the outsiders' market shares – weighted by their reaction parameters – is smaller than the insiders' market shares, i.e., $s_I > \sum_{i\in O}\lambda_i s_i$.

To discuss the total external effect, the integral of infinitesimal changes must be considered. As noted above and given by (6), "the net externality is a weighted integral of η along a path from $X_I^{initial}$ to X_I^{final}" (*Farrell* & *Shapiro*, 1990). A sufficient condition for the total effect on outsiders and consumers to be negative is fulfilled if $\eta < 0$ after the merger (*Farrell* & *Shapiro*, 1990). It is sufficient for an output-reducing merger because η increases as X_I falls (see proposition 5 in *Farrell* and *Shapiro* (1990); the authors give sufficient conditions for an increase of η as X_I falls). In this case, total welfare decreases as a result of an unprofitable merger. For η to be negative after the merger, it has to be sufficiently negative before the merger, i.e., $\sum_{i\in O}\lambda_i x_i \ll X_I$. The other possibility is that η changes its sign in the course of the "infinitesimal mergers", but the total external effect is negative. Both reflect the point that "big mergers" should be addressed with caution.

Converting η into market shares, this means that the insiders' market shares before the merger must be sufficiently large. In Fig. 1, this case is positioned in the southwestern quadrant δ.

If the total external effect of an unprofitable merger is positive, two possibilities must be considered:

A. the negative change in insiders' profits outweighs the positive external effect, which causes total welfare to fall *(area ε)*, or
B. the positive external effect is larger than the negative change in insiders' profits, which causes total welfare to rise *(area ζ)*.

In case A, the positive external effect must not be too large because the probability is increased that the profit change of the insiders will be outweighed. A sufficient condition for the external effect to be positive is given by $\eta \geq 0$ before the merger. First, the described situation is fulfilled the closer η lies to zero before the merger. Second, η changes its sign in the course of the "infinitesimal mergers", and the total effect is larger than zero. In both cases, the result is a fall in total welfare because the negative change in insiders' output amounts to more than the positive external effect. Both mentioned cases again address caution toward permission for "bigger mergers".

In case B, the positive external effect outweighs the change in insiders' profits. Despite the unprofitability of the merger, total welfare rises. Therefore, the total external effect must be sufficiently large. Due to the relationship between η and X_I, this means that η must be sufficiently large. The situation is most easily fulfilled if η is positive, both before and after the merger, i.e., the difference between the weighted market shares of the outsiders and the insiders' market shares is positive before the merger and rises after it. Given that η is positive both before and after the merger, this situation describes one possibility for the total external effect being large enough. Another possibility is that η changes sign, and the functional relation $\eta(X)$ is strong enough so that the total effect can outweigh the negative change in insiders' profits. This describes situations that are supported by sufficiently low market shares of the insiders (note that the reaction parameters λ of the outsiders would have to be considered as well; however, this complicates the analysis without altering the basic thought) and somewhat supports a cautious approach toward so-called "safe harbor" provisions.

4. Consequences for Merger Policy

Farrell and *Shapiro* (1990) draw their policy conclusions under the restrictive assumptions that only privately profitable mergers are proposed to the competition authorities. This implies that they (almost) exclusively look at the upper half of figure one. In doing so, their recommendation for merger policy reads: "Privately unprofitable mergers will not be proposed, so proposed mergers should be permitted unless their external effects are 'sufficiently' bad to outweigh their private profitability" (*Farrell & Shapiro,* 1990, pp. 116-117). The authors suggest a two-part procedure for merger review by competition authorities (*Farrell & Shapiro,* 1990). First, determine the external effect ($\Delta W - \Delta\pi^I$). If it is positive, allow the merger (area α). If it is negative, then, second, estimate the profit effect ($\Delta\pi^I$). If $|\Delta\pi^I| > |\Delta W - \Delta\pi^I|$, then allow the merger (efficiency defense; area β); otherwise, the merger should be prohibited (area γ).

Against the background of the empirics of mergers and acquisitions, however, the overall picture (according to section 3.3) must be interpreted to derive sound recommendations for competition authorities. Our interpretation of all six areas from the FSF (fig. 1), including the areas with unprofitable mergers (negative internal effect), reveals some concordance with *Farrell* and *Shapiro* but also some extensions and divergences.

Area (α): $\Delta\pi^I > 0 \wedge \Delta W - \Delta\pi^I > 0$, both the internal and the external effect are positive. In compliance with *Farrell* and *Shapiro*, *unconditional permission is recommended* from a total-welfare perspective. Note, however, that employing a different welfare standard might alter the assessment. For instance, within EU competition policy, a consumer welfare standard is applied. While the total welfare standard seeks the maximization of the sum of producers' and consumers' rent, the consumer welfare standard seeks to maximize the consumers' rent. The FSF does not allow for straightforward conclusions regarding such a consumer welfare standard because the external effect ($\Delta W - \Delta\pi^I$) comprises elements of producers' rents (the outsider firms to the merger) and the consumers' surplus: $\Delta W - \Delta\pi^I = \Delta\pi^O + CS$. Therefore, despite an overall positive external effect, consumers might be hurt, but their welfare loss is overcompensated by the increasing profits of the remaining competitors of the merging companies. The larger the external effect is, however, the less likely such a scenario becomes (if $\Delta W - \Delta\pi^I >> 0$, then $\Delta\pi^O >>> 0$ to allow for $CS < 0$). Vice versa, a negative external effect need not necessarily imply a reduction of consumer welfare because an increase in CS might be overcompensated by a loss in $\Delta\pi^O$. Again, this becomes less likely with an increasingly negative external effect.

Area (β): $\Delta\pi^I > 0$ and $\Delta W - \Delta\pi^I < 0$ with $|\Delta\pi^I| > |\Delta W - \Delta\pi^I|$, i.e., the positive internal effect outweighs the negative external effect. This is the area in which an efficiency defense is meaningful and becomes an important element of a welfare-maximizing merger policy. Despite anticompetitive effects (a reduction of the sum of consumers' rents and competitors' rents), total welfare is increased because the efficiency gains from the merger overcompensate them. Thus, *permission is recommended* from a total welfare perspective. Furthermore, even under a consumer welfare standard, some β-mergers might be approvable, namely, cases where the negative external effect results from a small increase in consumer welfare that is outweighed by a larger decrease in competitors' welfare. Therefore, prohibiting all β-mergers would be against welfare maximization even under a consumer welfare standard and, in some cases, protect competitors instead of consumers.

Area (γ): $\Delta\pi^I > 0$ and $\Delta W - \Delta\pi^I < 0$ with $|\Delta\pi^I| < |\Delta W - \Delta\pi^I|$, i.e., the negative external effect outweighs the positive internal effect. Mergers within this area are anticompetitive. Thus, *prohibition is recommended* from a total welfare perspective.

Area (δ): $\Delta\pi^I < 0 \wedge \Delta W - \Delta\pi^I < 0$, both the internal and the external effect are negative. This area consists of anticompetitive mergers: thus, *prohibition is recommended* from a total welfare perspective. This area is neglected by the original FSF. Therefore, a merger policy abstaining from the frequent occurrence of unprofitable mergers might err here. The FSF implies an asymmetric treatment: while a positive external effect suffices to allow a merger, a negative external effect is not sufficient to prohibit a merger, simply because the internal effect is assumed to be positive and, therefore, a trade-off inevitably arises. Consequently, δ-mergers would not be blocked automatically in the course of the two-part procedure suggested by *Farrell* and *Shapiro* (see above). Instead, their destiny would depend on the estimation of the internal effect that is – as *Farrell* and *Shapiro* (1990) admit – subject to some error risk. False positives (allowing a welfare-reducing merger) might, nevertheless, be rare because the competition authority should not find substantial efficiencies in such cases (that potentially outweigh the negative external effect) and thus should – in practice – prohibit these cases anyway. A residual might arise in cases where the negative external effect is very small, and the authority is thus willing to accept rather vague efficiencies because in a world without unprofitable mergers, almost every merger would be able to offset a small negative external effect. Then, false positives could occur to a certain extent if awareness of the frequent occurrence of privately unprofitable mergers is lacking.

Area (ε): $\Delta\pi^I < 0$ and $\Delta W - \Delta\pi^I > 0$ with $|\Delta\pi^I| > |\Delta W - \Delta\pi^I|$, i.e., the negative internal effect outweighs the positive external effect. In this case, a merger policy following the original FSF analysis commits errors, more specifically false positives. Due to the positive external effect, the merger is allowed although total welfare is reduced. In the modified interpretation, where unprofitable mergers are considered, ε-mergers are anticompetitive and *should be prohibited* under a total welfare standard. This leads to the important implication that the general recommendation of the original FSF – every merger with a positive external effect should be permitted – cannot be sustained in the modified FSF (inclusion of privately unprofitable mergers).

Result I: If unprofitable mergers are allowed to be proposed, a positive external effect does not represent a sufficient condition for the allowance of a merger anymore!

If a consumer welfare standard is considered, then the assessment of area *(*ε*)* becomes more difficult because of the positive external effect. The latter comprises the effect on competitors and consumers, so there can be a case where consumer welfare is positive. Therefore, while *Result I* stands that a positive external effect is not a sufficient condition to clear a merger proposal, ε-mergers are not generally prohibited under a strict consumer welfare standard – in contrast to a total welfare standard.

Area (ζ): $\Delta\pi^I < 0$ and $\Delta W - \Delta\pi^I > 0$ with $|\Delta\pi^I| < |\Delta W - \Delta\pi^I|$, i.e., the positive external effect outweighs the negative internal effect. Although the original FSF does not expect ζ-mergers to occur, a respectively styled merger policy would not make mistakes in such cases. Due to the positive external effect, ζ-mergers would be allowed, and this unwittingly corresponds to the resulting increase in total welfare. In a way, the right result is achieved for the wrong reasons.

However, if total welfare should be maximized consequently according to this framework, then the allowance of actually proposed ζ-mergers would not suffice. Instead, it would imply enforcing ζ-mergers even against the wishes of the firms because it increases total welfare and is Kaldor-Hicks-superior (*Farrell* and *Shapiro*, 1990 preferred to Pareto-optimality). As well as allowing an anticompetitive merger for efficiency reasons (area β) by assessing and judging the private profitability of a merger project, a competition authority in the FSF maximizes welfare if it evaluates and judges the external effect of possible mergers (that are not proposed voluntarily by the companies) and instructs them to merge in case it finds them located in area ζ. The same holds for privately profitable mergers that are not proposed due to the imperfections of the merger process and self-interested managers and advisers but that would increase total welfare (α- and β-mergers). Alternatively, the competition authority could apply subsidies as an instrument to promote ζ-mergers (*Dragone* et al., 2006; *Faulí-Oller*, 2002). The latter instrument might be viewed to be less controversial in regard to existing laws (private property rights) and related societal values (freedom of investment). However, from a strict welfare point of view, it is also less optimal because of the resulting burden on taxpayers.

Farrell and *Shapiro* (1990) explicitly reject compulsion or subsidies to implement ζ-mergers because "both of which would be enormous changes from our antitrust policy". We find this reasoning, however, not very convincing. In their article, *Farrell* and *Shapiro* draw policy conclusions and recommend certain merger policies, which implies that they intend to change hitherto antitrust policy in the first place. This stands in accordance with the widely held view that competition economics-research should be guiding the designing and reforming of practical competition policy. Moreover, a theory addressing why gradual changes will be recommended but not 'enormous' changes (wherever the delineation lies) is not provided. Furthermore, it lies at the heart of the FSF that a competition authority should maximize welfare by evaluating, assessing and eventually judging concrete merger projects. It cannot be derived from the framework why the welfare maximization activities of the competition authority should be restricted to voluntarily proposed merger projects. This line of argument becomes strengthened if firms are assumed to also engage in unprofitable mergers.

Despite rejecting *Farrell* and *Shapiro's* reasoning against enforcing welfare-enhancing mergers against the wishes of the companies, we share their concerns about a merger policy that instructs or subsidizes mergers. However, we find their reasons insufficient because the FSF does not include any element that rules out such a policy. Actually, the FSF on its own is compatible with a merger policy where the competition authority organizes and determines the market structure (instead of the competitive process) against the background of comprehensive evaluations of possible mergers and their welfare effects (*orchestrative merger policy*). Although this may appear to be too radical, there are actually tendencies toward a moderate version of this line of reasoning (*Dragone* et al., 2006 and *Faulí-Oller*, 2002 represent considerable steps in this direction.). The European Commission, for instance, has increasingly taken a constructive stance toward resolving anticompetitive merger proposals (without prohibiting them). In extensive negotiations with the merging companies and their competitors, the Commission seeks to develop remedies that mold the market structure in a way to maximize (consumer) welfare. This includes re-organizing market shares by orchestrated divestitures from the merging companies to (policy) selected competitors to rebuild the pre-merger market situation (*Budzinski* & *Kuchinke*, 2012). Thus, although the Commission 'only' intervenes when a merger is voluntarily proposed by the companies, in the course of the merger control procedure, remedies may be negotiated that include additional takeovers by (previous) outsiders of the mergers induced by the competition authority. The degree of active re-modeling of a market in the course of merger control has considerably increased and may represent a mild version of orchestrative merger policy.

However, before implementing FSF into merger control, additional assumptions must be relaxed and controlled for the subsequent effects. This includes ambitious assumptions about the knowledge of the competition authority and the measurability of the actual internal and external effects. Additionally, it touches on basic questions of the primacy of individual disposition about property rights (freedom of competition). Additionally, in a public choice view, the development toward a comprehensive 'merger control and instruction agency' would enhance the powers and resources of a competition authority as a bureaucracy, which could fuel the self-interested adoption of comparable reasoning.

Result II: An isolated application of the modified FSF implies far-reaching and controversial intervention opportunities for merger control authorities.

5. Conclusion

In this paper, we demonstrate that the popular FSF relies sensitively in its policy conclusions on the assumption that rational agents will only propose privately profitable mergers. If this assumption were held, a positive external effect of a proposed merger would represent a sufficient condition to allow the merger. However, the empirical picture on mergers and acquisitions reveals a significant share of unprofitable mergers, and economic theory, moreover, demonstrates that privately unprofitable mergers can be the result of rational action. Therefore, we extend the FSF by explicitly allowing unprofitable mergers to occur with some frequency. This exerts a considerable impact on merger policy conclusions: while several insights of the original FSF are corroborated (f.i., efficiency defense), a positive external effect does not represent a sufficient condition for the allowance of a merger any longer. Applying such a rule would cause a considerable amount of false positives. In addition, an isolated application of the modified FSF implies far-reaching and controversial intervention opportunities for merger control authorities.

References

Andrade, G., Mitchell, M. & Stafford, E. (2001). New evidence and perspectives on mergers. *Journal of Economic Perspectives*, 15(2), 103-120.

Barros, P. P., & Cabral, L. (1994). Merger policy in open economies. *European Economic Review*, 38 (5), 1041-1055.

Beigi, M., & Budzinski, O. (2013). Reservations on the use of event studies to evaluate economic policy decisions. *Intereconomics - Review of European Economic Policy*, 48 (3), 174-179.

Brueckner, J. K, & Spiller, P. T. (1991). Competition and mergers in airline networks. *International Journal of Industrial Organization*, 9 (3), 323-342.

Bruner, R. F. (1988). The use of excess cash and debt capacity as a motive for merger. *Journal of Financial and Quantitative Analysis*, 23 (2), 199-217.

Budzinski, O. (2003). Cognitive rules, institutions, and competition. *Constitutional Political Economy*, 14 (3), 215-235.

Budzinski, O., & Kuchinke, B. A. (2012). Deal or no deal: consensual arrangements as an instrument of european competition policy? *Review of Economics*, 63 (3), 265-292.

Cheung, F. K. (1992). Two remarks on the equilibrium analysis of horizontal merger. *Economics Letters*, 40 (1), 119-123.

Dickerson, A. P., Gibson, H., & Tsakalotos, E. (1997). The impact of acquisitions on company performance: Evidence from a large panel of UK firms. *Oxford Economic Papers*, 49 (3), 344-361.

Dragone, D., Lambertini, L., & Mantovani, A. (2006). Horizontal mergers with scale economies (Working Paper No. 571). Dipartimento Scienze Economiche, Universita' di Bologna.

Farrell, J., & Shapiro, C. (1990). Horizontal mergers: an equilibrium analysis. *American Economic Review*, 80 (1), 107-126.

Farrell, J., & Shapiro, C. (1991). Horizontal Mergers: Reply. *American Economic Review*, 81 (4), 1007-1011.

Faulí-Oller, R. (2002). Mergers between Asymmetric Firms: Profitability and Welfare. *Manchester School*, 70 (1), 77-87.

Firth, M. (1980). Takeovers, shareholders returns and the theory of the firm. *Quarterly Journal of Economics*, 94 (2), 315-347.

Fridolfsson, S. O. and Stennek, J. (2005). Why mergers reduce profits and raise share-prices: a theory of preemptive mergers. *Journal of the European Economic Association*, 3 (5), 1083-1104.

Fridolfsson, S. O. (2007). Anti- versus pro-competitive mergers (Working Paper No. 694). Research Institute of Industrial Economics. Retrieved from http://www.ifn.se/Wfiles/wp/wp694.pdf

Gugler, K., Mueller, D. C., Yurtoglu, B., & Zulehner, C. (2003). The effects of mergers: an international comparison. *International Journal of Industrial Organization*, 21 (5), 625-653.

Hennessy, D. A. (2000). Cournot oligopoly conditions under which any horizontal merger is profitable. *Review of Industrial Organization*, 17 (3), 277-284.

Jensen, M. C. (1986). Agency cost of free cash flow, corporate finance, and takeovers. *American Economic Review*, 76 (2), 323-329.

Kahneman, D. (2003a). A psychological perspective on economics. *American Economic Review*, 93 (2), 162-168.

Kahneman, D. (2003b). Maps of bounded rationality: psychology for behavioral economics. *American Economic Review*, 93 (5), 1449-1475.

Kaplan, S. N., & Weisbach, M. S. (1992). The success of acquisitions: evidence from divestitures. *Journal of Finance*, 47 (1), 107-138.

Levin, D. (1990). Horizontal mergers: the 50-percent benchmark. *American Economic Review*, 80 (5), 1238-1245.

Neven, D. J. (2006). Competition economics and antitrust in Europe. *Economic Policy*, 21 (48), 742-791.

Nilssen, T., & Sørgard, L. (1998). Sequential horizontal mergers. *European Economic Review*, 42 (9), 1683-1702.

Novshek, W. (1985). On the existence of Cournot equilibrium. *Review of Economic Studies*, 52 (1), 85-98.

Pautler, P. A. (2003). Evidence on mergers and acquisitions. *The Antitrust Bulletin*, 48 (1), 119-221.

Rau, P. R., & Vermaelen, T. (1998). Glamour, value and the post-acquisition performance of acquiring firms. *Journal of Financial Economics*, 49 (2), 223-253.

Ravenscraft, D. J., & Scherer, F. M. (1987). Mergers, sell-offs, and economic efficiency, Washington, DC: Brookings Institution.

Roll, R. (1986). The hubris hypothesis of corporate takeovers. *Journal of Business*, 59 (2), 197-216.

Röller, L. H., Stennek, J., & Verboven, F. (2006). Efficiency gains from mergers. In F. Ilzkovitz & R. Meiklejohn (Eds.), *European merger control: do we need an efficiency defence?* (pp. 84-101). Cheltenham, UK: Edward Elgar.

Salant, S. W., Switzer, S., & Reynolds, R. J. (1983). Losses from horizontal merger: the effects of an exogenous change in industry structure on Cournot-Nash equilibrium. *Quarterly Journal of Economics*, 98 (2), 185-199.

Shleifer, A., & Vishny, R. W. (1988). Value maximization and the acquisition process. *Journal of Economic Perspectives*, 2 (1), 7-20.

Spector, D. (2003). Horizontal mergers, entry, and efficiency defences. *International Journal of Industrial Organization*, 21 (10), 1591-1600.

Tichy, G. (2001). What do we know about success and failure of mergers? *Journal of Industry, Competition and Trade*, 1 (4), 347-394.

Trautwein, F. (1990). Merger motives and merger prescriptions. *Strategic Management Journal*, 11 (4), 283-295.

Verboven, F. (1995). Corporate restructuring in a collusive oligopoly. *International Journal of Industrial Organization*, 13 (3), 335-354.

Werden, G. J. (1991). Horizontal mergers: comment. *American Economic Review*, 81 (4), 1002-1006.

Acknowledgements

We thank all of the participants of the 29th HOS Conference (Marburg, November 2007), the 35th EARIE Conference (Toulouse, September 2008) and the Annual Meeting of the Verein für Socialpolitik (Graz, September 2008) for valuable and helpful discussion of earlier versions of this paper. Furthermore, we thank Barbara Güldenring for editorial assistance.

Appendix

We regard a simple model that is able to describe all possible types of mergers out of the graphical illustration in Figure 1 by referring to the analysis of *Salant*, Switzer and Reynolds (1983) in conjunction with *Dragone* et al. (2006).

Salant et al. (1983) regard the impact of mergers by referring to Cournot's classic example. Given the notation of section 3 of our paper, the inverse demand is given by $p(X) = \beta - X$, with $\beta > 0$, X denoting total industry output and p denoting the price. The number of firms is exogenous and given by n. Firm i's output is given by x_i. It is assumed that the n firms are identical with the same marginal costs c and fixed costs F. Thus, total industry output is given by $X = \sum_{i=1}^{n} x_i$, and $\sum_{j \neq i} x_j = X - x_i$ summarizes the aggregated output of all firms other than firm i.

Firm i now maximizes its profit by setting x_i, i.e., $\max_{x_i} \left[p(X) - c \right] x_i - F$. Assuming that the n firms are identical, the output of each firm will be the same in a symmetric Nash equilibrium, i.e., $x_i = x_j = x$ (*Salant* et al., 1983), which is given by $x = (\beta - c)/(n+1)$. Price and profit of each firm will, therefore, be given by $p(X) = (\beta + nc)/(n+1)$ and $\pi(x) = \left[(\beta - c)/(n+1) \right]^2 - F$, respectively.

Now, $m+1$ firms merge ("insiders"), and the number of independent firms decreases to $n-m$ ($n=m$ describes the limiting case of the monopolization of a market). Thereby, m can be interpreted as the size of the merger, i.e., the market share of the merging firms (*Dragone* et al., 2006; *Salant* et al., 1983). Different from the assumption of *Salant* et al. (1983) the merging firms do not totally shut down all of the plants but one. At this point, we rather refer to the analysis of *Dragone* et al. (2006). They assume that efficiency gains are "the outcome of an adjustment in fixed costs via the merger" (*Dragone* et al., 2006). The reduction in total fixed costs of the insiders following the merger amounts to a fraction smaller than mF because of a "restructuration of production plants within the resulting firm" (*Dragone* et al., 2006); the fixed costs of the resulting firm amount to $(1+e)F$ with $e \in (0, m-1)$. The parameter e thus describes the inefficiency of the merger, i.e., a higher value of e is equal to lower restructuration gains. Marginal costs are unchanged.

Industry output and price are now given by $\hat{X} = \sum_{i=1}^{n-m} \hat{x}_i$ and $p(\hat{X}) = \beta - \hat{X}$, respectively, whereas the roof denotes the post-merger situation. Each firm's output in the new symmetric Nash equilibrium is given by $\hat{x} = (\beta - c)/(n-m+1)$. The resulting price $p(\hat{X}) = \left[\beta + (n-m)c \right]/(n-m+1)$ is larger than $p(X)$ for $\beta > c$, which must be fulfilled to have a strictly positive industry output. Insiders' profits and the profits of the $n-m-1$ outsiders (non-merging firms) amount to $\pi^I(\hat{x}) = \left[(\beta - c)/(n-m+1) \right]^2 - (1+e)F$ and $\pi^O(\hat{x}) = \left[(\beta - c)/(n-m+1) \right]^2 - F$, respectively.

According to *Salant* et al. (1983), the profitability of a merger is given by the difference between the post-merger profit $\pi^I(\hat{x})$ and the sum of the pre-merger profits of the 2 insiders (The first derivative with respect to m is given by $\frac{\partial \Delta \pi^I}{\partial m} = 2(\beta - c)^2/(n-m+1)^3 - (\beta - c)^2/(n+1)^2 + F$):

$$\Delta \pi^I = \pi^I(\hat{x}) - (m+1)\pi(x) = $$
$$= (\beta - c)^2 \left\{ (n-m+1)^{-2} - (m+1)(n+1)^{-2} \right\} + (m-e)F. \quad (0.1)$$

Joint Profits of the outsiders and the consumer surplus (CS) change as follows:

$$\Delta \pi^O = (n-m-1)\left[\pi^O(\hat{x}) - \pi(x) \right] =$$
$$= \frac{\left[m^2(m-3n-1) + 2m(n^2-1) \right](\beta - c)^2}{(n+1)^2 (n-m+1)^2}, \text{ and} \quad (0.2)$$

$$\Delta CS = CS(\hat{X}) - CS(X) =$$
$$= \frac{\left[m^2(2n+1) - 2nm(n+1) \right](\beta - c)^2}{2(n-m+1)^2 (n+1)^2}, \text{ respectively.} \quad (0.3)$$

This results in the determination of the external effect due to *Farrell* and *Shapiro* (1990), i.e., the sum of the consumer surplus and joint outsiders' profits $(\Delta CS + \Delta \pi^O)$:

$$\Delta CS + \Delta \pi^O =$$
$$= \frac{\left[m^2(2m-1) - 4m - 2nm(1+2m-n) \right](\beta - c)^2}{2(n-m+1)^2 (n+1)^2}. \quad (0.4)$$

The change in total welfare due to a merger is thus given by:

$$\Delta W = \Delta \pi^I + \Delta \pi^O + \Delta CS =$$
$$= (\beta - c)^2 \left\{ \frac{n-m}{n-m+1} - \frac{n}{n+1} - \frac{1}{2}\left(\frac{n-m}{n-m+1} \right)^2 + \frac{1}{2}\left(\frac{n}{n+1} \right)^2 \right\} +$$
$$+ (m-e)F. \quad (0.5)$$

We can now describe the effect of a merger in settings that differ in the crucial parameters m, e and F. The first variation considers different sizes of mergers, the second variation considers the efficiency of restructuration due to mergers, and the third variation considers the possible amount of the second variation. Thereby, it is possible to describe all mergers out of the graphical illustration in Figure 1.

Generally, an increase in the inefficiency parameter e reduces the profitability of the merger. Given the merger of two firms, or even a few, the variation moves along the areas α, ζ, and ε. Thus, the change in total welfare is more likely to be positive but small, and at some point, it drops below the 45°-line into the negative area. However, the change in the external effect does not turn out to be negative due to a positive development of the outsiders' profits. In contrast, if many firms merge, the change in the external effect does not turn out to be positive due to the highly negative impact on consumer surplus. Then, an increase in the inefficiency parameter e also reduces the profitability of the merger, but the variation now moves along the areas β, γ, and δ. Thus, an efficiency defense is more likely for high efficiencies; the change in total welfare quickly drops below the 45°-line into the negative area.

The number of merging firms also has a clear impact, which can be shown in a counter-clockwise move along the areas. The effects of a smaller number of firms can more often be illustrated by areas ε, ζ, and α, whereas the effects of a higher number of merging firms can more often be illustrated by areas β, γ, and δ.

High fixed costs make the mergers more profitable, i.e., savings are possible in a higher amount. This result holds for a few as well as for many merging parties. Thereby, a higher inefficiency parameter e increases the amount of fixed costs needed to turn a merger to be profitable. Given two merging parties, or even a few, increasing fixed costs lead to a variation along the areas ε, ζ, and α. Thus, the change in total welfare turns from negative into positive, and the change in the external effect does not turn out to be negative due to a positive development of the outsiders' profits. In contrast, if many firms merge, the change in the external effect does not turn out to be positive due to the highly negative impact on consumer surplus. Then, an increase in the fixed costs F also increases the profitability of the merger, but the variation now moves along the areas δ, γ, and β. Furthermore, small changes in the amount of fixed costs now also have very high impacts, and the resulting effects of a merger quickly switch between the mentioned areas.

Unprofitability of a merger is possible in this simple framework if many firms merge (i.e., a high market share of the merging firms) and/or if the inefficiency parameter is high (i.e., a merger is unlikely to lead to efficiencies).

15

Franchise fairs: A relevant signal in franchise choice in social activity

Leonardo Martin Mastrangelo[1], Esther Calderon-Monge[2], Pilar Huerta-Zavala[2]

ABSTRACT

Potential franchisees encounter difficulties in gaining knowledge about a franchise before embarking on their first start-up venture. For this reason, it is necessary to research which information signals help potential franchisees choose the franchise chains with which they wish to enter into business. Working within the framework of signaling theory, this study's aim is to analyze the relationship between franchise choice and brand, price and participation in franchise fairs. The dynamic signaling model deployed to achieve the study´s aim draws on panel data methodology. This methodology allows us to analyze franchise chains over the period in which their parent franchises were using signaling to reveal information about their quality to potential franchisees. The results show that franchise fairs and up-front entry fees influence franchisee´s decisions. Therefore, it is concluded that potential franchisees prefer to garner information directly from franchise fairs, as opposed to heeding the other signals under study, and that when macroeconomic variables are exerting a strong influence on potential franchisees, up-front entry fees also constitute a signal that they consider. Finally, the managerial implications of the study are that franchise chains seeking franchisees should participate in franchise fairs to ensure that they are among the chosen franchises. Additionally, a franchisor should appropriately manage up-front entry fees as a signal, especially during periods of economic turmoil and recession.

KEY WORDS: Entrepreneurship; signals; price; franchising; GMM; franchise fairs

[1] Faculty of Economy, University of València, Spain; [2] Faculty of Economics and Business Studies, University of Burgos, Spain

1. Introduction

In recent years, franchises in Spain have been operating in an economy reeling from the effects of recession. This economic backdrop has forced franchises to move with the times, requiring them to demonstrate great flexibility and creativity. During this period, so-called low-cost franchises have surfaced that strive to limit investment, which is revolutionizing existing business concepts. Franchises have also launched new products and services to adapt to consumers' changing habits. Evidence of franchises' capacity to adjust in such a precarious environment can be observed in the high number of attendees at Spain's most well-established franchise fairs, such as SIF&Co and ExpoFranquicia. In 2012, these events welcomed 23,000 visitors through their doors, boasting the participation of approximately 500 franchise brands. Furthermore, of these 23,000 visitors, almost 80% attended these fairs with a view to accessing business opportunities by means of a fran-

Correspondence concerning this article should be addressed to: **Leonardo Martin Mastrangelo**, University of València, Faculty of Economy, Campus de los Naranjos, 46 021 Valencia, Spain. E-mail: leomastrangelo@hotmail.es

chise agreement. This reflects the role of franchising as an alternative for potential franchisees that provides a model not only for product distribution but also for starting up a new business. Accordingly, in 2012, the opportunity entrepreneurship rate (ventures that exploit a specific business opportunity) was 72.3% (Xavier, Kelley, Kew, Herrington, & Vorderwülbecke, 2012).

Budding entrepreneurs habitually view franchising as a chance to run a business, as franchising offers a guarantee of success, value added—as a business that has been tried and tested by the franchisor—an established brand image, initial and on-going training, economies of scale, and the so forth that permit the entrepreneur to develop and mature in a competitive environment.

The aim of the current study is to analyze the relationship between franchise choice and brand, price and franchise participation in franchise fairs. We test the hypotheses that appear in Section 2 using data from a database of 166 franchise chains that were operating across three sectors in Spain between 2006 and 2011. The dynamic signaling model deployed to achieve the above aim draws on panel data methodology. This methodology allows us to analyze franchise establishments over the period in which their parent franchises were using signaling to reveal information about their quality to potential franchisees. The results from the estimation of the model show that potential franchisees looking to start a business under a franchise agreement deem franchise fairs to be a signal that directly provides pertinent information about franchise chains.

This paper has five sections. Following the introduction, Section 2 presents a brief summary of signaling theory as a basis for later positing our hypotheses. Section 3 describes the study sample and the variables in the model, while Section 4 defines and estimates the model. Finally, Section 5 lays out the results and conclusions of the study.

2. Theoretical framework and hypotheses

In franchising, broadly understood as an exchange relationship, a potential franchisee encounters difficulties in gaining knowledge about the franchise before embarking on a relationship, giving rise to information asymmetries. We therefore pose the following research question: which information signals help potential franchisees resolve problems of information asymmetry with respect to the franchisor? The economics literature presents signaling theory as a strategy for potential franchisees to gather knowledge about franchise chains (Dant & Kaufmann, 2003). The majority of signaling models include the variable of quality (Janney & Folta, 2006). Potential franchisees choose chains with a certain level of quality, and this quality may be determined by signals such as brand recognition of the franchise (Weaven & Frazer, 2006) and price (Shane, Shankar & Aravindakshan, 2006; Wu, 1999) specifically, up-front entry fees, royalties, and investment. Additionally, quality may be perceived through visits to franchise fairs, which constitute an important communication channel that links the business to its current and potential clients (Baena & Cerviño, 2012).

2.1. Brand equity of a franchise

A readily accessible indirect indication of a commercial chain's current brand equity is longevity (Dant & Kaufmann, 2003). Longevity refers to the number of years a franchise has been operating in the marketplace (Mariz & García, 2009). Potential franchisees seek franchises with renowned brands because this attribute is a guarantee of future success. Better brand recognition increases a business's appeal, as it attracts clients, aids the company in differentiating itself from the competition, and reduces potential franchisees' costs of searching for information about the chain (Baena & Cerviño, 2012). Social venture franchising is liable to lead to increased selection costs because franchisees are organizations rather than individuals, and franchisees are assessed on their ability to achieve both social and commercial objectives (Tracey & Jarvis, 2007). Therefore, franchises with greater longevity have greater brand equity, which encourages potential franchisees to choose the franchise chain. We therefore posit the following hypothesis.

HI: Potential franchisees' choice of franchise is positively related to franchise brand equity.

2.2. Franchisees' initial investment

Meeting franchisees' expectations—in particular, those regarding the quality of a franchised outlet's daily operations and franchisees' perceptions of recovering their initial investment (Grace & Weaven, 2011)—causes the perceived risk of an investment when opening a franchise to fall dramatically and encourages future investment in the franchise. Thus, franchises that demand large amounts of initial investment will have fewer franchised outlets than other franchises that demand less initial capital from their franchisees (Shane et al., 2006). We therefore posit the following hypothesis.

H2: Potential franchisees' choice of franchise is negatively related to the initial investment demanded by the franchisor.

2.3. Franchises' up-front entry fees

Up-front entry fees act as a mechanism in a chain's quality control procedures. Therefore, the reputation of a franchise chain offers an alternative mechanism for attracting potential franchisees, with the franchisor able to set high up-front entry fees to attract potential franchisees (Shane et al., 2006). This argument leads to the following hypothesis.

H3: Potential franchisees' choice of franchise is positively related to up-front entry fees.

2.4. Franchise royalties

Franchisors justify charging royalties to franchisees on the basis of their commitment to transferring concepts and know-how and to promoting the franchise network (Fadairo, 2013). As stated by signaling theory, potential franchisees are more disposed to open an outlet with a franchise that demands higher royalties. Numerous scholars find a positive relation between the propensity to franchise and royalties (Shane et al., 2006). We therefore posit the following hypothesis.

H4: Potential franchisees' choice of franchise is positively related to royalties.

2.5. Franchises' participation in franchise fairs

Franchise fairs are an important communication channel (Blythe, 2010; Guilloux, Gauzente, Kalika & Dubost, 2004) in the sense that they act as a showcase for different business concepts, offer a meeting place for brands and investors, and serve as a platform for networking and obtaining information about the sector and new trends. Potential franchisees attend franchise fairs because they believe them to be an important medium for gathering information about new franchise business opportunities (Bennett, Frazer, & Weaven, 2010). The participation of franchises in franchise fairs is a key factor in introducing the business concept to and establishing a direct relationship with potential franchisees, which is impossible to do via the traditional press, brochures, and the like. The implication is that social franchising is more effective when franchisees are given a higher degree of autonomy (Tracey & Jarvis, 2007). Therefore, direct marketing is highly effective in attracting new franchisees (Perrigot, Basset, & Cliquet, 2011). This argument leads to the following hypothesis.

H5: Potential franchisees' choice of franchise is positively related to franchises' participation in franchise fairs.

3. Research

The data come from the Spanish Association of Franchisors and the consultancy Tormo and Associates. The sample consists of non-aggregated data for 166 franchise chains that were operative in Spain between 2006 and 2011 and that developed social activities. Using the year 2006 as a starting point, we performed simple random sampling from the population of franchises for that year. In subsequent years, we maintained the same franchises as those chosen for 2006—eliminating any that had since been rolled up—and added new franchises to ensure the representativeness of the sample for each of the six years under study.

Table 1 presents a summary of the variables—definition, nomenclature, and their metrics—that feature in the model below.

4. Findings

Table 2 shows the descriptive statistics for the variables described in Table 1.

In addition to the univariate analysis, we performed a bivariate analysis with the aim of uncovering the multiple correlation between the independent variables, thereby evaluating the model's collinearity. Table 3 shows that all Variance Inflation Factors (VIF) values are below 10 and that the tolerance values all indicate that collinearity explains a maximum of 10% of the variance of any independent variable.

The linear regression model that we aim to estimate to explain the relationship between franchise

Table 1. Variables and their metrics

Variable Name	Metric	References
	Dependent Variable	
[TEADO] Franchise choice	% of new franchised establishments opened by a first-time franchisee.	Ehrmann and Spranger, 2005
	Independent Variables	
[LNG] Brand equity	Number of years since the franchise began its operations with respect to the observation year.	Windsperger and Dant, 2006
[INVI] Initial investment	Amount (in euros) demanded by the franchisor, excluding up-front entry fees.	Shane et al., 2006
[DE] Up-front entry fees	Amount (in euros) that a franchisee must pay the franchisor as a single, one-time payment.	
[RYT] Royalties	% of sales that franchisees must pay the franchisor.	Kaufmann and Dant, 2001
[FSIF] Franchise fair (SIF&CO)	Participation in the SIF&CO franchise fair. Dichotomous variable that takes the value 1 if the franchise has participated and 0 otherwise.	Baena & Cerviño, 2012
[FEXPOF] Franchise fair (ExpoFranquicia)	Participation in the ExpoFranquicia franchise fair. Dichotomous variable that takes the value 1 if the franchise has participated and 0 otherwise.	
	Control Variables	
s = Sector (hostelry, retailing, and services)	Dummy variable that takes the value 1 if the chain belongs to one of the three sectors included in the study and 0 otherwise.	Michael, 2009
d = Time	Dummy variable that takes the value 1 for a given period and 0 otherwise.	Shane et al., 2006

signals and franchise choice by the franchisee is the following:

$$TEADO_{it} = \acute{\alpha}n + \acute{\alpha}1[LNG_{it}] - \acute{\alpha}2\,[INVI_{it}] + \acute{\alpha}3\,[DE_{it}] + \\ + \acute{\alpha}4[RYT_{it}] + \acute{\alpha}5[FSIF_{it}] + \acute{\alpha}6[FEXPOF_{it}] + \eta i + dt + \\ + si + vit \qquad (1)$$

The estimation of the model applies panel data methodology (using the Generalized Method of Moments (GMM) framework). We opt for this method to control for the unobservable heterogeneity of the potential franchisee, such as his managerial talent or personal traits, and to correct for any possible endogeneity between the dependent and independent variables (Shane et al., 2006). Furthermore, this methodology allows us to include in the model the effects of certain macroeconomic variables that may influence potential franchisees' choice of franchise.

Table 4 shows the results of the estimate of the dynamic linear model upon introducing the one-period

Table 2. Descriptive statistics for the sample

Var.	Mean	S.D.	Min.	Max.
TEADO	0.02	0.03	0	0.08
LNG	13.95	8.37	0	71.00
INVI	121,947.80	130,871.70	0	2020.99
DE	15,155.43	17,465.77	0	300.00
RYT	0.03	0.04	0	0.60
FSIF	0.04	0.21	0	1.00
FEXPOF	0.05	0.22	0	1.00

Table 3. Variance inflation factors and tolerance measures

Variable	VIF	(1/VIF)
LNG	1.02	0.985
INVI	1.21	0.830
DE	1.31	0.765
RYT	1.10	0.909
FSIF	1.31	0.765
FEXPOF	1.32	0.757
Mean VIF	1.21	

lagged variable, [TEADO_1] as an explanatory variable. Inclusion of this variable is advisable, as a potential franchisees' choice may be influenced by his choices in the previous year.

5. Conclusion

The limited literature that exists is practice oriented, focusing upon the key managerial challenges faced by social entrepreneurs in franchising. The results fail to corroborate the hypothesis linking franchise choice to brand equity [H1], initial investment [H2], and royalties [H4]. The results do, however, corroborate hypothesis [H3], which posits a direct relationship between up-front entry fees and the franchisee's decision. According to our results, the relationship in [H3] is significant and positive when the model accounts for the time dummy variables. The results also corroborate, in all three estimates, hypothesis [H5], which links franchise choice to franchises' participation in franchise fairs.

In terms of the control variables, the effects of the macroeconomic variables, represented by the time dummy variables, seem to exert an influence on franchise choice, with a greater influence existing between

Table 4. Estimates of the proposed model

Var.	I	II	III
$TEADO_{it-1}$	-0.490*** (0.000)	-0.511*** (0.000)	-0.511*** (0.000)
LNG_{it}	-0.009*** (0.000)	-0.013* (0.005)	-0.013* (0.005)
$INVI_{it}$	-3.790 (0.025)	5.260 (0.031)	5.260 (0.031)
DE_{it}	-6.880 (0.661)	6.200* (0.002)	6.200* (0.002)
RYT_{it}	-0.063*** (0.000)	-0.140*** (0.000)	-0.140*** (0.000)
$FSIF_{it}$	0.004* (0.044)	-0.013* (0.005)	-0.013* (0.005)
$FEXPOF_{it}$	0.030*** (0.000)	0.044*** (0.000)	0.044*** (0.000)
V.Temp.	----------	Deleted 2/6	Deleted 2/6
Z_1	76.69 (7) (0.000)	----------	----------
Z_2	----------	18.91 (4) (0.000)	18.91 (4) (0.000)
m_1	0.000	0.000	0.000
m_2	0.000	0.000	0.000
Hansen	0.220	0.810	0.810
Obs.	310	310	310
Chains	166	166	166

2008 and 2011. Moreover, the decisions from previous periods appear to have a negative effect on the current choice of franchise, as shown by the role of the lagged variable. Finally, franchises from the same sector do not compete with one another for franchisees—the quality of the chains in all sectors follows a continuous distribution. Consequently, evidence is lacking as to the differences in quality between chains, which means that sector is inadequate as a signal (Cheong & Kim, 2004).

In conclusion, potential franchisees seek information about the quality of franchises with which they are looking to enter into business through direct signals such as participation in franchise fairs. This is because these signals allow potential franchisees to gain knowledge directly from franchisors about new business concepts, as well as to obtain the information they are searching for. Beckmann and Zeyen (2014) noted that the idea of *friendchising* (friendship between the franchisor and the franchisees) is misleading in social franchising because in a complex social franchise system, there is too little contact and too little transparency. Therefore, direct marketing, mainly in the form of participation in franchise fairs, emerges as a potent information signal (Perrigot et al., 2011) that potential franchisees regard as important in their decision-making process. Up-front entry fees also constitute a signal that potential franchisees consider, particularly when macroeconomic variables are exerting a strong influence on these individuals.

It is noteworthy that the managerial implications of the study are that franchise chains seeking franchisees should participate in franchise fairs to ensure that they are among the chosen franchises. Additionally, a franchisor should appropriately manage up-front entry fees as a signal, especially when the potential franchisee is affected by macroeconomic variables, as is the case during periods of economic turmoil and recession.

Future research should use qualitative comparative analysis for this type of study. This would help in gaining an understanding of both the franchisor and franchisee perspective.

References

Baena, V., & Cervino, J. (2012). International franchise expansion of service chains: Insights from the Spanish market. *Service Industries Journal, 32*(7), 1121-1136.

Beckmann, M., & Zeyen, A. (2014). Franchising as a strategy for combining small and large group advantages (logics) in social entrepreneurship: A Hayekian perspective. *Nonprofit and Voluntary Sector Quarterly, 43*(3), 502–522.

Bennett, S., Frazer, L., & Weaven, S. (2010). What prospective franchisees are seeking. *Journal of Marketing Channels, 17*(1), 69-87.

Blythe, J. (2010). Trade fairs as communication: A new model. *Journal of Business & Industrial Marketing, 25*(1), 57-62.

Cheong, I., & Kim, J. Y. (2004). Costly information disclosure in oligopoly. *Journal of Industrial Economics, 52*(1), 121-132.

Dant, R. P., & Kaufmann, P. J. (2003). Structural and strategic dynamics in franchising, *Journal of Retailing, 79*(2), 63-75.

Ehrmann, T., & Spranger, T. (2005). Why do franchisors combine franchises and company-owned units? Social Science Research Net Work, Available at http://papers.ssrn.com/sol3/papers.cfm?abstract_id=807346

Fadairo, M. (2013).Why include royalties in distribution contracts? Evidence from France. *International Journal of Retail & Distribution Management, 41*(8), 566-583.

Grace, D., & Weaven, S. (2011). An empirical analysis of franchisee value-in-use, investment risk and relation satisfaction. *Journal of Retail, 87*(3), 366-380.

Guilloux, V., Gauzente, C., Kalika, M., & Dubost, N. (2004). How France's potential franchisees reach their decisions: A comparison with franchiser's perceptions. *Journal of Small Business Management, 42*(2), 218-224.

Janney, J. J., & Folta, T. B. (2006). Moderating effects of investor experience on the signalling value of private equity placements. *Journal of Business Venturing, 21*(1), 27-44.

Kaufmann, P. J., & Dant, R. P. (2001). The pricing of franchise rights. *Journal of Retailing, 77*(4), 537-45.

Mariz, R., & García, T. (2009). The internalization strategy of Spanish indigenous franchised chains: A resource-based view. *Journal of Small Business Management, 47*(4), 514-530.

Michael, S. C. (2009). Entrepreneurial signalling to attract resources: The case of franchising. *Managerial and Decision Economics, 30*(6), 405-422.

Perrigot, R., Basset, G., & Chiquet, G. (2011). Multichannel communication: The case of Subway attracting new franchisees in France. *International Journal of Retail & Distribution Management, 39*(6) 434-455.

Shane, S., Shankar, V., & Aravindakshan, A. (2006). The effects of new franchisor partnering strategies on franchise system size. *Management Science, 52*(5), 773 - 787.

Tracey, P., & Jarvis, O. (2007). Toward a theory of social venture franchising. *Entrepreneurship Theory and Practice, 31*(5), 667–685.

Weaven, S., & Frazer, L. (2006). Investment incentives for single and multiple unit franchisees. *Qualitative Market Research: An International Journal*, 9(3), 225-242.

Windsperger, J., & Dant, R. P. (2006). Contractibility and ownership redirection in franchising: A property rights view. *Journal of Retailing, 82*(3), 259-272.

Wu, L. (1999). The pricing of a brand name product: Franchising in the motel services industry. *Journal of Business Venturing, 14*(1), 87-102.

Xavier, S. R., Kelley, D., Kew, J., Herrington, M., & Vorderwülbecke, A. (2012). 2012 Global Report. Global Entrepreneurship Monitor. Retrieved from http://www.gemconsortium.org/report

16

A review of individual and systemic risk measures in terms of applicability for banking regulations

Katarzyna Sum[1]

ABSTRACT

The latest financial crisis has exposed substantial weaknesses in the bank risk models used by national regulators as well as the Basel Accords. The study is aimed at presenting the evolution and critique of risk measures and risk models in banking, with a special focus on the dynamically developing area of systemic risk measures. A discussion of the features of the respective measures allows us to draw conclusions for banking regulations based on the analyzed models and to present the main challenges for regulators in terms of bank risk measurement. The study shows that substantial challenges for regulators include compensating for the drawbacks of the Value at Risk (VaR) and expected shortfall risk models, resolving the pro-cyclicality in risk modeling, improving the techniques of stress testing, and addressing the fallacy of composition in banking (i.e., to model risk from a systemic point of view and not only from the perspective of an individual bank). As the discussion concerning proper risk measurement in regulatory frameworks, such as the Basel Accord or the European Banking Authority's (EBA) rules is in progress, the topic seems to be of particular importance; moreover, measures of systemic risk are not yet a subject of regulation.

KEY WORDS: bank risk, risk measures, risk models, systemic risk

[1] Warsaw School of Economics - Chair of International Finance, Poland

Introduction

For decades, bank risk modeling has been a challenge for managers of financial institutions and regulating authorities. The latest financial crisis has unleashed substantial weaknesses of the risk models used by national supervisors and the Basel Accords. These models are too arbitrary to evaluate the risk profiles of large banks. As such, they are prone to pro-cyclicality, which has contributed to incorrect risk measurement. Banking regulations derived from these models focus solely on individual bank risk without regard to the fallacy of composition problem; that is, even if individual banks function well, the banking system can fail. Hence, the focus of post-crisis regulations has shifted from a micro-prudential approach of banking supervision to a macro-prudential one.

While measuring individual bank risk is a complex process in itself, the difficulties in estimation and modeling increase dramatically when one takes systemic bank risk into account. This study is aimed at presenting the evolution and critique of risk measures

Correspondence concerning this article should be addressed to: **Katarzyna Sum**, Warsaw School of Economics - Chair of International Finance, ul. Madalińskiego 6/8, 02-513 Warszawa, Poland. E-mail: ksum@sgh.waw.pl

in banking, with a special focus on the dynamically developing area of systemic risk measurement. The discussion of the features of each measure allows to draw conclusions for banking regulations that are based on the mentioned models and to present the main challenges for regulators in terms of bank risk measurement. Because the measures capable of counteracting systemic risk are currently not a subject of regulation, this topic seems to be of particular importance.

The paper is structured as follows: the first section reviews the individual bank risk measures, the second presents the risk models based on the mentioned measures, and the third section focuses on systemic risk measurement.

Review of risk measures

Banking risk includes credit risk, market risk (i.e., the risk of price changes), and operational risk (i.e., related to the banks general activity). The measurement and quantification of the various risk types has been a substantial challenge for academics, bank managers, and regulators.

In most cases, risk measures are defined as functions of random variables, such as portfolio losses or returns. These types of measures require an arbitrary choice of the time horizon over which one analyses the losses and returns, as well as the assumed probability distribution (Basel Committee for Banking Supervision [BCBS], 2011). In contrast, risk measures that provide general information about the bank's financial soundness (e.g., the z-score) are based on accounting information and do not require assumptions about the distribution of losses. Determining which risk measurement to use depends on a number of factors, such as the simplicity of calculation, the mathematical properties of the measure, the ability to attribute risk to individual portfolio components, the ability to backtest, and the objectives of regulators/managers (BCBS, 2011).

The most common measure of bank risk is the Value at Risk (VaR). The theoretical foundations for VaR are based on the portfolio theory of Markowitz. VaR is defined as the maximum value of the loss on a given portfolio for an assumed probability of the loss over a specific time horizon. In other words, VaR defines how much money an institution should set aside to counteract a predicted loss. The computation of VaR is aimed at preventing a liquidity crisis triggered by a loss in the case of a low probability event. The term Value at Risk was first used officially by J. P. Morgan in 1995, referencing their RiskMetrics database, which enables public access to data on the variances of and covariances across various asset classes. It has been used by banks and regulators over the last two decades (Damodaran, 2010).

While there is no definition of how to compute VaR, its estimation requires assumptions about the profit and loss density function. To estimate the potential loss on a portfolio, the probability distributions of individual risks, as well as their correlation and their effect on the value of the potential loss, have to be defined, resulting in arbitrary risk modeling. Three solutions are applied to address this problem: estimation based on past values of the parameters, Monte Carlo methods, which require an assumption about the distribution of the portfolio values, and analytic methods, which are based on assumptions about the return distribution parameters (Damodaran, 2010).

The VaR measure has many drawbacks. First, it assumes a normal distribution of the values without accounting for fat tails. Thus, despite this fact the VaR concept is regarded as the worst case scenario, regulators and managers cannot focus on extreme events, which may result in excessive risk taking. Second, even if the assumption of the distribution is correct, another problem is the non-stationarity of variances and covariances across assets (BCBS, 2011). Third, the classical VaR assumes a linear relationship between risk and portfolio positions, which does not hold when derivate instruments are included in the portfolio. Finally, another drawback is the narrow focus on market risk.

Prior to the recent financial crisis, the use of VaR models contributed to the build-up of risk in the banking sector, as the models gave managers and regulators a false sense of security. A crucial criticism is that while VaR is the worst case scenario, it does not account for situations where the loss exceeds the VaR. The concept does not offer any solutions beyond the threshold of VaR, nor are there any implications regarding the distribution of losses beyond the VaR level. A possible solution to this problem is the concept of Conditional Value at risk (CVaR), also known as expected shortfall. The expected shortfall concept has substantial theoret-

Table 1.

VaR	Expected Shortfall/ CVaR
Abstracts from extreme events	Accounts for extreme events
Inferior mathematical properties	Superior mathematical properties
Backtesting possibility	No possibility of backtesting
Robust to estimation errors	Prone to estimation errors- accuracy of tail modeling is crucial

ical foundations (Acerbi & Tasche, 2002; Rockafellar & Uryasev, 2002; Yamai & Yoshiba, 2005). Its popularity among bank managers and regulators has increased. Because of its coherence, the Basel Committee included this concept, rather than the VaR used over the last decade, in its new regulatory framework Basel III (Chen, 2014).

The expected shortfall assumes losses in the tails of the distribution function i.e., beyond the value of VaR. The term conditional value at risk was introduced by Rockafellar and Uryasev in 2000 (Rockafellar & Uryasev, 2002). Larsen, Mausser and Uryasev (2002) define it as a weighted average of the VaR and losses exceeding the VaR. The expected shortfall is the expected loss on a given portfolio in the worst case scenario i.e., provided that the loss exceeds a given value. Hence, the evaluation of an investment is more conservative than in the case of VaR. This approach helps counteract excessive risk taking by managers. Compared to VaR, CVaR has superior mathematical properties. It also mitigates the effect of the arbitrary choice of a single confidence level on estimated losses (BCBS, 2011).

A drawback of CVaR is that it is more sensitive to estimation errors than VaR i.e., CVaR's accuracy depends largely on the accuracy of tail modeling. In the event when the tail modeling is inaccurate, the mixed CVaR concept can be applied. In the mixed CVaR concept, instead of penalizing extreme tail losses, different weights are attributed to different parts of the distribution. One should take into account that historical data may not carry the necessary information about the tails. In this case, adjustment of the tail modeling may be needed (Rockafellar & Uryasev, 2002). Another drawback of expected shortfall is the inability to backtest the model. In contrast to the VaR concept, expected shortfall forecasts cannot be verified through comparison with historical data (Chen, 2014). The main differences between VaR and CVaR are depicted in Table 1.

The economic literature improves upon the expected shortfall concept by proposing new spectral risk measures that generalize expected shortfall (BCBS, 2011). In addition to having desirable mathematical properties, these measures can also be adapted to investor behavior. The concept of generalized spectral measures implies that banks will be less risk averse towards small losses while more risk averse towards large losses. The highest weights are attributed to losses in cases where banks are unwilling to raise additional capital to absorb the loss. An advantage of general spectral measures is that, in contrast to VaR and expected shortfall, the outcome of the model does not depend on a single confidence level. Instead, the changes in the loss distribution will allow the risk measure to adapt (BCBS, 2011).

Another attempt to improve the risk measurement is the concept of the stressed value at risk. The measure has been proposed by the Basel Committee in 2009 within the so called Basel 2.5 framework. The main trigger of this concept is the financial crisis, during which the losses in banks' trading books largely exceeded the VaR-based capital requirements. In a stressed VaR framework, the value at risk is computed with the assumption of "a continuous 12-month period of significant financial stress" (BCBS, 2009b, p. 14).

The stressed VaR shows that current market conditions may lead to risk underestimation during times of financial stress (BCBS, 2011). Its purpose is to counteract the pro-cyclicality in capital provisioning. A problem related to the stressed VaR is the calibration of the reference period (European Banking Authority [EBA], 2012). According to the Basel Committee, the methodology banks use to identify a stressed period that is relevant to their current portfolios is either formulaic or judgment-based, which enables them to make arbitrary choices. It has been stressed in the literature that past events and crises are not a good indicator of future bank performance (Chen, 2014). During a financial crisis, the volatility of market prices rises to extreme levels, which causes the correlation of returns used in the VaR methodology to deviate from historical values. The concept of stressed VaR lacks theoretical underpinnings; consequently, its discussion in the academic literature is sparse.

The Basel Committee has tried to introduce a risk measure that would be resistant to fragility during periods of extreme financial stress and easily backtested. In these terms, the concepts proposed in Basel 2.5 and in Basel III are contradictory; they highlight the conflict between the elicit VaR and coherent expected shortfall. (Chen, 2014). Alternative risk measures to VaR are considered to be technological leaders; as a consequence, their popularity in the banking sector has increased (BCBS, 2011).

Review of risk models in banking regulations

The risk measures discussed are the basis for risk modeling for financial institutions and regulating agencies. A large number of risk models are derived from the Basel Accords.

The first Basel Accord from 1988 focuses on credit risk models attributed to the respective types of asset groups. The changes in the scope of banking activity enabled by deregulation make it apparent that regulators have to account for both credit and market risk. The Market Risk Amendment from 1996 introduces additional capital charges for banks' assets that are exposed to market risk. The capital requirements have been computed on the basis of two alternative models: the standardized approach or internal bank risk models. The former applies ready formulas for capital charges drawn from regulations, the latter uses VaR models that have been developed by the banks themselves and approved by the supervisory authorities. While the standardized approach is used primarily by small banks with limited exposure to market risk, it can also be applied in the event of internal model failure. Since the expansion of credit exposures securitization renders the construction of the regulatory trading book obsolete, the Market Risk Amendment from 1996 also specifies the risk charges to instruments in the banks' trading books. The risk charges do not adequately capture the market risk exposure of the assets. This has led to further reforms of the Basel framework, including the introduction of an incremental default risk charge to VaR models (BCBS, 2012).

One of the weaknesses of the Basel I framework is the various treatment of trading and banking books, particularly the inclusion of assets that are exposed to credit risk in the trading book. The regulations state how to estimate the correlations between different asset values to determine portfolio risk. In the case of the credit risk in the banking book, asset value correlations are derived from regulations, even for banks using internal models.

Moreover, the framework does not specify when to use the standardized approach or the model based approach. Even worse, although they did not necessarily work, the internal models cannot be changed during times of financial turmoil. Additionally, the measurement of risk raises some concerns. The standardized approach suffers from the portfolio invariance problem i.e., diversified portfolios are assigned the same risk weights as concentrated ones. Moreover, the standardized approach does not capture the risk exposure to complex instruments. On the other hand, the internal model approach is based on 10- day VaR i.e., it focuses on day-to-day risk exposures and did not account for tail events. The arbitrary choice of the models by individual banks may have limited individual bank risk, but is not equipped to counteract systemic risk (BCBS, 2012).

In 2004, Basel II strengthens the framework for risk models. The supervisory agencies are required to monitor both individual bank risk and systemic risk. Moreover, liquidity risk, concentration risk, and legal risk becomes the focus of supervisors.

Basel II maintains the basic features of Basel I, which has many drawbacks; one of which is the pro-cyclicality of risk assessment. The standardized approach uses external ratings which tend to be pro-cyclical, whereas the internal rating based approach is based estimating the parameters that conform to pro-cyclical formulas. The parameters that need to be estimated within the internal model based approach are: the probability of default for each individual credit, its loss-given-default, and the expected exposure at default. The three risk parameters are used to calculate the expected loss on a portfolio. All three elements are dependent on the economic cycle; they are driven by stock market and asset values, hence they contribute to the pro-cyclicality in risk assessment (Blundell-Wignall & Atkinson, 2010).

The Basel 2.5 revision of 2009 is an attempt to improve the market risk framework. Its major contribution is the introduction of three new risk models: the incremental risk charge (IRC), a comprehensive risk measure for default and migration risk arising from correlation trading (CRM), and the stressed VaR model (Chen, 2014). The stressed VaR measure has been discussed in the previous section. Its basic goal is to account for amplified portfolio losses during economic downturns. The second element – CRM – has been introduced to replace the surcharge models in the framework, which have been used in cases where the bank did not capture the incremental default risk prior to 2009. The CRM is an incremental risk measure that requires the measurement of additional risk factors: the cumulative risk from multiple defaults, the credit spread risk, the volatility of implied correlations, the cross effect between spreads and correlations, and benefits from dynamic hedging (BCBS, 2009b).

The IRC has attracted much attention, particularly from economists. It is aimed at measuring the default and migration risks of unsecuritized items over a one-year capital horizon while accounting for the liquidity horizons and estimating portfolio value changes resulting from spread changes, rating adjustments, and default events for specific trading book exposures (BCBS 2009b; Inanoglu, Jacobs & **Karagozoglu** 2014). It treats banks exposures in the trading book as equal to the ones in the banking books. The Committee does not specify the exact formula for calculating IRC. It suggests that banks develop their own models, which highlights the differences in risk assessment, especially in situations where there is no consensus regarding the risk measurement for illiquid trading positions (BCBS, 2009a). Given that the respective models imply different asset transition patterns, the choice of migration risk measure is also ambiguous (Inanoglu et al., 2014).

Another important change from the Basel 2.5 update is the equal treatment of securitized instruments in both the banking and trading books resulting from the standardized regulatory charges. An exception is that banks can estimate the risk of the correlation of trading activities by using comprehensive risk measures. In the case of the internal model based approach, banks are required to capture a broader scope of risk and abandon the application of the surcharge model for estimating the risk.

The Basel 2.5 framework still leaves some ambiguities to solve, such as a lack of a straightforward method to assess the risk in the trading book. The framework consists of hybrid elements used to calculate weighted risk. In some cases, the same positions in the banking and trading books are treated differently, with some securitized, highly illiquid credit risk exposures being included in the trading book. The application of both VaR and stressed VaR models leads to overlapping capital charges. The stressed VaR methodology faces limitations concerning liquidity requirements to a 10-day horizon, which renders it impossible to capture market illiquidity risk. Additionally, the stressed VaR specification implies that banks are able to hedge the risk within a 10-day period, which is an unrealistic assumption. The framework does not fully capture market liquidity risk. The additional risk measures introduced in Basel 2.5 i.e., IRC and CRM are focused only on credit risk.

Further changes to risk modeling are introduced by Basel III in 2010. One of the most important contributions of the Accord is the inclusion of counterparty risk, or credit valuation adjustment, in the models. Additional risk charges are attributed to assets exposed to the deterioration in the creditworthiness of a counterparty. The new risk measures also include unrealized gains at losses as a part of assets (BCBS, 2012). The Committee has proposed further changes in terms of risk measurement to replace VaR based models with expected shortfall based models (Chen, 2014).

Basel III offers a proposal to address pro-cyclicality. This regulation can counteract the build-up of risk resulting from mark-to-market accounting or the increased leverage in times of economic expansion. One of the proposed solutions is the estimation of the probability of default over a longer time horizon and the introduction of forward-looking, dynamic provisioning based on expected, rather than current, losses. The Committee also proposes bank capital deductions in cases of provision shortfall (Blundell- Wignall & Atkinson, 2010).

A commonly criticized element of the Basel III framework is the application of various risk measures that may lead to varied results in terms of capital levels. Moreover, differences in the outcomes of the standardized and model based approaches still exist. Blundell-Wignall and Atkinson (2010) find that while Basel III does not address the main problems of the risk-weighting approach in the calculation of capital requirements, it improves some aspects of the risk management process by introducing leverage ratios, countercyclical measures, and the promotion of settling derivatives to clearing houses. The authors stress that Basel III does not solve the problem of portfolio invariance, as there are no additional capital requirements for concentrated portfolios. Moreover, they stress that the risk modeling is too linear- it reflects a single global risk factor instead of local factors. As we have seen in the subprime crisis, shocks tend to originate locally and spread globally (Slovik, 2012).

An additional challenge for regulators is the aggregation of risk types into risk indicators that allow for the formulation of capital requirements. One way to do this is to take the sum of the computed capital requirements for credit, market, and operational risk. This approach ignores portfolio invariance i.e., it does not account for diversification benefits. Another way is to estimate all the risks within an integrated framework that accounts for possible correlations and interactions (BCBS, 2011).

These empirical models are used for regulatory purposes and are abstract from the theoretically funded models prevalent in academic literature. Popular models that assess bank risk are accounting-based models (Altman, 1968; Ohlson, 1980) or the structural distance to default model (Merton, 1974). The academic models rely on the cost of debt, rather than default data, to assess the bankruptcy risk. The rationale behind this approach is that some banks never experience bankruptcy. In addition, the lag between estimated and actual default can differ among banks such that quantifying default data may be problematic (Mansi, Maxwell & Zhang 2010).

The historically most significant model used for assessment of financial distress is the distance to default model (Merton 1974). The model extends the option pricing formula to predict company defaults. An advantage of this model is that it is not sensitive to the leverage ratio of other models that are aimed at estimating the probability of default (Mansi et al. 2010). Gropp, Vesala and Vulpes (2006) show that the distance to default measure outperforms other indicators of risk in predicting bank defaults in Europe. Moreover, the Financial Stability Board stresses the importance of this measure in determining systemically important banks (Vallascas & Keasey, 2012). While it does not account for tail events, the distance to default measure is appropriate for modeling central dependence. De Jonghe (2010) shows that risk indicators of tail dependence and central dependence may lead to substantially different outcomes. To measure bank risk in a stressed environment the literature proposes the concept of exceedances, which are defined as extreme increases of bank risk that are proxied by the daily changes of the distance to default measures (Vallascas & Keasey 2012).

This model refers to individual bank risk; it can also be used to model systemic risk. This issue is discussed in the next section.

Systemic risk measures

Risk measurement at the individual bank level as the basis for computing regulatory capital charges can lead to an increase of systemic risk in the banking sector. Banks do not consider the linkages of portfolios within the system; they also underestimate the risk that increases during times of economic expansion. This leads to pro-cyclicality and high correlation of asset returns that amplifies in boom and bust cycles (BCBS, 2011).

Systemic risk occurs if many institutions fail simultaneously. Even if the system consists of individually sound institutions, exogenous events may trigger the instability of the system and cause these institutions to fail. This situation is described by the term "fallacy of composition".

Following Danielsson, Shin and Zigrand (2013) one can define systemic risk as the sum of the risk of market volatility resulting from fundamental changes and the endogenous feedback of market participants i.e., trading patterns. Systemic risk is endogenous because while it depends on the behavior of market participants, this behavior depends on the perceived risk. If market players anticipate higher risk in the future, they will act upon this assumption, which contributes to market volatility. Patro, Qi, and Sun (2013) depict systemic risk as the probability of a broad-based breakdown of the financial system triggered by a systemic event e.g., the failure of a large financial institution. According to Adrian and Brunnemeier (2011) systemic risk consists of two elements: the risk which builds up during credit booms at times when perceived risk level is low and the spillover effects that amplify the shocks which occur during crises.

The economic literature identifies two basic ways of quantifying systemic risk from both macroeconomic and microeconomic points of view (Vallascas & Keasey, 2012). The macroeconomic perspective focuses on the contribution of each individual institution to the systemic risk. The microeconomic approach to measuring systemic risk focuses on how individual banks react to systemic shocks. These two approaches use various risk measures.

Table 2 presents an overview of systemic risk measures applied in the literature as well as the attribution method of systemic risk to individual institutions. Due to their importance for banking regulatory frameworks, the factors contributing to systemic risk for a majority of the studies are also listed.

From the overview presented in Table 2, one can conclude that measuring systemic risk has a number of difficulties. First of all, it requires high frequency data concerning stock returns, stock option prices, or CDS spreads of banks, i.e., data which is not always available for large banks samples, especially during times of crises (Iyer & Peydro, 2009). The high frequency of the data is needed to ensure the quick reactivity of the measure to market movements. Moreover, because the systemic risk measures serve as early warning indicators, they should have forward looking features, i.e., they should be based on detailed, properly extracted information from derivative markets.

Another problem is the determination of excessive systemic risk. The cited studies do not provide an answer of how to evaluate the proposed risk measures in terms of their impact on banking system instability. Systemic risk always exists and it is not the task of regulators to eliminate it. The focus of systemic risk analysis should not be on the level of systemic risk, rather, it should focus on the changes in the level over time (Patro et al., 2013).

A further difficulty is defining the factors of systemic risk to formulate proper regulations. While the studies point to various factors that contribute to systemic risk, there is no consensus as to which factors are domineering. A commonly held view is that bank size and the increase in non-traditional banking activities enhance systemic risk (de Jonghe, 2010). Because of large common exposures, big banks contribute to systemic risk more than small banks; moreover, the involvement of banks in activities other than deposit taking and lending enhances the transfer of risk from market segments that are not a subject of deposit insurance. The topic of systemic risk factors is widely researched and at the center of an intense debate among economists.

A very important feature of systemic risk that has to be considered is its endogeneity. The endogenous risk mechanism is as follows: a negative piece of information causes a decrease in capitalization or an increase in price volatility, which causes market participants to minimize their exposure to risk. An endogenous feedback loop occurs if this deterioration of financial conditions increases the risk aversion, which further worsens the financial conditions (Danielsson et al., 2013). The implication of endogeneity for systemic risk measurement is that the observed volatility should be modelled as two separate elements: the exogenous volatility and endogenous volatility while accounting for the multiplier effect in the latter element caused by the aforementioned feedback loop.

A problem in the application of the mentioned systemic risk measures and models for regulatory purposes arises because a large part of the measures is based on academic, theoretical models that have not been prevalent in regulatory practices. An additional challenge for regulators is the introduction of this new approach in the current framework.

Table 2.

Authors	Systemic risk measure	Systemic risk attribution to individual institutions	Systemic risk determinants
Acharya et al. (2010)	Marginal expected shortfall- the average return of each institution, based on high frequency data, measured over the worst 5% of the sample period.	Systemic expected shortfall- the propensity of an institution to be undercapitalized when the whole system is undercapitalized.	Leverage, expected loss.
Acharya, Engle, & Richardson (2012)	Capital shortfall based on equity returns.	Capital shortfall calculated via weighting assets by long run marginal expected shortfall and constant book values of debt.	Systemically risky assets, leverage.
Adrian & Brunnermeier (2011)	CoVaR, the value at risk of the whole system conditional on the distress of single institutions. Tail covariation between the risk of single institutions and the whole system based on high and low frequency data.	The difference between CoVaR of an institution in distress and CoVaR in the median state of the institution.	Size, leverage, maturity mismatch.
Bartram, Brown & Hund (2007)	3 measures of systemic risk: 1. Equity returns of banks with no direct exposure to the crisis during the time of the crisis. 2. The likelihood of systemic failure based on a structural credit risk model and distances to default. 3. Bank default probabilities based on equity option prices.	Micro approach. The difference between average pre-crisis and post-crisis probabilities for banks with no direct exposure to the crisis.	Market value, debt, deposits, and asset volatility.
Brownlees & Engle (2012)	Marginal expected capital shortfall during a crisis.	Expected capital shortage of a firm during a crisis as indication for the institutions' contribution to system wide capital shortage.	Leverage, size and marginal expected shortfall.
De Jonghe (2010)	The tail beta i.e., the probability of a decrease in a bank's stock price in the case of a banking index crash computed via extreme value analysis.	Micro approach. The probability computed for each institution.	Non-traditional banking activities, bank size, bank capitalization.
Drehmann & Tarashev (2013)	Expected shortfall based on Shapley values.	Two attribution methods based on Shapley values: to what extent a bank generates a shock and to what extent it propagates existing shocks besides generating ones.	n.a.

Table 2. (Continued)

Authors	Systemic risk measure	Systemic risk attribution to individual institutions	Systemic risk determinants
Huang, Zhou & Zhu (2010)	Insurance cost against losses in a banking system i.e., a measure including expected default risk of single banks, risk premia and their correlated defaults based on banks' CDS spreads and equity price co-movements, respectively applied to a portfolio credit risk model.	Computed for each bank individually.	Expected default risk, CDS spreads and equity price co-movements.
Puzanova & Düllmann (2013)	Expected extreme loss in banks' liabilities measured by expected shortfall and value at risk based on a structural credit risk model.	Marginal expected shortfall contributions based on Euler allocation principle.	Capitalization, correlation of assets, systemic size, banking concentration.
Tarashev, Borio, & Tsatsaronis (2010)	System wide Value at Risk and expected shortfall based on Shapley values.	Two attribution procedures based on Shapley values: the contribution of single institutions to systemic risk and their participation in systemic events.	Relative size, probability of default, exposure to common risk.
Vallascas & Keasey (2012)	Distance to default and tail measure conditional on the occurrence of market decline. The default risk is proxied by Merton's distance to default model.	Micro approach- reactions to shifts in the banking sector conditions computed for each bank based on the Merton's distance to default model.	Leverage ratio, liquidity requirements, bank size, the share of non-interest income and asset growth.

Conclusions

The latest financial crisis reveals many weaknesses of bank risk modeling. Due to their pro-cyclicality and lack of accounting for tail events, the commonly used VaR models are misleading. The economic literature proposes alternative risk measures e.g., the expected shortfall or generalized spectral measures. Each of these measures has its advantages and drawbacks; nevertheless, the expected shortfall and other spectral measures are viewed as more conservative in risk assessment and are favored by regulators.

The choice of the risk measurement method is crucial because regulators and bank managers base their risk models on these measures. The respective versions of the Basel Accords offer evolving risk models that attempt to resolve the problems of arbitrary model choices by banks, portfolio invariance issues, and the various treatment of banking and trading books. A challenge that still lies ahead for regulators is compensating for the drawbacks of the applied measures. An issue left to resolve is the pro-cyclicality in risk modeling and the improvement of the techniques of stress testing.

A substantial challenge of the financial crisis for risk modeling is also the revealed fallacy of composition in banking, which highlights the need for risk modeling from a systemic point of view in addition to an individual bank's perspective. Systemic risk models allow regulators to account for spillovers and correlated exposure among banks that can destabilize the whole banking system during times of market distress.

While the evolving risk measures and models are gradually being included in the banking regulatory frameworks, there are many systemic risk factors which have not yet been subjected to regulations. The challenge of adapting the regulations to changing risk profiles of banks and banking systems lies still ahead.

References

Acerbi, C., Tasche, D. (2002). On the coherence of expected shortfall. *Journal of Banking and Finance*, 26 (7), 1487–1503.

Acharya, V., Engle, R., & Richardson, M. (2012). Capital shortfall: a new approach to ranking and regulating systemic risks. *American Economic Review: Papers & Proceedings*, 102 (3), 59–64.

Acharya, V., Pedersen, L., Philippon, T., & Richardson, M. (2010). Measuring systemic risk (Working Paper No. 1002). Federal Reserve Bank of Cleveland.

Adrian, T. & Brunnermeier, M. (2011). CoVaR (Staff Report No. 348). Federal Reserve Bank of New York.

Altman, E. (1968). Final ratios, discriminant analysis and the prediction of corporate bankruptcy. *Journal of Finance,* 23 (4), 589-609.

Bartram, S. M., Brown, G. W., & Hund, J. E. (2007). Estimating systemic risk in the international financial system. *Journal of Financial Economics,* 86 (3), 835–869.

BCBS (2009a). Guidelines for computing capital for incremental risk in the trading book. Basel, Bank for International Settlements. Retrieved from http://www.bis.org/publ/bcbs159.pdf

BCBS (2009b). Revisions to the Basel II market risk framework. Bank for International Settlement. Retrieved from http://www.bis.org/publ/bcbs158.pdf

BCBS (2011). Messages from the academic literature on risk measurement for the trading book (Working Paper No. 19). Bank for International Settlement. Retrieved from http://www.bis.org/publ/bcbs_wp19.pdf

BCBS (2012). Fundamental review of the trading book. Basel, Bank for International Settlements. Retrieved from http://www.bis.org/publ/bcbs219.pdf

Blundell-Wignall, A., & Atkinson, P. (2010). Thinking beyond Basel III: necessary solutions for capital and liquidity. *OECD Journal: Financial Market Trends*,1, 1-23.

Brownlees, C. T., Engle, R. (2012). Volatility, correlation and tails for systemic risk measurement. Available at SSRN: http://ssrn.com/abstract=1611229.

Chen, J. (2014). Measuring market risk under the Basel accords: VaR, stressed VaR, and expected shortfall. *Aestimatio, The IEB International Journal of Finance*, 8, 184-201.

Damodaran, A. (2010), The value at risk. Available at: http://people.stern.nyu.edu/adamodar/

Danielsson, J., Shin, H., Zigrand, J. (2013). Endogenous and systemic risk. In J. Haubrich & Lo (Eds.), *Quantifying systemic risk* (pp. 73 – 94). Chicago, IL: University of Chicago Press.

De Jonghe, O. (2010). Back to the basics in banking? A micro-analysis of banking system stability. *Journal of Financial Intermediation,* 19 (3), 387–417.

Drehmann, M. & Tarashev, N. (2013) Measuring the systemic importance of interconnected banks. *Journal Financial Intermediation,* 22 (4), 586–607.

EBA (2012). EBA guidelines on stressed value at risk (Stressed VaR). EBA/GL/2012/2. London, EBA. Retrieved from https://www.eba.europa.eu/documents/10180/104547/EBA-BS-2012-78--GL-on-Stressed-VaR-.pdf

Gropp, R., Vesala, J., & Vulpes, G. (2006). Equity and bond market signals as leading indicators of bank fragility. *Journal of Money, Credit and Banking*, 38 (2), 399-428.

Huang, X., Zhou, H., & Zhu, H. (2010). Assessing the systemic risk of a heterogenous portfolio of banks during the recent financial crisis (Woking Paper No. 296). Bank for International Settlements.

Inanoglu, H., Jacobs, M., & Karagozoglu, A. (2014), Bank capital and new regulatory requirements for risks in trading portfolios. *The Journal of Fixed Income,* 23 (4), 71-88.

Iyer, R., Peydró, J. L. (2009). Interbank contagion at work: evidence from a natural experiment. *Review of Financial Studies*, 24 (4), 1337-1377.

Larsen, N., Mausser, H., Uryasev, S. (2002). Algorithms For optimization of value-at-risk. In P. M. Pardalos, & V. K. Tsitsiringos (Eds.), Financial engineering, e-commerce and supply chain (pp. 19-46). Norwell,

MA: Kluwer Academic Publishers. Research Report, ISE Dept., University of Florida, available at: www.ise.ufl.edu/uryasev/wp_VaR_minimization.pdf

Mansi, S. A., Maxwell, W. F., Zhang A. (2010). Bankruptcy prediction models and the cost of debt. *Journal of Fixed Income,* 21 (4), 25-42.

Merton, R. (1974). On the pricing of corporate debt: the risk structure of interest rates. *Journal of Finance,* 29 (2), 449–70.

Ohlson, J. (1980). Financial ratios and the probabilistic prediction of bankruptcy. *Journal of Accounting Research,* 18 (1), 109-131.

Patro, D. K., Qi, M., Sun, X. (2013). A simple indicator of systemic risk. *Journal of Financial Stability,* 9 (1), 105- 116.

Puzanova, N., & Düllmann, K. (2013). Systemic risk contributions: a credit portfolio approach. *Journal of Banking & Finance,* 37 (4), 1243–1257.

Rockafellar, R. T. & Uryasev, S. (2002). Conditional value-at-risk for general loss distributions. *Journal of Banking & Finance,* 26 (7), 1443–1471.

Slovik, P. (2012), Systemically important banks and capital regulation challenges (Working Papers No. 916). OECD Publishing.

Tarashev, N., Borio, C., & Tsatsaronis, K. (2010). Attributing systemic risk to individual institutions. Methodology and policy applications (Working Papers No. 308). Bank for International Settlements.

Vallascas, F., & Keasey, K. (2012). Bank resilience to systemic shocks and the stability of banking systems: Small is Beautiful. *Journal of International Money and Finance,* 31 (6), 1745–1776.

Yamai, Y., & Yoshiba, Y. (2005). Value-at-risk versus expected shortfall: a practical perspective. *Journal of Banking and Finance,* 29 (2), 997–1015.

17

Theoretical and Methodological Aspects of Innovation Development in Modern Economic Systems

Irina V. Gashenko[1], Svetlana G. Vokina[2], Dmitry G. Romanov[1], Tatiana L. Bezrukova[3], Yuri A. Kozenko[4]

ABSTRACT The purpose of this article is to classify existing approaches to analyzing theoretical and methodological aspects of innovation development in modern economic systems. We also present a new approach based on existing ones that combines advantages, eliminates drawbacks, and offers means of analyzing innovation development in modern economic systems and that presents optimal models of innovation development in modern economic systems.

The authors develop and approbate – based on the case of present-day Russia – proprietary methodologies for examining innovation development in modern economic systems. It involves the calculation of an index of innovation development that reflects current levels of innovation development in economic systems and possibilities and perspectives related to innovation development in economic systems in the near future.

The authors classify approaches to the analysis of theoretical and methodological aspects of innovation development in modern economic systems as criteria on innovation development in economic systems. Within this classification, the authors distinguish between and conduct comparative analyses of the following three main approaches: plan-factual, ranking, and indexing, which involve making various theoretical assumptions on innovation development in modern economic systems and on the use of various methodologies.

The authors present a new approach to the analysis of theoretical and methodological aspects of innovation development in modern economic systems that eliminate drawbacks of existing approaches and that present unique advantages (simple calculations and universal use). In turn, an optimal model of innovation development in modern economic systems is offered.

KEY WORDS: innovation development, modern economic system, human capital, economic growth

---

[1] Rostov State Economic University, Russia; [2] Plekhanov Russian University of Economics, Russia; [3] Voronezh State University of Forestry and Technologies named after G. F. Morozov, Russia; [4] Volgograd State Agrarian University, Russia

Introduction

A priority of any modern economic system and global economy is to improve the population living standards. This first involves increasing rates of economic growth and GDP per capita, in turn improving the set of goods and services accessible to each consumer. Second, it involves the creation of innovations that satisfy public needs even while preserving rates of economic growth and creating a stable set of goods and services accessible to consumers. Both processes involve innovation development.

Correspondence concerning this article should be addressed to: **Tatiana L. Bezrukova**, Voronezh State Academy of Forestry Engineering, 8 Timiryazeva St., Voronezh 394087, Russia.
E-mail: bezrukova_t_l@mail.ru

Absolute and relative increases in GDP occur through scientific research and the development of human resources enterprises, which increase intellectual capital, which promote capabilities for the development of innovations, and which promote adaptations to new technologies and equipment and their application through the creation of innovative technologies of production. Such technologies increase labor efficiency, and the modernization of equipment expands enterprise production capacities. This, in turn, facilitates innovation development within existing spheres of the economy and the refinement of existing products, technologies, and equipment.

The creation of innovations occurs through scientific and educational development in economic systems; through the financing of economic research at corporate and state levels for the development of new products, technologies, and equipment that satisfy consumer needs or existing needs more efficiently; and through the creation of new economic spheres. As a result, scientific revolutions occur, and technological modes change one another.

When taking into account capacities for innovation development in modern economic systems, the efforts of multiple representatives of scientific societies are aimed at theoretical considerations and instrumental developments for the provision of innovation development in modern economic systems. However, the results of previous studies often contradict one another, and accumulated knowledge in this sphere is scattered. This complicates the selection of optimal criteria and of practical applications of existing analysis methodologies focused on innovation development in modern economic systems, predetermining the necessity for their reconsideration and systematization.

The purpose of this article is to classify existing approaches to the analysis of theoretical and methodological aspects of innovation development in modern economic systems and to present a new approach based on existing methods that applies their advantages, eliminates their drawbacks, and includes means for analyzing of innovation development in modern economic systems and optimal models of innovation development in modern economic systems.

Literature review

Issues of innovation development have been thoroughly studied by scientists in recent years. Various organizational-, production-, and marketing-focused innovation activities employed in enterprises in various countries and economic spheres have been explored at the local scale to support or increase firm competitiveness while preserving or improving firm positions in the market (Allan, Crouchley, & Robertson 2012; Bayev & Podshivalova, 2013; Morozova & Vladimirivna, 2014; Nechaev & Antipina, 2015; Ryapukhina, Suprun, Doroshenko, Bukhonova, & Somina, 2015). Enterprise innovation activities are conducted through organizational, production, and marketing activities (Tovt, 2014) to support or increase competitiveness (Belkin & Belkina, 2013) while also preserving or improving firm market positioning (Imanbekova, 2014).

Other scientists have analyzed basic characteristics, essential peculiarities, and generalized features of innovation development processes at the macro level to determine the role of innovation in the provision of national economic growth and have studied ways of provisioning country competitiveness in the global economy through the creation and application of innovations into national production and through the stimulation of business innovation activities through state policies (Coccia, 2015; Donate, Peña, & Sánchez de Pablo, 2016; Kolychev & Prokhorov, 2015; Rumyantsev, 2015; Vasin & Gamidullaeva, 2015). Innovations play a key role in the provisioning of national economic growth (Ng, Kanagasundram, Wong, & Chandran, 2015). Increased state competitiveness in the global economy is largely achieved through the creation and application of innovations in national production (Filinova, Filinov, Pogodina, Lunev, & Luneva, 2015) and through the stimulation of innovative business activities through state policies (Turriago-Hoyos, Thoene, Bernal-Torres, & Alfonso-Lizarazo, 2015).

Numerous scientific studies have focused on global aspects of innovation development related to overcoming disproportionate economic growth in various countries through innovation and related to global economic growth not only through quantitative expression or an increase in GDP growth but also through qualitative expression through the application of innovations (e.g., (Al-Sudairi & Bakry, 2014; Machado Arroio, 2012; Parrilli, Nadvi, & Yeung, 2013; Popkova, Zubakova, Bogdanov, Yakoleva, & Nebesnay, 2013; Popkova, Yurev, Stepicheva, & Denisov, 2015; Voegtlin & Scherer, 2015). At the global scale, innovation involves overcoming disproportionate economic growth in various countries (Yakovleva, Azarova, & Titova, 2015) and ensuring global economic growth (Ryneiska, 2014) not only in quantitative terms through increases in GDP growth but also in qualitative terms (Voegtlin & Scherer, 2015).

Issues relating to the functioning and development of modern economic systems have been actively studied in the context of determining common features, unique possibilities, and key tendencies and in terms of identifying significant factors of development based on statistics of economic growth, dynamics of economic system change, models of current states and structures and forecasts of changes to occur in the near future (Hu, 2013; Mishra & Narayan, 2015; Oxenstierna, 2015; Rommel, 2015; Saikevych, 2012; Zakharova, Prokhorova, Shutilov, & Klochko, 2015). Modern economic systems develop according to market types involved, and this supposes free competition and minimal interference with market processes (Batkovskiy, Konovalova, Semenova, Trofimets, & Fomina, 2015). This also assumes the occurrence of periods of crisis and economic growth (Loasby, 2015). Innovations are some of the most significant developmental factors affecting modern economic systems (Okrepilov, Makarov, Bakhtizin, & Kuzmina, 2015).

Nevertheless, despite the numerous studies conducted on this topic, theoretical and methodological aspects of innovation development in modern economic systems have not been studied in a consistent or systemic way. Research conducted in this sphere is thus fragmented, raising the necessity for a systematization of accumulated knowledge for the creation of nuanced and comprehensive understandings of problems, perspectives, and methods related to the activation of innovation activities in modern economic systems. This is examined in this article.

Method

As methodological instruments, the authors apply induction, deduction, problem and systemic analysis, classification, formalization, economic modeling and forecasting. In addition to the above methods, we use the proprietary method of innovation development analysis in modern economic systems. This approach involves the calculation of indexes of innovation development, which reflect current levels of innovation development in economic systems and perspectives on innovation development in economic systems to develop in the near future:

$$Iinnov=(SE+SF+IT/CT)+(IE_5/IE_1+QP_5/QP_1+FS_5/FS_1) \quad (1)$$

where

Iinnov – index of innovation development in an economic system;

SE – share of innovation enterprises to the total number of enterprises in an economic system;

SF – share of expenditures for financing science in the form of GDP;

CT – number of leading production technologies created in the current year;

IT – number of leading production technologies applied through enterprise activities in the current year;

IE – number of innovation enterprises (1 – in the first year, 5 – in 5 years)

QP – quantity of personnel focused on scientific research and development (1 – in the first year, 5 – in 5 years)

FS – financing of science from state budget assets (1 – in the first year, 5 – in 5 years).

Indicators of innovation development and generated innovation development index values are evaluated using a special scale (Tables 1 and 2). The index generates values of 6 to 30. The higher the index value, the higher the level and the more significant perspectives on innovation development are in an economic system.

Results

In this study, the authors classify approaches to the analysis of theoretical and methodological aspects of innovation development in modern economic systems as criteria for innovation development in economic systems (Table 3). Within this classification, the following three main approaches are identified: plan-factual, ranking, and indexing approaches. These approaches involve applying various theoretical definitions of innovation development in modern economic systems and various methodologies.

Table 1. Scale for evaluating values of indicators of innovation development in modern economic systems

Indicators	Values assigned to indicators				
	1	2	3	4	5
SE	<1%	1%-9%	10%-24%	25%-50%	>50%
SF	<0.5%	0.5%-0.9%	1-2.9%	3%-5%	>5%
IT/CT	<0.50	>100	0.50-0.99	50-100	1-50
IE_5/IE_1	<0.80	0.80-0.99	1.00-1.19	1.20-1.49	>1.50
QP_5/QP_1	<0.80	0.80-0.99	1.00-1.19	1.20-1.49	>1.50
FS_5/FS_1	<0.80	0.80-0.99	1.00-1.19	1.20-1.49	>1.50

Table 2. Scale for evaluating values of indexes of innovation development in modern economic systems

Iinnov Values	Innovation development: current levels and perspectives
6-10	critical lack and absence of innovation development perspectives
11-14	limited or absent innovation development perspectives
15-20	limited but good innovation development perspectives
21-26	high-level but insignificant innovation development perspectives
27-30	high-level and significant innovation development perspectives

As Table 3 shows, when applying a plan-factual approach, innovation development in an economic system can be understood as the degree of plan realization. Rather, a model of innovation development in an economic system is created first and is then compared to reality. When applying a ranking approach, innovation development in an economic system is measured through rankings. While this allows one to compare economic systems, it hinders the determination of causal relations. Through the indexing approach, innovation development in an economic system is understood as the value of a certain index. This approach is limited due to challenges associated with procuring statistical data and calculating indices.

Existing approaches to the analysis of theoretical and methodological aspects of innovation development in modern economic systems are most limited in their focus on previous (plan-factual approaches) or current trends (ranking and index approaches) without accounting for future possibilities for innovation development in economic systems and in their basis in economically developed countries, rendering them inapplicable developing countries.

To overcome these drawbacks, we present a new proprietary approach to the analysis of theoretical and methodological aspects of innovation development in modern economic systems that involves not only the evaluation of current levels but also the determination of potential avenues of innovation development in economic systems. Furthermore, unlike existing approaches, this approach can be applied at the national, regional, and global levels, making it universally applicable.

The proposed approach is based on the calculation of integral indicators of innovation development, en-

Table 3. Classification of approaches to the analysis of theoretical and methodological aspects of innovation development in modern economic systems

Criteria of comparison	Approaches to the analysis of theoretical and methodological aspects of innovation development in modern economic systems		
	Plan-factual approach	Ranking approach	Index approach
Approach representatives	(Vasin & Gamidullaeva, 2015), (Ng et al., 2015)	(Donate et al., 2016), (Turriago-Hoyos et al., 2015), (Filinova et al., 2015)	(Coccia, 2015), (Rumyantsev, 2015), (Kolychev & Prokhorov, 2015)
Determination of innovation development in modern economic systems through the approach	Innovation development in economic systems – plan realization	Innovation development in economic systems –ranking position	Innovation development in economic systems –index values
Levels of innovation development in modern economic systems considered through the approach	Comparison between factual levels of innovation development and normative values and previously compiled models and plans on innovation development in economic systems	- Knowledge assessment methods (KAM – the Knowledge Assessment Methodology) (The World Bank, 2015); - ranking countries on innovativeness (Economist Intelligence Unit, 2015).	- Index of scientific & technical potential as a component of integral indicators for evaluating a country's competitiveness (World Economic Forum, 2014); - System for evaluating innovation activity in a country based on indicators of the European innovation scoreboard (European Commission, 2014); Global innovation index (Management Today, 2013).

suring compatibility with the index approach. However, the new approach involves completing simpler calculations based on generally accessible statistical information on economic systems, and it generates results faster, creating additional advantages and making it more attractive when conducting research.

Let us conduct an evaluation of levels and perspectives of innovation development in present-day Russia using the proposed approach. To calculate the necessary indicators and index of innovation development for the Russian economy, let us use official Federal State Statistics Service statistics for 2010-2014. Statistical information and analysis results are given in Table 4.

Table 4 shows that in present-day Russia, according to 2010-2014 data, a small share of enterprises conduct scientific research and development and apply innovations – innovation enterprises (less than 1%). A small share of GDP expenditures is dedicated to financing scientific research (less than 0.5%), causing the number of innovations applied to significantly exceed the number of innovations created (135 times). This shows that in Russia, innovation development does not receive enough attention from the state or businesses.

At the same time, there has been growth in the number of innovation enterprises (2% over 5 years) and significant growth in scientific research financing (almost doubling over 5 years). However, in view

Table 4. Results of our analysis on innovation development in present-day Russia based on the proprietary methodology proposed

Indicators of innovation development in Russia	2010	2014	Integral	Assigned values
Indicators of current levels of innovation development in economic systems				
IE	3,536	3,605	-	-
Number of enterprises in thousands	4,823.3	4,886	-	-
SE, %	-	**0.07**	<1%	**1**
FS	225.762	425.302	-	-
GDP of Russia, RUB billion	82,055	126,186	-	-
SF, %	-	**0.34**	<0.5%	**1**
CT	-	1,409	-	-
IT	-	191,372	-	-
IT/CT	-	**135.82**	>100	**2**
Indicators of possibilities and perspectives on innovation development in economic systems for the near future				
IE_{2014}/IE_{2010}	-	**1.02**	1.00-1.19	**3**
QP, one thousand people	742	727	-	-
QP_{2014}/QP_{2010}	-	**0.98**	0.80-0.99	**2**
FS_{2014}/FS_{2010}	-	**1.88**	>1.50	**5**

Note: Adapted from "*Russia in numbers. Scientific research and innovations 2015: Bulletin of Rosstat*" by Rosstat (2015). Retrieved from Retrieved from http://www.gks.ru/free_doc/doc_2015/rusfig/rus-15.pdf

of inflation, this growth trend is brought down to zero and is thus nominal, and this is aggravated by a decline in the number of employees conducting scientific research (a 2% decline over 5 years). The equation for the 2014 index of innovation development in Russia takes the following form:

Iinnov(Russia2014)=1+1+2+3+2+5=14.

The retrieved index of innovation development value shows low current levels and a lack of views on innovation development. Russian economic modernization strategies and an orientation toward innovation development have positive effects and should improve conditions in future years. From the developed approach, we propose the following optimal model of innovation development for modern economic systems (Fig. 1).

Fig. 1 shows that the proposed model can be visualized as a pyramid reflecting the dependence of past and current levels of innovation development in economic systems and their current potential and future development. This format allows one to conduct complex analyses in view of dynamics and tendencies of innovation development, modeling, and change forecasting. The model applies instruments of innovation development such as the financing of science and the creation and application of innovations by means of the development of economic system human capital.

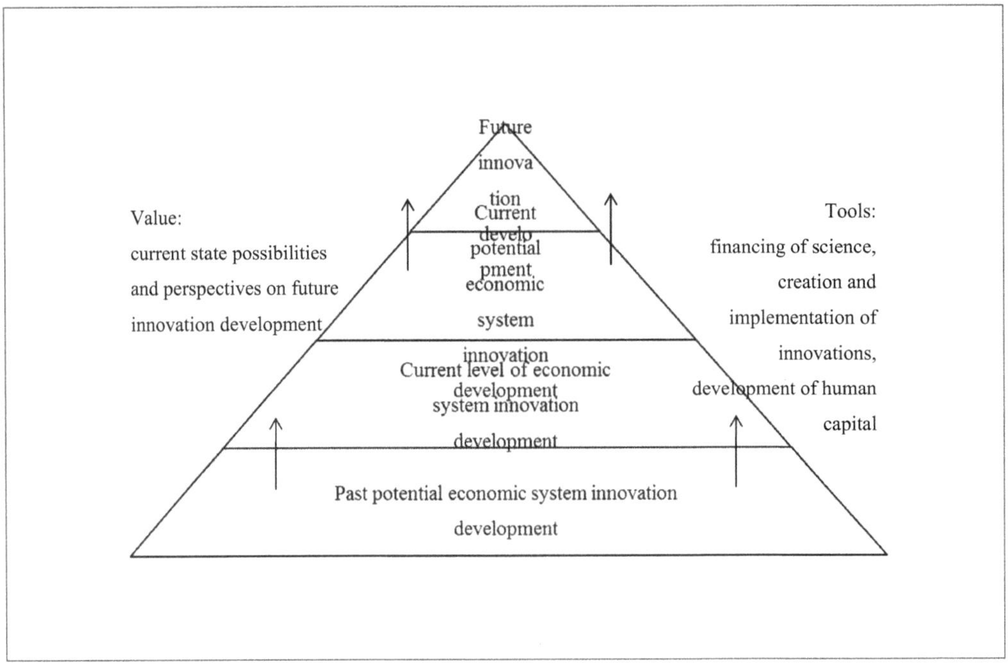

Figure 1. Optimal model of innovation development in modern economic systems

Conclusion

We conclude that at present, there are three approaches to the analysis of theoretical and methodological aspects of innovation development in modern economic systems. These methods can be classified based on theoretical views of innovation development in modern economic systems and certain methods as follows: the plan-factual approach, whereby innovation development in economic systems is understood as the degree of plan realization; the ranking approach, through which innovation development in economic systems is measured based on rankings; and the index approach, by which innovation development in an economic system is understood as an index value.

These approaches present unique advantages and serious disadvantages by disregarding future innovation development and orientation in economically developed countries. As a means of overcoming these drawbacks, we presented a new approach that involves the simultaneous evaluation of current levels and determinations of potential innovation development in economic systems. We apply the proposed methodology through an analysis of innovation development in modern economic systems based on the case of present-day Russia, revealing limited perspectives on future innovation development and probable improvements as a result of state modernization programs and innovation development strategies.

We present a new methodology for the analysis of innovation development in modern economic systems that involves the calculation of an index of innovation development that reflects current levels of innovation development in economic systems and possibilities for and perspectives on innovation development in economic systems to emerge in the near future.

Our validation of the proposed methodology through the case of present-day Russia revealed the country's weak innovation development plans but probable improvements to this situation as a result of state modernization programs and innovation development strategies. Our calculation of the 2014 index of innovation development for Russia revealed that innovation development does not receive enough attention in Russia from the state and businesses.

The developed approach involves the use of an optimal model of innovation development in modern economic systems. The model applies instruments of innovation development such as the financing of science and the creation and application of innovations by means of the development of economic system human capital.

Our approval of the proposed methodology was ensured for the provision of its clarity and is limited the presented analysis of the Russian economy; the proposed model of optimal innovation development in economic systems is practically oriented but is theoretical in nature, limiting the results of the research conducted. Hence, in future research studies, the proposed approach should be used for the analysis of state views on innovation development in various economic systems and the creation of innovation development strategies for modern economic systems.

References

Allan, R., Crouchley, R., Robertson, A. (2012). Collaborative and distributed innovation and research in business activity. In A. A. Juan, T. Daradoumis, M. Roca, S. E. Grasman, & J. Faulin (Eds.), Collaborative and distributed e-research: Innovations in technologies, strategies and applications (pp. 310-329). Hershey, PA: IGI Global.

Al-Sudairi, M., Bakry, S.H. (2014). Knowledge issues in the global innovation index: Assessment of the state of Saudi Arabia versus countries with distinct development. *Innovation: Management, Policy and Practice, 16*(2), 176-183

Batkovskiy, A. M., Konovalova, A. V., Semenova, E. G., Trofimets, V. J., Fomina, A. V. (2015). Study of economic systems using the simulation-based statistical modeling method. *Mediterranean Journal of Social Sciences, 6*(4), 369-380.

Bayev, I. A., Podshivalova, M. V. (2013). Tasks of institutional support to increase innovation activity of small business in the region. *Economy of Region, 2013*(1), 189-198.

Belkin, V.N., Belkina, N.A. (2013). Ways of increasing enterprises' innovation activity. *Economy of Region, 2013*(1), 238-242.

Coccia, M. (2015). General sources of general purpose technologies in complex societies: Theory of global leadership-driven innovation, warfare and human development. *Technology in Society, 42*, 199-226.

Donate, M. J., Peña, I., Sánchez de Pablo, J. D. (2016). HRM practices for human and social capital development: effects on innovation capabilities. *International Journal of Human Resource Management, 27*(9), 928-953.

Economist Intelligence Unit (2015). New global classification of the most innovationally developed countries. Retrieved from http://www.enter.ie.edu/cms/en/o/6469/1

European Commission (2014). European innovation scoreboard 2014. Retrieved from http://ec.europa.eu/growth/industry/innovation/facts-figures/scoreboards_en

Filinova, N. V., Filinov, V. P., Pogodina, O.N.,Lunev, V.A., Luneva, E. V. (2015). The socio-economic foundations of the development of contemporary economic innovations. *Asian Social Science, 11*(6), 150-160.

Hu, Z. P. (2013). On the value orientation of modern market economic system. In D. Li (Ed.), Values of Our Times: Contemporary Axiological Research in China (pp. 231-238). Berlin: Springer Verlag.

Imanbekova, M. (2014). The use of foreign experience in forming system state regulation of innovation activities of enterprises in the Republic of Kazakhstan. *World Applied Sciences Journal, 30*(5), 630-634.

Kolychev, V. D., Prokhorov, I. V. (2015). Conception, technology and methods of development of university system of innovation projects commercialization based on effectuation. *Asian Social Science, 11*(8), 44-51.

Loasby, B. J. (2015). Knowledge and Organisation in Economics and Economic Systems: A Research Tradition. *Managerial and Decision Economics, 36*(1), 6-15.

Machado Arroio, A. C. (2012). Governance of science, technology and innovation programmes for development is global financing getting it right? *Institutions and Economies, 4*(2), 45-64.

Management Today (2013). Global innovational index: More on methodology. Retrieved from http://www.managementtoday.co.uk/news/610009

Mishra, S., Narayan, P. K. (2015). A nonparametric model of financial system and economic growth. *International Review of Economics and Finance, 39*, 175-191.

Morozova, I.A. Poluyufta, L.V. (2014). (2014). The use of subcontracting mechanisms in education as means of the increase of business and innovation activity of higher education institutions. *World Applied Sciences Journal, 31*(5), 884-888.

Nechaev, A., Antipina, O. (2015). Tax stimulation of innovation activities enterprises. *Mediterranean Journal of Social Sciences, 6*(1S2), 42-47.

Ng, B. K.,Kanagasundram, T., Wong, C. Y., Chandran, V. G. R. (2015). Innovation for inclusive development in Southeast Asia: The roles of regional coordination mechanisms. *The Pacific Review, 29*(4), 573-602.

Okrepilov, V. V., Makarov, V. L., Bakhtizin, A. R., Kuzmina, S. N. (2015). Application of supercomputer technologies for simulation of socio-economic systems. *Economy of Region, 2015*(2), 301-313.

Oxenstierna, S. (Ed.). (2015). The Challenges for Russia's Politicized Economic System. London, UK: Routlege.

Parrilli, M. D., Nadvi, K.,Yeung, H. W. C. (2013). Local and regional development in global value chains, production networks and innovation networks: A comparative review and the challenges for future research. *European Planning Studies, 21*(7), 967-988.

Popkova, E. G, Zubakova, N. N., Bogdanov, D. V., Yakovleva, E. A, Nebesnay, A. Y. (2013). Measurement of economic growth as a factor of development of strategies of economic transformation. *World Applied Sciences Journal, 25*(2), 264-269.

Popkova, E. G., Yurev, V., Stepicheva, O., Denisov, N. (2015). Transformation and concentration of intellectual capital as a factor of economic growth in the modern economy. *Regional and Sectoral Economic Studies, 16*(1), 53-60.

Rommel, J. (2015). What can economic experiments tell us about institutional change in social-ecological systems? *Environmental Science and Policy, 53*, 96-104.

Rosstat. (2015). *Russia in numbers. Scientific research and innovations 2015: Bulletin of Rosstat.* Retrieved from http://www.gks.ru/free_doc/doc_2015/rusfig/rus-15.pdf

Rumyantsev, A. A. (2015). Science and innovation space of a macroregion: Prospects of innovative territorial development. *Studies on Russian Economic Development, 26*(4), 379-387.

Ryapukhina, V. N., Suprun, E. V.,Doroshenko, Y. A., Bukhonova, S. M., Somina, I. V. (2015). Strategy of effective management for small businesses at different stages of innovation activity. *Journal of Applied Engineering Science, 13*(2), 117-125.

Ryneiska, L. (2014). The world innovation economy: Modern trends of development. Economic Annals-XXI, 7-8, 8-11.

Saikevych, M. I. (2012). Dualism of modern economic system. *Actual Problems of Economics, 132*(6), 9-15.

The World Bank (2015). Knowledge for Development Program. Retrieved from https://openknowledge.worldbank.org/bitstream/handle/10986/22550/WBAnnualReport2015EN.pdf

Tovt, T. I. (2014). Regulation mechanism for investment support of innovation activities of enterprises. *Actual Problems of Economics, 152*(2), 211-218.

Turriago-Hoyos, A., Thoene, U., Bernal-Torres, C., Alfonso-Lizarazo, E. (2015). Product innovation, research and development and technology acquisition: A case study of the industrial sector in Colombia. *Institutions and Economies, 7*(2), 85-119.

Vasin, S. M., Gamidullaeva, L. A. (2015). Development a basic model of the innovation system. *Review of European Studies, 7*(11), 175-183.

Voegtlin, C., Scherer, A. G. (2015). Responsible innovation and the innovation of responsibility: Governing sustainable development in a globalized world. *Journal of Business Ethics.* Doi: 10.1007/s10551-015-2769-z.

World Economic Forum (2014). Report on global competitiveness for 2014. Retrieved from http://www.weforum.org/en/initiatives/gcp/Global%20Competitiveness%20Report/index.htm

Yakovleva, E. A., Azarova, N. A., Titova, E. V. (2015). Innovation as a vector of regional economic development and a necessary condition for the progress of the world economy. *Asian Social Science, 11*(20), 90-96.

Zakharova, E. N., Prokhorova, V. V., Shutilov, F. V., Klochko, E. N. (2015). Modern tendencies of cluster development of regional economic systems. Mediterranean Journal of *Social Sciences, 6*(5S3), 154-163.

Permissions

All chapters in this book were first published in Contemporary Economics, by University of Finance and Management, Warsaw; Vistula University; hereby published with permission under the Creative Commons Attribution License or equivalent. Every chapter published in this book has been scrutinized by our experts. Their significance has been extensively debated. The topics covered herein carry significant findings which will fuel the growth of the discipline. They may even be implemented as practical applications or may be referred to as a beginning point for another development.

The contributors of this book come from diverse backgrounds, making this book a truly international effort. This book will bring forth new frontiers with its revolutionizing research information and detailed analysis of the nascent developments around the world.

We would like to thank all the contributing authors for lending their expertise to make the book truly unique. They have played a crucial role in the development of this book. Without their invaluable contributions this book wouldn't have been possible. They have made vital efforts to compile up to date information on the varied aspects of this subject to make this book a valuable addition to the collection of many professionals and students.

This book was conceptualized with the vision of imparting up-to-date information and advanced data in this field. To ensure the same, a matchless editorial board was set up. Every individual on the board went through rigorous rounds of assessment to prove their worth. After which they invested a large part of their time researching and compiling the most relevant data for our readers.

The editorial board has been involved in producing this book since its inception. They have spent rigorous hours researching and exploring the diverse topics which have resulted in the successful publishing of this book. They have passed on their knowledge of decades through this book. To expedite this challenging task, the publisher supported the team at every step. A small team of assistant editors was also appointed to further simplify the editing procedure and attain best results for the readers.

Apart from the editorial board, the designing team has also invested a significant amount of their time in understanding the subject and creating the most relevant covers. They scrutinized every image to scout for the most suitable representation of the subject and create an appropriate cover for the book.

The publishing team has been an ardent support to the editorial, designing and production team. Their endless efforts to recruit the best for this project, has resulted in the accomplishment of this book. They are a veteran in the field of academics and their pool of knowledge is as vast as their experience in printing. Their expertise and guidance has proved useful at every step. Their uncompromising quality standards have made this book an exceptional effort. Their encouragement from time to time has been an inspiration for everyone.

The publisher and the editorial board hope that this book will prove to be a valuable piece of knowledge for researchers, students, practitioners and scholars across the globe.

List of Contributors

Nurudeen Abu and Mohd Zaini Abd Karim
Othman Yeop Abdullah Graduate School of Business, Univeristi Utara Malaysia, 06010 Sintok, Kedah, Malaysia

Mukhriz Izraf Azman Aziz
School of Economics, Finance and Banking, Univeristi Utara Malaysia, 06010 Sintok, Kedah, Malaysia

Natalia G. Vovchenko, Olga B. Ivanova, Elena D. Kostoglodova, Marina O. Otrishko and Olga S. Dzhu
Rostov State Economic University, Russia

Wiesław Dębski
University of Finance and Management in Warsaw - Management and Finance, Poland

Bartosz Świderski
Warsaw University of Life Sciences - Faculty of Applied Informatics and Mathematics, Department of Applied Informatics, Poland

Sheilla Nyasha and Nicholas M Odhiambo
University of South Africa, Department of Economics, South Africa

Michele Sabatino
KORE University of Enna, Italy

Sukanya Chetty, Rebekah Naidoo and Yudhvir Seetharam
University of the Witwatersrand - School of Economic and Business Sciences, South Africa

Svetlana S. Morkovina
Voronezh State University of Forestry Engineering named after G.F. Morozov, Russia

Alexandr S. Natsubidze
Moscow International Academy, Russia

Margarita S. Irizepova
Volgograd State University, Russia

Nikolai G. Sinyavsky
Volgograd State Agricultural University, Russia
Financial University under the Government of the Russian Federation, Russia

Vladimir V. Chashchin
Ural State Institute of Stock Market, Russia

Natalia Medrano and Cristina Olarte-Pascual
Universidad de La Rioja, Spain

Irina S. Zinovyeva
Voronezh State University of Forestry and Technologies named after G.F. Morozov, Russia

Yuri A. Kozenko and Margarita S. Irizepova
Volgograd State University Russia

Kirill B. Gerasimov
Samara National Research University, Russia

Yulia I. Dubova
Volgograd State Technical University, Russia

Kee Tuan Teng
Tunku Abdul Rahman University College, Malaysia

Siew Hwa Yen, Soo Y. Chua and Hooi Hooi Lean
Universiti Sains Malaysia, Malaysia

Marinko Škare and Romina Prziklas Druzeta
Juraj Dobrila University of Pula - Faculty of economics and Tourism "Dr. Mijo Mirkovic", Croatia

Svetlana G. Vokina
Plekhanov Russian University of Economics, Russia

Yulia S. Zima
Rostov State Economic University, Russia

Nikolai G. Sinyavsky
Volgograd State Agricultural University, Russia
Financial University under the Government of the Russian Federation, Russia

Vadim Meshkov
Perm Institute of Economics and Finance, Russia

Aleksandra V. Sultanova
Samara State Technical University, Russia

Jan Vlachý
Czech Technical University in Prague - Masaryk Institute of Advanced Studies, Czech Republic

Oliver Budzinski
Ilmenau University of Technology, Institute of Economics, Germany

Jürgen-Peter Kretschmer
Federal Cartel Office, Germany

Leonardo Martin Mastrangelo
Faculty of Economy, University of València, Spain

Esther Calderon-Monge and Pilar Huerta-Zavala
Faculty of Economics and Business Studies, University of Burgos, Spain

Katarzyna Sum
Warsaw School of Economics - Chair of International Finance, Poland

Irina V. Gashenko1, Dmitry G. Romanov
Rostov State Economic University, Russia

Svetlana G. Vokina
Plekhanov Russian University of Economics, Russia

Tatiana L. Bezrukova
Voronezh State University of Forestry and Technologies named after G. F. Morozov, Russia

Yuri A. Kozenko
Volgograd State Agrarian University, Russia

Index